CIVIL LITIGATION
FOR
PARALEGALS

ELIZABETH C. RICHARDSON, J.D.

ADJUNCT FACULTY

CENTRAL PIEDMONT COMMUNITY COLLEGE

MILTON C. REGAN, JR., J.D.

ASSOCIATE PROFESSOR

GEORGETOWN UNIVERSITY LAW CENTER

LQ40AA
PUBLISHED BY
SOUTH-WESTERN PUBLISHING CO.
CINCINNATI, OH   DALLAS, TX   LIVERMORE, CA

ISBN 0-538-70371-7

3 4 5 6 7 8 9 0 MT 0 9 8 7 6 5 4 3
Printed in the United States of America

Acquisitions Editor: Betty Schechter
Editorial Production Manager: Linda R. Allen
Production Editor: Martha G. Conway
Designer: James DeSollar
Production Artist: Sophia Renieris
Photo Researcher: Devore M. Nixon
Marketing Manager: Shelly Battenfield

PHOTO CREDITS

p. 1   Charles Gupton/Stock, Boston
p. 25   Eric Carle/Superstock
p. 57   American Petroleum Institute
p. 109 Unisys Corporation
p. 195 R. Michael Stuckey/Comstock
p. 295 R. Lewellyn/Superstock
p. 325 Billy E. Barnes/Stock, Boston
p. 341 Superstock

Library of Congress Cataloging-in-Publication Data

Richardson, Elizabeth C.
    Civil litigation for paralegals / Elizabeth C. Richardson, Milton
C. Regan, Jr.
        p.   cm.
    Includes index.
    ISBN 0-538-70371-7
    1. Civil procedure—United States.   2. Legal assistants—United
States   I. Regan, Milton C.   II. Title.
    KF8841.R525   1991
    347.73'5—dc20
    [347.3075]   90-26274
                                                        CIP

PREFACE

Civil litigation instructors may recall some uneasy moments in their first-year law school civil procedure courses. They may recall sitting in class thinking that the concept of federal question jurisdiction is well and good, but what does it really mean—how do you apply it in a real live lawsuit?

Civil Litigation for Paralegals answers those uneasy questions for paralegal students, giving them a practical introduction to civil litigation. It is a comprehensible guide to civil procedure for students in all types of paralegal programs. There are many approaches for teaching civil litigation—as one basic course, as a basic and then an advanced course, and in conjunction with other areas of law, such as personal injury. *Civil Litigation for Paralegals* is suitable for all approaches.

ABOUT THE TEXTBOOK

One goal of *Civil Litigation for Paralegals* is to enable students to understand the rules that govern civil procedure and to apply the rules to actual lawsuits. To accomplish this goal, *Civil Litigation for Paralegals* applies the rules of civil procedure to two sample cases. The text tracks the primary case, involving product liability, from the initial client conference through the trial and post-trial procedures, enabling students to follow a lawsuit through the entire litigation process and grasp an overview of civil procedure.

A second goal of *Civil Litigation for Paralegals* is to enable students to understand the principles that underlie the rules that govern civil litigation. An important principle underlying the Federal Rules of Civil Procedure is to provide for the fair and orderly disposition of lawsuits, and this is illustrated throughout the text. *Civil Litigation for Paralegals* devotes an entire chapter to the rules of evidence. Although paralegals will not actually try cases, they must understand the goals of the rules—to ensure fairness and to ascertain the truth. Chapter 4 focuses on these basic principles that underlie the rules of evidence and applies them to factual situations so that paralegal students can grasp the practical application of the rules of evidence as well.

Civil Litigation for Paralegals focuses another of its chapters on legal ethics. Chapter 2 explains the importance of the rules of ethics for paralegals and attorneys and discusses the rules most pertinent to litigation.

There are several important organizational features in the textbook. First, the text focuses on the Federal Rules of Civil Procedure, because these rules give a cohesive overview of the litigation process and because many states have rules that are the same as or similar to the Federal Rules. Throughout, the text emphasizes the importance of state rules of civil procedure and local rules of court as well. Second, the text follows a sample case (product liability) throughout the litigation process, and supplements this with a second case involving employment discrimination. Finally, to help students grasp an overview of the litigation process, each chapter begins with a Litigation Extract, which recaps the stages of litigation through which the sample lawsuit has already proceeded and puts in perspective the topic discussed in the chapter at hand.

Another special learning aid throughout the text is the appearance of Pointers—practical observations for paralegals. Pointers not only clarify the text, but also prepare paralegals to be useful litigation team members from the outset of their careers. For example, paralegals often prepare numerous exhibits to attach to the complaint. A Pointer tells students that it is helpful to tab each exhibit so that judges do not have to plow through a mass of papers to sort out exhibit numbers.

ABOUT THE STUDENT RESOURCE MANUAL

For each chapter of the text, the Resource Manual features a summary that reviews the important rules and concepts covered. The summary is a helpful aid for test review. Each summary is followed by a series of Study Questions and a section entitled Test Your Knowledge, which presents short-answer, multiple choice, and true/false questions. These exercises are also excellent review and test preparation tools. Answers to all questions appear at the end of the chapter.

ABOUT THE INSTRUCTOR'S MANUAL

Designed for the busy instructor, the Instructor's Manual features a lecture guide in the form of an Annotated Outline for each chapter. It also contains Teaching Suggestions, which give supplemental explanatory material for difficult concepts, point out appropriate places to discuss state and local rules, suggest classroom exercises, and give other practical suggestions for teaching civil litigation. The manual also contains a list of Behavioral Objectives for each chapter. Because every busy instructor needs test questions, the manual provides tests for each chapter, including objective questions and short essay questions.

ABOUT THE AUTHORS

Elizabeth C. Richardson earned her Juris Doctor degree from the University of North Carolina School of Law, where she was a member of the Jessup Cup International Moot Court Team and the Order of Barristers. Ms. Richardson earned her B.A. from the University of North Carolina at Greensboro, where she was inducted into Phi Beta Kappa. She also earned a Master's degree from the University of Cincinnati, where she was a Louise Taft Semple Fellow.

Elizabeth Richardson is an adjunct instructor in the Paralegal Program at Central Piedmont Community College. Ms. Richardson is an attorney in Charlotte, North Carolina, and her areas of concentration have been civil litigation and administrative law. She has published articles in the *North Carolina Law Review* and *Outside* Magazine.

Milton C. Regan, Jr., earned his Juris Doctor degree from Georgetown University Law Center, where he was articles editor of the *Georgetown Law Journal*. Mr. Regan earned his B.A. from the University of Houston and his M.A. from the University of California at Los Angeles. Mr. Regan served as a law clerk to the Honorable Ruth Bader Ginsburg of the United States Court of Appeals for the District of Columbia Circuit. Mr. Regan also was a law clerk to the Honorable William J. Brennan, Jr., of the United States Supreme Court. He served as a litigation associate at Davis Polk & Wardwell in Washington, D.C., before becoming an associate professor at Georgetown University Law Center.

ACKNOWLEDGEMENTS

We extend our special thanks to Janis L. Walter, J.D., assistant professor of legal studies and director of the Legal Assisting Program at the University of Cincinnati, for her outstanding suggestions, which contributed greatly to make this an effective learning and teaching package. Other colleagues, students and friends have enhanced the text with their knowledge and experience, and we are grateful to them all. Although these persons are too numerous to mention, Ms. Richardson extends special thanks to the law firm of Hartsell, Hartsell, & Mills, P.A., for sharing their litigation experience, knowledge, and friendship.

Finally, we express our boundless gratitude to our spouses, Michael Pawlyk and Nancy Sachs. Their patience and understanding know no bounds. We are likewise indebted to our parents, R.C. and Stuart Richardson, and Milton and Lucie Regan, who have inspired us throughout our lives. Without the understanding and guidance that our spouses and parents have so generously given, this book would not have been possible, and to them we gratefully dedicate our work.

Elizabeth C. Richardson
Milton C. Regan, Jr.

SUMMARY
OF CONTENTS

CONTENTS

CIVIL LITIGATION: OVERVIEW OF THE LITIGATION PRO-CESS, 1; The Litigation Process, 2; Rules that Govern Civil Litigation, 5; *The Federal Rules of Civil Procedure, 5; State Rules of Civil Procedure, 6; Federal Local Court Rules, 6; State Local Court Rules, 6; General Remarks about Procedural Rules, 7; Federal and State Rules of Evidence, 7; Rules of Professional Responsibility, 7;* Types of Lawsuits, 7; *Torts, 8; Contracts, 8; Corporate, 8; Property, 9; Civil Rights, 9; Domestic Relations, 9;* Remedies Available in Civil Litigation, 10; *Money Damages, 10; Equitable Remedies, 10;* **THE LAW OFFICE, 10;** Law Office Personnel and Organization, 10; The Litigation Atmosphere, 11; Working with Lawyers, 12; Important Office Procedures: Billing/Timekeeping, 12; *Timekeeping Procedures, 12; Disbursements, 14;* Time Management Techniques, 14; Important Office Procedures: Docket Control, 15; *Examples of Docket Control Systems, 15; Sources of Information for Docket Control, 16; Important Deadlines and Dates, 17;* **COMMUNICATING WITH CLIENTS, 19;** The Importance of Regular Communication, 19; Telephone Contact, 19; Letters to Clients, 19; The Memorandum to the File, 20; **THE ROLE OF THE PARALEGAL ON THE AT-TORNEY/PARALEGAL TEAM, 20;** The Importance of Paralegals, 20; Litigation Tasks for Paralegals, 20; *Prior to Commencement of the Action, 21; Commencement of Action, 21; Motions and Responsive Pleadings, 21; Discovery, 21; Motions for Entry of Judgment Without Trial, 21; Pretrial Conferences and Settlement, 22; Trial Preparation, 22; Trial, 22; Post-Trial, 22.*

INTRODUCTION, 25; SOURCES OF ETHICAL GUIDELINES, 26; ABA Model Code of Professional Responsibility, 26; ABA Model Rules of Professional Conduct, 30; State Guidelines, 30; **EFFECT OF ETHICAL GUIDELINES ON ATTORNEYS AND PARALEGALS, 30;** Consequences of Violating Ethical Guidelines, 30; Application of Ethical Rules to Conduct of Paralegals, 32; **PROHIBITION AGAINST UNAUTHORIZED PRACTICE OF LAW, 32;** What Constitutes the Unauthorized Practice of Law, 34; The Importance of Identifying

Depositions, 259; **PHYSICAL AND MENTAL EXAMINATIONS, 260; REQUESTS FOR ADMISSION, 263;** Procedure, 263; Format of Requests for Admission, 265; Drafting Requests for Admission, 265; Responding to Requests for Admission, 265; **MOTIONS FOR CONTROLLING THE DISCOVERY PROCESS, 267;** Procedure to Compel Discovery, 267; Discovery Sanctions, 269.

CASES FOR LITIGATION: AN INTRODUCTION

The best way to understand civil litigation is to follow a lawsuit throughout its course. We will follow *Bryson Wesser v. Woodall Shoals Corporation and Second Ledge Stores, Incorporated*, a lawsuit arising from a fire allegedly caused by defects in an electric blanket. As a result of that fire Mr. Wesser suffered injury to his person and damage to his home.

A second lawsuit that we will consider is *Equal Employment Opportunity Commission v. Chattooga Corporation.* This lawsuit involves an engineer who claims that her employment was terminated for reasons that constitute a violation of Title VII of the Civil Rights Act of 1964.

Read the fact situations for our two sample cases. You may need to refer back to these fact situations as we follow these cases throughout our discussion of civil litigation.

WESSER V. WOODALL SHOALS CORPORATION AND SECOND LEDGE STORES, INCORPORATED

On January 16, 1986, Bryson Wesser drove through the snow to Second Ledge, a local department store, to purchase an electric blanket. He chose an electric blanket manufactured by Woodall Shoals Corporation, a company whose products he had used before. That night Mr. Wesser read the instructions that accompanied the blanket. He put the blanket on his bed, plugged it in, and slept soundly beneath the warm blanket. Shortly after the first cold snap the next winter, Mr. Wesser resumed use of the blanket. The blanket worked fine, and Mr. Wesser noticed nothing unusual.

On the evening of January 3, 1987, Mr. Wesser went to bed around 11:30, turned on the electric blanket, and soon was asleep. About two hours later Mr. Wesser was awakened by flames leaping from the electric blanket. He threw the blanket off, jumped out of bed, and ran from his room. The fire had ignited a bedspread that lay crumpled on the floor at the foot of the bed and near it a newspaper that Mr. Wesser had been reading before he fell asleep. Mr. Wesser sustained burns both while he was in his bed and as he ran through the burning bedspread and newspaper on his way out of the bedroom. He ran to the kitchen and called the fire department and then waited outside the house until firefighters arrived about eight minutes later.

By the time the fire was extinguished, Mr. Wesser's bedroom was gutted and his house damaged by smoke throughout.

EQUAL EMPLOYMENT OPPORTUNITY COMMISSION V. CHATTOOGA CORPORATION

Chattooga Corporation, located in Charleston, North Carolina, is a consulting firm that serves utilities that operate nuclear power plants. On June 23, 1988, Chattooga Corporation hired Sandy Ford as a consulting engineer. This position involved going on-site at nuclear power plants and rendering advice on safe plant operation and on inspections by the Nuclear Regulatory Commission.

Before Sandy Ford was hired, she was advised at length in an interview about specific qualifications for the position of consulting engineer. One requirement was that she have no felony convictions, and this was clearly delineated as a condition of employment in her employment contract. A Chattooga personnel representative explained that nuclear plants have rigid security requirements and will not allow on the premises anyone with a felony conviction. Sandy Ford filled out the job application and signed it. To the specific question "Have you ever been convicted of a felony?" Ms. Ford checked "no." In fact, she had been convicted of a felony eight years earlier.

At the bottom of the application, in bold type, was the following statement: "I hereby certify that the facts set forth in the above employment application are true and complete. I understand that if employed, falsified statements on this application shall be considered sufficient cause for dismissal."

Chattooga Corporation hired Sandy Ford as a consulting engineer. She received five weeks of training before she was permitted to visit a nuclear plant. During this time, Ms. Ford helped a fellow employee file a claim of employment discrimination against Chattooga Corporation with the Equal Employment Opportunity Commission. Both Ms. Ford's supervisor and the director of personnel knew this.

Although her security check had not been completed, Ms. Ford made her first visit to a nuclear facility about six weeks after she was hired. Ms. Ford and her supervisor arrived at the nuclear plant, where according to usual procedure, plant personnel ran their own security check, which included checking local police records. Security officials refused to let Ms. Ford enter the plant. The reason: she had a felony conviction.

As the two traveled back to their office, Ms. Ford's supervisor explained that because Ms. Ford had the felony conviction and had falsified her application, she could not continue employment with Chattooga Corporation. The supervisor explained that Ms. Ford would not have been hired had the felony conviction been known, because the nuclear plants where she would work would not allow her to enter. Sandy Ford stated that she understood and that she would resign, effective one week later.

Four days later Sandy Ford attempted to rescind her resignation. Chattooga Corporation refused to accept the withdrawal of the letter of resignation, and Ms. Ford was forced to leave the company that day. Ms. Ford filed a charge with the Equal Employment Opportunity Commission alleging that Chattooga Corporation had violated Section 704(a) of Title VII of the Civil

Rights Act of 1964, as amended, which prohibits retaliation against an employee who has opposed an unlawful employment practice or has participated in an investigation, proceeding or hearing involving a Title VII matter. (See 42 U.S.C §2000-e for the complete text of the retaliation section of Title VII.)

Attempts at conciliation failed, and the Equal Employment Opportunity Commission filed suit on behalf of Sandy Ford.

1 INTRODUCTION TO CIVIL LITIGATION AND THE LAW OFFICE

LITIGATION EXTRACT: You have just been hired as a litigation paralegal in the law firm of Heyward and Wilson. Leigh Heyward, one of the partners, calls you into her office to discuss a case that she has just been hired to litigate—the claim involving Bryson Wesser. You know the basic facts of Mr. Wesser's case, which you read in the introductory material.

Ms. Heyward has examined the facts and determined that Mr. Wesser probably has a claim worth pursuing through the litigation process. She has already had the initial interview with Mr. Wesser. Ms. Heyward wants you to assist her throughout the litigation, and because you are new, she feels that an overview of the entire litigation process would be instructive. You listen eagerly while Ms. Heyward explains the steps involved in pursuing Mr. Wesser's claim for damages stemming from the electric blanket fire.

CIVIL LITIGATION: OVERVIEW OF THE LITIGATION PROCESS

Before you explore the steps in the litigation process, it is important to understand just what civil litigation is. **Litigation** is the process of carrying on a lawsuit—that is, the process of seeking a remedy or enforcing a right in a court of law.[1] **Civil litigation** refers to lawsuits that involve only noncriminal matters. Note that another term for a lawsuit is an **action**; these two terms are used interchangeably in this text.

1

The Litigation Process

Ms. Heyward is ready to explain the litigation process for Mr. Wesser's action involving the electric blanket fire. You may wish to refer to Figure 1-1, which is a short outline of that process.

FIGURE 1-1 THE LITIGATION PROCESS

Occurrence of the cause of action
Initial client conference
Preliminary investigation
Complaint and summons: prepare and serve
Responsive pleadings: answer, motions to dismiss, etc.
Discovery
Motions for entry of judgment without trial and other pretrial motions
Sometimes further discovery
Settlement attempts
Pretrial conferences
Trial preparation
Trial
Appeal (if necessary)
Enforcement of judgment

The basis for the litigation process has already occurred. It is the fire that injured Mr. Wesser and damaged his home. This is the **cause of action**, the event or state of facts that gives rise to a claim for which a party seeks relief from a court. The facts that give rise to Mr. Wesser's cause of action are the fire, which occurred because the blanket ignited, and the injuries suffered by him as a result, as well as the damages to his house. Mr. Wesser is the **plaintiff**—that is, the party to the lawsuit who is seeking relief from the court. He seeks damages from Woodall Shoals Corporation, the manufacturer of the blanket, and Second Ledge Stores, Incorporated, the seller of the blanket.

Woodall Shoals and Second Ledge are the **defendants**—that is, the parties from whom recovery is sought in the lawsuit.[2] Mr. Wesser seeks to recover **damages**: monetary compensation for the injuries he has suffered and the damage to his property.

The initial client interview has already been conducted. At that interview Ms. Heyward asked Mr. Wesser about the basic facts—what occurred the night of the fire, where the blanket was purchased, the name of the manufacturer, where he received medical treatment and how extensive the treatment was, and other facts necessary to determine whether Mr. Wesser has a viable claim. Ms. Heyward explained to Mr. Wesser the way the litigation will proceed, and they entered a fee agreement.

Your first task will be to set up the file. Next, you and Ms. Heyward will conduct a preliminary investigation to ascertain more facts about the case. For example, you will contact the insurance carrier for the defendants. In the Wesser case, the same carrier represents both defendants, and the defendants have chosen to defend the action together and use the same attorney, David Benedict. Note that in some cases codefendants use different attorneys, and codefendants may even assert claims against each other, as well as defending against the plaintiff's charges. You will also review Mr. Wesser's expenses for medical treatment and the records of that treatment. You will conduct further investigation and interview witnesses, as described in Chapter 5.

Your preliminary investigation will involve more than finding out the basic facts. You may also need to research the law to make sure that your client has a legally sufficient claim. One important point to research at the beginning is the **statute of limitations**. Statutes establish a specific number of years within which a lawsuit must be filed. For instance, a statute may state that a lawsuit for personal injury must be filed within two years of the date the injury occurred. If a party fails to commence the lawsuit within the period specified in the statute (the statute of limitations), then the party is barred from ever filing the lawsuit. Obviously clients can lose important legal rights if a lawsuit is not filed within the statute of limitations, so it is imperative that the attorney/paralegal team check the applicable statute of limitations right away.

The next step is to draft the **complaint**, the document filed by the plaintiff to commence the lawsuit. When we speak of **filing** a document in litigation, we mean taking the document to the office of the clerk of court, where it is received by the clerk's personnel and placed in the clerk's file. When you file a complaint, the clerk assigns the lawsuit a case number, which must then appear on every subsequent document filed. The clerk maintains a file for every pending lawsuit. After the complaint and other essential documents (see Chapter 6) are filed in the clerk's office, the complaint and summons are served on the defendants. The **summons** is a form that accompanies the complaint and explains in simple terms to the defendants that they have been sued and must file an answer with the clerk of court within a prescribed period of time. The delivery of the summons and complaint to the defendants is called **service of process** and must be accomplished in accordance with Rule 4 of the Federal Rules of Civil Procedure. The complaint is the first pleading filed in a lawsuit. **Pleadings** are the formal documents in which the parties allege their claims and defenses.[3]

After the defendants receive the complaint and summons, they conduct their own preliminary investigation and then file pleadings, responding to the complaint. The defendants may file several types of motions seeking dismissal of the plaintiff's complaint.[4] The defendants also file an **answer**, which is the defendants' formal written statement stating the grounds of their defense.[5]

The next stage in the litigation process is the **discovery** phase. **Discovery** is the primary means for gathering facts in the litigation process in order to prepare for trial; it includes several methods for obtaining information from the opposing party. **Interrogatories** are written questions submitted to the opposing party, who must answer the questions and sign a sworn statement that the answers are true. Another common discovery device is the **deposition**, where an attorney orally examines a witness, who takes an oath that the answers given will be truthful.

A court reporter transcribes the testimony and sends copies of the questions and answers to all the parties. There are other discovery devices, which will be discussed in Chapter 9.

The next step in the litigation process involves motions by parties requesting that a judgment be entered in their favor without having to go through a trial. The plaintiff may seek a **default judgment** when the defendant fails to respond to the complaint within the allotted time period. Either party may seek a **judgment on the pleadings**, requesting that the court examine the facts set forth in the pleadings and enter judgment in that party's favor based only on the pleadings. A motion frequently made is a motion for **summary judgment**. Here the court looks at facts beyond the pleadings and determines whether the moving party is entitled to judgment as a matter of law based on the undisputed material facts in the lawsuit.[6]

After the court makes a ruling on these pretrial motions, there may be further discovery, if the parties request it and the court allows it. Bear in mind that the parties can discuss and agree on a settlement at any stage in the litigation. A **settlement** is an agreement between the parties to resolve the lawsuit without having a trial. When parties settle a lawsuit, they enter into a written settlement agreement stating the terms of their settlement—for example, how much money Mr. Wesser would receive for personal injury and property damage. When a lawsuit is settled, the parties also agree to dismiss the lawsuit and file with the court a formal dismissal.

The final pretrial conference takes place after the completion of discovery and before the final stage of trial preparation. At the final pretrial conference the attorneys for the parties meet with the judge and determine which facts are in dispute and try to narrow the issues. The attorneys may also settle the case at this point, and some judges actively encourage the parties and their attorneys to do so. If the lawsuit cannot be settled, the attorneys determine the witnesses and exhibits they will use at trial. The judge may also rule on some pretrial motions, such as motions concerning the admission of certain evidence. The decisions reached by the judge and attorneys are written up in a pretrial order.

The final few weeks before the actual trial are busy with pretrial preparations. You must prepare witnesses for their testimony, arrange exhibits in order and make the proper number of copies of each exhibit, issue subpoenas if necessary, and do everything else necessary to prepare for the trial.

Throughout the trial you will help keep track of exhibits, take notes of testimony, and perform other activities to assist your employer.

If the judgment entered at trial is not satisfactory, it can be appealed. As we will discuss at greater length in Chapter 3, an appellate court is different from a trial court.[7] A trial court hears the testimony of witnesses and examines the exhibits that the parties present. In contrast, appellate courts hear no testimony. The appellate court reviews the record of the trial to determine whether the trial judge made any mistakes that warrant a new trial. Paralegals help to compile the **record on appeal**, which consists of copies of the pleadings and judgment entered, the transcript of the trial with notations as to which pieces of evidence were objected to, a statement of the questions presented to the appellate court for review, and all other documents from the litigation that are necessary for understanding the issues before the appellate court. If a satisfactory judgment is entered in Bryson Wesser's favor at the trial level, no problems enforcing the judgment are anticipated. That is, the defendants' insurance company is expected to pay promptly, although it too has the option to appeal the judgment.

Rules that Govern Civil Litigation

The preceding overview of the litigation process shows you that a lawsuit proceeds in a predictable pattern. The entire litigation process—from the filing of the complaint to commence the lawsuit to the entry of judgment at the conclusion of the lawsuit—is governed by detailed rules. Several sets of rules must be followed. The goal of all the rules that govern civil procedure is well described in Rule 101 of the Rules of Practice and Procedure of the United States District Court for the Middle District of North Carolina. Rule 101 states the philosophy of the rules as follows: "These rules shall be construed and enforced in such manner as to avoid technical delay, permit just and prompt determination of all proceedings, and promote the efficient administration of justice."

When you consider the tremendous number of lawsuits filed in our federal and state court systems, it becomes obvious why detailed rules of court are essential. Without the strict enforcement of rules of procedure, the court system would be extraordinarily chaotic.

The consequences of failure to follow the rules of procedure are drastic. In particular, failure to meet filing deadlines can have devastating consequences. For instance, a party may have a constitutional right to trial by jury. However, if the party does not request a jury trial within the time limitations of Rule 38 of the Federal Rules of Civil Procedure, the party waives his or her right to a jury trial. As another example, after judgment is entered, a party may seek relief from the judgment for certain reasons, but only within one year from entry of the judgment, as set forth in Rule 60 of the Federal Rules of Civil Procedure. Do not be disturbed if you do not yet understand the intricacies of these examples. For now, just remember that the rules that regulate civil litigation must be followed, or else your client will lose important rights.

The Federal Rules of Civil Procedure. Throughout this text we will concentrate on the Federal Rules of Civil Procedure, which are printed in 28 United States Code. The Federal Rules of Civil Procedure (FRCivP) apply to all civil actions filed in the United States District Courts, that is, the trial courts in the federal court system.

The Federal Rules of Civil Procedure regulate the course of the lawsuit from start to finish. Rules 3 through 5 concern the commencement of a lawsuit.[8] The Federal Rules of Civil Procedure provide numerous deadlines for filing certain documents. FRCivP 6 explains how to compute the time limits prescribed.[9] Rules 7 through 16 govern the various pleadings filed after the complaint, the pleading that commences the lawsuit.[10] Rules 17 through 25 deal with the parties to a lawsuit.[11]

Rules 26 through 37 govern the discovery process, delineating the types of information that can be elicited through discovery and the various discovery procedures for obtaining the information.[12] Rules 38 through 53 apply to the trial, covering such topics as right to jury trial, dismissal of actions, subpoenas, and instructions to the jury.[13] Rules 54 through 63 concern entry of judgment.[14] These rules delineate the various ways a party can obtain a judgment, such as a default judgment when the defendant does not respond to the complaint.[15] FRCivP 56 governs summary judgment, which entitles a party to judgment without having a full-blown trial.[16] Other rules discuss how to obtain relief from a judgment entered against a party.

The remainder of the rules are termed "miscellaneous." Probably the most important of these is FRCivP 65, which deals with temporary restraining orders and preliminary injunctions.[17]

State Rules of Civil Procedure. For civil actions filed in state court, you must follow that state's rules of civil procedure. Most state rules of civil procedure are modeled closely after the Federal Rules of Civil Procedure. However, there may be important differences, so you must consult the state rules of civil procedure. You can find the state rules in the state statutes. You can also find the state rules of civil procedure in commercial publications that contain the rules of court (procedure, evidence, appellate procedure, etc.) for a specific state.

Federal Local Court Rules. Federal district courts have their own local rules of procedure, which serve to supplement the Federal Rules of Civil Procedure. For example, the United States District Court for the Southern District of New York publishes its own rules of practice and procedure. The local rules generally cover topics such as requirements for initial pretrial orders and the procedure for final pretrial conferences. In addition, the local rules set forth practical requirements, such as how many copies to file with the clerk, paper size, format, and rules for case citations.

Note that specialized federal courts, such as bankruptcy court, may have their own local procedural rules. For instance, the Federal District Court for the Middle District of North Carolina has its Rules of Practice and Procedure for actions filed in that district, and there are separate Local Bankruptcy Rules for the United States Bankruptcy Court for the Middle District of North Carolina.

State Local Court Rules. You must also check your state's general rules of practice for its state trial courts. The state rules of practice supplement the state rules of civil procedure. The state general rules of practice govern the mechanics of a lawsuit, such as what size paper to use for pleadings. Topics may also include procedure for pretrial conferences and enlargement of time for filing motions. The state court rules of general practice are also contained in the state statutes and in commercial publications.

Finally, judicial districts within a state often have local rules of practice. In North Carolina, for instance, Mecklenburg County comprises Judicial District 26, which publishes its local court rules in the *Mecklenburg Bar Handbook*. These rules address procedural matters such as how cases are scheduled, how to submit proposed orders to the judge, and how to schedule emergency hearings.

General Remarks about Procedural Rules. The preceding description may sound like an unworkable maze of rules. However, all the rules are easy to understand. Just remember that in federal court you follow the Federal Rules of Civil Procedure. For more mechanical procedural questions, consult the local rules for the district in which your action is filed. For state court actions, follow the state rules of civil procedure; and for the more mechanical procedural questions, consult the state general rules of practice. For very specific questions, such as how to calendar (schedule) a case, check the local procedural rules for your judicial district.

 POINTER: If your state judicial district does not have written rules, consult the office of the clerk of court or trial court administrator, or consult your supervising attorney or another paralegal in the firm.

Federal and State Rules of Evidence. The rules we have discussed so far concern procedure. Another very important set of rules concerns the evidence that can be presented at trial. Evidence includes the testimony of witnesses, documents related to the event in question, and objects such as the control unit of the electric blanket in the Wesser case. Evidence will be discussed more fully in Chapter 4.

Not every piece of evidence is admissible. A piece of evidence is **admissible** if it is proper information for the decision maker to consider in reaching a decision at trial and if the judge determines that it may be introduced at trial. Litigators must look to the rules of evidence to determine whether evidence is admissible. The Federal Rules of Evidence govern proceedings in federal court. You can find the Federal Rules of Evidence in Title 28 of the United States Code (28 U.S.C.) and in commercial publications. In state court, you must follow the rules of evidence for the state in which the action is tried. Most states have rules similar to the Federal Rules of Evidence. However, there can be important differences, so you must consult the state rules of evidence, which can be found in state statutes and in commercial publications.

Rules of Professional Responsibility. There is a final set of rules to consider. The rules of professional responsibility govern the conduct of attorneys during litigation and in every transaction they undertake. The penalties for conduct in violation of the rules of professional responsibility range from a private letter of reprimand to revocation of a lawyer's license to practice law. Although paralegals cannot be disciplined directly for violations of the rules of professional conduct, the attorneys with whom they work can be penalized for the paralegals' conduct. Thus it is imperative that paralegals know and obey the rules of professional conduct, which are discussed at length in Chapter 2.

Types of Lawsuits

As part of the paralegal/attorney team, you will probably work on lawsuits involving a wide range of subject matter. You may work on anything from a property division in connection with a divorce action to an action to collect a debt owed a hospital or an action challenging the constitutionality of a new law. We will discuss some of the most common types of lawsuits. In the course of your career, you will work on these and many other types of litigation.

Torts. One of the largest areas of litigation involves **torts**, which are injuries to a person or property. Torts are usually the result of a person's negligent conduct or his or her intentional conduct. **Negligence**, the source of a large percentage of these lawsuits, involves the concept that all people have a duty to exercise due care in their conduct toward others so that others are not injured. A person's careless behavior can result in a negligent act, as when an inattentive driver runs a stop sign and causes a car accident.

Litigation concerning torts is frequently **personal injury** litigation. Personal injury cases occur when a person has been physically injured by the wrongful act of another person, as in a car accident. Another area of tort litigation is **product liability**, when a person is injured by a defective product. The Wesser case involves product liability: Mr. Wesser contends that Woodall Shoals manufactured and Second Ledge sold a defective electric blanket, which ignited and caused injury to him and damage to his home.

When we discuss torts, remember that these are civil cases, not criminal cases. A person does not necessarily break a law every time he or she injures another person. For instance, if you make a left turn and hit another person's car, you have not necessarily broken a law, even if you injure the other person. However, you can commit a tort and break a law at the same time. Suppose you make the left turn because you are driving under the influence of alcohol. Now you have committed a tort *and* committed a criminal offense. The personal injury litigation will involve the tort only. The criminal offense will be handled by a prosecutor in criminal court.

Contracts. A **contract** is an agreement between two or more parties that one party is obliged to perform an act in exchange for something from the other party. For example, if you enter a contract with your bank to finance your car, the bank agrees to lend you the money to pay for the car, and you agree to pay the bank back through a series of payments. When one party fails to honor his or her obligation, this is a **breach of contract**. Contract litigation arises when one party breaches the contract.

Another example of contract litigation is when a person enters a hospital and signs a statement promising to pay the hospital for the services rendered. If the person fails to pay the hospital, the hospital may sue to collect the debt. A frequent subject of contract litigation involves construction of buildings. Suppose you enter a contract with a builder to construct your home to certain specifications for a certain price. If the builder does not complete the house or build it to the agreed specifications, you may sue the builder, asking that the house be finished to meet the agreed-upon specifications or that you be allowed to pay the builder less than the agreed-upon price because the house was not constructed according to the terms of the contract.

Corporate. Lawsuits involving corporations come in many varieties and often involve contract disputes. They may also involve trademark violations and actions against persons who reveal trade secrets. Other corporate lawsuits may arise from personnel matters, such as overtime pay, terminating an employee, or declining to promote an employee. If an employee feels that the action is the result of discrimination, a lawsuit such as the Chattooga case may arise. Lawsuits based on charges of discrimination are discussed under Civil Rights, following the next section.

Property. Disputes over the ownership of property can give rise to litigation. For instance, if two neighbors have a boundary dispute they cannot settle, they may go to court for a resolution. Disputes over the possession of property can also result in lawsuits. For example, two people may disagree as to whether one gave or simply lent the other a very expensive piece of jewelry. Disputes between landlord and tenant can also result in litigation.

Civil Rights. Civil rights cases involve violations of personal rights protected by the United States Constitution and state constitutions and by certain federal and state laws. An example of such a federal law is Title VII of the Civil Rights Act of 1964, as amended, which is the statute involved in the Chattooga case. Title VII prohibits discrimination ''against any individual with respect to his compensation, terms, conditions, or privileges of employment, because of such individual's race, color, religion, sex, or national origin...'' (42 U.S.C. 2000e-2).

There exist a host of other civil rights statutes, designed to give force to basic personal rights guaranteed by the Constitution. Just a few examples include the Voting Rights Act; the Age Discrimination in Employment Act; and the Equal Pay Act.

There are often prerequisites to filing a lawsuit in court to enforce a right under a civil rights statute. Title VII is a good example. Before a lawsuit can be filed in federal court, certain procedures must be completed within the Equal Employment Opportunity Commission (EEOC), the federal agency responsible for enforcing Title VII. First, the aggrieved party visits the EEOC office and files a charge of discrimination. The EEOC investigates the charge. If the EEOC determines that there is ''reasonable cause'' to believe Title VII has been violated, the EEOC must attempt conciliation, with the aim of eliminating the practices that violate Title VII. Conciliation involves corresponding and meeting with the party against whom the charge is made, as well as an informal hearing to determine the facts. If conciliation is unsuccessful and the EEOC is convinced that the charging party has a legitimate claim, the EEOC can file suit on the charging party's behalf. If the EEOC chooses not to file suit, the charging party may sue in federal court, using his or her own attorney and proceeding at his or her own expense. The completion of the procedures within the administrative agency (here, the EEOC) before filing a lawsuit is known as **exhaustion of administrative remedies**.

Domestic Relations. The termination of a marriage can spawn extensive litigation. Besides obtaining a divorce, the spouses must resolve issues including division of property, child custody, child support, and sometimes alimony. Aside from obtaining a court judgment granting a divorce, the other matters can often be settled by the parties and their attorneys outside court. If not, litigation ensues and can continue for a long time. This is especially true when young children are involved, because the issues of custody, visitation, and the amount of child support can arise repeatedly until the children are no longer minors.

Remedies Available in Civil Litigation

Plaintiffs file lawsuits because they seek relief from the court. That is, plaintiffs ask the court to enter judgment directing the defendants to remedy the wrong they have inflicted upon the plaintiffs.

Money Damages.   Plaintiffs frequently seek **money damages**—that is, monetary compensation from the defendants for the injuries and losses suffered. For example, Mr. Wesser requests in his complaint that the defendants be ordered to compensate him for his injuries and property loss. A creditor suing a debtor on a promissory note requests that the court order the debtor to pay the money and interest owed. Various types of monetary damages are discussed in Chapter 5.

Equitable Remedies.   When a plaintiff's loss cannot be compensated by monetary damages, the plaintiff seeks equitable remedies. An **injunction**, which is a court order forbidding a party from a particular activity, is an equitable remedy. For instance, your neighbor may want to cut down a 100-year-old tree in your yard because it casts too much shade on the neighbor's house. You do not want monetary compensation for the timber value. You want an order forbidding your neighbor from cutting down the tree, so you seek an injunction.

The contrast between monetary relief and injunctive relief can be seen in the complaint in the Chattooga case. The plaintiff seeks monetary relief in the form of back pay for Sandy Ford. The plaintiff also seeks injunctive relief—that is, an order that the defendant cease from retaliation against employees who complain of acts believed to be unlawful under Title VII.

Another type of equitable relief is **specific performance**, where the court orders a party to comply with the terms of a contract. For instance, the court may order the defendant to sell to the plaintiff a piece of real estate, as agreed in a contract. This remedy is used only when the thing to be purchased is unique.

This is by no means an exhaustive discussion of equitable remedies. However, you should now understand the difference between equitable remedies and monetary damages.

THE LAW OFFICE

Every law office has its own special office procedures, personnel categories, and personnel management techniques. However, an understanding of certain common characteristics and procedures will help you jump right in on your first day in your law firm.

Law Office Personnel and Organization

Usually there are two types of lawyers in a firm—partners and associates. **Partners** are owners of the firm; they share in the profits of the firm rather than work for a straight salary. Partners also participate in the management of the firm. A larger firm may also have **senior partners**, lawyers who have been partners for the longest time and who share in the largest portion of the firm's profits.

Associates are the more recently hired lawyers, who are not partners. They are paid salaries, with occasional bonuses depending on the firm's profitability in a given year. In a litigation firm, the newer attorneys participate in the pretrial aspects of litigation, such as discovery and arguing simple motions in court, before they gain enough experience to conduct an entire trial.

As you no doubt know, **paralegals** are persons who possess legal skills and work under the supervision of attorneys.[18] The particular duties commonly assigned to paralegals are discussed at the end of this chapter.

Law clerks are persons not yet licensed to practice, usually law students, who work in law firms during breaks from law school. They perform research and writing tasks and often are hired by the firm as associates after they graduate from law school and pass the bar examination.

Depending on its size, a law firm may employ a wide variety of support personnel. Obviously, legal secretaries are essential for word processing and other duties. A large law firm may have persons who do word processing exclusively, employing legal secretaries for other duties. A firm may also have employees responsible solely for billing matters. The time that the lawyers and paralegals spend on a particular case is carefully recorded, and the amount of the client's bill depends on how much time is spent on the case, when the client is paying an hourly rate for legal services. Obviously, a case involving a simple divorce will be far less expensive for a client than a case defending against a medical malpractice suit. For further discussion of billing, see the upcoming material on timekeeping procedures.

The Litigation Atmosphere

The atmosphere in which a litigation attorney/paralegal team works is different from many other types of law. Litigators cannot control their schedules to the extent that some other types of lawyers can. The trial court administrator or clerk of court, not the attorney, generally sets the date for trials. The attorney must be ready when the case is scheduled. Typically, the administrative office of the court in a state court publishes a **calendar**, sometimes called a **docket** or **trial list**, which lists a number of cases to be heard on a certain day or during a certain week. When the court's calendar is published, it has an amazing effect on the rate at which cases on the calendar are settled. A calendar may contain a list of 50 cases to be heard during a week-long session of court, and your case may be 30th on the list. The attorney must still be ready to try that case, because the 29 cases before it may settle. Attorneys have a little more control over their schedules in federal court, where the trial calendar tends to be more carefully tailored for a particular day and hour for a trial to begin.

The point of this example is that litigators often have little control over their schedules. This causes a fair amount of stress and even frustration. An attorney may spend days preparing for trial, only to have the court **continue** it—that is, move the trial to a later date.

Litigators also have to work at a fast pace. As you progress through this text, you will learn more and more about the importance of deadlines. Attorneys often have many important documents due at the same time. On a given day, an attorney may have to file an answer to a complaint, mail a memorandum of law in an appellate case, and travel to another city to conduct a deposition. Thus you can see how essential litigation paralegals are! On this busy day you can go to the courthouse to file the answer and be sure that copies are mailed to all the parties to the lawsuit. After the attorney has approved the memorandum of law, you can make sure that all the copies are made, that everything is in order, that the letter to the office of the clerk of court is included, and that the package is sent out in the express mail. If you were not there to help while the attorney went out of town for a deposition, the attorney would have a very stressful day indeed.

Working with Lawyers

In many ways working with lawyers is no different from working with any other group of persons. Lawyers come in all varieties and all personality types. You may work with a litigator who is the calmest individual you have ever met—a person who is not upset when there are two clients waiting (without appointments), three phone calls on hold, and two people in the lawyer's office asking questions. On the other hand, you may work with litigators who find such situations extremely stressful and become a bit testy. There is no magic formula for working with lawyers. Like all persons, no two are alike. Your best approach is to be a keen observer of human nature and learn how best to deal with each lawyer. If there is a lawyer in the firm with whom you have problems working, consult with your supervisor immediately.

Important Office Procedures: Billing/Timekeeping

When a client hires a lawyer, they enter a fee agreement specifying how the lawyer will be compensated. Fee agreements are discussed in detail in Chapter 5. The two most common fee arrangements are **hourly rate** and **contingent fee**. In the hourly rate system, the number of **billable hours** spent on the client's case is multiplied by the hourly rate agreed on. In the contingent fee arrangement, the lawyer's compensation is an agreed percentage of the amount recovered by the client. A common arrangement is for the attorney to receive one-third the amount awarded.

In addition to the fee for professional services rendered, the fee agreement usually provides that the client will pay certain costs, or out-of-pocket expenses, such as xerox copies, long-distance calls, postage, and filing fees. These expenses are sometimes referred to as disbursements.

Obviously, a careful record must be kept of all time spent on a client's case and of all disbursements made. The paralegal's time is also figured into the billable hours, so you must keep careful records.

Timekeeping Procedures. The methods for keeping track of time spent on a client's case vary among law firms. A variety of forms can be used, and some law firms make extensive use of computers for timekeeping. You must carefully review your firm's written procedures for timekeeping and discuss them with your supervisor.

No matter what type of forms you use, the same basic timekeeping information must be recorded. Examine Figure 1-2, which illustrates the time sheet used by the law firm Heyward and Wilson. This particular form consists of an 8 1/2-× 11-inch sheet with a series of rows of information with the same headings for each row. Every day every attorney and paralegal record the work they performed, putting the appropriate information under each heading. This particular form has a sheet underneath it on which a carbon copy is made of everything entered on the face sheet. Heyward and Wilson uses a combination of handwritten and computer systems for billing. Each row on the form is detachable, and usually at the end of each day you give the individual slips to the clerk in charge of billing, who puts the billing entries in the computer. At the end of the month, a statement is sent to the client. If the fee agreement is for an hourly rate, the monthly bill is calculated by the number of billable hours times the hourly rate.

POINTER: It is important to write your entries on the time sheet throughout the day. At the end of a hectic day, you may not be able to remember every task you performed that day, much less how much time it took. You can fill in the rows as you complete the task.

FIGURE 1-2   TIME SHEET OF HEYWARD AND WILSON

TC telephone conference	LF letter from	I investigation	
R review	C conference	Misc miscellaneous	
RV revision of	CA court appearance	NC no charge	
P preparation	TR travel	RS research	
LT letter to			

Date	File No.	Client	Atty/ Par Code	Description of Services	Time Spent

Because the amount of space on the time sheet is limited, the firm uses a series of abbreviations to describe services rendered. The abbreviations appear at the top of the form. The columns for information entered are straightforward. Enter the date the work was performed. Under file number, insert the number the law firm has assigned to that file.

POINTER: Do not confuse the firm's file number, used to keep track of the file within the firm only, with the file number assigned by the clerk of court when the lawsuit is commenced. The clerk's file number—for example, C-89-1293-B in the Wesser case—identifies the location of the file in the clerk's office and ensures that court documents are filed properly in the clerk's office.

Under the Client column, enter the client's name, and be consistent, always using the last name for an individual and the proper designation for a corporation. In the Attorney/Paralegal column, enter your initials. The column designated

Code is filled in with an abbreviation to indicate the type of task done—telephone conference, for example, or letter. Description of Services elaborates on this information, describing to whom the call was made or letter written as well as its subject matter. The detail in which services are described varies among law firms; some require a finely detailed description and others require only a brief notation. Under Time Spent, write the amount of time it took to perform the task. For increments of time less than a full hour, most law firms record the time spent by one-tenth of the hour. Thus, if a phone conversation took 18 minutes, you would enter .30.

There are many other methods of timekeeping. For instance, some attorneys keep a manual journal, which looks more like a daily diary. A typical entry might be the following:

1.50   File 0832-A   R of discovery documents.

Here the letter *R* stands for review.

Disbursements. As we noted, clients are billed for expenses such as postage and copying. There are many systems for keeping track of disbursements. Slips similar to those for timekeeping are frequently used. As with timekeeping slips, you enter the date, file number, client's name, and your initials. Then you designate the nature of the expense and the amount. Each slip may be torn off at the end of the day and placed in the client's file in an envelope or subfile. Disbursements are also entered on the computer and included in the client's bill.

Time Management Techniques

Because the number of hours paralegals spend on a case is so important, it is essential to develop time management techniques. Among reading material available on this subject are publications of the American Bar Association's section on Law Practice Management.[19] Here are just a few tips:

- Always fill out time slips promptly. Otherwise, at the end of the day, you may not be able to account for all the time you worked.
- Keep a list of tasks you must perform, arranged by importance and/or date due. Consult the list every morning and plan your day accordingly.
- Use the tickler system (discussed later in this section) for reviewing files. If you request a reasonable number of files each day, you may be able to concentrate on just a few files and wrap up several tasks.
- If you have to draft a difficult document, work on it early in the morning. Not only will your mind be fresher, but you will have fewer interruptions.
- Meet regularly with the attorneys on your team and determine who can handle certain matters most quickly and efficiently. While a heavy workload may be expected, if yours becomes unmanageable, discuss the problem with the attorneys.
- Review your time sheets to be sure that you have sufficient billable hours. If you have been at the office for eight hours, and have done only three hours' worth of billable work, you have probably wasted a good

bit of time. Of course, there will be days when you have to spend a substantial amount of time on nonbillable matters, such as attending professional meetings or training.

Important Office Procedures: Docket Control

Docket control means maintaining a system for keeping track of deadlines. While the docketing of deadlines is important for all types of law practice, it is particularly crucial for litigation. As our discussion will emphasize, there are a multitude of deadlines to be tracked in the course of litigation, from the statute of limitations to the trial date to the deadline for filing an appeal. Docket control is one of the most important tasks assigned to paralegals.

Examples of Docket Control Systems. A variety of docket control systems are used by law firms. A firm may use more than one system, with one or more systems serving as backup for the others. Because there are so many permutations, you must become familiar with all the details of your firm's docket control system(s).

Computer Systems. Many firms, especially larger ones, use a computerized docket control system. When paralegals enter the appropriate information into the computer system, the deadlines are readily available. For instance, if you represent Chattooga Corporation, you enter the date that the summons and complaint were served and the date that a responsive pleading is due. The computer can generate a calendar of deadlines for all the cases the firm is litigating. You may wish to put the calendar on the wall or in some other conspicuous place in your office. The computer may be programmed to flash upcoming deadlines on your personal computer first thing in the morning. Ideally, the computer will give multiple warnings that become more frequent as the deadline nears.

Tickler Forms. One manual type of docket control system is the use of tickler forms. Examine Figure 1-3. This shows a simple tickler form. The paralegal fills out the file number, client's name, action to be completed, and deadline for the action to be completed. Then the paralegal writes three dates on which to be reminded of the action to be completed. The tickler form has three carbon copies, and on each of the three dates the employee in charge of the tickler system gives the reminder to the paralegal.

FIGURE 1-3 TICKLER FORM

File No.	Client	Action to be Completed	Deadline

1st reminder_____
2d reminder_____
3d reminder_____

The purpose of a tickler system is for you to receive a copy of the tickler form at specified times to remind you to complete a task. Assume that you have to prepare the first draft of an answer to a complaint. You indicate on the tickler form three dates on which you want to receive a copy to remind you to draft the answer. On those dates, the employee in charge of the tickler system will give you the written reminders.

Calendars. Here we are referring to regular month-by-month calendars. (Remember that a court's schedule of hearings and trials is called a *court calendar.* Also helpful in tracking deadlines, the court calendar is discussed later in this section.) Paralegals and attorneys may use regular calendars to record deadlines. For instance, if an answer is due on January 27, write ''answer due'' on that date on your calendar. This system may cause problems if you do not also enter reminders well in advance of the date the answer is due. You may become busy and forget to review the coming weeks. If January 27 falls on a Monday and you have forgotten to check the calendar in advance, you will have a rude surprise first thing Monday morning. Regular calendars are best used in conjunction with other backup systems. Small calendars may be handy for checking deadlines when you are away from your office, suddenly get a sinking feeling, and need to check a deadline immediately.

Sources of Information for Docket Control. Obviously, in order to keep a record of deadlines, first you have to determine the deadlines. Whenever a document related to one of the files assigned to you arrives—whether it is a pleading, a notice of motion, or a notice of a scheduled deposition—you must note the deadline immediately in your docketing system. Entering deadlines and scheduled events is like recording the information in your checkbook register. If you do not do it immediately, you may forget.

Records of Proceedings in the File. In the file itself, you need to keep a readily viewable record of everything that transpires in the course of litigation. You should be able to open the file and quickly find what pleadings have been filed, when depositions are scheduled, dates that motions are scheduled, and any other transaction in the course of litigation. In this way, when your docket control system alerts you that a deadline is approaching, you can both double-check the proper date and see whether the transaction has already been completed. Enter deadlines promptly in this same record of proceedings, even though the docket control system will generate reminders.

One important component of the record of proceedings is the **pleading record**. This may be part of the larger record of proceedings, or it may be easier to follow if maintained as a separate document. The pleading record tracks every pleading filed and received and the response date. For the pleadings that you file, you record the date the pleading was filed, the date it was served on the other party or parties, and the date that a response is due. For pleadings served on your client, enter the name of the pleading, the date it was served, and the date a response is due.

POINTER: A good way to review the record of proceedings is to establish a tickler system for file review. The method can be simple. When you finish the work you are doing with a file, mark on the outside of the file the date that you want to see the file again. Have the filing clerks maintain a calendar on which they enter the date you and the attorneys want to see files again. The clerks will enter the date in the calendar before refiling each file. First thing each morning, the file clerks will pull and distribute to each paralegal and attorney the files they have requested for review that day. This is yet another backup system to make sure you do not neglect any files. Even if there are no deadlines within the next few weeks, you can still monitor the progress of the litigation—for example, settlement negotiations—and keep the client informed.

Review the Clerk of Court's Records. The clerk of court keeps a record of all documents filed in the clerk's office. Usually in the front of the clerk's file you can find the record of the date all documents were filed in that case. This method helps you double-check the dates you have entered in the firm's docket control system.

While you are checking the dates, you should also check for proof of service. Suppose that you have multiple defendants in a federal court action. You have 120 days to effect service of process on each defendant, or else the action may be dismissed as to each defendant not served. Proof of service will be in the clerk's file, and you must monitor it closely for all defendants in order not to miss the 120-day deadline. See Chapter 6 for a discussion of service of process under FRCivP 4.

Court Calendars. As we noted earlier, the **court calendar** is a court's schedule for hearings, pretrial conferences, and trials. One important task for paralegals is to check the calendars for all courts in which you have actions pending. You may have actions pending in state and federal courts, and each court may have its own system of publishing its calendar. In many cities, calendars are published in periodicals to which attorneys subscribe. You may be assigned the task of reviewing the periodicals to find all references to cases your firm is litigating. Other courts mail their calendars directly to the attorneys involved. Still others may require that you go by the office of the clerk of court or trial administrator to pick up copies of the court calendars. Become familiar with all the methods for distributing court calendars in the courts in which you are involved, and monitor the calendars carefully.

Important Deadlines and Dates. A wide array of deadlines and dates must be docketed for a litigation practice. Some of the most important ones are discussed here.

Statutes of Limitations. This is the first date you should determine when a client comes in to discuss potential litigation. We discussed it earlier in the chapter, but it is important enough to reemphasize: a **statute of limitations** is the time within which a lawsuit must be commenced, or else the plaintiff can never bring suit. For example, the applicable law may provide that an action for breach of contract must be filed within two years of the breach. If your lawsuit will be filed in state court, check the applicable state statutes concerning statutes of limitations. The amount of time allowed for filing suit differs according to the type of action involved, and some states have fairly complex statutes of limitations. In federal court actions, check the applicable federal laws. Remember that even if a plaintiff has a case that is almost certain to win, if the lawsuit is not commenced before the statute of limitations expires, the plaintiff is forever barred from filing suit. If the law firm is responsible for the failure to file the action within the time allowed, a malpractice suit is likely to ensue.

Dates for Filing Pleadings.   As you have seen, the rules of civil procedure, both state and federal, provide a certain number of days within which a response to a pleading must be filed. For example, under the Federal Rules of Civil Procedure, a defendant has 20 days from date of service of the complaint to file an answer. There are also deadlines for responding to counterclaims and other pleadings. (These deadlines are discussed in Chapters 7 and 8.) Mark the reminder of the deadline well in advance so that the attorney/paralegal team may make a timely request for an extension, if necessary.

Discovery Deadlines.   Often a judge enters a pretrial order setting forth the dates by which discovery must be completed. Many courts have applicable local court rules that impose deadlines for discovery deadlines—for example, discovery must be completed within 120 days of the filing of the complaint unless the court specifies otherwise. Check all applicable discovery deadlines and enter them in the docket control system. (See Chapter 9 for details on discovery.)

Deadlines for Filing and Responding to Motions.   As we will discuss in Chapters 7 and 8, many motions are filed before a lawsuit goes to trial. Both state and federal rules of civil procedure, as well as local court rules, impose deadlines for filing certain motions and for responding to motions. For example, certain motions to dismiss under FRCivP 12 must be filed within the time allowed to file an answer. Local court rules may impose rules for filing responses to motions. For example, a court may consider a motion unopposed if a response is not filed within 10 days of service of the motion. Because pretrial motions are such an important part of the litigation process, all deadlines regarding motions must be monitored very carefully, in order to ensure that your client does not lose the right to make important assertions.

Court Appearances.   Enter dates for court appearances well in advance. The attorney/paralegal team needs as much time as possible to prepare for hearings on motions, pretrial conferences, and the trial itself. Monitor the mail for notices of motions, and monitor the court calendars as discussed above.

Appeals and Post-Trial Motions.   At the conclusion of a trial, prompt action must be taken to preserve the right to appeal the verdict and to file other post-trial motions. You must consult the applicable state and federal rules of civil procedure, as well as the rules of appellate procedure for the court in which the appeal will be taken.

Other Deadlines.   There are a host of other deadlines that paralegals must monitor. For instance, in open court at a motion hearing, the judge may orally impose deadlines for filing memoranda of law or other documents. Thus, if the attorney on your team makes a court appearance and you do not accompany him or her that day, be sure to find out if any response deadlines were announced. Federal and state rules of civil procedure and local rules of courts are full of various deadlines, and you must take care to monitor all of them.

COMMUNICATING WITH CLIENTS

Paralegals are in constant contact with clients. Ideally, they are introduced to one another at the initial conference; thus the client feels comfortable with the paralegal thereafter. Paralegals interview clients and frequently communicate with them by phone and letter. There are important guidelines to keep in mind in all your communications with clients, as well as with witnesses and other persons.

The Importance of Regular Communication

Few things make clients more unhappy than thinking that the law firm representing them is neglecting their case. In fact, this is one of the most common bases for grievances filed against attorneys.

However, avoiding grievances is not the only reason that regular communication with clients must be maintained. You need to obtain much information from clients in order to draft pleadings, answer interrogatories, and perform tasks at all stages of litigation. As we discussed, all this must be accomplished in a timely manner, so obviously you have to give clients plenty of lead time to compile and forward information. Regular communication ensures that you advise clients of upcoming deadlines well in advance.

Telephone Contact

You may talk to some clients even more often than the attorney does. Often the attorney is out of the office or otherwise unavailable, and the paralegal will receive the telephone calls from clients.

There are some important guidelines to keep in mind when you communicate with clients, especially on the telephone. Clients often call because they have a question that requires legal advice. As Chapter 2 will clearly explain, paralegals are not permitted to give legal advice. Therefore you must take down the information and give it to the attorney for a response. One method is to dictate a memorandum to the attorney, outlining the conversation and the client's question. The attorney can contact the client and render the necessary legal advice. If the attorney is involved in a trial or otherwise unavailable for an extended period, the paralegal will be authorized to relay the attorney's responses to the client.

Letters to Clients

You will frequently correspond with clients through letters. Letters are a particularly effective method for explaining detailed information that you need from the client. Be sure to keep the letters simple and to the point. At times a letter may need to be lengthy to explain much detailed information, but it need not be convoluted.

You must always indicate in the way you sign the letter that you are a paralegal. Chapter 2 will explain how your letters should be signed.

If you need a response by a certain date, be sure to include the deadline in the letter. Then note the deadline to follow up with a phone call, if necessary. If you are asking the client to fill out forms, be sure to enclose the forms, with an explanation of how to fill them out.

The Memorandum to the File

After a telephone conversation or a meeting with a client, you need to make a record of what transpired. This is important for several reasons. First, you may have learned information important to the case, and you need a written record of the precise information you got. Second, if there is a question later about what you said or what the client said, you have a record. This can be very important if a client suggests that you neglected to convey certain facts or that you conveyed the wrong information.

Route the memo to the file to the attorneys working on the case, if the memo contains information they should know before their next review of the file. If the information is extremely significant, bring it to their attention immediately.

THE ROLE OF THE PARALEGAL ON THE ATTORNEY/PARALEGAL TEAM

It is important to understand the importance of your position as a litigation paralegal and the assignments you will perform.

The Importance of Paralegals

The importance of paralegals cannot be overemphasized. This is especially true in the area of litigation. Attorneys who litigate work on many cases simultaneously, and the activities in one case do not cease just because the attorney is in court trying another case. This is one reason litigation paralegals are particularly valuable. Paralegals can keep the files moving and current when the attorney is tied up in court or in depositions. Litigation attorneys are often out of the office, especially when they are involved in lawsuits in other geographical regions. Paralegals are essential in tracking the many deadlines encountered in litigation.

Paralegals are invaluable for the delivery of competent, cost-efficient legal services. Paralegals handle a wide range of very important duties in the litigation process. Short of rendering legal advice and making court appearances, the range of duties delegated to a trained paralegal can be very expansive.

Litigation Tasks for Paralegals

The variety of tasks performed by litigation paralegals varies according to the law firm and the paralegal's level of experience. The following list describes tasks commonly assigned to litigation paralegals sequentially according to the stage in the litigation at which they are usually performed. This overview is not all-inclusive but is designed to give you an indication of the duties that may be assigned to you.[20]

Prior to Commencement of the Action

- Attend initial client conference.
- Informal investigation (interview potential witnesses, check public records, etc.).
- Make preliminary arrangements for expert witnesses.
- Set up file.
- Follow up with client on any documents or other information needed to prepare complaint.

Commencement of Action

- Prepare initial draft of complaint for attorney review.
- Prepare summons for attorney review.
- Assemble any exhibits to the complaint.
- Prepare civil cover sheet.
- Arrange for service of process.
- Ensure that proof of service of process is in clerk's file.
- Now and throughout litigation process, enter deadlines in docket control system.

Motions and Responsive Pleadings

- If you represent defendant, prepare initial draft of answer and/or other responsive motions such as motions to dismiss or to strike.
- If applicable, prepare initial draft of counterclaim and cross-claim for attorney review.
- If applicable, prepare initial draft of amended pleadings and motions to amend.

Discovery

- Draft for attorney review interrogatories, requests for admission and production.
- Depositions: arrange place and court reporter, send notices and prepare any necessary subpoenas. At the deposition, take notes and help with exhibits.
- Producing documents: organize, screen and number documents to be produced. Make an index of documents. Make arrangements for copies to be made.
- Documents produced by other parties: review, organize, and index.
- Prepare digests of documents and of testimony from depositions.

Motions for Entry of Judgment Without Trial

- If defendant filed no response to complaint, prepare documents for default judgment.
- If attorney/paralegal team deems it warranted, prepare for attorney review initial drafts of motion for judgment on the pleadings or summary judgment.
- Assist with supporting exhibits, affidavits, and memoranda of law.

Pretrial Conferences and Settlement

- Monitor court calendar and correspondence for dates of pretrial conferences.
- Review and organize file in preparation for pretrial conference and settlement discussions.
- Assist with determining settlement value and assist with settlement brochure or letter.
- If settlement is reached, prepare for attorney review settlement documents such as release, settlement agreement, stipulation to dismiss, and so on.

Trial Preparation

- Monitor court calendar for trial date.
- Confer with witnesses regarding trial date and their availability.
- Assist with witness preparation.
- Review organization of all documents and ensure that they are easily retrievable.
- Organize, label, and index exhibits for trial.
- Ensure sufficient copies of all exhibits.
- Prepare demonstrative evidence (e.g., charts).
- If videotape testimony will be used, make technical arrangements.
- Jury investigation.
- Prepare subpoenas for witnesses.

Trial

- Ensure that witnesses arrive on time.
- Take notes of testimony.
- Arrange and give to attorney exhibits in proper order.
- Keep track of exhibits admitted into evidence.
- Share observations with attorney.

Post-Trial

- If appeal is taken:

  Assist with preparation of record on appeal and ensure that necessary exhibits and transcripts are appended.

  Assist with timely filing of notice of appeal.

  For appellate brief, check case cites and any attachments.

- If no appeal is taken:

  Assist with enforcement of judgment (e.g., execution, garnishment).

In addition, there are certain duties litigation paralegals perform at all stages of litigation, such as ensuring regular communication with clients, keeping files updated and organized, following all deadlines, conducting legal research, and other tasks as assigned by the supervising attorney.

ENDNOTES

1 *Black's Law Dictionary* 841 (5th ed. 1979).

2 *Black's Law Dictionary* 377 (5th ed. 1979).

3 *Black's Law Dictionary* 1037 (5th ed. 1979).

4 See Chapter 7, pp. 162–166 for a discussion of motions to dismiss.

5 In addition to the answer, a defendant may file a counterclaim against the plaintiff. Counterclaims are claims asserted by a defendant against a plaintiff and are discussed in Chapter 7, pp. 173–180. We do not anticipate that the defendants in the Wesser case will assert counterclaims.

6 The standards for granting these motions are fairly technical and are discussed in Chapter 8.

7 See Chapter 3 for a discussion of the federal and state court systems.

8 The commencement of a lawsuit is discussed in detail in Chapter 6.

9 This rule is discussed in Chapter 7, pp. 160–161.

10 See Chapters 6, 7 and 8.

11 The discussion of these rules is largely outside the scope of this text. The denomination of the proper parties can be complex and will be determined by your supervising attorney or in conjunction with your supervising attorney.

12 See Chapter 9 for a detailed discussion of discovery.

13 See Chapter 12 for a discussion of the trial.

14 See Chapter 13 for a discussion of judgments.

15 See Chapter 8, pp. 207–219.

16 See Chapter 8, pp. 221–231.

17 See Chapter 6, pp. 156–157.

18 *Black's Law Dictionary* 1001 (5th ed. 1979).

19 The American Bar Association Section on Law Practice Management publishes *Law Practice Management*, which contains articles on time management and a wide array of other law office practice techniques. An audiocassette on time management for lawyers is also available. You may wish to pursue these resources now so that you are ready to be effective from day one in the law office.

You may wish to become an Associate of the American Bar Association. The ABA offers associate affiliations for legal assistants. You may obtain information by calling or writing: ABA Membership Department, 750 North Lake Shore Drive, Chicago, Illinois 60611, 312-988-5522.

20 For additional paralegal tasks, see Thomas W. Brunner, Julie P. Hamre, and Joan F. McCaffrey, *The Legal Assistant's Handbook* (Washington, D.C.: Bureau of National Affairs), 1982.

2 LEGAL ETHICS

LITIGATION EXTRACT: You have been introduced to Mr. Wesser's lawsuit and to the organization of law offices and important office procedures. Before beginning even the investigation preliminary to preparing the complaint, there are more important rules to learn that apply to every stage of litigation. These are the rules of professional ethics and conduct. The rules directly govern the conduct of lawyers, and violations can bring disciplinary sanctions as severe as permanent revocation of a lawyer's license to practice law. Paralegals cannot be directly disciplined for conduct that violates the rules of ethics. However, the attorneys for whom a paralegal works can be disciplined for a paralegal's conduct. Therefore it is imperative that you understand the rules of ethics. This chapter focuses on the rules most directly applicable to litigation and to prohibitions against nonlawyers engaging in the practice of law.

INTRODUCTION

The power to regulate the legal profession rests with the individual states. Each state supreme court has the ultimate power to regulate the practice of law in that state. Each state has a code of ethics based largely on rules promulgated by the American Bar Association (ABA). The ABA rules will be discussed in the section that follows this introduction.

Every state has requirements that a person must meet before he or she can be licensed to practice law in that state. A lawyer licensed to practice law in a particular state is considered a member of the state bar. In addition to controlling the admission of attorneys to practice, the state bar also controls the discipline, disbarment, and restoration of attorneys. Another function of the state bar is to adopt rules of professional ethics and conduct.

A bar association is in many states separate from the state bar. The state bar association is usually active in providing continuing legal education, coordinating *pro bono* services—that is, volunteer work for clients with no resources—

and similar activities to enhance the legal profession. In some states membership in the state bar association is optional. In other states the state bar and the state bar association are combined into one; this is called an "integrated" bar.

The American Bar Association is a nationwide lawyers' organization. Membership is voluntary. The ABA has many goals and functions, including sponsoring continuing legal education programs and monitoring legislation affecting the legal profession. The ABA has numerous committees that work to develop lawyers' knowledge in specific areas of law and to improve our system of justice. The ABA publishes legal treatises, as well as a monthly magazine, *The ABA Journal*, with features on current legal issues and regular articles on legal ethics.

One important project of the ABA is the development of model standards of professional conduct. These standards do not themselves directly regulate lawyers. Rather, individual states follow the ABA standards, with some variations, in promulgating their own rules of professional conduct to which lawyers are subject. In 1969, the ABA promulgated the Model Code of Professional Responsibility (Model Code), which was subsequently adopted with some changes by most states. In 1977, the ABA began revising the Model Code and developed the ABA Model Rules of Professional Conduct. In 1983, the ABA adopted the Model Rules of Professional Conduct (Model Rules), which have now been adopted in some form by more than 35 states. Because many states' ethics rules contain elements of both the Model Code and the Model Rules, and because some states have not adopted the Model Code, it is important to know both.

The ABA also publishes Ethics Opinions, which address specific questions of interpretation and application of the Model Rules and Model Code as submitted by practicing attorneys. The format consists of a specific question followed by a detailed answer. See Figure 2-1 for an example. Courts cite the ABA Code, ABA Rules, and Ethics Opinions as evidence of the standard of conduct for the legal profession.

 POINTER: The *ABA/BNA Lawyers' Manual on Professional Conduct* contains the ABA Model Rules, ABA Model Code, ABA Ethics Opinions, and digests of state ethics opinions. It also has discussions of the application of ethics rules to problems encountered in the practice of law, including discussion of pertinent court decisions.

SOURCES OF ETHICAL GUIDELINES

ABA Model Code of Professional Responsibility

The purpose of the ABA Model Code is to provide guidelines for conduct and rules to help determine when a lawyer should be disciplined for failing to meet those guidelines. As noted in the Preliminary Statement to the ABA Code, the "Code is designed to be adopted by appropriate agencies both as an inspirational guide to the members of the profession and as a basis for disciplinary action when the conduct of a lawyer falls below the required minimum standards stated. . . ."

It is important to understand the format of the ABA Code. Figure 2-2 illustrates its three basic components: *Canons, Ethical Considerations* (ECs), and *Disciplinary Rules* (DRs). The ABA Code contains nine **Canons**, which are broad statements "expressing in general terms the standards of conduct expected of lawyers . . ."[1] Canons set forth the general concepts from which ethical considerations and

FIGURE 2-1   AN EXAMPLE OF ETHICS OPINION FORMAT

Informal Opinion 1367
Correspondence Signed by   June 15, 1976
Paralegals on Firm Letterhead

You have inquired whether it is ethical for a law firm to allow "paralegals" or "legal assistants" to conduct correspondence on behalf of the firm on firm letterhead. The Committee has previously held (1) that such persons may ethically be employed by law firms if their performance is properly directed by a lawyer (Informal Opinion 909); (2) that such persons may not be listed on the firm's letterhead, but may have business cards designating their title and identifying them as employed by the firm (Informal Opinion 1185); (3) that it is not in violation of a Disciplinary Rule of the Code to allow a secretary certified as a member of the Legal Assistant Section of the National Association of Legal Secretaries (International) to sign with the designation "Legal Assistant," but that caution should dictate deferral of its use until the class of persons who qualify as "Legal Assistants" is better defined (Informal Opinion 1278).

The Ethics Committee of the Philadelphia Bar has responded to an inquiry similar to yours by indicating that such persons as you describe may use firm stationery under the lawyer's supervision and may sign the legal assistant's own name as long as he indicates his capacity with clarity (*i.e.,* office manager, investigator, administrative assistant and the like) (Opinion 69-2 of the Philadelphia Bar Association, April 23, 1969). The Florida Bar has reached a similar conclusion (Fla. Ops. 384 [Opinion 66-40, August 1, 1966]). The New York County Lawyer's Association has indicated that substantial, non-routine letters on firm stationery must be signed by lawyers (N.Y. Co. L.A. 806 [Opinion 420, 1953]).

The lawyers' use of assistants to perform specialized tasks such as you describe in your letter, to wit:

1. Graduates of the Paralegal Institute, Philadelphia, Pennsylvania. These employees under the supervision of lawyers in our firm index depositions, coordinate filing systems in connection with complex litigation, assist in gathering information in connection with the administration of successions and matters generally of this type;
2. Employees who have been trained by us to abstract titles which are used as a preliminary basis for the final issuance by our firm of title opinions regarding real estate;
3. Employees trained by us who act as investigators and in this connection take statements in matters such as maritime collisions and the like. These employees also occasionally serve subpoenas where service of process has been difficult to obtain by those responsible for service of process.

is becoming increasingly common, and, indeed, essential to the efficient practice of law. The Committee is of the opinion that it is appropriate for legal assistants to sign correspondence which is incident to the proper conduct of his or her responsibilities but care should be taken to identify accurately the capacity of the person who signs the letter so that the receiver is not misled.

FIGURE 2-2   COMPONENTS OF THE ABA CODE

CANON 3
A Lawyer Should Assist in
Preventing the Unauthorized
Practice of Law

ETHICAL CONSIDERATIONS

EC 3-1 The prohibition against the practice of law by a layman is grounded in the need of the public for integrity and competence of those who undertake to render legal services. Because of the fiduciary and personal character of the lawyer-client relationship and the inherently complex nature of our legal system, the public can better be assured of the requisite responsibility and competence if the practice of law is confined to those who are subject to the requirements and regulations imposed upon members of the legal profession.

EC 3-2 The sensitive variations in the considerations that bear on legal determinations often make it difficult even for a lawyer to exercise appropriate professional judgment, and it is therefore essential that the personal nature of the relationship of client and lawyer be preserved. Competent professional judgment is the product of a trained familiarity with law and legal processes, a disciplined, analytical approach to legal problems, and a firm ethical commitment.

EC 3-3 A non-lawyer who undertakes to handle legal matters is not governed as to integrity or legal competence by the same rules that govern the conduct of a lawyer. A lawyer is not only subject to that regulation but also is committed to high standards of ethical conduct. The public interest is best served in legal matters by a regulated profession committed to such standards.[1] The Disciplinary Rules protect the public in that they prohibit a lawyer from seeking employment by improper overtures, from acting in cases of divided loyalties, and from submitting to the control of others in the exercise of his judgment. Moreover, a person who entrusts legal matters to a lawyer is protected by the attorney-client privilege and by the duty of the lawyer to hold inviolate the confidences and secrets of his client.

EC 3-4 A layman who seeks legal services often is not in a position to judge whether he will receive proper professional attention. The entrustment of a legal matter may well involve the confidences, the reputation, the property, the freedom, or even the life of the client. Proper protection of members of the public demands that no person be permitted to act in the confidential and demanding capacity of a lawyer unless he is subject to the regulations of the legal profession.

EC 3-5 It is neither necessary nor desirable to attempt the formulation of a single, specific definition of what constitutes the practice of law.[2] Functionally, the practice of law relates to the rendition of services for others that call for the professional judgment of a lawyer. The essence of the professional judgment of the lawyer is his educated ability to relate the general body and philosophy of law to a specific legal problem of a client; and thus, the public interest will be better served if only lawyers are permitted to act in matters involving professional judgment. Where this professional judgment is not involved, non-lawyers, such as court

FIGURE 2-2   COMPONENTS OF THE ABA CODE (continued)

clerks, police officers, abstracters, and many governmental employees, may engage in occupations that require a special knowledge of law in certain areas. But the services of a lawyer are essential in the public interest whenever the exercise of professional legal judgment is required.

EC 3-6 A lawyer often delegates tasks to clerks, secretaries, and other lay persons. Such delegation is proper if the lawyer maintains a direct relationship with his client, supervises the delegated work, and has complete professional responsibility for the work product.[3] This delegation enables a lawyer to render legal service more economically and efficiently.

DISCIPLINARY RULES

DR 3-101   Aiding Unauthorized Practice of Law.

(A) A lawyer shall not aid a non-lawyer in the unauthorized practice of law.

(B) A lawyer shall not practice law in a jurisdiction where to do so would be in violation of regulations of the profession in that jurisdiction.

DR 3-102   Dividing Legal Fees with a Non-Lawyer.

(A) A lawyer or law firm shall not share legal fees with a non-lawyer,[13] except that:

   (1) An agreement by a lawyer with his firm, partner, or associate may provide for the payment of money, over a reasonable period of time after his death, to his estate or to one or more specified persons.[14]

   (2) A lawyer who undertakes to complete unfinished legal business of a deceased lawyer may pay to the estate of the deceased lawyer that proportion of the total compensation which fairly represents the services rendered by the deceased lawyer.

   (3) A lawyer or law firm may include non-lawyer employees in a compensation or retirement plan, even though the plan is based in whole or in part on a profit sharing arrangement providing such plan does not circumvent another Disciplinary Rule.

DR 3-103   Forming a Partnership with a Non-Lawyer.

(A) A lawyer shall not form a partnership with a non-lawyer if any of the activities of the partnership consist of the practice of law.[14]

disciplinary rules derive. Canon 3, for example, states as its premise, ''A Lawyer Should Assist in Preventing the Unauthorized Practice of Law.''

With each canon are several **Ethical Considerations**, which expand and explain the principles set forth in that canon. The ABA Code Preliminary

Statement describes the ethical considerations as "aspirational in nature" and "a body of principles upon which the lawyer can rely for guidance in many specific situations."[2] Figure 2-2 shows Ethical Considerations 3-1 through 3-6.

The **Disciplinary Rules** that appear with each canon are mandatory in character. They "state the minimum level below which no lawyer can fall without being subject to disciplinary action." Figure 2-2 shows DRs 3-101–103 under Canon 3.

ABA Model Rules of Professional Conduct

The format of the ABA Model Rules consists of a rule followed by a series of comments. Figure 2-3 reprints Rule 5.3, Responsibilities Regarding Nonlawyer Assistants. Like those of the Model Code, some portions of the ABA Model Rules are obligatory and some are advisory. As explained in the Preliminary Statement, "(s)ome of the Rules are imperatives, cast in the terms 'shall' or 'shall not.'. . . Others, generally cast in the term 'may,' are permissive and define areas under the Rules in which the lawyer has professional discretion."[3] The **Comments** that follow each rule illustrate its meaning and are intended as guides to interpretation rather than definitive statements of the rule. Figures 2-3 and 2-4 illustrate comments.

State Guidelines

As we explained previously, each state has its own set of ethics rules, most of which are modeled after the ABA Model Rules of Professional Conduct or the ABA Model Code of Professional Responsibility. It is imperative that you read and understand your state's rules. Like the ABA Model Rules and Model Code, your state's rules will likely have comments to guide interpretation. Case law has developed in the area of legal ethics and can aid you in researching ethical questions. There are also state statutes that address ethics issues such as the attorney-client privilege.

EFFECT OF ETHICAL GUIDELINES ON ATTORNEYS AND PARALEGALS

It is important to understand the sanctions that may be imposed on attorneys who engage in unethical conduct. As we have noted, while paralegals may not be directly sanctioned, their conduct may subject the attorneys for whom they work to sanctions.

Consequences of Violating Ethical Guidelines

It is mandatory that a lawyer obey the DRs and Model Rules cast in the terms "shall" and "shall not." Violation of a mandatory rule subjects a lawyer to disciplinary actions. In most states, reports of violations are directed to the state bar. A bar ethics committee then reviews the complaint and recommends whether disciplinary measures should be implemented or whether the complaint should be dismissed. If the committee recommends imposition of a penalty, an appeal can usually be made to an appellate board within the state bar and ultimately to the state court.

FIGURE 2-3   FORMAT OF THE ABA RULES

RULE 5.3 Responsibilities Regarding Non-lawyer Assistants

With respect to a nonlawyer employed or retained by or associated with a lawyer:
(a) a partner in a law firm shall make reasonable efforts to ensure that the firm has in effect measures giving reasonable assurance that the person's conduct is compatible with the professional obligations of the lawyer;
(b) a lawyer having direct supervisor authority over the nonlawyer shall make reasonable efforts to ensure that the person's conduct is compatible with the professional obligations of the lawyer; and
(c) a lawyer shall be responsible for conduct of such a person that would be a violation of the rules of professional conduct if engaged in by a lawyer if:
    (1) the lawyer orders or, with the knowledge of the specific conduct, ratifies the conduct involved; or
    (2) the lawyer is a partner in the law firm in which the person is employed, or has direct supervisory authority over the person, and knows of the conduct at a time when its consequences can be avoided or mitigated but fails to take reasonable remedial action.

COMMENT

Lawyers generally employ assistants in their practice, including secretaries, investigators, law student interns, and paraprofessionals. Such assistants, whether employees or independent contractors, act for the lawyer in rendition of the lawyer's professional services. A lawyer should give such assistants appropriate instruction and supervision concerning the ethical aspects of their employment, particularly regarding the obligation not to disclose information relating to representation of the client, and should be responsible for their work product. The measures employed in supervising nonlawyers should take account of the fact that they do not have legal training and are not subject to professional discipline.

Excerpts from the Model Rules of Professional Conduct, Model Code of Professional Responsibility and Informal Opinion, copyrighted by the American Bar Association. All rights reserved. Reprinted with permission.

    The ABA Model Code and Model Rules do not set forth specific penalties for particular violations. Rather, the severity of the penalty depends on the severity of the violation and all surrounding circumstances.[4] The least severe penalty is a private reprimand—that is, a letter to the attorney warning him or her of the impropriety of the conduct. More serious is a public reprimand or censure, where the warning is placed in public records. Still more serious is suspension from practice for a designated period. The most severe penalty is disbarment, which means that an attorney can no longer practice law in the state.

Both the ABA Model Code and Model Rules cite conduct that is disciplinable even if lawyers are not engaging in the practice of law when they commit the wrong. Conduct involving dishonesty, fraud, deceit, or misrepresentation is disciplinable (DR 1-102(A)(4) and Model Rule 8.4). Such conduct can include commission of a crime.

Generally speaking, the commission of a crime is disciplinable if the crime involves dishonesty or otherwise reflects adversely on a lawyer's fitness to practice law. Thus, if a lawyer receives a traffic citation for traveling 75 miles an hour in a 45-mph zone, this indicates that the lawyer is a bad driver but does not indicate that he or she lacks the moral fiber to practice law. On the other hand, willful failure to file an income tax return may result in disciplinary proceedings because it reflects adversely on the lawyer's fitness to practice law.

POINTER: Read the first paragraph of the Comment to Model Rule 8.4 (Figure 2-4). It explains more fully the concept of illegal conduct that reflects adversely on fitness to practice law.

Application of Ethical Rules to Conduct of Paralegals

The ABA Model Rules and Model Code and the state ethics rules based on them apply directly only to lawyers. Even though nonlawyers cannot be disciplined under the rules, the rules nevertheless apply as guidelines to nonlawyers' conduct. The Model Code Preliminary Statement makes it clear that the Code "do(es) define the type of ethical conduct that the public has a right to expect not only of lawyers but also of their . . . employees and associates in all matters pertaining to professional employment." Comment 1 to Model Rule 5.3 states that a lawyer's nonlawyer assistants are not subject to professional discipline. However, the comment emphasizes the duty of lawyers to ensure that their nonlawyer assistants abide by ethical standards. A paralegal's misconduct may result in sanctions against the supervising attorney and the law firm.

A person who will not follow the ethical obligations applicable to lawyers simply will not be a suitable employee for a law firm. Thus paralegals must know and follow the ethics rules for their jurisdiction.

PROHIBITION AGAINST UNAUTHORIZED PRACTICE OF LAW

Both the Model Code and the Model Rules provide that a lawyer shall not assist a nonlawyer in the performance of activity that constitutes the unauthorized practice of law. This is not a prohibition against a lawyer employing nonlawyers and delegating certain tasks to them. As the comment to Model Rule 5.5 states, a lawyer may employ the services of paraprofessionals and delegate functions to them, as long as the lawyer supervises and retains the ultimate responsibility for the delegated work.[5] The various rationales for the requirement that only duly licensed lawyers practice law are expressed in the ethical considerations accompanying Canon 3 in the Model Code. EC 3-5 states that the "essence of the professional judgment of the lawyer is his educated ability to relate the general body and philosophy of law to a specific legal problem of a client; and thus, the public

FIGURE 2-4 MODEL RULE 8.4

RULE 8.4 Misconduct

It is professional misconduct for a lawyer to:
(a) violate or attempt to violate the rules of professional conduct, knowingly assist or induce another to do so, or do so through the acts of another;
(b) commit a criminal act that reflects adversely on the lawyer's honesty, trustworthiness or fitness as a lawyer in other respects;
(c) engage in conduct involving dishonesty, fraud, deceit or misrepresentation;
(d) engage in conduct that is prejudicial to the administration of justice;
(e) state or imply an ability to influence improperly a government agency or official; or
(f) knowingly assist a judge or judicial officer in conduct that is a violation of applicable rules of judicial conduct or other law.

COMMENT

Many kinds of illegal conduct reflect adversely on fitness to practice law, such as offenses involving fraud and the offense of willful failure to file an income tax return. However, some kinds of offense carry no such implication. Traditionally, the distinction was drawn in terms of offenses involving "moral turpitude." That concept can be construed to include offenses concerning some matters of personal morality, such as adultery and comparable offenses, that have no specific connection to fitness for the practice of law. Although a lawyer is personally answerable to the entire criminal law, a lawyer should be professionally answerable only for offenses that indicate lack of those characteristics relevant to law practice. Offenses involving violence, dishonesty, or breach of trust, or serious inteference with the administration of justice are in that category. A pattern of repeated offenses, even ones of minor significance when considered separately, can indicate indifference to legal obligation.

A lawyer may refuse to comply with an obligation imposed by law upon a good faith belief that no valid obligation exists. The provisions of Rule 1.2(d) concerning a good faith challenge to the validity, scope, meaning or application of the law apply to challenges of legal regulation of the practice of law. . . .

will be better served if only lawyers are permitted to act in matters involving professional judgment." EC 3-3 points out that nonlawyers are not subject to the same rules that govern the conduct of lawyers and thus the "public interest is best served in legal matters by a regulated profession" subject to the stringent standard of conduct imposed on lawyers.

What Constitutes the Unauthorized Practice of Law

There is no universal definition of what activity constitutes the ''practice of law.''[6] The definition is determined by state law and can differ from state to state. For example, in North Carolina the practice of law is defined as follows:

> The phrase ''practice law'' as used in this Chapter is defined to be performing any legal service for any other person, firm or corporation, with or without compensation, specifically including the preparation or aiding in the preparation of deeds, mortgages, wills, trust instruments, inventories, accounts or reports of guardians, trustees, administrators or executors, or preparing or aiding in the preparation of any petitions or orders in any probate or court proceeding; abstracting or passing upon titles, the preparation and filing of petitions for use in any court, or assisting by advice, counsel, or otherwise in any such legal work; and to advise or give opinion upon the legal rights of any person, firm or corporation. . . .[7]

It is often difficult for a paralegal to know when he or she ''crosses the line'' into the forbidden realm of giving legal advice. A general rule of thumb is that persons engage in the practice of law when they apply the law to the particular facts of a client's case. For example, suppose that you are talking with a client who wishes to apply for political asylum in the United States. Your assignment is to find out the reasons why the client wishes to seek political asylum. In order to ascertain the pertinent facts, you must inform the client of the standards for gaining political asylum in the United States. You may state that a person must be a ''refugee'' within the statutory meaning in order to attain political asylum in the United States. You may then explain that a person is considered a refugee when she cannot return to her country of nationality or last residence because of persecution or a well-founded fear of persecution on account of race, religion, nationality, membership in a particular social group, or political opinion.[8] You may then question the client to find out why she feels she might be persecuted if forced to return to her country of nationality. Suppose that the client then asks you whether she meets the definition of a refugee. If you give your opinion about whether she is a refugee, then you have crossed the line into the realm of rendering legal advice. It is not permissible for you to apply the law to the facts. Instead of stating your opinion, you should say that that is a question that Ms. Smith, the attorney, must answer when she joins you in a few minutes.

 POINTER: It is sometimes difficult to know how much you can say to a client without crossing the line into the giving of legal advice. The situation can be particularly difficult when you are on the telephone with the client and the attorney is not available for consultation at that moment. Always err on the side of caution, and tell the client that you cannot answer the question but will be glad to relay the question to Ms. Smith, the attorney, and let her answer it. You may well know the answer, but if you suspect that furnishing it might constitute the provision of legal advice, you should consult with the attorney with whom you are working before responding to the client. Make it clear that you are stating the attorney's opinion and not your own.

In other instances it is much easier to determine when a person is engaging in the practice of law. A paralegal cannot appear in court on behalf of a client. This is true even when the court appearance is only to present a very simple motion to continue the case until the following week. Nor can a paralegal prepare and sign a legal document. You will often be asked to prepare drafts of legal documents such as complaints or motions for extension of time to file an answer. However, the attorney must always review the legal documents you have prepared and make any necessary additions or corrections. It is always the attorney, not the paralegal, who signs the legal document.

The Importance of Identifying Yourself as a Paralegal

It is very important that in all telephone conversations and correspondence you identify yourself as a paralegal. Sometimes a client will call the attorney and the call will be transferred to you when the attorney is not available. Be sure to identify yourself and state that you are a paralegal at the very beginning of the conversation to avoid the appearance of holding yourself out as a lawyer. This is equally true when you talk with persons other than clients.

At times you will send your own letters to request material or relate information to clients and others. For instance, you may be asked to write to the plaintiff that your firm represents to inform him that counsel for the defendant has scheduled his deposition for a certain date and time. When you sign the letter, you must make it clear that you are a paralegal. See Figure 2-5 for an illustration of the proper way to sign letters.

FIGURE 2-5   THE PROPER WAY FOR A PARALEGAL TO SIGN LETTERS

> Please provide the requested information as soon as possible. We look forward to hearing from you.
>
> Sincerely yours,
>
> Leslie A. Armstrong
> Paralegal

LAWYERS' RESPONSIBILITIES REGARDING NONLAWYER ASSISTANTS

Inherent in the ethical obligation not to assist in the unauthorized practice of law is the duty to supervise paralegals' work and conduct. Attorneys who fail to supervise their nonlawyer employees' work and to maintain a relationship with clients may be subject to sanctions.

Lawyers' Duty to Supervise Paralegals' Work

Both the Model Code and the Model Rules impose on lawyers a duty to supervise the work of their nonlawyer assistants. Model Rule 5.3 (Figure 2-3) specifically addresses these responsibilities. Its comment explains some of the lawyer's specific duties. A lawyer should instruct nonlawyer assistants concerning the ethical aspects of their employment, especially the duty not to reveal information relating to the firm's representation of the client.

The comment further states that a lawyer should be responsible for the nonlawyer assistants' work product. This is an important requirement. Paralegals prepare the drafts of many crucial legal documents. It is essential that attorneys review all work that they delegate to paralegals; they have an ethical obligation to do so. This obligation is reinforced in the comment to Rule 5.5, which states that a lawyer is allowed to delegate tasks to paraprofessionals so long as the lawyer supervises and retains responsibility for their work.

POINTER: With training and experience, you will acquire the knowledge to draft substantial legal documents. Once you gain that experience, be sure that your supervising attorney continues to review all your work. It is tempting to skip the review when your work team is in a hurry to meet a late afternoon deadline. Your team can prevent this temptation from even forming. The key is to complete the work well ahead of the deadline.

The ABA Model Code is less specific about lawyers' duties to supervise. It contains no separate rule about responsibilities regarding nonlawyer assistants. This is probably because the Model Code was drafted much earlier, before paralegals were employed as extensively as they now are. The lawyer's responsibilities regarding nonlawyer assistants under the Model Code are concerned mainly with the preservation of confidential information about the client. DR 4-101(D) makes it mandatory for lawyers to "exercise reasonable care to prevent" employees and other persons whose services they utilize from disclosing confidential client information. EC 4-2 emphasizes that a lawyer must carefully select and train employees "so that the sanctity of all confidences and secrets of his clients may be preserved."

EC 3-6 states more specifically the obligations of lawyers when tasks are delegated to nonlawyer assistants. The lawyer must maintain a direct relationship with the client, supervise the delegated work, and maintain complete professional responsibility for the work product. For example, in a real estate closing, it would not be proper for an attorney to allow a paralegal to perform a title search and prepare all the closing documents without the attorney supervising and reviewing the paralegal's work.

Lawyers' Liability for Conduct of Paralegals

Although paralegals are not subject to professional discipline under the Model Code and the Model Rules, a lawyer may be disciplined for a paralegal's misconduct in some instances. Model Rule 5.3(c) (Figure 2-3) states that a lawyer is responsible for a nonlawyer assistant whose conduct violates the rules of professional conduct if the lawyer orders the conduct or gains knowledge of the conduct and then ratifies the conduct.

In addition, a lawyer who has direct supervisory responsibility for the paralegal or is a partner in the firm and who knows about the conduct and fails to take "reasonable remedial action" is subject to discipline. Suppose that lawyer Martinez hires paralegal Turner and gives Turner thorough instructions regarding the obligation not to disclose confidential information about clients. Despite adequate instruction, paralegal Turner discloses confidential information about a client to a friend who works in the law firm that represents the adversary in a lawsuit. The disclosed information damages the client's case. Soon after the disclosure, attorney Martinez finds out about the disclosure but neither reprimands Turner nor admonishes Turner to refrain from disclosing information. Attorney Martinez is subject to discipline, even though he carefully instructed paralegal Turner regarding the importance of confidentiality. Attorney Martinez is subject to discipline because he is the paralegal's supervisor and because he failed to take action to mitigate the damage. By his inaction, he also ratified the conduct of paralegal Turner.

CONFIDENTIALITY OF CLIENT INFORMATION

The remainder of this chapter discusses in more detail some of the specific ethical duties of which the paralegal should be aware. One of the most important duties is to preserve confidential client information.

Duty to Preserve Confidential Information

Both the ABA Model Code and the ABA Model Rules state that the duty to preserve confidential client information is mandatory. Both state that with certain exceptions a lawyer *must* not disclose confidential client information. As we noted previously, this duty applies equally to paralegals. The duty to preserve confidential client information continues after the termination of employment. Thus, when a lawsuit is over and the case file is closed, the information gained in representation of the client remains confidential.

What Constitutes Confidential Information

The ABA Model Code defines confidential information in DR 4-101(A) and divides it into two types of client information. DR 4-101(A) provides that a lawyer must preserve the "confidences" and "secrets" of a client. See Figure 2-6 for the precise definitions. Note that a "confidence" is information covered by the attorney-client privilege. (Chapter 4 contains a full discussion of the attorney-client privilege.) The attorney-client privilege applies in judicial proceedings where a lawyer may be called as a witness or asked to produce evidence about the client. It is a rule of evidence that prevents a court from compelling an attorney to disclose communications between lawyer and client. The scope of the attorney-client privilege is fairly narrow and can differ under state law. Basically, the attorney-client privilege protects written and oral communications between lawyer and client that were intended to be confidential. For example, when an attorney writes a client a letter discussing trial strategy and the defenses they will raise, the letter is protected by the attorney-client privilege.

A "secret" is much broader in scope than client information protected under the attorney-client privilege. Note that client information may be considered a

FIGURE 2-6   DR 4-101

DR 4-101   Preservation of Confidences and Secrets of a Client.[10]

(A) "Confidence" refers to information protected by the attorney-client privilege under applicable law, and "secret" refers to other information gained in the professional relationship that the client has requested be held inviolate or the disclosure of which would be embarrassing or would be likely to be detrimental to the client.

(B) Except when permitted under DR 4-101(C), a lawyer shall not knowingly:
   (1) Reveal a confidence or secret of his client.[11]
   (2) Use a confidence or secret of his client to the disadvantage of the client.
   (3) Use a confidence or secret of his client for the advantage of himself[12] or of a third person,[13] unless the client consents after full disclosure.

(C) A lawyer may reveal:
   (1) Confidences or secrets with the consent of the client or clients affected, but only after a full disclosure to them.[14]
   (2) Confidences or secrets when permitted under Disciplinary Rules or required by law or court order.[15]
   (3) The intention of his client to commit a crime[16] and the information necessary to prevent the crime.[17]
   (4) Confidences or secrets necessary to establish or collect his fee[18] or to defend himself or his employees or associates against an accusation of wrongful conduct.[19]

(D) A lawyer shall exercise reasonable care to prevent his employees, associates, and others whose services are utilized by him from disclosing or using confidences or secrets of a client, except that a lawyer may reveal the information allowed by DR 4-101(C) through an employee.

"secret," regardless of whether the attorney-client privilege encompasses it, if the client requests that the information be kept inviolate, or if disclosure would embarrass or be detrimental to the client.[9] Figure 2-6 contains the Model Code definition of "secret."

The definition of protected information in the ABA Model Rules is even broader than that in the Model Code. Rule 1.6 includes as confidential "information relating to representation of a client...." (See Figure 2-7.) The comments to Rule 1.6 explain the breadth of confidential information, stating that "[t]he confidentiality rule applies not merely to matters communicated in confidence by the client but also to all information relating to the representation, whatever its source."[10]

FIGURE 2-7   MODEL RULE 1.6

RULE 1.6 Confidentiality of Information

(a) A lawyer shall not reveal information relating to representation of a client unless the client consents after consultation, except for disclosures that are impliedly authorized in order to carry out the representation, and except as stated in paragraph (b).

(b) A lawyer may reveal such information to the extent the lawyer reasonably believes necessary:

(1) to prevent the client from committing a criminal act that the lawyer believes is likely to result in imminent death or substantial bodily harm; or

(2) to establish a claim or defense on behalf of the lawyer in a controversy between the lawyer and the client, to establish a defense to a criminal charge or civil claim against the lawyer based upon conduct in which the client was involved, or to respond to allegations in any proceeding concerning the lawyer's representation of the client.

COMMENT

The lawyer is part of a judicial system charged with upholding the law. One of the lawyer's functions is to advise clients so that they avoid any violation of the law in the proper exercise of their rights.

The observance of the ethical obligation of a lawyer to hold inviolate confidential information of the client not only facilitates the full development of facts essential to proper representation of the client but also encourages people to seek early legal assistance.

Almost without exception, clients come to lawyers in order to determine what their rights are and what is, in the maze of laws and regulations, deemed to be legal and correct. The common law recognizes that the client's confidences must be protected from disclosure. Based upon experience, lawyers know that almost all clients follow the advice given, and the law is upheld.

A fundamental principle in the client-lawyer relationship is that the lawyer maintain confidentiality of information relating to the representation. The client is thereby encouraged to communicate fully and frankly with the lawyer even as to embarrassing or legally damaging subject matter. . . .

Why Confidentiality Is Essential

The comments to Model Rule 1.6 (paragraphs 1–4) explain the importance and the purpose of confidentiality. The duty to preserve confidential information is a "fundamental principle in the client-lawyer relationship." A client must know that the lawyer will preserve confidential information in order to be willing to tell the lawyer all the facts, including embarrassing and legally damaging information. Only with full disclosure can the lawyer find out all the pertinent facts and fully develop a case. EC 4-1 of the ABA Model Code justifies confidentiality for the same reasons, stating that "[t]he observance of the ethical obligation of a lawyer to hold inviolate the confidences and secrets of his client not only facilitates the full development of facts essential to proper representation of the client but also encourages laymen to seek early legal assistance." To understand the importance of the client disclosing all the pertinent facts, consider a lawsuit involving alimony. When an attorney undertakes representation of a client in a lawsuit involving alimony, the attorney needs to know whether the client has engaged in conduct that is a ground for alimony, such as adultery or spousal abuse. It would be embarrassing for a client to admit to such conduct, but the lawyer must know about the conduct to prepare the case.

Discussion of Confidential Information with Firm Personnel

You will be privy to confidential information both in discussions with the attorneys in your firm and in review of client files. The ABA Model Code acknowledges that nonlawyer assistants have access to confidential information, and EC 4-2 states that this necessitates careful selection and training of employees to ensure preservation of confidential information. Both the ABA Model Code and the ABA Model Rules provide that lawyers may share information as necessary, unless the client requests that information be confined to specific lawyers.[11] The sharing of information within the firm is necessary to develop a case fully and represent clients adequately. However, the wisest course is to discuss a case only with the employees in the firm with whom you are working on that particular case. The best approach to preserving client information is to discuss it no more than is necessary to provide adequate representation. You will enhance your professional position by not talking about cases more than is necessary within the firm, although the temptation can be great when you are working on a particularly flashy case.

Exceptions to the Rule: When an Attorney Can Disclose Confidential Information

There are limited exceptions to the prohibition against disclosing confidential client information. These exceptions vary in some respects between the Model Code and the Model Rules. The exceptions may vary among states as well. They are discussed only generally in this text, so you must know the definitive exceptions accepted in your jurisdiction.

POINTER: Although you should be familiar with the exceptions, you should never consider revealing client information without consulting your supervising attorney. This is very important in a litigation context. For example, in the discovery portion of litigation, your firm may well reveal some confidential client information to the other side. However, you can be sure that this will be disclosed only if it is permissible under your state's ethics rules. Therefore you will review carefully with your attorney work team any information that you give to the other side in the discovery process.

A lawyer may reveal confidential client information under the following circumstances.

1. Client Consent.   (DR 4-101(C)(1) and Rule 1.6(a)) Disclosure is proper when the client consents to disclosure, but only after the attorney has fully informed the client of the consequences of disclosure. Model Rule 1.6 specifically states that implied consent justifies disclosure, provided that disclosure is necessary to carry out the representation of the client. Paragraph 7 in the comments to Rule 1.6 gives an example specifically dealing with litigation. It states that "[i]n litigation . . . a lawyer may disclose information by admitting a fact that cannot properly be disputed, or in negotiation by making a disclosure that facilitates a satisfactory conclusion." For example, in a lawsuit involving damages to an automobile, a lawyer may disclose the model of the car and the mileage on the odometer at the time of the accident. When the lawyer undertook representation of the client, the client probably did not expressly say that you have permission to disclose the model and number of miles on the odometer. However, it may reasonably be implied that the client consented to the disclosure of this information, because it is so basic to the resolution of the case.

2. Dispute about Lawyer's Conduct.   (DR 4-101(C)(4) and Rule 1.6(b)) Lawyers may reveal confidential information when they are accused of wrongdoing in connection with representing a client. A lawyer may be faced with a charge of wrongdoing against the client or a third person; for example, a person may claim to have been defrauded by the lawyer and client acting in complicity. In such an instance, the comments to Rule 1.6 (paragraph 18) explain that "the rule of confidentiality should not prevent the lawyer from defending against the charge."[12] A lawyer is also permitted to use confidential information to prove services rendered if necessary to collect fees. For example, suppose that a client did not tell the lawyer a very important but embarrassing fact when she and the client entered a fee agreement. This fact caused the litigation to be more complex and protracted than the lawyer initially anticipated. The attorney may need to disclose the fact and the additional work it caused, in order to establish entitlement to the fee. For instance, a client may come in and say that she seeks a divorce. The attorney explains that living separate and apart for one year is grounds for a divorce, and the client nods and says that will be fine. The attorney and client agree on a flat fee for a simple divorce. It later becomes evident that there is a serious factual dispute about whether the parties had actually lived separate and apart for one year, and this causes a considerable amount of extra work for the attorney. The client refuses to pay any more money for the many hours of extra work, and a fee dispute arises.

No matter what type of dispute is involved, ethical rules dictate that the lawyer disclose no more confidential information than is necessary to protect the lawyer's interest. The lawyer should try to minimize potential harm to the client.

3. To Prevent Commission of Future Crime.   (DR 4-101(C)(3) and Rule 1.6(b)(1)) An attorney may reveal a client's intention to commit a crime and information necessary to prevent the crime. Rule 1.6 limits disclosure to crimes that are "likely to result in imminent death or substantial bodily harm." However, the Model Code applies to any crime. Some states that have adopted a version of the Model Rules did not adopt the limitation on the type of crime, choosing instead to include all crimes.

It is important to distinguish between past crimes and future crimes. The exception does not apply to past crimes. Thus, if a client confesses a murder he has already committed, the rule of confidentiality applies. However, if the client says he is going to murder Mrs. Stone tomorrow, the attorney is allowed to disclose this information to prevent the murder.

4. When Permitted under Disciplinary Rules or Required by Court Order. (DR 4-101(C)(2) and paragraph 20 of Comments to Model Rule 1.6) DR 4-101(C)(2) specifically states that other sections of the Model Code can override the confidentiality requirement. DR 4-101(A)(4) provides that a lawyer shall not knowingly use perjured testimony or false evidence. For example, a lawyer in a divorce action presented to the court an affidavit she prepared for her client stating that the whereabouts of the client's husband was unknown and could not with due diligence be ascertained. However, the attorney failed to disclose to the court that she had a letter that contained the husband's return address. The attorney was found to have engaged in conduct involving fraud, dishonesty, deceit and misrepresentation.[13]

Although none of the Model Rules mirror the language of DR 4-101(C)(2), the comments to Rule 1.6 state that other rules may "permit or require a lawyer to disclose information relating to the representation." The Model Rules do not discuss specific situations where other provisions of law supersede Rule 1.6, noting instead that this is a matter of interpretation beyond the scope of the Model Rules.

A lawyer may be ordered by a court to reveal confidential information. As stated in the comments to Rule 1.6, the attorney should invoke the attorney-client privilege when it is applicable. The attorney may contest the court order and appeal it, but once the order is final, the attorney should obey it.

CONFLICT OF INTEREST

A lawyer has a mandatory duty to avoid conflicts of interest. Conflicts of interest can take many forms, and numerous ethical rules relate to conflicts of interest. Only the conflicts most frequently encountered in litigation are discussed here, but you should become familiar with all the conflict of interest rules.[14]

Clients with Adverse Interests

In litigation a frequent potential conflict is representation of a client when that representation would be directly adverse to another client. The general rule forbidding representation of clients with adverse interests is stated most succinctly in Model Rule 1.7(a) (see Figure 2-8). The comments to Rule 1.7 elaborate on

FIGURE 2-8   MODEL RULE 1.7(a)

> RULE 1.7 Conflict of Interest: General Rule
>
>   (a) A lawyer shall not represent a client if the representation of that client will be directly adverse to another client, unless:
>   (1) the lawyer reasonably believes the representation will not adversely affect the relationship with the other client; and
>   (2) each client consents after consultation.
>
>   ───────────────
>

the general rule, stating that "loyalty to a client prohibits undertaking representation directly adverse to that client without that client's consent." The Model Code states the duty not to represent clients with adverse claims in DR 5-101(A) and DR 5-105 (see Figures 2-9 and 2-10).

POINTER: The definition of what is "directly adverse" may differ among jurisdictions. The attorney will make the final decision and interpretation. Your most helpful role is to bring to the attorney's attention any situation you perceive as a potential conflict.

   A litigator may be asked to represent multiple clients—for example, coplaintiffs or codefendants—in one lawsuit. Determining the propriety of multiple representation can be complex. Lawyers must determine whether they can adequately represent the multiple parties, and then obtain the consent of each party, having fully disclosed "the implications of common representation and the advantages and risks involved."[15] The comments to Rule 1.7 explain that an impermissible conflict can exist where parties' testimony is substantially discrepant, or the parties' views of what constitutes a good settlement are substantially different. EC 5-15 discusses multiple representation, noting that an attorney must weigh the possibility that his or her judgment may be impaired or loyalty divided. The attorney must then weigh the degree to which the parties' interests differ, and decline representation if propriety seems doubtful. If a lawyer has already undertaken representation of multiple parties, and the parties' interests become divergent, the attorney should withdraw from the case. Whenever lawyers have to withdraw, they should strive to minimize the disruption to the client.[16] The potential for disruption is one reason a lawyer should decline multiple representation if a conflict appears likely.

Conflicts with Interests of Former Clients

Model Rule 1.9 delineates a lawyer's continuing duty to protect the interests of former clients (see Figure 2-11). Rule 1.9(a) prohibits representation of another person "in the same or a substantially related matter" when the other person's

FIGURE 2-9   MODEL CODE DR 5-101(A)

DR 5-101   Refusing Employment When the Interests of the Lawyer May Impair
           His Independent Professional Judgment.

(A) Except with the consent of his client after full disclosure, a lawyer shall not
    accept employment if the exercise of his professional judgment on behalf
    of his client will be or reasonably may be affected by his own financial,
    business, property, or personal interests.[20]

Excerpts from the Model Rules of Professional Conduct, Model Code of Professional Responsibility and Informal Opinion, copyrighted by the American Bar Association. All rights reserved. Reprinted with permission.

FIGURE 2-10   MODEL CODE DR 5-105

DR 5-105   Refusing to Accept or Continue Employment if the Interests of Another
           Client May Impair the Independent Professional Judgment of the
           Lawyer.

(A) A lawyer shall decline proffered employment if the exercise of his independent professional judgment in behalf of a client will be or is likely to be adversely affected by the acceptance of the proffered employment,[35] or if it would be likely to involve him in representing differing interests, except to the extent permitted under DR 5-105(C).[36]

(B) A lawyer shall not continue multiple employment if the exercise of his independent professional judgment in behalf of a client will be or is likely to be adversely affected by his representation of another client, or if it would be likely to involve him in representing differing interests, except to the extent permitted under DR 5-105(C).[37]

(C) In the situations covered by DR 5-105(A) and (B), a lawyer may represent multiple clients if it is obvious that he can adequately represent the interest of each and if each consents to the representation after full disclosure of the possible effect of such representation on the exercise of his independent professional judgment on behalf of each.

(D) If a lawyer is required to decline employment or to withdraw from employment under a Disciplinary Rule, no partner, or associate, or any other lawyer affiliated with him or his firm, may accept or continue such employment.

Excerpts from the Model Rules of Professional Conduct, Model Code of Professional Responsibility and Informal Opinion, copyrighted by the American Bar Association. All rights reserved. Reprinted with permission.

FIGURE 2-11   MODEL RULE 1.9

RULE 1.9 Conflict of Interest: Former Client

(a) A lawyer who has formerly represented a client in a matter shall not thereafter represent another person in the same or a substantially related matter in which that person's interests are materially adverse to the interests of the former client unless the former client consents after consultation.

(b) A lawyer shall not knowingly represent a person in the same or a substantially related matter in which a firm with which the lawyer formerly was associated had previously represented a client

   (1) whose interests are materially adverse to that person; and

   (2) about whom the lawyer had acquired information protected by Rules 1.6 and 1.9(c) that is material to the matter;
unless the former client consents after consultation.

(c) A lawyer who has formerly represented a client in a matter or whose present or former firm has formerly represented a client in a matter shall not thereafter:

   (1) use information relating to the representation to the disadvantage of the former client except as Rule 1.6 or Rule 3.3 would permit or require with respect to a client, or when the information has become generally known; or

   (2) reveal information relating to the representation except as Rule 1.6 or Rule 3.3 would permit or require with respect to a client.

interests are ''materially adverse'' to the interests of a former client. Because the definitions of the terms in quotes are subject to interpretation, you should refer to the rules and case law governing your jurisdiction. A former client can consent to the adverse representation, but only after the lawyer discloses the adverse interest and the lawyer's role in representing the new client. Like the rules that protect confidential information concerning former clients, this rule protects the interests of former clients.

Note that a lawyer may not use confidential information to the detriment of the former client, even if the lawyer does not share the confidential information with other persons. The Model Code does not directly state the rule concerning former clients, but ethics opinions have construed the Code to afford this protection.

Duty to Avoid Conflicts with the Lawyer's Own Interests

Lawyers also have a duty not to represent a person when the lawyers' own interests prevent them from exercising independent judgment. As DR 5-101(A) explains, a lawyer's own financial, business, property, or personal interests can interfere with professional judgment. In such a case, the lawyer must decline employment. Model Rule 1.7(b) and DR 5-101(A) both permit representation if the client consents after full disclosure or consultation. Model Rule 1.7(b) adds that the lawyer must believe that the adverse interest will not adversely affect his representation of the client. However, the comments to Rule 1.7 and the ethical considerations under Canon 5 make it clear that lawyers should decline employment if there is serious possibility that they cannot give detached advice.

After lawyers undertake representation, they have a duty to refrain from transactions that may interfere with their professional judgment. The prohibited transactions are too numerous to discuss in detail, so you should review carefully Model Rule 1.8 and DR 5-103, 5-104, and 5-107. In general, a lawyer must limit any business dealings with clients where the lawyer and client may have differing interests, unless the client consents after disclosure. A lawyer may not exploit to the client's disadvantage information relating to the representation of the client. The comments to Rule 1.8 cite as an example a lawyer's acquisition of real estate next to property he knows the client is buying, where the lawyer's purchase would adversely affect the client's plan for investment.

Office Procedures to Prevent Conflicts of Interest

One of your responsibilities may be to screen cases to ensure that representation of a person will not create a conflict of interest. As we noted previously, a conflict may arise because a client seeks representation in a matter that is adverse to the interests of another client. Recall that this applies to former clients as well. Cases must also be screened to ensure that none of the attorneys in the firm has a conflict, either because of personal reasons or because an attorney has represented a client in a matter directly adverse. It is important to consider all attorneys in the firm, because the disqualification of one attorney is imputed to the other attorneys in the firm. See Model Rule 1.10 and DR 5-105(D).

Your firm should have an index of every client and every party that is or has been adverse to that client in a lawsuit. Indices must cover both present and past clients. A manual index system for a small firm may have an alphabetical list of clients arranged under these headings:
1. Our clients: open files
2. Our clients: closed files
3. Adverse parties: open files
4. Adverse parties: closed files

A large firm will probably require a computer check for conflicts because of the huge number of cases handled. When a potential matter comes in, the law firm ascertains the name of the potential client and of all parties. For instance, in a large landlord-tenant dispute, the plaintiffs may include several of the tenants plus the tenants' association. The defendants may include the property owner, realty company manager, and building manager.

After gathering the names of all parties, one method for checking potential conflicts is to run a computer search of all stored documents (pleadings, discovery documents, etc.). The search is for the names of all parties involved in the new case. All documents on which any of the names appear are printed and read by attorneys and paralegals who assess the degree of involvement of that party in a former case. If a new party is brought into the litigation later, the same search must be done for documents with that party's name.

In a small law firm, the lawyers and paralegals may know enough about all the clients and cases to review the indices without having to review the documents in the files, but it is always best to take the utmost precaution in preventing conflicts. Remember that it is imperative that the system be absolutely up-to-date and all parties to a lawsuit be cross-referenced.

Special considerations arise when your firm represents corporate clients. Model Rule 1.13 and EC 5-18 make clear that an attorney who represents a corporation or other organization owes allegiance to the organization or corporation and not to its shareholders, directors, officers, or other persons connected with the entity. A lawyer may represent persons connected with the entity, but only if the lawyer believes that differing interests are not present. Thus you must take care to cross-reference all corporations and other organizations that your firm represents.

POINTER: At this time, read Chapter 5, pages 109–113, which discusses opening new files. When you open a new file, it is important to indicate that the new matter has been checked for conflicts of interest. Identifying a conflict at the outset eliminates the confusion and inconvenience to the client that arise when an attorney has to withdraw from a matter.

OTHER GENERAL DUTIES TO CLIENTS

Diligence

Model Rule 1.3 states very directly a lawyer's duty of diligence. It reads: "A lawyer shall act with reasonable diligence and promptness in representing a client." This rule sounds almost simplistic, but it encompasses many of the lawyer's duties, including the duties to be competent, prompt, and diligent. These duties apply equally to paralegals, and many times the burden will be on you to ensure that a case moves along properly. This is particularly true in the litigation context, where lawyers are in court often and have little control over their own schedule because of the unpredictability of court scheduling. Your work is crucial in ensuring that deadlines are met and that clients are promptly informed of developments in their case.

Competence

DR 6-101 spells out in more detail the lawyer's duty to act competently. It provides that lawyers shall not undertake a matter that they do not have the expertise to handle unless they associate another lawyer who has the proper expertise. For instance, if a lawyer in general practice does routine corporation work, such as drafting contracts, and one of the corporate clients becomes involved in a complex situation involving alleged violations of securities laws, the attorney should associate another attorney with knowledge of this complex area of law.

It further provides that a lawyer must prepare adequately for a case. This becomes very challenging for the busy litigator who may have to try several cases in a month plus keep up with discovery schedules and settlement offers. Here paralegals play a crucial role in tracking deadlines, assisting with discovery, and preparing for trial. Finally, DR 6-101 notes the duty of lawyers not to neglect a legal matter entrusted to them. Rarely does an attorney willfully neglect a case, but to a client involved in a protracted lawsuit it may appear that the attorney is being neglectful. This is one reason why it is important to maintain steady communication with every client, even if you merely inform them that there have been no new developments in the past month.

Communication

The duty to keep clients informed is stated in Model Rule 1.4(a), which reads: ''A lawyer shall keep a client reasonably informed about the status of a matter and promptly comply with reasonable requests for information.'' Lawyers must keep clients informed of developments so that clients can make decisions, in conjunction with the lawyers' advice, about matters concerning their case, such as whether to accept an offer of settlement. A lawsuit can go on for years, and this is particularly true of complex litigation. Thus it is important to communicate with clients regularly to inform them of the status of their case, even if there have been no recent developments.

A lawyer and a client may have different opinions as to what constitutes ''reasonable'' communications. Some clients want to talk with the attorney about their case every day. This is particularly true of clients in very stressful situations, such as those who are involved in a divorce and property settlement. Because the attorney is often in court, the paralegal frequently is the one who talks with the client. It is important to explain to the client, especially when time is billed by the hour, that the client will be charged for all time spent on the case. The client must understand that daily calls to inquire whether anything has happened will result in a larger bill for services rendered. Many clients do not realize the amount of time spent on pretrial matters such as discovery and settlement negotiations. In particular, they do not realize that time on the telephone constitutes billable time. After several weeks of daily calls, you may be the one who explains to the client why daily calls are not necessary or wise. One approach is to explain that when an attorney has 200 active files, she cannot talk to every client every day, even for five minutes. If she did, she would have no time to make progress on anyone's case, including the case of the frequent caller.

Regular written communications with every client are essential. Particularly with lengthy litigation, you should mark every file for review at least once a month. At that time, send a letter to each client to inform the client of the status of his or her case. If nothing has developed since the prior month, it is sufficient to state that there have been no new developments since your last communication and that you will inform the client promptly of all new developments. This not only lets the client know that you are keeping close track of the case, but provides written proof of diligence in the event that the client ever accuses the lawyer of neglect.

TRANSACTIONS WITH PERSONS OTHER THAN CLIENTS

Rules of professional responsibility extend beyond communications with clients. Communications with other parties and with the court are also governed by specific rules.

Truthfulness in Statements to Others

Both the Model Code and Model Rules dictate truthfulness in statements made to the court and to other persons, including the opposing party. See Model Rule 4.1 (Figure 2-12) and DR 7-102 (Figure 2-13) and read the specific prohibitions. In general, a lawyer must not make a false statement of material fact or law and must not conceal information that he is required by law to disclose. In addition, lawyers must not use evidence that they know to be false, including testimony that the lawyer knows is perjured.

FIGURE 2-12   MODEL RULE 4.1

TRANSACTIONS WITH PERSONS OTHER THAN CLIENTS

RULE 4.1 Truthfulness in Statements to Others

In the course of representing a client a lawyer shall not knowingly:
(a) make a false statement of material fact or law to a third person; or
(b) fail to disclose a material fact to a third person when disclosure is necessary to avoid assisting a criminal or fraudulent act by a client, unless disclosure is prohibited by Rule 1.6.

Excerpts from the Model Rules of Professional Conduct, Model Code of Professional Responsibility and Informal Opinion, copyrighted by the American Bar Association. All rights reserved. Reprinted with permission.

FIGURE 2-13   MODEL CODE DR 7-102

DR 7-102   Representing a Client Within the Bounds of the Law.

(A) In his representation of a client, a lawyer shall not:
  (1) File a suit, assert a position, conduct a defense, delay a trial, or take other action on behalf of his client when he knows or when it is obvious that such action would serve merely to harass or maliciously injure another.[69]
  (2) Knowingly advance a claim or defense that is unwarranted under existing law, except that he may advance such claim or defense if it can be supported by good faith argument for an extension, modification, or reversal of existing law.
  (3) Conceal or knowingly fail to disclose that which he is required by law to reveal.
  (4) Knowingly use perjured testimony or false evidence.[70]
  (5) Knowingly make a false statement of law or fact.
  (6) Participate in the creation or preservation of evidence when he knows or it is obvious that the evidence is false.
  (7) Counsel or assist his client in conduct that the lawyer knows to be illegal or fraudulent.
  (8) Knowingly engage in other illegal conduct or conduct contrary to a Disciplinary Rule.

Excerpts from the Model Rules of Professional Conduct, Model Code of Professional Responsibility and Informal Opinion, copyrighted by the American Bar Association. All rights reserved. Reprinted with permission.

Communication with a Person Represented by Counsel

Both Model Rule 4.2 and DR 7-104(A)(1) provide that a lawyer shall not communicate about the subject of the representation with a party the lawyer knows to be represented by another lawyer in the matter, unless the lawyer has the consent of the other party's lawyer or is authorized by law to communicate with the other party. A lawyer is not prohibited from discussing with an opposing party a matter unrelated to the matter in controversy between the parties. For example, suppose a lawyer in a small town represents Ms. Cardoza in a contract dispute with Mr. Hamadi's corporation. If the lawyer and Mr. Hamadi meet at a social event, the lawyer may discuss with Mr. Hamadi the weather, sports, or anything else unrelated to the matter in controversy.

When you work as a paralegal, you may receive a phone call from the opposing party in a lawsuit. If you know that the party is represented by counsel, you must advise the party that you cannot talk with her without the prior consent of her attorney. If you are uncertain whether the party has an attorney, check with your supervising attorney before you talk with her.

Communication with an Unrepresented Person

Model Rule 4.3 and DR 7-104(A)(2) address dealing with a person unrepresented by counsel. DR 7-104(A)(2) states that if the interests of the unrepresented person have a "reasonable possibility of being in conflict with the interests of his client," the attorney can give no advice to the unrepresented persons except to advise them to secure their own attorney. Rule 4.3 states that a lawyer has a duty to inform the unrepresented person that the lawyer is not disinterested in the matter. This protects unrepresented persons from disclosing information injurious to their own case.

CONDUCT SPECIFICALLY RELATED TO LITIGATION

Several ethical rules apply specifically to litigation. It is imperative that litigation paralegals be especially familiar with these rules.

Meritorious Claims and Contentions

Model Rule 3.1 provides that a lawyer shall not advance a claim or defense that is "frivolous." The definition of "frivolous" can vary among jurisdictions. The comment to Rule 3.1 states that a position is not frivolous just because the lawyer thinks the client is unlikely to prevail. However, a claim or defense is frivolous if the purpose of the action is primarily to harass or maliciously injure a person; the lawyer cannot make a good-faith argument on the merits of the action; or the lawyer cannot make a good-faith argument for an extension, modification or reversal of existing law.

DR 7-102(A)(1) also provides that a lawyer may not take an action that is designed merely to harass or maliciously injure another. Such action includes filing a suit, asserting a position, conducting a defense, and delaying a trial, when it is obvious or the attorney knows the action is for the purpose of harassment.

DR 7-102(A)(2) provides that a lawyer may advance a claim or defense that is "unwarranted under existing law" only if it can be supported by a good-faith argument for modification of the existing law.

For example, assume that Congress has passed a new law. An attorney sincerely believes that the new law deprives a client of due process and is therefore unconstitutional. The plaintiffs in three similar lawsuits in different states have lost. If the attorney can make a good faith argument that the law is unconstitutional, the lawsuit is not frivolous, even though plaintiffs in other jurisdictions have lost similar claims.

In addition to ethical rules, Rule 11 of the Federal Rules of Civil Procedure is designed to deter the filing of frivolous claims and defenses. FRCivP 11 requires an attorney to sign all pleadings filed with the court. The attorney's signature "constitutes a certificate by him that he has read the pleading; that to the best of his knowledge, information, and belief there is good ground to support it; and that it is not interposed for delay." FRCivP 11 provides that if a pleading or motion is signed in violation of this rule, the court "shall impose" upon the person who signed it "an appropriate sanction," which may include payment of the expenses, including attorney's fees, to the party that was forced to respond.

Expediting Litigation

DR 7-102(A), as noted above, imposes a duty not to delay litigation. Model Rule 3.2 states the obligation clearly: "A lawyer shall make reasonable efforts to expedite litigation consistent with the interests of the client." An attorney may seek extensions for answering discovery and rescheduling of hearings when more time is needed to gather facts for the client's case or for some other legitimate reason that is in the best interest of the client. However, there must exist some substantial purpose other than the delay. The comment to Rule 3.2 states that "realizing financial or other benefit from otherwise improper delay in litigation is not a legitimate interest of the client."

A lawyer who seeks numerous delays in litigation will soon see the patience of the judge wear thin. Paralegals can help avoid delays by making sure that documents are ready well ahead of the deadline and by giving witnesses ample notice when they must appear for a deposition or trial.

Candor Toward the Tribunal

Model Rule 3.3 is similar to Rule 4.1, which requires truthfulness in statements to others. "Others" certainly includes the court. Rule 3.3 specifies that a lawyer shall not knowingly make a false statement of material fact to the court, fail to disclose a material fact necessary to avoid assisting a criminal or fraudulent act by the client, or offer evidence that the lawyer knows to be false. DR 7-102(A) states basically the same requirements.

In addition, Model Rule 3.3 requires an attorney to disclose to the court "legal authority in the controlling jurisdiction known to the lawyer to be directly adverse to the position of the client and not disclosed by opposing counsel." DR 7-106(B)(1) states the same requirement. EC 7-23 notes that once attorneys have disclosed the adverse law, they may challenge the soundness of the law. Paralegals must be careful in their legal research to report both the favorable and unfavorable law related to any case. It will serve no purpose to try to ignore law unfavorable to your client's position. In fact it will harm your client's case, because the court is likely to be aware of the adverse law anyway and will not look kindly on any effort to hide the adverse authority. The best approach is to bring the adverse authority to the attention of your supervising attorney and then help find ways to distinguish your own case or attack the soundness of the law.

Fairness to Opposing Party and Counsel

Ethical duties related to fairness to the opposing side deal mainly with the presentation of evidence. We have already discussed the duty not to allow the submission of false evidence. DR 7-109(A) and Model Rule 3.4(a) state a lawyer's duty not to suppress, alter, destroy or unlawfully obstruct another party's access to evidence. Rule 3.4(b) states the prohibition against falsifying evidence or counseling a witness to testify falsely.

Model Rule 3.4(d) states a very important prohibition for paralegals to keep in mind. That is the duty not to make frivolous discovery requests and the affirmative duty to comply with a legally proper discovery request from the opposing side (see Figure 2-14). The comment explains that obtaining evidence through discovery or subpoena is an important procedural right that is frustrated by the alteration, concealment, or destruction of relevant material. See Chapter 9 for more discussion of how to comply fairly with the discovery process.

Other Ethical Obligations Regarding Trial Conduct

Model Rule 3.4(c) and DR 7-106(A) both require lawyers to obey the rules of the tribunal. Both also provide that a lawyer may in good faith contest a rule. This means that a lawyer must follow the local rules of a court. As we noted in Chapter 1, courts have procedural rules with which litigants must comply. It is imperative that paralegals know and obey the local rules. ECs 7-19 and 7-20 explain well the need for procedural rules in the litigation process. They essentially state that in the adversary system, lawyers must be able to present their clients' cases to an impartial fact finder who must be able to receive all relevant evidence. This can be achieved only when the litigation is governed by rules that assure an "effective and dignified process."

DR 7-106(A) and Model Rule 3.4(c) also require lawyers to follow the court's rulings (see Figure 2-15). As the trial proceeds, the judge will make rulings regarding the admission of evidence and will rule on various motions made by the lawyers. For example, if your firm represents the defendant, when the plaintiff has presented all her evidence, your supervising attorney may make a motion to dismiss the plaintiff's case for failure to show a right to relief. If the judge denies defendant's motion to dismiss, the defendant's attorney objects on the record. However, the trial must continue, and the attorney must abide by the judge's ruling. If the plaintiff wins a favorable verdict, the defendant's attorney can include in the grounds for appeal the failure to grant defendant's motion to dismiss.

FIGURE 2-14   MODEL RULE 3.4

RULE 3.4 Fairness to Opposing Party and Counsel

A lawyer shall not:

(a) unlawfully obstruct another party's access to evidence or unlawfully alter, destroy or conceal a document or other material having potential evidentiary value. A lawyer shall not counsel or assist another person to do any such act;

(b) falsify evidence, counsel or assist a witness to testify falsely, or offer an inducement to a witness that is prohibited by law;

(c) knowingly disobey an obligation under the rules of a tribunal except for an open refusal based on an assertion that no valid obligation exists;

(d) in pretrial procedure, make a frivolous discovery request or fail to make reasonably diligent effort to comply with a legally proper discovery request by an opposing party;

(e) in trial, allude to any matter that the lawyer does not reasonably believe is relevant or that will not be supported by admissible evidence, assert personal knowledge of facts in issue except when testifying as a witness, or state a personal opinion as to the justness of a cause, the credibility of a witness, the culpability of a civil litigant or the guilt or innocence of an accused; or

(f) request a person other than a client to refrain from voluntarily giving relevant information to another party unless:

(1) the person is a relative or an employee or other agent of a client; and

(2) the lawyer reasonably believes that the person's interests will not be adversely affected by refraining from giving such information.

DR 7-106(C) and Model Rule 3.4(e) preclude an attorney from asserting personal knowledge about facts in issue unless she is a witness. Nor may an attorney give a personal opinion about a person's guilt or innocence or credibility or about the justness of a person's cause. In addition, a lawyer is not allowed to allude to any matter that he does not reasonably believe to be relevant or that is not supported by admissible evidence. Model Rule 3-5 and DR 7-108 prohibit a lawyer from communicating with jurors before or during a trial, except when formally addressing them as a group in the courtroom. DR 7-106 and Rule 3.4 contain other prohibitions that you should read (Figures 2-14 and 2-15).[17]

Although as a paralegal you will not actually try any cases yourself, it is essential that you understand the ethical obligations that govern conduct in the courtroom. Your understanding will make you better able to help the attorney prepare for trial. Finally, you should be aware that any trial publicity is handled by the attorney and is governed by DR 7-107 and Model Rule 3.6.

FIGURE 2-15   MODEL CODE DR 7-106

DR 7-106   Trial Conduct.

(A) A lawyer shall not disregard or advise his client to disregard a standing rule of a tribunal or a ruling of a tribunal made in the course of a proceeding, but he may take appropriate steps in good faith to test the validity of such rule or ruling.

(B) In presenting a matter to a tribunal, a lawyer shall disclose:[78]
   (1) Legal authority in the controlling jurisdiction known to him to be directly adverse to the position of his client and which is not disclosed by opposing counsel.[79]
   (2) Unless privileged or irrelevant, the identities of the clients he represents and of the persons who employed him.[80]

(C) In appearing in his professional capacity before a tribunal, a lawyer shall not:
   (1) State or allude to any matter that he has no reasonable basis to believe is relevant to the case or that will not be supported by admissible evidence.[81]
   (2) Ask any question that he has no reasonable basis to believe is relevant to the case and that is intended to degrade a witness or other person.[82]
   (3) Assert his personal knowledge of the facts in issue, except when testifying as a witness.
   (4) Assert his personal opinion as to the justness of a cause, as to the credibility of a witness, as to the culpability of a civil litigant, or as to the guilt or innocence of an accused;[83] but he may argue, on his analysis of the evidence, for any position or conclusion with respect to the matters stated herein.
   (5) Fail to comply with known local customs of courtesy or practice of the bar or a particular tribunal without giving to opposing counsel timely notice of his intent not to comply.[84]
   (6) Engage in undignified or discourteous conduct which is degrading to a tribunal.
   (7) Intentionally or habitually violate any established rule of procedure or of evidence.

ENDNOTES

1 ABA Model Code of Professional Responsibility, Preliminary Statement.
2 *Id.*
3 The Preliminary Statement of the ABA Model Rules of Professional Conduct includes the following sections: Preamble: A Lawyer's Responsibilities; Scope; and Terminology. All three are helpful in understanding the scope and meaning of the Model Rules.

4 Preliminary Statements, ABA Model Code of Professional Responsibility and ABA Model Rules of Professional Conduct (under Scope).

5 See comment to Model Rule 5.5.

6 EC 3-5 suggests that persons engage in the practice of law when they ''relate the general body and philosophy of law to a specific legal problem of a client.''

7 N.C. Gen. Stat. 84-2.1 (1988).

8 8 U.S.C. Sections 1101(a)(42)(A) and 1158(a).

9 Paragraph 5 of the comment to Model Rule 1.6 further explains the attorney-client privilege and its relationship to ethical rules regarding confidentiality.

10 Only part of the comments to Rule 1.6 are reprinted in Figure 2-6. This quote is from a portion of the comments discussing the attorney-client privilege.

11 EC 4-2; paragraph 8 of comments to Model Rule 1.6.

12 Paragraph 18 of comments to Model Rule 1.6.

13 *North Carolina State Bar v. Wilson*, 74 N.C. App. 777, 330 S.E.2d 280 (1985).

14 Model Rules 1.7 through 1.13; Canon 5, including DR 5-101 through 5-107.

15 Model Rule 1.7(b) and DR 5-105(C).

16 DR 2-110(A), DR 5-105(A)-(C), Model Rule 1.16(d).

17 Excerpts from the Model Rules of Professional Conduct, Model Code of Professional Responsibility and Informal Opinion, copyrighted by the American Bar Association. All rights reserved. Reprinted with permission.

3 COURT ORGANIZATION AND JURISDICTION

LITIGATION EXTRACT: Before we can commence our lawsuit in the Wesser case, we have to determine where to file the action. A lawsuit filed in the wrong court can be dismissed, so it is imperative that we choose a proper court. In Chapter 3, we consider the concept of jurisdiction—which court can hear this type of case and has the power to bring the defendants into court and enter a binding judgment. First we have an overview of the federal and state court systems in order to understand which courts we consider for filing our action. After examining jurisdiction, we consider the proper venue—in which geographical district it is fair to litigate.

INTRODUCTION

The lawsuits in which you participate will not all be tried in the same court. Some cases will be heard in a federal court, others in a state court. There exist a number of different types of courts within both the federal and state systems. Many factors determine in which court a case is tried. These factors are discussed in the section headed Jurisdiction. **Jurisdiction** is the authority of a court to preside over claims in a judicial proceeding. If a court does not have proper jurisdiction over a case, the case can be dismissed at any time during the course of the litigation. This is true even on appeal, after a judgment has been entered. If too much time has passed since the cause of action, the plaintiff may not be able to refile a claim in the appropriate court because the statute of limitations will have expired. Furthermore, any judgment the court enters in a case where it has no jurisdiction is void and unenforceable. Thus it is imperative that a plaintiff file the lawsuit in the correct court.

As a paralegal, you may work with the attorney on your team to determine in which court a case should be filed. Even if the question of jurisdiction has been determined before you start working on the case, you must understand the way the state and federal court systems are organized and understand the types of cases over which the courts may exercise jurisdiction.

DEFINITIONS

Every state has its own court system. Within every state there is also a separate federal court system. In order to understand how both systems work, you must be familiar with certain terms that pertain to both systems. If you do not grasp the practical meaning of each term simply by reading the definition, do not panic. The practical meanings will become clear as you study the court organization and apply the definitions to the federal and state court systems.

Both the state and federal court systems have trial courts and appellate courts. The **trial court** is the court in which the lawsuit is commenced. The trial court is where both parties present their case—lawyers make opening arguments, witnesses testify, the judge rules on motions made at trial, and the judge or jury (if it is a jury trial) renders a verdict.

The trial courts in the federal court system are called United States district courts. Trial courts in the state court system have different names in different states. Common names include state, district, superior, county, or common pleas, to name a few.

After judgment is entered, a losing party may appeal an unfavorable outcome. The losing party requests an **appellate court** to review and overturn the trial court's decision. In contrast to the trial court, the appellate court hears no testimony. The appellate court bases its decision on the record of the trial court. The **record** consists of the testimony at trial, the pleadings, discovery materials, and other documents from the litigation at the trial level. The appellate court reviews the record to determine whether the relevant law was properly applied. It does not readjudicate the facts of the case. The attorneys for both the party that brings the appeal (**appellant**) and the party that opposes the appeal (**appellee**) present briefs to the appellate court arguing why their side should prevail on appeal. The attorneys also present oral arguments, unless the appellate court waives oral argument. The role of the appellate court is to review the record and determine whether the appellant received a fair trial and whether the evidence supports the verdict. See Chapter 13 for more details on appeals.

In discussing appeals, one often refers to the trial or decision "below." Trial courts are often referred to as **inferior courts**. This is just another way of describing the distinction between trial courts and appellate courts. The inferior (trial) court is where the case is first heard and judgment entered. The appellate court is superior to the trial court in that it can overrule the trial court, and the appellate court's decision is binding on the trial (inferior) court. Thus, if the appellate court determines that the trial judge committed an error that justifies a new trial, the trial court must conduct a new trial whether it cares to or not.

Two other terms often are used in reference to the trial court. The trial court is often called the **court of original jurisdiction**. Again, this merely means that the case is initiated and heard at this level, not reviewed and appealed. The trial court, at least in the federal system, is a **court of record**. This means that all transactions and arguments that take place in the courtroom are recorded by a stenographer, the court reporter. If a court is not a court of record, no recording or stenographic transcription is made. Some state courts at certain levels are not courts of record, as we will discuss later.

Another important distinction is a **court of limited jurisdiction** as opposed to a **court of general jurisdiction**. A court of limited jurisdiction can hear only specific types of cases. For instance, federal district courts have jurisdiction only over the types of cases that Congress has authorized them to hear. (See the section headed Subject Matter Jurisdiction later in this chapter.) An example is the bankruptcy court, which obviously has jurisdiction only over matters related to bankruptcy. A state court system may have a traffic court that hears only traffic cases. A court with general jurisdiction is not limited in the type of cases it can hear. Most state courts are courts of general jurisdiction, except for certain specialized courts such as traffic court or juvenile court.

THE FEDERAL COURT SYSTEM

At the outset it is important to understand that federal trial courts are not superior to state trial courts. Federal courts are a separate, independent system of courts.

Three basic groups comprise the federal court system: the United States district courts, the United States courts of appeal, and the United States Supreme Court. The district courts are trial courts, and the courts of appeal and U.S. Supreme Court are appellate courts.

United States District Courts

U.S. district courts are courts of original jurisdiction—that is, lawsuits are commenced and tried at this level. Every state has a federal district court. The more populous states have more than one federal district court. For example, New York has four federal district courts—the U.S. District Court for the Southern District of New York, the U.S. District Court for the Eastern District of New York, the U.S. District Court for the Western District of New York, and the U.S. District Court for the Northern District of New York. For states that have only one federal district court—for example, New Mexico—that court is called the U.S. District Court for the District of New Mexico or the particular state in question.

Federal district courts are courts of limited jurisdiction; that is, they can hear only the types of cases that federal law authorizes them to hear. Congress has defined certain types of cases as falling within federal court jurisdiction. Two of the most common categories are cases involving a **federal question** and cases with **diversity of citizenship**. Briefly defined, federal question jurisdiction includes cases that involve federal laws or the United States Constitution. For example, the plaintiff in the Chattooga case claims that the defendant violated federal law prohibiting employment discrimination; therefore federal question jurisdiction exists. Diversity of citizenship jurisdiction involves cases where the plaintiffs and the defendants are from different states and the claim involves more than $50,000.

Both the Wesser and Chattooga cases are federal district court actions, so you will become familiar with the procedure for litigation in federal district court as we follow the proceedings in these cases in subsequent chapters. Many, though not all, of the decisions rendered by federal district judges are published in *Federal Supplement* (F. Supp.). A decision is published if it may provide useful guidance for other courts dealing with the issue in the future.

United States Courts of Appeal

The U.S. courts of appeal hear appeals from the federal district courts. They are the intermediate appellate courts in the federal system. That is, a party dissatisfied with the decision of a U.S. court of appeals can appeal to a higher appellate court—the United States Supreme Court.

The U.S. Court of Appeals is divided into twelve geographical regions, termed **circuits**. Refer to Figure 3-1, which shows the states covered by each circuit. You see, for example, that the 11th Circuit encompasses Florida, Georgia, and Alabama. The 11th Circuit Court of Appeals hears appeals from the federal district courts in these three states. Note that the District of Columbia has its own Circuit Court of Appeals, because many of the cases involving the federal government are litigated in Washington, D.C.

FIGURE 3-1 CIRCUIT COURTS OF APPEAL

	Areas Covered
First	Maine, New Hampshire, Massachusetts, Rhode Island, Puerto Rico
Second	New York, Connecticut, Vermont
Third	New Jersey, Pennsylvania, Delaware, Virgin Islands
Fourth	Maryland, Virginia, West Virginia, North Carolina, South Carolina
Fifth	Texas, Louisiana, Mississippi, Canal Zone
Sixth	Michigan, Ohio, Kentucky, Tennessee
Seventh	Illinois, Indiana, Wisconsin
Eighth	Minnesota, North Dakota, South Dakota, Iowa, Nebraska, Missouri, Arkansas
Ninth	Washington, Oregon, California, Idaho, Nevada, Montana, Arizona, Hawaii, Alaska, Guam
Tenth	Colorado, New Mexico, Utah, Wyoming, Kansas, Oklahoma
Eleventh	Alabama, Georgia, Florida
District of Columbia	District of Columbia
Federal Circuit	Appeals from specialized federal courts

In addition to the twelve circuit courts based on geographical regions, there is the United States Court of Appeals for the Federal Circuit. This is a specialized court of limited jurisdiction, which can hear only the types of cases enumerated in 28 U.S.C. §1295. The Court of Appeals for the Federal Circuit is authorized to hear appeals from federal courts of any district, where the case relates to certain copyright, trademark, and patent issues. It may also hear appeals of certain decisions concerning contracts with government agencies, as well as appeals of final decisions of the United States Court of International Trade, and certain other types of appeals as delineated in 28 U.S.C. §1295. This is only a general description of the appeals that the Federal Circuit Court of Appeals can hear; there is no substitute for reading 28 U.S.C. §1295 when you are involved in a case over which this court may have appellate jurisdiction.

Some decisions of administrative agencies can be appealed directly to the circuit courts of appeal, without having to appeal first to the federal district court, which is the usual avenue of appeal. The direct appeal of an administrative agency decision is created by specific statutes. For example, 7 U.S.C. §§135b(d) and 136n(b) provide for direct appeal of orders of the Administrator of the Environmental Protection Agency with respect to registration of economic poisons and pesticides.

As with other appellate courts, the circuit courts of appeal base their decisions on the record from the trial court below. The appellant and appellee present memoranda of law supporting their arguments, and the attorneys present oral arguments. A panel of judges, usually three to a panel, considers the case and renders an opinion. If the opinion is a published one, it can be found in *Federal Reporter* (F. or F.2d). If a party does not appeal to the U.S. Supreme Court, the decision of the circuit court of appeals stands as the final decision.

POINTER: The various circuits have their own court rules. The rules can differ significantly among circuits, so it is imperative that you consult the court's own rules.

United States Supreme Court

The United States Supreme Court is the highest court in the country. It is comprised of nine justices—one chief justice and eight associate justices. The justices exercise a great deal of discretion in choosing the cases the Court will hear. If a party wants the U.S. Supreme Court to hear its appeal, that party must file a **petition for certiorari**, asking the Court to hear its appeal and explaining why the Court should hear the appeal.[1] If the Court decides that the case involves an important enough question of law, the Court will issue a **writ of certiorari**, which is an order by the Court stating that it has decided to hear the appeal and ordering the lower appellate court to send up the record. If the Court denies the petition for certiorari, the lower court decision stands as the final decision in the case.

The U.S. Supreme Court often chooses to hear a case when there is a conflict among the U.S. courts of appeal on a specific question of law. For example, in the case of *Immigration and Naturalization Service v. Cardoza-Fonseca*, the U.S. Supreme Court granted certiorari because there was a conflict among the circuit courts regarding a question of law concerning persons seeking political asylum in the United States. To gain political asylum, persons must establish that they have a ''well-founded fear of persecution''—that is, a well-founded fear that if they were forced to return to their home country, they would be persecuted because of their race, religion, nationality, membership in a particular social group, or political opinion. Different circuit courts had arrived at different conclusions about the degree of proof necessary to establish a well-founded fear of persecution, so the U.S. Supreme Court granted certiorari to resolve this conflict.[2]

The United States Supreme Court has original jurisdiction in a few very limited types of cases. These types of cases are enumerated in 28 U.S.C. §1251. They include controversies between two states, controversies between the United States and a state, and actions by a state against the citizens of another state or against aliens. An **alien** is not a person from outer space. This is the common legal term for a person who is not a citizen of the United States. The U.S. Supreme Court also has original jurisdiction over ''actions or proceedings to which ambassadors, other public ministers, consuls, or vice consuls of foreign states are parties.''

Specialized Federal Courts

Several specialized federal courts were created by statute to hear specific types of cases. We have already discussed the Federal Circuit Court of Appeals and its limited jurisdiction. Other examples include the United States Court of Claims, which hears cases concerning claims against the United States when such claims arise from a federal law or the U.S. Constitution, or involve a contract with the United States; and the United States Tax Court, which decides actions concerning federal income, death, or gift taxes.

STATE COURT SYSTEMS

Each state has its own court system, established and governed by the constitution and statutes of that state. There is a great deal of variety from state to state in the names assigned to various levels and divisions of courts in the state systems. However, the general structure is basically the same—trial courts and appellate courts. There are various divisions within each of these two basic court levels. Our discussion is intended to give you a broad overview of state court structure. You must learn the names, jurisdiction, and operating procedures of each level and division in your state.

State Trial Courts

Commonly, one primary trial court is the nucleus of a state trial court system. Various names are given to this trial court: district, circuit, county, superior, or common pleas, for a few examples. It is a court of general jurisdiction as opposed to the federal trial courts, which have limited jurisdiction.

This core trial court system is often split into two sets of trial courts—one that hears cases involving amounts exceeding, for example $10,000, and the other hearing cases involving amounts less than that. For instance, a case involving damages of $10,000 or less may be filed in the ''district court,'' and cases involving more than $10,000 may be heard in the ''superior court.'' The district court has its own set of judges, as does the superior court. Trials are conducted similarly in both trial courts. However, there may be some differences, such as whether the proceedings are recorded by a court reporter. The courts dealing with the lesser amounts are sometimes not courts of record.

A state trial court of general jurisdiction hears cases involving issues such as contract disputes, personal injury, property damage, and divorce-related matters. Some states also have specialized courts that deal only with specific issues. There may be a separate court division that hears only divorce-related issues such as custody and child support. There may be special courts exclusively for juvenile matters or probate (trusts and estates) matters. It is common to have a separate division for all criminal trials.

Another common special court is one that deals exclusively with cases involving no more than a small dollar amount: say, $1,500. This court is often called small claims, municipal, or magistrate's court. Cases heard frequently include those dealing with issues such as past-due rent, money owed on promissory notes, and other contract disputes involving small sums. Often parties litigate these small claims by themselves—that is, without attorneys. The filing fee is usually small, and simple forms are used to file a complaint. The employees in the clerk of court's office usually help people with their questions about filing a claim and initiating a lawsuit. The court hearings are usually simple, and the pretrial procedure is not complex. That is, the pleadings usually include just a complaint and answer, with none of the more intricate pretrial motions and discovery procedures that occur in more complex litigation.

A party who loses in small claims court can usually appeal to the next highest trial court. The party is generally entitled to an entirely new trial at the next level. This is termed a trial *de novo*.

 POINTER: It is important to grasp the distinction between a trial *de novo* and a regular appeal. At a trial *de novo* the entire case is heard again. The witnesses testify again, and the judge makes a decision on the evidence he or she actually hears and reads. In contrast, in a regular appeal no new testimony is given, and the appellate court bases its decision on the record made at the trial below. The appellate court reviews the trial below for errors; it does not conduct a new trial.

State Appellate Courts

When a final judgment has been entered in the highest state trial court, a dissatisfied party may seek appeal with a state appellate court. A state appellate court system usually has two levels of appellate courts. The first level of appeal is to the intermediate appellate court, often called the court of appeals, and the second level is to the highest court in the state, usually called the state supreme court. Some states split the intermediate court into the court of civil appeals and the court of criminal appeals.

A party usually has an appeal as of right to the intermediate appellate court (court of appeals). An **appeal as of right** means that by statute the party is granted an appeal to the next level and does not have to petition the court to hear its case. Usually a panel of three or more judges hear oral argument and sign the court's decision. If one of the members of the panel dissents from the court's decision, there is often an appeal as of right to the state supreme court.

A party dissatisfied with the decision of the court of appeals may then ask the highest state court (supreme court) to review the decision. In most types of cases, review by the supreme court is not automatic. Instead, a party must file a petition for certiorari or petition for discretionary review. State statutes sometimes provide for an appeal as of right to the state supreme court. Such an appeal may be available when the case involves an important constitutional question.

In rare instances, state statutes provide for appeal of a trial court judgment directly to the state supreme court. The most common example is the appeal of a criminal conviction that imposes the death penalty.

Decisions rendered by state administrative agencies may also be appealed to the appellate courts. This may involve special rules of appellate procedure and state statutes. It is important to remember that all appeals within the administrative agency itself must be exhausted before an appeal can be made to a court.

JURISDICTION

You now understand that there exist many types of courts in both the state court systems and the federal court system. A particular court can hear a case and enter a judgment only if it has jurisdiction over the case. As we noted earlier, **jurisdiction** is defined as a court's power to decide a case or controversy. State statutes define the power of state courts, and federal statutes delineate the types of cases that federal courts can hear. As we discussed previously, some courts, particularly federal courts, have the authority to hear only certain types of cases.

In order to adjudicate a case, the court must have authority over both the type of case and the parties involved in the case. The authority to hear a particular type of case is called **subject matter jurisdiction**. The power of the court to bring a party before it and enter a judgment against that party is called **personal jurisdiction**. You should note at the outset that a plaintiff submits to the court's jurisdiction by filing the lawsuit in the court. Thus the issue of personal jurisdiction involves the court's authority to make a defendant come into that court.

Subject matter jurisdiction and personal jurisdiction are two separate analyses. The analysis for subject matter jurisdiction focuses on whether the court has the authority to hear this type of case. The focus of the analysis for personal jurisdiction is twofold. The first is whether the defendants can be brought into the court without violating their constitutional right to due process. The second is whether the defendants received proper notice that they are being sued. This involves giving the defendant proper written notice, or service of process, which is discussed in Chapter 6.

The concepts of subject matter jurisdiction and personal jurisdiction are best understood by examining how they are applied at the state and federal trial court level.

Subject Matter Jurisdiction

Subject matter jurisdiction is an extremely important matter. A case may be dismissed at any time if the court does not have subject matter jurisdiction. Even if all parties wish to have a case litigated in a certain court because it would be convenient, that court cannot hear the case if subject matter jurisdiction is not conferred on the court by statute. Furthermore, even if neither party raises the issue, a court may on its own (*sua sponte*) dismiss a case for lack of subject matter jurisdiction.

Subject Matter Jurisdiction in State Courts. Because most state courts are courts of general jurisdiction, subject matter jurisdiction is not as finely delineated by statute as it is in federal courts. As we discussed earlier, in state courts the trial court's jurisdiction is frequently limited by the amount in controversy. If a small amount is involved, the claim may have to be brought in small claims court. A state may have two or three levels of trial courts, with jurisdiction based on the amount in controversy. When a court's jurisdiction is based on the amount at issue in the case, that amount is called the **jurisdictional amount**.

State courts do have some specialized courts that handle only certain types of cases, such as traffic court and juvenile court. These are exceptions, however, to the practice that most state courts are courts of general jurisdiction.

Subject Matter Jurisdiction in Federal Courts. The federal court system was created by Article III, Section 1, of the United States Constitution, which states that "[t]he judicial Power of the United States, shall be vested in one supreme Court, and in such inferior Courts as the Congress may from time to time ordain and establish."

Congress created the federal district courts, which have jurisdiction as set forth in several federal statutes.

Numerous statutes confer on the federal courts jurisdiction over particular types of cases. Some of the most important types of jurisdiction are as follows:

Statute	Type of Case
28 U.S.C. §1333	admiralty
28 U.S.C. §1336	Interstate Commerce Commissioner's orders
28 U.S.C. §1337	commerce and antitrust regulations
28 U.S.C. §1338	patents, copyrights, trademarks and unfair competition
28 U.S.C. §1340	Internal Revenue, customs duties
28 U.S.C. §1343	civil rights and elective franchise
28 U.S.C. §1345	United States as plaintiff
28 U.S.C. §1346	United States as defendant

Although this list is by no means exhaustive, it names some of the major jurisdictional statutes. Various grants of jurisdiction are contained in 28 U.S.C. §§1331 through 1364.

The bulk of the cases heard by federal district courts are those in which jurisdiction is based either on a federal question under 28 U.S.C. §1331 or on diversity of citizenship under 28 U.S.C. §1332.

Federal Question Jurisdiction. According to 28 U.S.C. §1331, "[t]he district courts shall have original jurisdiction of all civil actions arising under the Constitution, laws, or treaties of the United States." This is the broadest grant of jurisdiction of all federal statutes. Obviously it is not as specific as, for example, 28 U.S.C. §1346, which grants jurisdiction whenever the United States is a defendant. The meaning of "arising under" is in some circumstances open to interpretation. The many litigated interpretations are beyond the scope of this text. We will concentrate on the more obvious examples so that you can understand the concept of federal question jurisdiction.

The general meaning of federal question jurisdiction is that a claim is based on federal law. The Chattooga case involves a federal statute. The plaintiff's claim of employment discrimination is based on an alleged violation of Title VII of the Civil Rights Act of 1964 (42 U.S.C. §2000e *et seq.*). This claim clearly arises under a law of the United States.

A party may also initiate a federal question lawsuit based on a claim that its rights have been violated under the U.S. Constitution. For example, a plaintiff may claim that a zoning ordinance has deprived it of property in violation of the due process protection of the Fifth and Fourteenth Amendments to the Constitution. This claim arises under the U.S. Constitution, and thus also constitutes a federal question.

Plaintiffs who base their claims on a federal question must state affirmatively in the complaint the law, treaty, or section of the U.S. Constitution on which their claim is based.

Diversity Jurisdiction. Diversity jurisdiction is the second major category of federal subject matter jurisdiction. It is based on diversity in the citizenship of the parties to a lawsuit. According to 28 U.S.C. §1332(a) diversity of citizenship exists when the action is

1. between citizens of different states;
2. between citizens of a state and citizens or subjects of a foreign state;
3. between citizens of different states and in which citizens or subjects of a foreign state are additional parties; and
4. between a foreign state as plaintiff and citizens of a state or of different states.

Categories 2, 3, and 4 apply when a party is a foreign state or citizen of a foreign state. Because United States law refers to noncitizens of the United States as aliens, these three categories are sometimes called the *alienage sections.*

By far the most commonly used category is the first: when plaintiffs and defendants are citizens of different states. This is the only category that we will explore in detail.

Determining Citizenship. Because diversity is determined by the **citizenship** of the parties, one must first understand the meaning of the term. Persons are considered to be citizens of the state where they have their **domicile**—that is, the place where a person has his or her permanent home and intends for the permanent home to remain.[3] A person can have only one domicile at a time.

Note that the word "state" is defined by 28 U.S.C. §1332(d) to include the District of Columbia and the Commonwealth of Puerto Rico.

Corporations are considered to be citizens for purposes of diversity jurisdiction; 28 U.S.C. §1332(c) states that a corporation is deemed to be a citizen of the state where it is incorporated and of the state where it has its principal place of business. **Principal place of business** is generally considered to mean the place where the majority of the corporation's business takes place or where the corporate headquarters is located. A corporation can be a citizen of more than one state; 28 U.S.C. §1332(c) also provides rules to determine the citizenship of a liability insurer and the legal representative of the estate of a decedent. See Figure 3-2.

In the Wesser case, both Woodall Shoals and Second Ledge are incorporated in Delaware and have their corporate headquarters in New York. Both companies are considered citizens of Delaware and of New York. They are not considered

FIGURE 3-2 DIVERSITY OF CITIZENSHIP EXPLAINED IN 28 U.S.C. §1332

§ 1332. Diversity of citizenship; amount in controversy; costs

(a) The district courts shall have original jurisdiction of all civil actions where the matter in controversy exceeds the sum or value of $50,000, exclusive of interest and costs, and is between—

(1) citizens of different States;

(2) citizens of a State and citizens or subjects of a foreign state;

(3) citizens of different States and in which citizens or subjects of a foreign state are additional parties; and

(4) a foreign state, defined in section 1603(a) of this title, as plaintiff and citizens of a State or of different States.

(b) Except when express provision therefor is otherwise made in a statute of the United States, where the plaintiff who files the case originally in the Federal courts is finally adjudged to be entitled to recover less than the sum or value of $50,000, computed without regard to any setoff or counterclaim to which the defendant may be adjudged to be entitled, and exclusive of interest and costs, the district court may deny costs to the plaintiff and, in addition, may impose costs on the plaintiff.

(c) For the purposes of this section and section 1441 of this title—

(1) a corporation shall be deemed to be a citizen of any State by which it has been incorporated and of the State where it has its principal place of business, except that in any direct action against the insurer of a policy or contract of liability insurance, whether incorporated or unincorporated, to which action the insured is not joined as a party-defendant, such insurer shall be deemed a citizen of the State of which the insured is a citizen, as well as of any State by which the insurer has been incorporated and of the State where it has its principal place of business; and

(2) the legal representative of the estate of a decedent shall be deemed to be a citizen only of the same State as the decedent, and the legal representative of an infant or incompetent shall be deemed to be a citizen only of the same State as the infant or incompetent.

citizens of North Carolina. Although they do business in North Carolina, North Carolina is not their principal place of business.

Diversity jurisdiction requires **complete diversity**, which means that each plaintiff must have a citizenship different from each defendant. If there are multiple parties, and one plaintiff and one defendant are citizens of the same state, diversity is destroyed. For example, if the plaintiffs in a lawsuit are citizens of Arkansas and Oklahoma and the defendants are citizens of Texas and Missouri, complete diversity exists. However, if citizens of Arkansas and Oklahoma bring an action against citizens of Texas, Missouri, and Oklahoma, complete diversity does not exist.

If plaintiffs are citizens of the same state, this does not destroy diversity, so long as no defendant is a citizen of the same state as a plaintiff. Likewise, diversity exists where two defendants are citizens of the same state, but the defendants are not citizens of the same state as any of the plaintiffs.

POINTER: Sometimes diversity jurisdiction can become confusing as you try to sort out the parties. A simple way is to make a chart in which you list on one side each plaintiff and the state of that plaintiff's residence. Do the same on the other side of the chart for each defendant.

Diversity Jurisdiction: the Jurisdictional Amount.   Read again 28 U.S.C. §1332 in Figure 3-2. You will see that even if there is complete diversity between or among the parties, this alone is not enough to confer diversity jurisdiction on the federal court. The lawsuit must also meet the second requirement for diversity jurisdiction: the jurisdictional amount. As 28 U.S.C. §1332(a) states, the amount in controversy must exceed the sum or value of $50,000, exclusive of costs and interest. The purpose of the jurisdictional amount is to limit the federal court caseload to the more significant cases.

To determine whether more than $50,000 is at issue, the court looks at the plaintiff's complaint. If the amount at issue is clearly not in excess of $50,000, the plaintiff cannot rely on diversity jurisdiction. The burden is on the defendant to show that the amount in controversy does not exceed $50,000. Courts are usually liberal in assessing whether the $50,000 test is met. However, the plaintiff's assertion of damages in excess of $50,000 must be well-founded. That is, the plaintiff cannot merely state that the damages meet the jurisdictional amount just for the sake of getting into federal court.

Some complex questions arise in multiparty litigation as to whether parties can aggregate, or lump together, their claims when individually the claims do not exceed $50,000 and do not meet the jurisdictional amount. This issue is beyond the scope of this text, but usually the propriety of aggregation depends on how many plaintiffs and how many defendants are involved in the lawsuit and whether the claims the plaintiff wishes to aggregate are separate and distinct claims or involve only one right or title. For example, in a lawsuit with one plaintiff and two defendants, the plaintiff may not aggregate two claims if the claims arise from two separate contracts. However, if the two defendants are jointly liable, as with partners in a business, the plaintiff may aggregate the amounts in controversy to attain the jurisdictional amount.[4]

Concurrent and Exclusive Jurisdiction

When a court has **exclusive jurisdiction**, that court is the *only* court that has jurisdiction. The authorization of one court to hear a certain type of case, to the exclusion of all other courts, is often specified by statute. For example, 28 U.S.C. §1338(a) provides for exclusive federal jurisdiction over patent, copyright, and trademark cases.

As a general rule, when there is no statute explicitly stating that the federal or the state court has exclusive jurisdiction, then federal and state courts have **concurrent jurisdiction**. That is, subject matter jurisdiction is not limited to just one court. However, sometimes there exists implied exclusive jurisdiction, when no statute establishes exclusive jurisdiction but the courts nonetheless determine that jurisdiction is exclusive. An example is Title VII of the Civil Rights Act (42 U.S.C. 2000e *et seq.*), the statute involved in the Chattooga case. No statute explicitly states that federal courts have exclusive jurisdiction over Title VII claims. However, numerous court decisions have held that Congress intended that Title VII cases be filed exclusively in federal court.[5] Obviously, it is very important that the attorney/paralegal team carefully consider the issue of exclusive jurisdiction in preparing a lawsuit.

Consider the Wesser case. Here concurrent jurisdiction exists. There is no statute or judicial decision stating that any type of court has exclusive jurisdiction. The attorney/paralegal team representing Mr. Wesser decided to file the lawsuit in federal court, with diversity jurisdiction as its basis because none of the defendant corporations is a citizen of the same state as Mr. Wesser. The amount in controversy exceeds $50,000, so the jurisdictional amount requirement is met. Thus diversity jurisdiction in federal court exists.

However, Mr. Wesser could have filed this action in state court, if he had chosen. There is no applicable statute requiring that this case be heard in federal court. Mr. Wesser might have chosen state court for a number of reasons. The court might be closer and more convenient for him and the witnesses. He might wish to avoid a certain judge. He might be able to have a very receptive jury in his county. There are numerous reasons that parties choose a certain court. As part of the paralegal/attorney team, you will probably have occasion to analyze these choice-of-court decisions.

PERSONAL JURISDICTION

After it is determined that a court has jurisdiction over the subject matter, one must determine whether the court has jurisdiction over the parties in the lawsuit. As we noted earlier, personal jurisdiction means that the court has the power to bring a defendant into that court and enter a judgment against that person.

Recall that personal jurisdiction over the plaintiff is not at issue, because the plaintiff submits to the court's jurisdiction by filing a complaint with the court. Nor is personal jurisdiction a problem when the defendant is a resident of the state in which the lawsuit is filed. A state has the power to adjudicate claims concerning the persons and property within the state. Note that the state in which the lawsuit is commenced is called the **forum state**.

The underlying principle of personal jurisdiction is fairness to the defendant. The rules for personal jurisdiction are designed to protect defendants from having to go to distant states to defend a lawsuit when they have very little connection with that state. The rules that govern personal jurisdiction have evolved from the requirement that a person cannot be deprived of life, liberty, or property without **due process of law**. The right to due process is founded in the Fifth and Fourteenth Amendments of the U.S. Constitution. The concept of due process simply means that persons must be given notice of lawsuits against them and be given the opportunity to be heard in order to defend their position.

Determining Whether the Court Has Personal Jurisdiction over a Defendant

The easiest way to determine whether a court has personal jurisdiction over a nonresident is to answer three questions. The first question is whether there is an applicable **long-arm statute**. A long-arm statute is a law authorizing jurisdiction over an out-of-state defendant because the defendant has been involved in certain transactions in the forum state. For example, states have nonresident motorist statutes, which provide that if an out-of-state motorist is involved in an accident in that state, the local resident may sue the out-of-state motorist in the state where the accident took place. The theory behind this law is that the out-of-state motorist submits to the jurisdiction of the state through which he drives.

Long-arm statutes vary greatly from state to state. Some long-arm statutes are very broad and basically provide that if a defendant has minimum contacts with a state and jurisdiction would not offend the defendant's due process rights, the defendant may be sued in the forum state. (The concept of minimum contacts is discussed below.) Other states have specific long-arm statutes. For example, North Carolina's long-arm statute provides for jurisdiction in the following instance:

> . . . (5) Local Services, Goods, or Contracts.—In any action which:
> a. Arises out of a promise, made anywhere to the plaintiff or to some third party for the plaintiff's benefit, by the defendant to perform services within this State or to pay for services to be performed in this State by the plaintiff . . . [6]

When a state has a broadly worded long-arm statute, the courts have great latitude to decide whether a transaction falls within the statute; with a very specific statute, the courts have less discretion.

In federal court actions, one should first check to see whether there are any specific federal long-arm statutes that are applicable. While they are few in number, such statutes are wide in scope. Statutes that pertain to jurisdiction in antitrust actions, for instance, contain no geographical restrictions. Unless there is a specifically applicable federal statute, the court looks to the long-arm statute of the state in which the court sits. The U.S. District Court for the Southern District of New York, for instance, looks to New York law.

Even if a party is involved in a transaction that arguably falls within a state's long-arm statute, a second question arises: Can the defendant be compelled to defend the lawsuit in the forum state without violating the defendant's right to due process? This is where the concept of minimum contacts applies. The concept of minimum contacts has evolved over the years through a series of U.S. Supreme Court decisions. The classic statement concerning minimum contacts is in the case of *International Shoe Co. v. State of Washington*, 326 U.S. 310, 316 (1945). There the Court held that jurisdiction was proper when a corporation's minimum contacts within the forum state were such that being forced to defend a lawsuit in that state would not offend "traditional notions of fair play and substantial justice."

This general rule is best understood by considering a specific example. If a defendant who is a resident of Arizona cashes a check in North Carolina, and the check bounces, is it fair to make the defendant come into court in North Carolina? This will depend on whether the defendant has other connections with North Carolina. If the defendant has no bank account in North Carolina, has entered into no contracts in North Carolina, and was just passing through on vacation when she wrote the check, then the defendant probably does not have sufficient contacts with North Carolina to require her to defend a lawsuit in North Carolina. This means that the plaintiff will have to sue the defendant in Arizona.

A final question is whether the defendant was given adequate notice of the lawsuit. This is answered by determining whether the defendant received adequate service of process—that is, written notification of the action against her. Service of process is a straightforward act so long as the plaintiff knows the address of the defendant. A discussion of service of process is found in Chapter 6.

VENUE

By now you understand that in order to enter a binding judgment a court must have subject matter jurisdiction over the type of controversy in a lawsuit and personal jurisdiction over the parties. The court also needs venue. **Venue** designates the particular county or court district in which a court with jurisdiction may hear a lawsuit.

The Relationship of Venue to Jurisdiction

Venue is the third determination you must make to identify the court in which a lawsuit may be heard. First you determine whether to file the case in federal or state court. If there are different levels within the trial court, such as district and superior court in a state court system, you must determine in which level to file. This is the subject matter jurisdiction analysis. Second, you must determine in which state you can obtain personal jurisdiction over the defendant. Third, you must examine the venue statutes to determine in which geographical district within the state or federal court system venue is proper. In state courts, you must decide in which county the action will be filed. In federal court, you must decide in which federal court district within a state the action will be filed, if there is more than one district in the state.

Consider the following example. Suppose that Mrs. Hearne wants to file a complaint seeking a divorce from Mr. Hearne. Mrs. Hearne is a resident of Carteret County in the state of North Carolina. Mr. Hearne is a resident of

Buncombe County, also in the state of North Carolina but hundreds of miles away. The North Carolina venue statutes provide that any county district court in North Carolina has subject matter jurisdiction to hear a divorce action when one party is a resident of North Carolina. Therefore, subject matter jurisdiction is not a problem. Mr. Hearne lives in the same state, and we know his address for service of process, so we have no problem with personal jurisdiction. The next question is which county district court has venue. The North Carolina venue statute provides that venue is proper in the county where the plaintiff resides or the county where the defendant resides. Therefore, Mrs. Hearne may file the action in Buncombe or Carteret County. In all likelihood, Mrs. Hearne's own county is most convenient, so she will choose Carteret County.

The Purpose of the Venue Requirement

The aim of venue statutes is to ensure that the lawsuit is heard in a geographical location that is fair to the defendant. Bear in mind that when a party must litigate in a distant location, it can be both inconvenient and expensive. For a trial, the parties and witnesses incur travel expenses and have to take more time off work. Unless the party's local lawyer is licensed to practice in the distant state, the party has to hire an attorney in the forum state to handle the case entirely or to serve as associate counsel. These are just some of the inconveniences and expenses of litgating in a distant forum.

How to Determine Venue

As we have discussed, venue is governed by statute. There are two types of venue statutes: special venue statutes and general venue statutes.

Special Venue Statutes. First you must check to see whether a special venue statute covers the type of case in question. For instance, 42 U.S.C. §2000e5(f)(3) is a special venue statute for Title VII employment discrimination cases. It reads as follows:

> (3) Each United States district court and each United States court of a place subject to the jurisdiction of the United States shall have jurisdiction of actions brought under this subchapter. Such an action may be brought in any judicial district in the State in which the unlawful employment practice is alleged to have been committed, in the judicial district in which the unemployment records relevant to such practice are maintained and administered, or in the judicial district in which the aggrieved person would have worked but for the alleged unlawful employment practice, but if the respondent is not found within any such district, such an action may be brought within the judicial district in which the respondent has his principal office. For purposes of sections 1404 and 1406 of Title 28, the judicial district in which the respondent has his principal office shall in all cases be considered a district in which the action might have been brought.

This special venue statute applies to the Chattooga case, which is a Title VII claim. The Chattooga Corporation office where Sandy Ford worked is in

Charleston, in the Middle District of North Carolina. The United States District Court for the Middle District of North Carolina is the appropriate venue, because the alleged unlawful employment practice took place in this district and the relevant employment records for Chattooga Corporation are located in this district.

General Venue Statutes. If there is no special venue statute, refer to the general venue statute. For federal district courts, the general venue statute is 28 U.S.C. §1391. Section 1391(a) governs cases based solely on diversity jurisdiction. It states that venue is proper in the district where

1. all plaintiffs reside; or
2. all defendants reside; or
3. where the cause of action arose.

For example, suppose that a plaintiff who is a resident of Georgia wants to sue two defendants, one a resident of Michigan and one a resident of Ohio, for damages incurred in an automobile accident in Florida. Venue is proper in Georgia, where the only plaintiff lives, or in Florida, where the cause of action arose. Venue is not proper in Michigan or Ohio, because only one of the two defendants resides in each of the two states.

If the lawsuit is not based on diversity jurisdiction, 28 U.S.C. §1391(b) governs. It provides for venue

1. where all plaintiffs reside; or
2. where the cause of action arose.

Determining a Party's Residence. Obviously, the means for determining a party's residence is crucial. For purposes of venue, residence is based on the party's domicile. As you recall, referring to a party's domicile is also how to determine a party's citizenship for purposes of diversity jurisdiction. Remember, domicile means the place where a person lives and intends to have his or her permanent home.

In 28 U.S.C. §1391(c) is an explanation of how corporate residence is determined for purposes of venue. Section §1391(c) provides as follows:

> (c) For purposes of venue under this chapter, a defendant that is a corporation shall be deemed to reside in any judicial district in which it is subject to personal jurisdiction at the time the action is commenced. In a State which has more than one judicial district and in which a defendant that is a corporation is subject to personal jurisdiction at the time an action is commenced, such corporation shall be deemed to reside in any district in that State within which its contacts would be sufficient to subject it to personal jurisdiction if that district were a separate State, and, if there is no such district, the corporation shall be deemed to reside in the district within which it has the most significant contacts.

Thus we must consider under what circumstances a corporation is amenable to jurisdiction in a certain judicial district. This must be evaluated in conjunction with FRCivP 4(d)(3), which explains how to obtain service of process on a corporation. (See Chapter 6.) As a practical matter, one may obtain jurisdiction over a corporation in the district in which it is incorporated, in which it is licensed to do business, and in which it is doing business, because one can find an agent of the corporation to receive service of process in those locations. A corporation is also deemed a resident of a state for purposes of venue when that state's long-arm statute establishes personal jurisdiction over the company.

Consider the Wesser case. Venue is proper in the Middle District of North Carolina, where both Woodall Shoals and Second Ledge are subject to personal jurisdiction. Both companies have agents to receive service of process in North Carolina. Even if they did not, assume that North Carolina has a long-arm statute that would allow service of process out of state—that is, at corporate headquarters in New York—because of the companies' extensive contractual dealings in North Carolina.

For further determinations, 28 U.S.C. §1391(d) addresses venue when the defendant is an unincorporated association, and 28 U.S.C. §1391(e) governs venue when the defendant is the United States or one of its agencies, officers, or employees. A detailed discussion is beyond the scope of this text, but you should refer to these sections when litigation involves those types of defendants.

Change of Venue

A determination of where venue is proper is made at the outset of a lawsuit. A party may challenge venue either with a motion under FRCivP 12(b)(3) or in the answer. (Chapter 7 presents a discussion of answers and Rule 12 motions.) Remember that the defendant is the party that challenges venue, because the plaintiff has already chosen venue by filing the lawsuit in a certain district. Pursuant to 28 U.S.C. §1406, a court may dismiss or transfer a case when the original venue is improper. Transfer is preferred over dismissal. Courts have the discretion to transfer venue ''for the convenience of parties and witnesses, in the interest of justice'' under 28 U.S.C. §1404.

In a case in which venue is proper in more than one district, and the court determines that one district is more convenient overall, the court may transfer the case from the district in which the plaintiff filed the lawsuit to the more convenient district. Section 1404(a) provides that the district to which the case is transferred be a district in which the plaintiff could have brought the action initially. Thus the court may not transfer the case to a state where the plaintiff could not have obtained personal jurisdiction over the defendant at the outset.

ENDNOTES

1 There is a narrow exception in 28 U.S.C. §1253 concerning decisions of three-judge courts.
2 The Court's decision in *INS v. Cardoza-Fonseca* is found in 480 U.S. 421, 107 S. Ct. 1207, 94 L. Ed. 2d 434 (1987).
3 *Black's Law Dictionary* 435 (5th ed. 1979).
4 See Thomas A Mauet, *Fundamentals of Pretrial Techniques* 66(1988).
5 See, e.g., *Dickinson v. Chrysler Corp.*, 456 F. Supp. 43 (E.D. Mich. 1978); *Valenzuela v. Kraft, Inc.*, 739 F.2d 434 (9th Cir. 1985).
6 N.C. Gen. Stat. §1–75.4(5)a (1988). This is only one specific instance contained in the North Carolina long-arm statute; it provides numerous other situations in which North Carolina courts have jurisdiction.

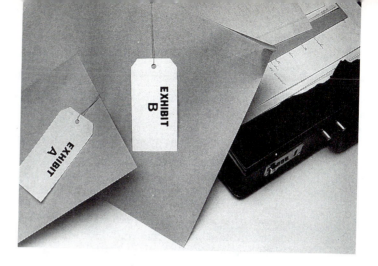

4 EVIDENCE

LITIGATION EXTRACT: You are now aware that an understanding of legal ethics and the structure of the court system is essential to an effective litigation paralegal. Before you can effectively help to gather the pertinent facts and to prepare Mr. Wesser's case for trial, it is also essential that you have a basic understanding of the rules of evidence. Chapter 4 explores the rules of evidence most applicable to your work as a litigation paralegal. Your task is not to memorize every rule of evidence and all the exceptions to the rule. Rather, you must understand the basic principles that underlie the rules and the application of these principles to the tasks that you perform.

INTRODUCTION

When you think of the rules of evidence, you probably envision a dramatic courtroom scene where an attorney leaps from a chair and actually yells "I object!" while a stunned witness is rendered speechless by the abrupt interruption. Your next thought may be "How do the rules of evidence affect me, if I cannot go to court and try a case myself?"

The rules of evidence affect paralegals and lawyers at every stage of the litigation process, not just at trial. The attorney/paralegal team may decide early that a particular piece of evidence would be inadmissible and that their efforts would be better spent pursuing evidence more likely to be admissible at trial. As paralegals screen documents during the discovery process, they must keep in mind that certain documents are privileged— that is, the information in them is protected from disclosure and cannot be obtained by the opposing party. A paralegal who does not understand the principles of privileged information may mistakenly divulge to an opposing party information that should never have been revealed.

DEFINITIONS AND TYPES OF EVIDENCE

We will discuss various definitions as we explore different concepts of evidence. However, some definitions are so basic to an understanding of the rules of evidence that we address them at the outset.

The first and most obviously important term is *evidence*. Evidence includes testimony of witnesses, documents, and physical objects that a party presents at trial to prove a fact.[1] When we speak of the evidence in a case, we refer to the testimony, documents, and objects that we wish the finder of fact to consider in determining which party is entitled to a favorable judgment. The finder of fact is the jury in a jury trial and the judge in a nonjury (or "bench") trial.

At trial, all the parties present their own version of the facts, and it is the duty of the finder of fact to determine which facts are true. The finder of fact does this by considering which evidence is persuasive—which witnesses seem more credible, which documents seem most conclusive, and other factual conclusions. For instance, in the Wesser case, Mr. Wesser asserts that the fire was caused by defects in the electric blanket. The defendants contend that Mr. Wesser misused the electric blanket and damaged it, thus causing the fire by his own actions. The finder of facts must assess the evidence and determine which version of the story is true.

Evidence is either direct or circumstantial. **Direct evidence** is evidence that a witness personally observed, and the evidence directly establishes a fact. For instance, Mr. Wesser testifies that he woke up and saw the electric blanket on fire and that he saw no fire in any other area of his room. This is direct evidence that the fire started in the area around the electric blanket.

Circumstantial evidence is evidence not based on personal observation. The evidence does not directly establish the fact in dispute. Rather, from the circumstantial evidence you must infer your conclusion about the fact in dispute. For instance, when Mr. Wesser testifies that the fire was only in the area of the electric blanket, you may infer that the blanket was the cause of the fire. If the fire inspector prepares a report stating that the fire began in the vicinity of the electric blanket, this too is circumstantial evidence that the blanket caused the fire, since the report is not based on the fire inspector's personal observation.

Although direct evidence is generally considered more reliable, both direct and circumstantial evidence can be important in proving your case. As you gather evidence, do not become preoccupied with classifying your evidence as direct or circumstantial. The label is not important. Rather, you should concentrate on gathering all evidence that may be helpful in proving the facts necessary to win the lawsuit. At the same time, you will hear the terms "direct" and "circumstantial" evidence often, so it is important to understand the concepts.

As you gather any type of evidence, there is one important question that you must always consider: Is the evidence admissible? A piece of evidence is **admissible** if the judge determines that the evidence may be introduced at trial and considered by the finder of fact.

The actual procedure for presenting evidence is discussed in Chapter 12. However, a quick overview will help you understand the basic rules of evidence.

Assume that we are in the process of trying the Wesser case. The fire inspector is on the witness stand and Leigh Heyward has just asked him to state his opinion about the cause of the fire. Before he has a chance to answer, the defense attorney, David Benedict, says "I object." Mr. Benedict states why he objects to the admission of this evidence, the fire inspector's opinion. Ms. Heyward then states why the evidence should be admitted. The judge decides whether the evidence is admissible. If the judge decides that the fire inspector should be allowed to state his opinion in response to Ms. Heyward's question, this means that the judge has ruled that the evidence is admissible.

As we proceed through the various stages of litigation, you will see that there are many types of evidence that we can present to prove our case. We will present **testimonial evidence**—that is, witnesses such as Mr. Wesser and the fire inspector will talk about what they have seen and observed about the fire. We will present **documentary evidence**—that is, documents such as the written warranty that came with the blanket. We will also present **physical** (or "real") **evidence**—that is, objects that a jury can actually touch and handle, such as the remains of the electric blanket and its control unit. In some lawsuits you may use **demonstrative evidence**—that is, charts, photographs, or other means of illustrating a scene or incident. For instance, in the Wesser case, you may prepare a chart showing the location of items in Mr. Wesser's room such as the bed with the blanket, the door through which he escaped, and the location of other objects that could conceivably ignite.

As we have noted, you should not be obsessed with categorizing by type every piece of evidence. The important consideration is whether the piece of evidence will be helpful to prove your case.

THE RULES OF EVIDENCE

How do judges, attorneys, and paralegals know whether a piece of evidence is admissible? They consult the rules of evidence. The Federal Rules of Evidence govern lawsuits in federal courts. In state court, you follow the rules of evidence for the state in which the lawsuit is tried.

Federal Rules of Evidence

You can find the Federal Rules of Evidence (FRE) in Title 28 of the United States Code (28 U.S.C.) and in commercial publications. You may find it helpful to use the United States Code Annotated (28 U.S.C.A.). The meaning and application of the rules of evidence are not always apparent from merely reading the rules. To understand many of the rules, you need to read the judicial opinions that apply the rules to the facts of particular cases. The cases discussed in the annotations to the U.S. Code provide a starting point for finding helpful cases.

State Rules of Evidence

You can find state rules of evidence in the state's statutes and in commercial publications. For example, the North Carolina Rules of Evidence appear in

Chapter 8C of the North Carolina General Statutes. They are also found in commercial publications that print the rules of evidence together with other court rules, such as the North Carolina Rules of Civil Procedure.

You may also need to read commentaries and treatises on evidence to understand some of the more difficult concepts. One well-known treatise is *McCormick on Evidence*. There are also treatises on the rules of evidence in particular states. For instance, *Brandis on North Carolina Evidence* is the standard text for questions about the rules of evidence in that state. Check your law library for treatises on the rules of evidence in your state.

The discussion in this chapter focuses solely on the Federal Rules of Evidence. Most states have rules similar to the Federal Rules of Evidence. However, there can be important differences between state and federal rules, so you must consult your state rules of evidence when the state rules are applicable.

THE PURPOSE OF THE RULES OF EVIDENCE

The Federal Rules of Evidence have two primary goals: to ensure fairness to all parties and to ascertain the truth. As FRE 102 states:

> These rules shall be construed to secure fairness in administration, elimination of unjustifiable expense and delay, and promotion of growth and development of the law of evidence to the end that the truth may be ascertained and proceedings justly determined.

Our discussion focuses on these two underlying principles of the rules of evidence. A discussion of every rule of evidence, and every exception to the rules, would fill volumes. The purpose of this chapter is to give paralegals a useful understanding of the underlying principles of the rules of evidence and the specific rules most frequently encountered by paralegals. This serves as a foundation for your research and your application of the rules of evidence to the lawsuits you will work on.

The Federal Rules of Evidence ensure fairness by the requirement that evidence must be relevant. As we will soon discuss more fully, evidence is **relevant** if it tends to prove the existence of a fact that is important to the outcome of the dispute. Several rules of evidence stem from the relevance requirement.

Closely related to the concept of relevance is the term **probative evidence**. Probative evidence is simply evidence that proves or tends to prove an issue in dispute. If a piece of evidence is totally unrelated to the issues in the lawsuit, there is no need to present that evidence.

The Federal Rules of Evidence ensure truthfulness by the requirement that evidence must be reliable. Evidence is generally considered to be reliable when the person asserting a fact has firsthand knowledge of the fact and has not made previous statements that are inconsistent with the fact asserted. Many rules of evidence stem from the reliability requirement, including the hearsay rule, rules requiring personal knowledge, rules regarding opinions, and rules regarding the authenticity of documents. We will first discuss the rules related to relevance.

The Requirement of Relevance

Only relevant evidence is admissible to resolve the issues in a lawsuit. (See FRE 402.) This is because the requirement of fairness dictates that the trier of fact consider only evidence that has a logical bearing on the issues in dispute. For instance, suppose that Mr. Wesser's dog frequently digs up his neighbor's garden, causing the neighbor to conclude that Mr. Wesser is a bad person. This has nothing to do with the cause of the fire in Mr. Wesser's home and therefore is not relevant to a resolution of Mr. Wesser's lawsuit against Woodall Shoals and Second Ledge. However, if the neighbor sued Mr. Wesser for damages because the dog destroyed vegetables worth hundreds of dollars, the fact that Mr. Wesser let his dog roam in his neighbor's garden would be relevant in that lawsuit.

The Definition of Relevant Evidence

FRE 401 defines relevant evidence as ''evidence having any tendency to make the existence of any fact that is of consequence to the determination of the action more probable or less probable than it would be without the evidence.'' This definition embodies several important concepts.

First, in order for evidence to be relevant, it does not have to address the one ultimate fact that proves the issue in dispute. Much background evidence is necessary to understand and establish the ultimate fact. Rule 401 allows the introduction of background facts necessary to understand the ultimate fact.

Consider, for example, the Wesser case. One of the ultimate issues is whether Second Ledge Stores, Incorporated, failed to inspect the electric blanket and whether an inspection would have revealed the defects that allegedly started the fire. Many background facts are necessary before the trier can decide the ultimate fact of whether Second Ledge failed to inspect and whether an inspection would have revealed defects. Some of these background facts include when Second Ledge received the blanket from the manufacturer; who was working in the stockroom that day; the procedures that Second Ledge employees use when merchandise arrives; the condition of the blanket when it was received—for example, whether it appeared to have been damaged in transit; and what happened to the blanket between the time Second Ledge received it and Mr. Wesser bought it. Another basic background fact that Mr. Wesser must establish is that Second Ledge is the store where he bought the blanket. All these facts are necessary to understand and decide the ultimate issue.

Another important concept in FRE 401 is that evidence is relevant if it has ''any tendency'' to establish a fact of consequence. Consider the background facts discussed in the previous paragraph. Each background fact does not in and of itself tend to prove the ultimate fact of consequence. However, all the background facts have a tendency to help determine the fact of consequence—whether Second Ledge failed to perform an inspection that would have revealed defects in the blanket.

Thus FRE 401 requires only that evidence have a logical bearing on the dispute. It does not require that a piece of evidence by itself convince the trier of fact that a particular fact is true. It is sufficient if the piece of evidence helps the trier of fact understand and reach a conclusion about the fact in issue.

Exclusion of Relevant Evidence

Just because evidence is relevant does not mean that it is admissible. FRE 403 provides that relevant evidence may be excluded when "its probative value is substantially outweighed by the danger of unfair prejudice, confusion of the issues, or misleading the jury, or by considerations of undue delay, waste of time, or needless presentation of cumulative evidence."

When it appears that a piece of evidence has any of these undesirable characteristics, the court must determine whether the undesirable characteristic outweighs the probative value of the evidence. For instance, after two witnesses give virtually the same testimony, the court may ask the lawyer whether the next witness will testify about the facts already stated. If the answer is yes, the court may determine that the testimony would be needlessly cumulative. There obviously is no rule that states how many witnesses may testify about similar facts before the testimony is deemed cumulative, so the court must exercise considerable discretion in deciding this issue.

Similar discretion is required in determining whether evidence is unduly prejudicial. For instance, Leigh Heyward may try to introduce photographs of Mr. Wesser's burns right after the fire occurred. The defense attorney may object to their admission, arguing that the photographs are unduly prejudicial because they are too gruesome, especially compared to Mr. Wesser's condition after treatment and plastic surgery. The judge must then weigh the probative value of the photographs against their potentially prejudicial nature in order to decide if the evidence should be excluded under FRE 403.

Character Evidence

One type of evidence that can be excluded under certain circumstances is character evidence. **Character evidence** is evidence of a person's reputation in the community or of a particular trait that a person possesses, such as honesty or dishonesty. FRE 404 states the general rule for the admissibility of character evidence. It provides that character evidence is not admissible for the purpose of proving that a person "acted in conformity" with his character traits on a particular occasion. For example, assume that Mr. Wesser keeps a rather sloppy house and that he does not maintain his car properly. From this one could infer that he has the characteristics of sloppiness and failure to maintain his possessions. However, defense counsel cannot use these characteristics as evidence that Mr. Wesser does not take care of his belongings and therefore did not take proper care of the blanket.

When Character Evidence is Admissible.   Character evidence is admissible when a person's character or trait is an essential element of a claim or defense, according to FRE 405(b). In such a case, it is said that character is in issue. The classic example is a case involving defamation—that is, making a statement that damages a person's reputation. Suppose that Ms. Stanfield makes a statement that her ex-husband is a thief and Mr. Stanfield sues her for defamation. Truth is a defense, so evidence that Mr. Stanfield committed several thefts would be admissible.

Distinguish Character Evidence Used for Impeachment. So far we have discussed character evidence that constitutes **substantive evidence**—that is, evidence introduced to prove a fact in issue. Another type of evidence is **impeachment evidence**—that is, evidence introduced to attack the credibility of a witness. The purpose of impeachment is to discredit the witness, causing the trier of fact to question whether the witness's version of the facts is correct. There are several ways to impeach a witness, such as pointing out inconsistencies in the witness's prior statements and questioning whether the witness actually had firsthand knowledge of the facts. Impeachment is discussed later in this section.

The important point about impeachment evidence in the context of character evidence is that even in civil cases, character evidence may be introduced to impeach a witness. FRE 608 provides that the credibility of a witness may be attacked, but that the impeachment evidence may refer only to the witness's character for truthfulness or untruthfulness. Suppose that the defense attorney, David Benedict, questions Mr. Wesser about the events of the day the fire occurred, specifically, whether Mr. Wesser had folded the blanket or placed objects on it after he turned it on, and whether he had left it on for several days prior to the fire. Mr. Benedict then introduces public records to show that Mr. Wesser was convicted of embezzlement one year earlier. The conviction may be admissible as impeachment evidence—that is, to show that Mr. Wesser has been convicted of a crime involving dishonesty and thus may be an untruthful person. However, the conviction is not admissible as substantive evidence—that is, to show that Mr. Wesser is not a responsible person and thus probably handled the blanket carelessly.

Distinguish Evidence of Habit. Evidence of habit is different from evidence of character. Character evidence refers to a person's general traits or disposition—honesty, peacefulness, prudence, and so on. However, a **habit** is a person's consistent response to a particular situation. For instance, Mr. Wesser may live on a street that has little traffic. He may fail to stop and look for traffic every time that he backs out of his driveway. It is his habit not to stop, because he fails to stop every time that he backs out.

FRE 406 provides that ''evidence of the habit of a person or of the routine practice of an organization . . . is relevant to prove that the conduct of the person or organization on a particular occasion was in conformity with the habit or routine practice.'' For instance, Mr. Wesser's testimony may include the fact that every morning he not only turns the electric blanket off, but also unplugs it. This is evidence of Mr. Wesser's habit. The basis for deeming evidence of the habit to be relevant is that the habit is an automatic response, which Mr. Wesser invariably follows. The key to admission of evidence of a person's habit is to introduce sufficient evidence of the repeated pattern of behavior.

Other Rules Concerning Relevance in Civil Cases

You will encounter other rules of relevance in civil litigation. Four of these are Rules 407, 408, 409 and 411 of the Federal Rules of Evidence. You should be familiar with their basic provisions.

FRE 407 provides that evidence that remedial measures were taken after an accident is not admissible to prove negligence. The rule states further, however, that evidence of the repairs may be admissible when offered for other purposes. These purposes include "proving ownership, control, or feasibility of precautionary measures" when these issues are in controversy, or impeachment.

For example, if a tenant falls on the steps of an apartment building, and the landlord subsequently repairs the steps, the repairs may not be admitted as evidence that the landlord was negligent. The reason for this rule is to avoid creating a disincentive for persons to remedy conditions that may be dangerous. However, if the landlord had previously asserted that he did not own the area where the accident occurred, evidence of the repairs by the landlord may be introduced to show ownership. The landlord would have no incentive to repair the steps if he did not own them.

FRE 408 provides that offers to settle a dispute are not admissible to show liability or nonliability. The rationale for this rule is to encourage settlement discussions. However, evidence of settlement offers may be "offered for another purpose, such as proving bias or prejudice of a witness, negativing a contention of undue delay, . . ."

FRE 409 states that "evidence of furnishing or offering or promising to pay medical, hospital, or similar expenses occasioned by an injury is not admissible to prove liability for the injury." Similarly, the rule is intended to avoid creating any disincentive for tendering such assistance. Like the above rules, there may be times when the evidence is admissible for purposes other than proving liability.

FRE 411 provides that evidence as to whether a person had liability insurance is not admissible to show that a person acted negligently. This rule is designed to avoid creating a disincentive for obtaining insurance. However, evidence of insurance may be admissible "when offered for another purpose, such as proof of agency, ownership, or control, or bias or prejudice of a witness."

As we can see, each of these four rules reflects a public policy judgment that the limited relevancy of the evidence is outweighed by the desire to encourage certain socially useful behavior. As with other rules of evidence, paralegals must study the rules and exceptions to understand them, and must research variations in the rules among various jurisdictions. However, understanding the principle underlying the rules helps to understand their application.

The Requirement of Reliability

As we discussed, one of the primary goals of the rules of evidence is to ascertain the truth. If the truth is to be ascertained, the evidence that the trier of fact considers must be reliable. The reliability requirement has generated rules applicable both to documents and to testimony.

Rules for Witnesses. We will consider first the reliability rules applicable to the testimony of witnesses.

The Requirement of Oath or Affirmation. Before testifying, witnesses must declare that they will testify truthfully. FRE 603 requires that every witness take an oath or affirmation ''in a form calculated to awaken his conscience and impress his mind with his duty to do so.'' The purpose of this requirement is to impress upon the witness the duty to tell the truth.

The Requirement of Personal Knowledge. One way to ensure that the testimony is reliable is to require that the witness have firsthand knowledge of the facts. For instance, testimony by Mr. Wesser that he awoke and discovered a fire burning at the foot of his bed, where the electric blanket lay, is reliable testimony as to the area where the fire started. However, testimony by Mr. Wesser's neighbor that he smelled smoke and saw Mr. Wesser's house on fire is not reliable evidence as to the area where the fire started, because the neighbor has firsthand knowledge only that there was a fire, not where the fire started.

The requirement of personal knowledge is set forth in FRE 602, which states that a ''witness may not testify to a matter unless evidence is introduced sufficient to support a finding that he has personal knowledge of the matter.'' Because of this requirement, at trial the attorney will first ask a witness questions to establish that the witness has personal knowledge of a fact before asking the witness about that fact. For instance, before asking Mr. Wesser where the fire originated, Leigh Heyward will first ask questions to establish his personal knowledge of this fact. Such questions include where Mr. Wesser lives, whether he spent the night at home on the night the fire occurred, in which room he slept, whether he was using the electric blanket on the night of the fire, and similar questions to establish firsthand knowledge. This process of asking background questions to establish a witness's personal knowledge of the facts to which the witness testifies is known as laying a **foundation**.

The requirement to lay a foundation to establish firsthand knowledge affects the way paralegals interview potential witnesses. Paralegals and attorneys must find out more than just the facts that the witnesses purport to know. They must also find out how the witnesses know the facts—that is, whether the witnesses have firsthand knowledge. For instance, suppose that Mr. Wesser's neighbor tells you that the fire started in the bedroom. You must ask the neighbor how he knows. He may say that he actually saw flames coming from the bedroom, but from no other room. On the other hand, he may say that he just thought that was the probable place for the fire's origin because the fire happened late at night, showing that he did not have firsthand knowledge of the fact.

 POINTER: Do not confuse the requirement of personal knowledge with the hearsay rule, discussed later in this chapter. The hearsay rule applies when a witness testifies about a statement another person made. When witnesses testify about something that the witnesses themselves supposedly saw or did, the objection is lack of personal knowledge.

Opinion Testimony

In addition to allowing witnesses to testify about facts they have observed, the Federal Rules of Evidence also allow witnesses to testify about their opinions. An opinion is the witness's conclusion or belief about the facts in dispute, as opposed to the witness's statement of the facts observed. For instance, if Mr. Wesser's neighbor testifies that he saw Mr. Wesser's house on fire, this is a statement of the fact observed. However, if Mr. Wesser's neighbor testifies that he believes that the electric blanket caused the fire, this is a statement of an opinion.

To discuss opinion testimony, it is helpful to divide witnesses into two types—expert witnesses and lay witnesses. An **expert witness** is a person who has "scientific, technical, or other specialized knowledge" that will "assist the trier of fact to understand the evidence or to determine a fact in issue" (FRE 702). The expert is qualified "by knowledge, skill, experience, training, or education" to explain and give an opinion about technical subjects that average lay persons generally do not understand.

Expert witnesses explain technical matters and give their opinions in order to help the trier of fact understand the evidence. For instance, in the Wesser case, Ms. Heyward will present an expert witness to explain how wiring in an electric blanket can short-circuit or how an electric blanket may contain certain design defects. The expert will also state an opinion as to whether the blanket had defects that caused the fire. Because the average lay person does not possess technical knowledge about electrical wiring and design criteria for electric blankets, the expert witness's testimony is helpful.

The other type of witness is the **lay witness**, that is, a person without expert knowledge. Basically, witnesses who are not expert witnesses are lay witnesees. There are separate rules regarding opinion testimony by lay witnesses and expert witnesses. We will discuss lay witnesses first.

Opinion Testimony by Lay Witnesses. FRE 701 provides that lay witnesses may testify about their opinions, but only if the opinions or inferences "are (a) rationally based on the perception of the witness and (b) helpful to a clear understanding of his testimony or the determination of a fact in issue." Obviously lay witnesses should not be allowed to state an opinion unless they have perceived the facts on which to form an opinion. It would not be proper for Mr. Wesser's neighbor to testify that the blanket caused the fire just because he saw Mr. Wesser run out of his house during the fire. The requirement that the opinion be helpful to understanding the facts in issue is a refinement of the relevance requirement. There is simply no need to allow opinion testimony about matters that do not facilitate an understanding of the facts in issue. In fact, such testimony would probably be prejudicial. For instance, a statement by Mr. Wesser's neighbor that Mr. Wesser is a bad neighbor because he does not mow his lawn regularly is not only unhelpful, but potentially prejudicial; from it a jury could infer that Mr. Wesser does not not take care of his possessions and thus probably misused the blanket.

Before a lay witness may state an opinion, a foundation must be laid establishing that the witness has personal knowledge of the events that form the basis of the opinion. This meets both the rational basis requirement of FRE 701 and the personal knowledge requirement of FRE 602.

POINTER: Throughout your study of the rules of evidence, remember that multiple rules are applicable at the same time. For instance, FRE 701 states certain requirements for opinion testimony. However, the testimony must also be relevant (FRE 402), and the witness must have personal knowledge of the facts (FRE 602).

Opinion testimony of lay witnesses is most helpful to describe an event succinctly and in a manner the finder of fact can understand. For example, Mr. Wesser's neighbor may testify that when Mr. Wesser ran out of his house during the fire, he (Mr. Wesser) was frightened but rational enough to explain calmly what happened. This is more effective than saying that Mr. Wesser was wide-eyed, spoke fairly quickly, looked like his heart was beating fast, but maintained a fairly even tone of voice. Opinion testimony can be helpful to give the finder of fact an understandable description of the events in issue, provided the testimony meets the requirements of being based on the witness's perception of the events and being helpful to an understanding of those events. When you interview lay witnesses, they will no doubt express a number of opinions. Your primary goal is to question the witnesses to determine that their opinions meet the requirements that make opinion testimony admissible.

Opinion Testimony by Expert Witnesses. Recall that FRE 702 describes expert witnesses as persons with scientific, technical, or other specialized knowledge that will assist the trier of fact to understand a fact in issue. In the Wesser case both the plaintiff and the defendants will have expert witnesses testify about the cause of the fire. These expert witnesses will have knowledge of electronic design and the causes of short circuits. Both will offer opinions as to whether the electric blanket caused the fire.

Expert testimony about many subjects may be appropriate in various types of lawsuits. As we will discuss in Chapter 5, it is possible to find expert witnesses for a wide range of subjects. Doctors frequently testify in personal injury lawsuits concerning the extent of clients' injuries and the prognosis for their recovery. For instance, in the Wesser case, Leigh Heyward may arrange to have a neurologist testify about the severity of the pain Mr. Wesser has suffered from his burns.

Two Requirements for Admissibility of Expert Testimony. FRE 702 provides two basic requirements for expert testimony to be admissible. First, the subject matter must be appropriate for expert testimony. As we have seen, expert testimony is generally proper for a wide range of subject matter. FRE 702 states the underlying principle for the subject matter that is appropriate: the testimony must assist the finder of fact "to understand the evidence or to determine a fact in issue." Obviously, the testimony of a neurologist would help a jury understand the issue of the severity of Mr. Wesser's pain, because the average lay person does not possess detailed knowledge about the nervous system and the effect of burns and scar tissue on the body.

At the same time, FRE 702 does not require that the subject matter be so technical that the average person would know nothing about it. For instance, one issue in the Wesser case is the amount of the damage to Mr. Wesser's house. Ms. Heyward may present a real estate appraiser to testify about the decrease in value of Mr. Wesser's house after the fire and a contractor to testify about the cost of repairs to the house. Some members of the jury may already have some knowledge in these areas because they recently bought houses or made home repairs. Even though the members of the jury have some background knowledge, the specialized knowledge of the appraiser and contractor are helpful to the jury to determine issues in the litigation. As you help to determine what kind of expert testimony would help your client's case, remember the general principle that the testimony should be helpful to the finder of fact to understand the issues in your case.

The second requirement for expert testimony to be admissible is that the expert witness must have sufficient "knowledge, skill, experience, training, or education" to qualify as an expert witness. Thus, when attorneys and paralegals arrange for expert witnesses, they must be sure that the expert has sufficient credentials and experience. For example, in choosing a neurologist, you and Ms. Heyward will consider the degrees the neurologist holds as well as the type of residencies and fellowships completed, further research conducted, how many years the neurologist has practiced, any articles or books published, and any other qualifications.

However, degrees and publications are not always necessary to qualify an expert. An expert may be qualified by many years of experience. For instance, the contractor who testifies about the repairs to Mr. Wesser's house may qualify as an expert by virtue of 30 years' experience making similar repairs.

One of your duties as a paralegal may include researching the qualifications of not only your expert witnesses, but also the expert witnesses of the opposition. You may discover that a proposed witness lacks sufficient expertise to qualify as an expert witness.

POINTER: There are many resources available to help you locate expert witnesses. See Chapter 5 for a discussion of these resources.

Rules Regarding Bases and Form of Expert Testimony. Recall that when lay witnesses state opinions, the Federal Rules of Evidence require personal observation of the events or facts on which the opinion is based. The Federal Rules of Evidence do not impose this requirement on expert witnesses. FRE 703 provides that expert witnesses can base their opinions on observations of other persons. FRE 703 further provides that the evidence on which the expert bases an opinion does not have to be admissible evidence, if it is "of a type reasonably relied upon by experts in the particular field in forming opinions or inferences upon the subject." For instance, a doctor may base an opinion on a physical examination of a client and discussions with the client and her relatives about the client's limitations as the result of the injuries in issue. The doctor's discussions with the relatives are probably not admissible evidence, but the doctor may still consider the discussions in forming an opinion.

The rules regarding the bases for expert testimony may differ under state rules of evidence. In particular, the interpretations of which type of evidence is "reasonably relied upon" may vary widely. When paralegals investigate an expert witness, they should explore the expert's background and the bases for the expert's opinion as fully as possible. Expert testimony can become quite complex, and the attorney/paralegal team will need to discuss all its aspects. Therefore you should have ample opportunity to discuss with your supervising attorney any questions about the bases of the experts' testimony and other complex issues related to expert testimony.

FRE 705 provides that an expert does not have to disclose the facts upon which the opinion is based unless the court requires it. On cross-examination, of course, opposing counsel may require the expert to disclose the underlying facts or data. As we discuss in Chapter 12, the purpose of cross-examination is to bring out weaknesses in a witness's testimony. An attorney may ask an expert questions that tend to show that the expert's opinion is not based on reliable evidence. One way to undermine a witness's testimony, for instance, is to point out inconsistencies in his or her statements. Both during trial and in statements made before trial, a witness may make contradictory assertions. Paralegals frequently read and summarize an expert's prior statements, including publications, to find inconsistencies.

Impeachment

Asking questions to undermine the credibility of a witness is known as **impeachment**. Impeachment is not limited to the testimony of expert witnesses. In fact, FRE 607 states that the credibility of any witness may be attacked. The purpose of impeachment is to test the witness's reliability and ensure that testimony is true. Several factors may indicate that a witness is not telling the truth.

Contradictory and Inconsistent Statements. One way to impeach a witness is to point out contradictory and inconsistent statements. For instance, if a witness testified in court that a stoplight was red, and ten minutes later said that it was green, you would wonder whether this witness was telling the truth. A witness may also make statements before trial that are inconsistent with the testimony during the trial. As we discuss in Chapter 9, witnesses may make many statements during the discovery phase of the litigation. For example, a witness may provide written statements in answering interrogatories and may make oral statements during a deposition. Suppose that during a deposition Mr. Wesser says that he occasionally folded the blanket or tucked it in at the foot at the bed. If Mr. Wesser testifies at the trial that he never folded the blanket and tucked it in, the defense attorney may impeach Mr. Wesser by pointing out his prior inconsistent statements. FRE 613 specifically allows the impeachment of witnesses by their prior inconsistent statements. FRE 613 provides that attorneys do not have to show a witness the prior inconsistent statement before questioning the witness about it; however, they must allow the witness an opportunity to explain or deny the inconsistent statement.

Attorneys must deal at trial with more technical considerations about inconsistent statements. The important duty for paralegals is to be attentive to possible inconsistencies in witnesses' statements throughout the litigation process. A witness may make a statement in your initial interview, only to contradict that statement in a deposition. Your job is to bring such inconsistencies and contradictions to the attorneys' attention. Look for inconsistencies everywhere: from oral statements in interviews to letters and documents that surface during the discovery process.

Bias. A witness may have a motive for being less than truthful. There are many bases for suspecting that a witness is biased and therefore not telling the truth. One obvious example is when a witness has accepted a bribe, but usually the basis for suspicion is much more mundane. For instance, a relationship between the witness and one of the parties may cause the witness either to lie or to be so partial that she or he simply cannot recognize the truth. If there is a close family relationship, the witness may be unable to accept the fact that a family member did something bad. If there is a business relationship, one partner may hesitate to admit being deceived by the other, who took excessive money out of the partnership. A witness may be prejudiced against a party or have a long-standing grudge.

These are just a few of the reasons why a witness may be biased. Paralegals must always think about possible bases for bias and discuss them with the attorneys. When paralegals interview witnesses, they should be particularly alert for bias and subtly ask questions to determine whether bias actually exists.

Other Methods of Impeachment. As we discussed earlier in this chapter, character evidence may be used to imply that a witness is not a truthful person. Character evidence may include a person's criminal convictions, with limitations provided in FRE 609. As in many areas of evidence, limitations on the admissiblity of character evidence may be quite complex and can vary among jurisdictions. Your goal as a paralegal is to investigate a witness's character, including convictions, and inform the lawyer of your findings. The lawyer can then address the fine points of how to use the evidence at trial.

As we noted earlier, evidence rules do not exist in isolation from one another. Rather, you may have to apply more than one rule to a piece of evidence. For example, recall that FRE 602 requires that witnesses have personal knowledge of the facts to which they testify. If a witness lacks personal knowledge, the evidence is objectionable because of the requirement of FRE 602. However, the lack of knowledge is also a basis to impeach the witness's testimony. Remember that testimony does not have to be an outright lie in order to be grounds for impeachment. A person may be impeached even if there is no conscious effort to tell less than the truth. A person simply may not know the facts, but this is still grounds for questioning the witness's credibility.

Special Reliability Rules for Documents

So far we have discussed only the rules that relate to reliability of oral testimony. No less subject to the reliability requirement is documentary evidence. There are two primary rules to ensure the reliability of documents: the first rule requires that the document be authentic, and the second expresses a preference for original documents.

Authentication. FRE 901(a) sets forth the requirement of authentication or identification. To authenticate a document, the person presenting the document as evidence must establish that the document is what it purports to be. In the Wesser case, Ms. Heyward will present the warranty that came with the electric blanket. Before that warranty can be admitted into evidence, Ms. Heyward must present evidence to show that this is in fact the warranty that came with the electric blanket. The concept of authentication is basically the same as the more common word "identification." The person presenting a document must identify the document. Ms. Heyward will ask Mr. Wesser, "Is this the warranty that came with the electric blanket that you purchased?" Mr. Wesser will reply, "Yes, that is the warranty."

In the Chattooga case, Nancy Reade Lee, who represents Chattooga Corporation, will present Sandy Ford's employment application and ask the personnel manager, "Is this the application that Sandy Ford filled out and signed?" The personnel manager will state that it is Sandy Ford's application.

Methods of Authentication. FRE 901(b) gives ten examples of acceptable authentication methods. See Figure 4-1. The examples we have cited use the first method—testimony of a witness with knowledge. The figure is largely self-explanatory, but bear in mind a few observations. First, note that FRE 901(b) does not require expert testimony to identify documents and signatures. FRE 901 accepts identification of a person's handwriting by either an expert or by a lay person who has personal knowledge of the writer's handwriting. Second, the authentication rules apply to voice identification as well as documents. A person familiar with a speaker's voice may identify the voice.

Note FRE 901(b)(8), which refers to "Ancient documents." A document need not be the Rosetta Stone to qualify for this method of authentication. FRE 901(b)(8) provides that a document may be authenticated by evidence that it is at least 20 years old, that it is free from suspicion concerning its authenticity, and that it was found in the place where it would likely be kept. This method is most often applied to documents such as deeds and wills.

FRE 901(b)(7) provides one way to authenticate public documents. Using this method, the attorney presents the original document, with testimony by an employee in the public office to confirm that the document came from that office. There are other, simpler methods to authenticate public documents.

Self-Authentication. It is not necessary to present testimony to establish the authenticity of all documents. FRE 902 sets forth several types of documents that are self-authenticating—that is, documents that are deemed authentic on their face, without the necessity of a witness to state that the documents are what they purport to be. Figure 4-2 sets forth the types of documents that are self-authenticating pursuant to FRE 902. One of the most common methods of self-authentication is to present a certified copy of public records.

This method illustrates the rationale behind the self-authentication rule. Real estate, for example, is a frequent subject of litigation. It would be impractical to require the Register of Deeds to come to court every time ownership of property is in dispute and identify the deed as a document kept in the Register

FIGURE 4-1   FRE 901: EXAMPLES OF AUTHENTICATION METHODS

Rule 901.   Requirement of Authentication or Identification
(a) General provision
The requirement of authentication or identification as a condition precedent to admissibility is satisfied by evidence sufficient to support a finding that the matter in question is what its proponent claims.
(b) Illustrations
By way of illustration only, and not by way of limitation, the following are examples of authentication or identification conforming with the requirements of this rule:
(1) Testimony of witness with knowledge
Testimony that a matter is what it is claimed to be.
(2) Nonexpert opinion on handwriting
Nonexpert opinion as to the genuineness of handwriting, based upon familiarity not acquired for purposes of the litigation.
(3) Comparison by trier or expert witness
Comparison by the trier of fact or by expert witnesses with specimens which have been authenticated.
(4) Distinctive characteristics and the like
Appearance, contents, substance, internal patterns, or other distinctive characteristics, taken in conjunction with circumstances.
(5) Voice identification
Identification of a voice, whether heard firsthand or through mechanical or electronic transmission or recording, by opinion based upon hearing the voice at any time under circumstances connecting it with the alleged speaker.
(6) Telephone conversations
Telephone conversations, by evidence that a call was made to the number assigned at the time by the telephone company to a particular person or business, if (A) in the case of a person, circumstances, including self-identification, show the person answering to be the one called, or (B) in the case of a business, the call was made to a place of business and the conversation related to business reasonably transacted over the telephone.
(7) Public records or reports
Evidence that a writing authorized by law to be recorded or filed and in fact recorded or filed in a public office, or a purported public record, report, statement, or data compilation, in any form, is from the public office where items of this nature are kept.
(8) Ancient documents or data compilation
Evidence that a document or data compilation, in any form, (A) is in such condition as to create no suspicion concerning its authenticity, (B) was in a place where it, if authentic, would likely be, and (C) has been in existence 20 years or more at the time it is offered.
(9) Process or system
Evidence describing a process or system used to produce a result and showing that the process or system produces an accurate result.
(10) Methods provided by statute or rule
Any method of authentication or identification provided by Act of Congress or by other rules prescribed by the Supreme Court pursuant to statutory authority.

FIGURE 4-2   FRE 902: SELF-AUTHENTICATING DOCUMENTS

Rule 902.   Self-authentication

Extrinsic evidence of authenticity as a condition precedent to admissibility is not required with respect to the following.

(1) Domestic public documents under seal

A document bearing a seal purporting to be that of the United States, or of any State, district, Commonwealth, territory, or insular possession thereof, or the Panama Canal Zone, or the Trust Territory of the Pacific Islands, or of a political subdivision, department, officer, or agency thereof, and a signature purporting to be an attestation or execution.

(2) Domestic public documents not under seal

A document purporting to bear the signature in the official capacity of an officer or employee of any entity included in paragraph (1) hereof, having no seal, if a public officer having a seal and having official duties in the district or political subdivision of the officer or employee certifies under seal that the signer has the official capacity and that the signature is genuine.

(3) Foreign public documents

A document purporting to be executed or attested in an official capacity by a person authorized by the laws of a foreign country to make the execution or attestation, and accompanied by a final certification as to the genuineness of the signature and official position (A) of the executing or attesting person, or (B) of any foreign official whose certificate of genuineness of signature and official position relates to the execution or attestation or is in a chain of certificates of genuineness of signature and official position relating to the execution or attestation. A final certification may be made by a secretary of an embassy or legation, consul general, consul, vice consul, or consular agent of the United States, or a diplomatic or consular official of the foreign country assigned or accredited to the United States. If reasonable opportunity has been given to all parties to investigate the authenticity and accuracy of official documents, the court may, for good cause shown, order that they be treated as presumptively authentic without final certification or permit them to be evidenced by an attested summary with or without final certification.

(4) Certified copies of public records

A copy of an official record or report or entry therein, or of a document authorized by law to be recorded or filed and actually recorded or filed in a public office, including data compilations in any form, certified as correct by the custodian or other person authorized to make the certification, by certificate complying with paragraph (1), (2), or (3) of this rule or complying with any Act of Congress or rule prescribed by the Supreme Court pursuant to statutory authority.

(5) Official publications

Books, pamphlets, or other publications purporting to be issued by public authority.

(6) Newspapers and periodicals

Printed materials purporting to be newspapers or periodicals.

FIGURE 4-2   FRE 902: SELF-AUTHENTICATING DOCUMENTS (Cont.)

(7) Trade inscriptions and the like
   Inscriptions, signs, tags, or labels purporting to have been affixed in the course of business and indicating ownership, control, or origin.
(8) Acknowledged documents
   Documents accompanied by a certificate of acknowledgment executed in the manner provided by law by a notary public or other officer authorized by law to take acknowledgments.
(9) Commercial paper and related documents
   Commercial paper, signatures thereon, and documents relating thereto to the extent provided by general commercial law.
(10) Presumptions under Acts of Congress
   Any signature, document, or other matter declared by Act of Congress to be presumptively or prima facie genuine or authentic.

of Deeds office. One of your duties in trial preparation may be to go to the Register of Deeds office and obtain a certified copy of a deed. The process is usually quite simple. Just tell an employee in the office that you need a certified copy of the deed. The employee locates the deed in the book where it is recorded and makes a copy. The employee then stamps the deed with a short statement of certification, signs the statement, and enters the date.

There is little chance that the documents specified in FRE 902 have been fabricated. Of course, opposing counsel is free to introduce evidence that the document is not authentic.

POINTER: Often parties agree before trial that certain documents are genuine, and they stipulate to their authenticity. A **stipulation** is a statement that the parties agree on a certain issue and will not contest it. This is an efficient way to weed out the issues that are not in dispute and to expedite the litigation. Judges encourage the parties to stipulate to issues on which they agree, and the parties often state their stipulations in a pretrial order.

The Original Writing Rule

So far we have proved only that the document is what it purports to be—a warranty, a deed, or the like. Sometimes there remains a dispute as to whether the content of a document is genuine. FRE 1002 states the original writing rule, often called the best-evidence rule. FRE 1002 requires that "to prove the content of a writing, recording, or photograph, the original writing, recording or photograph is required, except as otherwise provided in these rules or by statute." This means that when the content of a document is directly in issue, the Federal Rules of Evidence require the original document, unless the original is unavailable or unless another evidence rule or statute permits submission of a copy.

An original is often required when the contents of the document state the terms of what the parties have agreed to do. Examples include when the terms of a contract, or the contents of a will or deed, are in dispute. Consider a deed that has been recorded in the Register of Deeds office. We have already examined how to authenticate the deed—by getting a certified copy. The copy is fine to show that a deed was recorded. However, assume that a dispute arises about the size of the parcel of land that was transferred in that deed, with the persons who sold the land asserting that the buyer altered the description of the land before recording the deed. Now the content of the original deed is in question. The original writing rule requires that the original deed be produced, if possible, before the court can hear oral testimony about the contents of the deed.

To understand the rationale for requiring the original, consider how a description in a deed sounds—30 degrees north to the large elm, 20 degrees northwest along the creek, and so on. You can imagine that a person may not be able to recite the exact metes and bounds of the deed by memory. It would be unrealistic for the sellers to state that they are certain the original deed read 10 north to the large oak instead of 30 north to the large elm. The buyers' testimony is likely to be less accurate than the deed, so the Federal Rules of Evidence prefer production of the original deed.

If the original document is not available, the witness may still be able to testify about its contents. Before testifying, the witness must give sufficient reason for not producing the original. For example, the original may have been destroyed, or it may be in the possession of a person in another state and the court unable to compel that individual to produce the document. See FRE 1004 for other acceptable reasons.

As a practical matter, an original document will be more persuasive to the trier of fact than a copy. However, FRE 1003 permits admission of a duplicate unless "(1) a genuine question is raised as to the authenticity of the original or (2) in the circumstances it would be unfair to admit the duplicate in lieu of the original." Thus, if the original of a person's will cannot be located, a photostatic copy may be admissible unless there is a genuine question about the authenticity of the will. One party may contend that the other party took the copy of the will and added a paragraph. The authenticity of the will is now in issue, because one party asserts that the document is not what it purports to be: that is, the testator's statement of how the estate should be distributed.

Hearsay

The hearsay rule is a rule commonly invoked to ensure reliable testimony. The application of the hearsay rule is sometimes complex. However, once you understand the basic principles that underlie the rule, you can apply the principles to the evidence you encounter during litigation without undue difficulty.

Rules 801 through 806 of the Federal Rules of Evidence address hearsay. Basically, the rules provide that if a statement is hearsay, it is not admissible as evidence unless it fits into an exception to the hearsay rule. Thus you must understand what hearsay is and know the exceptions to the rule.

Definition of Hearsay and Principles Underlying the Rule. Hearsay is testimony in court about a statement made out of court, where the out-of-court statement is offered to prove the truth of the matter asserted in the out-of-court statement. For instance, Mr. Wesser may testify in court that the fire inspector came to his house immediately after the fire and told him that the electric blanket caused the fire. If the fire inspector's statement is offered as proof that the blanket started the fire, it is hearsay.

The best way to understand the definition of hearsay is to grasp the principles underlying the rule. The purpose of the rule is to ensure that testimony is truthful. At trial, attorneys test witnesses' truthfulness through cross-examination. Attorneys question whether witnesses have adequate personal knowledge of the facts about which they testify. Attorneys also question the accuracy of a witness's memory. Witnesses may remember events incorrectly, especially when the events occurred perhaps two years before the trial. In addition, the credibility of witnesses is important. Recall that there are many factors that may make a witness seem less than credible—bias, prejudice, and so on.

If Mr. Wesser were allowed to repeat the fire inspector's statement to prove the cause of the fire, it would be unfair to deprive the defendants of the opportunity to cross-examine the fire inspector. Obviously, the statement of the fire inspector about the cause of the fire is far more reliable when the fire inspector himself states his opinion in court. When the fire inspector testifies about the cause of the fire, the defense attorney can explore the basis for the fire inspector's opinion and can probe his testimony, looking for inconsistencies or other weaknesses in his conclusions. To allow Mr. Wesser to state the fire inspector's opinion and deprive the defense attorney the opportunity to cross-examine the inspector would obviously be unfair.

Assume that Mr. Wesser testifies about the inspector's statement for some purpose other than to establish the cause of the fire. For instance, Ms. Heyward may offer the out-of-court statement to establish the fact that the fire inspector came to Mr. Wesser's home immediately after the fire. Here, the out-of-court statement is offered not to prove the truth of the facts in the statement. Rather, the purpose is to show that the statement was made by the fire inspector immediately after the fire, establishing that the inspector was present immediately after the fire. In this instance, the statement would not be regarded as hearsay.

Hearsay is not limited to oral statements. Documents may also be hearsay. A document must also be reliable if the document is offered as evidence to prove that the matters in the document are true.

Exceptions to the Hearsay Rule. There are many exceptions to the hearsay rule. This means that there are many types of hearsay that fit into an exception and thus are admissible.

The exceptions to the hearsay rule are set out in FRE 803 and FRE 804. You should become familiar with all the exceptions. We will discuss some of the exceptions that paralegals frequently encounter.

But first you should be aware that FRE 801(d) sets forth certain types of evidence that by definition are not hearsay. Because FRE 801(d) defines these types of evidence as not hearsay, you do not need to fit them into an exception. You should become familiar with all the categories in 801(d). However, the categories you will encounter most frequently are prior inconsistent statements and admissions of a party opponent.

A witness's prior inconsistent statement fits the definition of nonhearsay when the statement was made under oath at a prior trial or hearing or in a deposition. It is important for paralegals to stay constantly alert for prior inconsistent statements. One important task paralegals often perform is to review witnesses' depositions or other statements to find inconsistencies in their testimony. Such inconsistencies greatly undermine the witness's credibility.

Paralegals should also be alert for admissions by a party opponent. When a party to the litigation makes a statement admitting a fact, that statement can be used against the party at trial. For instance, if Mr. Wesser said that he often folded the blanket and forgot to turn it off in the morning, these statements could be used against him at trial when he testified that he never folded the blanket and turned it off every morning.

POINTER: State rules of evidence sometimes consider the ''nonhearsay'' categories in FRE 801(d) to be hearsay exceptions rather than ''nonhearsay.'' Do not dwell too long on the definition the state uses. Rather, concentrate on your primary consideration—whether the statement is admissible at trial.

FRE 803 and 804 set forth the exceptions to the hearsay rule. If you can fit a hearsay statement into one of these exceptions, then it may be admissible. It is important to remember that a statement is not automatically admissible just because it fits an exception to the hearsay rule. The statement must still comply with the other rules of evidence, such as relevance.

Examine Figure 4-3, which shows FRE 803. One exception frequently encountered is the excited utterance (FRE 803(3)). Suppose that Mr. Wesser's neighbor heard Mr. Wesser when he ran out of his burning home, shouting ''My electric blanket caught on fire!'' This is an excited utterance and should be admissible. The rationale behind this exception is that the person was so excited that he would not have had time to fabricate the statement.

FRE 803(4) provides that statements made for the purpose of medical diagnosis or treatment constitute a hearsay exception. The rationale here is that a person wants to be treated and helped by the doctor and thus will likely tell the doctor the truth.

FRE 803(6) contains a very important exception, commonly called the business records exception. Records kept in the course of a regularly conducted business activity generally fit this exception. The rationale is that businesses require accurate records for their operation. In addition, business employees cannot be expected to remember every fact recorded in business records. For instance, a large hospital may have several thousand former patients who owe money to the hospital. You cannot expect the collections manager to remember the name of all former patients and the amount of money they owe. However, the hospital keeps accurate records, so the hospital's business records accurately reflect the information needed.

Many types of public records fall within hearsay exceptions. See FRE 803(8)

FIGURE 4-3   RULE 803

Rule 803.   Hearsay Exceptions: Availability of Declarant Immaterial
The following are not excluded by the hearsay rule, even though the declarant is available as a witness.
(1) Present sense impression
   A statement describing or explaining an event or condition made while the declarant was perceiving the event or condition, or immediately thereafter.
(2) Excited utterance
   A statement relating to a startling event or condition made while the declarant was under the stress of excitement caused by the event or condition.
(3) Then existing mental, emotional, or physical condition
   A statement of the declarant's then existing state of mind, emotion, sensation, or physical condition (such as intent, plan, motive, design, mental feeling, pain, and bodily health), but not including a statement of memory or belief to prove the fact remembered or believed unless it relates to the execution, revocation, identification, or terms of declarant's will.
(4) Statements for purposes of medical diagnosis or treatment
   Statements made for purposes of medical diagnosis or treatment and describing medical history, or past or present symptoms, or sensations, or the inception or general character of the cause or external source thereof insofar as reasonably pertinent to diagnosis or treatment.
(5) Recorded recollection
   A memorandum or record concerning a matter about which a witness once had knowledge but now has insufficient recollection to enable the witness to testify fully and accurately, shown to have been made or adopted by the witness when the matter was fresh in the witness' memory and to reflect that knowledge correctly. If admitted, the memorandum or record may be read into evidence but may not itself be received as an exhibit unless offered by an adverse party.
(6) Records of regularly conducted activity
   A memorandum, report, record, or data compilation, in any form, of acts, events, conditions, opinions, or diagnoses, made at or near the time by, or from information transmitted by, a person with knowledge, if kept in the course of a regularly conducted business activity, and if it was the regular practice of that business activity to make the memorandum, report, record, or data compilation, all as shown by the testimony of the custodian or other qualified witness, unless the source of information or the method or circumstances of preparation indicate lack of trustworthiness. The term ''business'' as used in this paragraph includes business, institution, association, profession, occupation, and calling of every kind, whether or not conducted for profit.
(7) Absence of entry in records kept in accordance with the provisions of paragraph (6)
   Evidence that a matter is not included in the memoranda reports, records, or data compilations, in any form, kept in accordance with the provisions of paragraph (6), to prove the nonoccurrence or nonexistence of the matter, if the matter was of a kind of which a memorandum, report, record, or data compilation was regularly made and preserved, unless the sources of information or other circumstances indicate lack of trustworthiness.

FIGURE 4-3 RULE 803 (Cont.)

(8) Public records and reports

Records, reports, statements, or data compilations, in any form, of public offices or agencies, setting forth (A) the activities of the office or agency, or (B) matters observed pursuant to duty imposed by law as to which matters there was a duty to report, excluding, however, in criminal cases matters observed by police officers and other law enforcement personnel, or (C) in civil actions and proceedings and against the Government in criminal cases, factual findings resulting from an investigation made pursuant to authority granted by law, unless the sources of information or other circumstances indicate lack of trustworthiness.

(9) Records of vital statistics

Records or data compilations, in any form, of births, fetal deaths, deaths, or marriages, if the report thereof was made to a public office pursuant to requirements of law.

(10) Absence of public record or entry

To prove the absence of a record, report, statement, or data compilation, in any form, or the nonoccurrence or nonexistence of a matter of which a record, report, statement, or data compilation, in any form, was regularly made and preserved by a public office or agency, evidence in the form of a certification in accordance with rule 902, or testimony, that diligent search failed to disclose the record, report, statement, or data compilation, or entry.

(11) Records of religious organizations

Statements of births, marriages, divorces, deaths, legitimacy, ancestry, relationship by blood or marriage, or other similar facts of personal or family history, contained in a regularly kept record of a religious organization.

(12) Marriage, baptismal, and similar certificates

Statements of fact contained in a certificate that the maker performed a marriage or other ceremony or administered a sacrament, made by a clergyman, public official, or other person authorized by the rules or practices of a religious organization or by law to perform the act certified, and purporting to have been issued at the time of the act or within a reasonable time thereafter.

(13) Family records

Statements of fact concerning personal or family history contained in family Bibles, genealogies, charts, engravings on rings, inscriptions on family portraits, engravings on urns, crypts, or tombstones, or the like.

(14) Records of documents affecting an interest in property

The record of a document purporting to establish or affect an interest in property, as proof of the content of the original recorded document and its execution and delivery by each person by whom it purports to have been executed, if the record is a record of a public office and an applicable statute authorizes the recording of documents of that kind in that office.

(15) Statements in documents affecting an interest in property

A statement contained in a document purporting to establish or affect an interest in property if the matter stated was relevant to the purpose of the document, unless dealings with the property since the document was made have been inconsistent with the truth of the statement or the purport of the document.

FIGURE 4-3   RULE 803 (Cont.)

(16) Statements in ancient documents
Statements in a document in existence twenty years or more the authenticity of which is established.

(17) Market reports, commercial publications
Market quotations, tabulations, lists, directories, or other published compilations, generally used and relied upon by the public or by persons in particular occupations.

(18) Learned treatises
To the extent called to the attention of an expert witness upon cross-examination or relied upon by the expert witness in direct examination, statements contained in published treatises, periodicals, or pamphlets on a subject of history, medicine, or other science or art, established as a reliable authority by the testimony or admission of the witness or by other expert testimony or by judicial notice. If admitted, the statements may be read into evidence but may not be received as exhibits.

(19) Reputation concerning personal or family history
Reputation among members of a person's family by blood adoption, or marriage, or among a person's associates, or in the community, concerning a person's birth, adoption, marriage, divorce, death, legitimacy, relationship by blood, adoption, or marriage, ancestry, or other similar fact of personal or family history.

(20) Reputation concerning boundaries or general history
Reputation in a community, arising before the controversy, as to boundaries of or customs affecting lands in the community, and reputation as to events of general history important to the community or State or nation in which located.

(21) Reputation as to character
Reputation of a person's character among associates or in the community.

(22) Judgment of previous conviction
Evidence of a final judgment, entered after a trial or upon a plea of guilty (but not upon a plea of nolo contendere), adjudging a person guilty of a crime punishable by death or imprisonment in excess of one year, to prove any fact essential to sustain the judgment, but not including, when offered by the Government in a criminal prosecution for purposes other than impeachment, judgments against persons other than the acccused. The pendency of an appeal may be shown but does not affect admissibility.

(23) Judgment as to personal, family, or general history, or boundaries
Judgments as proof of matters of personal, family or general history, or boundaries, essential to the judgment, if the same would be provable by evidence of reputation.

(24) Other exceptions
A statement not specifically covered by any of the foregoing exceptions but having equivalent circumstantial guarantees of trustworthiness, if the court determines that (A) the statement is offered as evidence of a material fact; (B) the statement is more probative on the point for which it is offered than any other evidence which the proponent can procure through reasonable efforts; and (C) the general purposes of these rules and the interests of justice will best be served by admission of the statement into evidence. However, a statement may not be admitted under this exception unless the proponent of it makes known to the adverse party sufficiently in advance of the trial or hearing to provide the adverse party with a fair opportunity to prepare to meet it, the proponent's intention to offer the statement and the particulars of it, including the name and address of the declarant.

through (17). The key to these exceptions is that the records are regularly kept by an agency or organization, thus there is usually no reason to doubt their trustworthiness. An example is a deed recorded in the Register of Deeds' office. Note that if circumstances indicate a lack of trustworthiness, then the records do not fit the hearsay exceptions.

Examine Figure 4-4, which shows FRE 804. Note that in order to use the exceptions in FRE 804, the declarant must be unavailable. This means that the person who made the out-of-court statement (the declarant) is unable to be present—that is, is dead or ill; or the subject matter of the person's statements is privileged; or the person persistently refuses to testify; or the witness cannot remember the subject matter of the statement; or the court cannot secure the presence of the witness.

FRE 804(b)(1) contains an important exception to the hearsay rule. If a witness is unavailable at trial, former testimony at another hearing or in a deposition is generally admissible if the party against whom the testimony is offered had the opportunity to question the witness. Often when attorneys fear that a witness may be dead by the time of the trial, or too ill to attend, they take the witness's testimony to preserve it. This may also be necessary with witnesses who are likely to disappear.

Another noteworthy exception is a statement against interest, in FRE 804(b)(3). When persons have made previous statements that are against their financial, legal, or business interests, we assume that the statements must be true, because persons presumably have no motive to fabricate statements that are detrimental to them.

The attorneys on your team must make the final decisions about the admissibility of hearsay. However, it is important for paralegals to recognize hearsay and try to fit the hearsay into an exception for the attorneys to consider.

PRIVILEGES

The rules of evidence discussed so far focus on disclosing evidence relevant to the lawsuit. In contrast, the purpose of the rules related to privileges is to prevent the disclosure of certain types of information.[2] Privileged communications are statements that are protected from forced disclosure because the statements were made between persons who have a confidential relationship with each other. The public policy in favor of protecting these confidential communications overrides the need for full disclosure of all evidence related to the litigation. For example, communications between an attorney and client are privileged—that is, protected from disclosure. This privilege exists because it is essential that the client tell the attorney all the facts, even the damaging and embarrassing ones, in order for the attorney to provide adequate representation.

Sources of Rules Regarding Privileges

The Federal Rules of Evidence do not contain specific rules regarding what types of information are privileged. Instead, FRE 501 leaves to the courts and state

FIGURE 4-4   RULE 804

Rule 804.   Hearsay Exceptions: Declarant Unavailable
(a) Definition of unavailability
Unavailability as a witness'' includes situations in which the declarant—

(1) is exempted by ruling of the court on the ground of privilege from testifying concerning the subject matter of the declarant's statement; or

(2) persists in refusing to testify concerning the subject matter of the declarant's statement despite an order of the court to do so; or

(3) testifies to a lack of memory of the subject matter of the declarant's statement; or

(4) is unable to be present or to testify at the hearing because of death or then existing physical or mental illness or infirmity; or

(5) is absent from the hearing and the proponent of a statement has been unable to procure the declarant's attendance (or in the case of a hearsay exception under subdivision (b)(2), (3), or (4), the declarant's attendance or testimony) by process or other reasonable means.

A declarant is not unavailable as a witness if exemption, refusal, claim of lack of memory, inability, or absence is due to the procurement or wrongdoing of the proponent of a statement for the purpose of preventing the witness from attending or testifying.

(b) Hearsay exceptions
The following are not excluded by the hearsay rule if the declarant is unavailable as a witness:

(1) Former testimony
Testimony given as a witness at another hearing of the same or a different proceeding, or in a deposition taken in compliance with law in the course of the same or another proceeding, if the party against whom the testimony is now offered, or, in a civil action or proceeding, a predecessor in interest, had an opportunity and similar motive to develop the testimony by direct, cross, or redirect examination.

(2) Statement under belief of impending death
In a prosecution for homicide or in a civil action or proceeding, a statement made by a declarant while believing that the declarant's death was imminent, concerning the cause or circumstances of what the declarant believed to be impending death.

(3) Statement against interest
A statement which was at the time of its making so far contrary to the declarant's pecuniary or proprietary interest, or so far tended to subject the declarant to civil or criminal liability, or to render invalid a claim by the declarant against another, that a reasonable person in the declarant's position would not have made the statement unless believing it to be true. A statement tending to expose the declarant to criminal liability and offered to exculpate the accused is not admissible unless corroborating circumstances clearly indicate the trustworthiness of the statement.

FIGURE 4-4   RULE 804 (Cont.)

(4) Statement of personal or family history
(A) A statement concerning the declarant's own birth, adoption, marriage, divorce, legitimacy, relationship by blood, adoption, or marriage, ancestry, or other similar fact of personal or family history, even though declarant had no means of acquiring personal knowledge of the matter stated; or (B) a statement concerning the foregoing matters, and death also, of another person, if the declarant was related to the other by blood, adoption, or marriage or was so intimately associated with the other's family as to be likely to have accurate information concerning the matter declared.

(5) Other exceptions
A statement not specifically covered by any of the foregoing exceptions but having equivalent circumstantial guarantees of trustworthiness, if the court determines that (A) the statement is offered as evidence of a material fact; (B) the statement is more probative on the point for which it is offered than any other evidence which the proponent can procure through reasonable efforts; and (C) the general purposes of these rules and the interests of justice will best be served by admission of the statement into evidence. However, a statement may not be admitted under this exception unless the proponent of it makes known to the adverse party sufficiently in advance of the trial or hearing to provide the adverse party with a fair opportunity to prepare to meet it, the proponent's intention to offer the statement and the particulars of it, including the name and address of the declarant.

legislatures the task of developing the rules for privileges. In other words, the Federal Rules of Evidence do not adopt certain privileges that apply uniformly to every case litigated in federal court.

Thus you must first determine which rules apply to your case. If your lawsuit is in state court, you use that state's rules. A state's rules regarding privileges may be found in the state's statutes and case law.

For lawsuits in federal court, the basic rule is that when your lawsuit is based on federal question jurisdiction, you apply the privilege rules developed by the federal courts. When jurisdiction is based on diversity of citizenship, you apply the privilege rules of the state in which the federal court is located.

Thus you have to look beyond the Federal Rules of Evidence to determine whether evidence is protected by a privilege. This requires detailed and accurate legal research. You may be confused initially when you try to figure out whether federal law or state law applies. Discuss your questions with the other members of the attorney/paralegal team and clarify whether federal law or state law applies. Then you can conduct your research and discuss the results with the attorney to determine whether the evidence in question is privileged and thus protected from disclosure.

How Privilege Rules Direct Paralegals' Work

Whether you are using federal or state privilege rules, it is important to remember that the rules apply throughout the litigation. Obviously, if a client's statement is privileged, the client cannot be forced to testify about the statement at trial. In fact, the privileged statement is protected from disclosure throughout the litigation process. This means that an opposing party cannot find out the contents of the statement during informal investigation or through formal discovery.

A primary responsibility of the paralegal is to ensure that protected information is not disclosed. This is particularly critical during the discovery phase of the litigation, when the parties sometimes exchange huge numbers of documents. As we discuss in Chapter 9, one of your tasks is to screen the documents to make sure that no privileged evidence is released to other parties.

Thus you must be able to spot evidence that may be privileged. Once you recognize the evidence that you think is privileged, you can discuss with the attorney the exact federal or state rules of privilege that apply. These rules differ among jurisdictions. Not every privilege is recognized in every jurisdiction. The important goal for now is that you understand the basic and more common privileges.

The Attorney-Client Privilege

The privilege you will encounter most frequently is the attorney-client privilege. The **attorney-client privilege** protects from disclosure confidential communications between the client and attorney. The effect of the privilege is that attorneys cannot be forced to testify about confidential communications with their clients. Also, the client can refuse to testify about the confidential communications and can prevent anyone else from testifying as well. For instance, suppose that you, Mr. Wesser, and Ms. Heyward met to discuss how Mr. Wesser handled the electric blanket—that is, whether he folded it or misused it in any way that would have damaged the blanket. At no stage in the litigation can you, Mr. Wesser, or Ms. Heyward be forced to testify about the content of your conversation. To illustrate how the client asserts the attorney-client privilege, suppose that at trial the defense attorney asked Mr. Wesser, ''Did you ever fold the blanket, contrary to the instructions that came with the blanket?'' Mr. Wesser would have to answer this question. However, the defense attorney might ask, ''What did you tell Ms. Heyward when you were preparing for trial and discussed how you handled the electric blanket?'' Mr. Wesser is entitled to refuse to answer this question, based upon the attorney-client privilege.

The attorney-client privilege is closely related to the ethical duty to preserve confidential information, which we discussed in Chapter 2. Recall that the Model Code directs that an attorney may not disclose the client's ''secrets'' and ''confidences,'' and that Model Rule 1.6 protects all information relating to the representation of the client. The communications protected by the attorney-client privilege are somewhat narrower. However, we will not dwell on the differences among the various definitions. Rather, we will concentrate on the practical way to recognize the kind of evidence that the attorney-client privilege covers.

Determining when the Attorney-Client Privilege Applies

In order for the attorney-client privilege to apply, two primary factors must exist: First, the purpose of the communications must be to render legal advice to the client. Second, the communications must be confidential.

When the Purpose of Communications Is to Render Legal Advice. The attorney-client privilege attaches only to communications concerning legal advice. If your best friend is a lawyer and you discuss the local basketball team or the weather, your conversation is not covered by the attorney-client privilege. But if Mr. Wesser and Ms. Heyward discuss the weather on the night of the fire because there was a thunderstorm during which Mr. Wesser's house was struck by lightning, this concerns the cause of the fire and is protected by the attorney-client privilege.

Suppose that Mr. Wesser is talking to Ms. Heyward at their initial conference and he is not yet sure that he will hire Ms. Heyward as his lawyer. Are their statements covered by the attorney-client privilege? Yes. Communications made in the course of determining whether to hire a lawyer are privileged, regardless of whether the lawyer is actually hired. The protection is needed from the very beginning so that both the attorney and the potential client can get enough information to determine whether it is worthwhile to pursue the litigation.

When Communications Are Confidential. Communications between attorney and client are considered to be confidential when the speakers intend that their communications not be heard by persons other than the persons they are addressing. The primary factor in determining the speakers' intent is the presence of persons other than the attorney and client. The presence of third parties can destroy the confidentiality of the communication. For instance, if the attorney and client are discussing the facts of the case in an elevator crowded with persons they do not know, one may safely assume that they do not intend that their conversation be confidential.

However, the presence of persons employed by the attorney, such as paralegals and clerks, does not destroy confidentiality. This is because the third parties are representatives of the attorney, and their purpose is to assist with rendering legal services to the client.

Confidential Communications Include Documents. So far we have discussed only spoken communications between attorney and client. It is imperative to understand that confidential communications also include documents exchanged between the attorney and the client. For instance, if Ms. Heyward writes a letter to Mr. Wesser explaining that the defendants have asserted that he misused the blanket and asking for information about how he handled the blanket, this letter is a confidential communication.

However, a document that existed before the attorney-client relationship was established does not become privileged simply because the client gives the document to the lawyer. If Mr. Wesser gives to Ms. Heyward the warranty that came with the blanket, that does not make the warranty a privileged document.

It is very important that paralegals understand that documents can be covered by the attorney-client privilege. One danger paralegals must avoid is turning over documents that contain confidential information to the opposing party during the discovery process. Paralegals may screen thousands of documents during discovery, and it is imperative that each document be carefully reviewed for confidential information.

Determining when the Attorney-Client Privilege Does Not Apply to Client Communications

The attorney-client privilege does not prevent the disclosure of all communications between the attorney and client. There exist a number of exceptions to the attorney-client privilege, and the client may waive the privilege. These subjects are discussed below.

Exceptions to the Attorney-Client Privilege. We discuss the exceptions you will encounter most frequently in litigation. Other exceptions exist, such as disputes over a deceased client's will when all the parties claim through the deceased client. Remember that the rules and exceptions may vary among jurisdictions, since the Federal Rules of Evidence do not dictate uniform rules to apply in all jurisdictions.

1. Future Crimes or Fraud. Communications between the attorney and client are not privileged when the purpose of the communications is to help a person commit a crime or fraud. Obviously, it would be against public policy to allow clients to consult attorneys for advice on how they might successfully commit a crime or perpetrate a fraud on another person. This is the same exception that applies to the ethical obligation to protect confidential client information. As with the ethics exception, be sure to distinguish between acts the client has already committed and future crimes or fraud.

2. Disputes Between the Attorney and Client. Suppose that a client asserts that the attorney did not perform the services agreed on. In order to defend against the accusation, the attorney may have to reveal some of the confidential communications that transpired between them. The attorney may have to testify about the exact nature of the work that the client hired him to perform. This exception is like the exception to preserving confidential information that we discussed on page 41. As with the ethics exception, the attorney should reveal no more confidential client information than is necessary to assert a defense.

3. Disputes Between Joint Clients. As we noted in Chapter 2, an attorney may undertake representation of multiple parties to a lawsuit when it appears that the parties do not have adverse interests. However, as the litigation progresses, the parties may have a falling out. For instance, in the Wesser case, David Benedict represents both defendants. Suppose that during the litigation Second Ledge decides that Woodall Shoals is at fault and decides to file a cross-claim against Woodall Shoals.

As we discussed in Chapter 2, Mr. Benedict would have to withdraw from representing either of the codefendants. In regard to the attorney-client privilege, communications between Mr. Benedict and the corporate officers of Woodall Shoals and Second Ledge, when they were both meeting with Mr. Benedict, are not covered by the attorney-client privilege.

Waiver of the Attorney-Client Privilege. The client may waive the attorney-client privilege. This happens when the client voluntarily discloses to others communications with the attorney. Consider again the example of an attorney and a client discussing facts on a crowded elevator. As we observed, the communications are clearly not confidential because other people are right there listening. In this example, the client has waived the attorney-client privilege in regard to the facts discussed on the elevator by voluntarily disclosing the facts to third parties.

In contrast, assume that the defense attorney asks Mr. Wesser, "Did you ever fold the blanket, contrary to the instructions?" and that Mr. Wesser answers this question. Even though Mr. Wesser had discussed this fact with his attorney prior to trial, he has not waived the attorney-client privilege protecting their conversation. When a client takes the stand and testifies about facts that he has discussed with his lawyer previously, but does not reveal what he actually discussed in his conversation with the lawyer, this does not constitute a waiver.

Similarly, consider our example of Mr. Wesser testifying at trial about how he handled the blanket. Suppose that the defense attorney asks Mr. Wesser, "What did you tell Ms. Heyward when you were preparing for trial and discussed how you handled the electric blanket?" If Mr. Wesser answers this question, revealing the contents of his conversation, then he has waived the attorney-client privilege in regard to this conversation. He has testified about his actual conversation with his attorney, and this constitutes a waiver. As a practical matter, Ms. Heyward would object to this question before Mr. Wesser answered it, so he would not unwittingly waive the privilege. If Mr. Wesser nonetheless answered the question after being alerted that it called for privileged information, he would be deemed to have waived the privilege.

You will often read that the privilege belongs to the client and thus the client can waive the privilege. This means that the attorney cannot waive the privilege for the client. However, you must not confuse this with asserting the privilege. Attorneys can assert the attorney-client privilege on a client's behalf to protect their confidential communications.

Duration of the Attorney-Client Privilege. The attorney-client privilege attaches to the confidential communications from the very outset of the discussion between attorney and client. As we discussed above, the privilege covers the communications even at the initial conference when the client has not yet decided whether to employ the attorney. Once the privilege attaches, it covers the communications forever, unless the client waives the privilege. The attorney-client privilege continues even after termination of the attorney's employment, protecting all the confidential communications made during the attorney-client relationship.

The Work Product Privilege

Suppose that David Benedict, lawyer for the defendants in the Wesser case, knows that Leigh Heyward has interviewed Mr. Misenheimer, the fire inspector. Mr. Benedict requests a copy of Ms. Heyward's interview notes. These notes are not protected by the attorney-client privilege, because they are not communications between the client and attorney. However, the notes are protected by the work product privilege.

The work product privilege is very important in the discovery phase of the litigation, and we will discuss it at greater length in Chapter 9. The privilege is set forth in FRCivP 26(b)(3). We are referring to the work product of the attorney, and the privilege affords protection to two types of work product.

First, the rule provides absolute protection to the "mental impressions, conclusions, opinions on legal theories" that the attorney forms in preparing for trial. Thus, if Ms. Heyward wrote a memorandum describing how Mr. Misenheimer's statements could be helpful at trial, this memorandum is absolutely protected by the work product privilege.

Second, there is a qualified privilege for other documents "prepared in anticipation of litigation" by a party's "representative." A representative can include the party's attorney, as well as other of the party's agents, such as paralegals or claims investigators. Thus a report on the reason the electric blanket caught fire, prepared for the defense attorney by the insurance claims investigator, would be protected. The protected trial preparation documents may be obtained by another party only if the other party has a "substantial need" and cannot obtain a "substantial equivalent" of the documents "without undue hardship." Thus these documents do not enjoy absolute protection, but may qualify for the more limited privilege. We will explore the meaning of these phrases further in Chapter 9.

Husband-Wife Privilege

Federal law and the law in most states recognize a privilege protecting confidential marital communications. The husband-wife privilege applies to confidential communications made during the course of the marriage. There are two basic requirements in order for the husband-wife privilege to apply. First, a valid marriage must exist. Second, the communications must be confidential. The method for determining whether the communications were intended to be confidential is the same as for attorney-client communications. That is, the presence of third parties generally destroys the confidentiality.

The husband-wife privilege applies to communications during the marriage. Thus a conversation before the couple was married or after they were divorced would not be protected. However, a conversation during the marriage would continue to be protected even if the spouses subsequently divorced. In addition to surviving divorce, the privilege also survives annulment of a marriage and death of a spouse.

There are exceptions to the husband-wife privilege. When a case involves crimes against a spouse or the children of either spouse, the privilege does not apply. Nor does the privilege apply in lawsuits between the spouses.

In many states there is also a second type of marital privilege, which applies only in criminal cases. Although we are addressing civil cases, you should be aware of the privilege in criminal cases and some quasi-criminal cases. Many states grant criminal defendants a privilege to keep the spouse from testifying against them in criminal cases. The privilege does not apply when the defendant is accused of crimes against the spouse or their children.

Physician-Patient Privilege

Most jurisdictions recognize a physician-patient privilege, which protects disclosure of information a physician obtains in treating a patient. There are variations on this privilege among jurisdictions, but generally the privilege protects all information that a doctor obtains about a patient.

For the privilege to attach, the patient must consult the doctor on his or her own accord for treatment or diagnosis. Sometimes a patient is directed by another to consult a doctor, in which case the privilege does not apply. Court-ordered examinations and insurance physicals are two examples of unprivileged examinations.

As with other privileges, the presence of third parties destroys the privilege because the communications are not confidential. However, when the third persons are agents of the doctor, such as nurses and x-ray technicians, the privilege is generally not destroyed. The privilege may also be preserved when the third party is a close family member. However, there are variations among jurisdictions, so you must research the applicable law.

Waiver of the Physician-Patient Privilege. The physician-patient privilege is frequently and easily waived. Often attorneys must have the doctor's records to assess and prove a client's claim. When a client signs an authorization for a doctor to release information to the client's attorneys, this is an effective waiver of the privilege. Patients often waive the privilege for insurance companies. You have probably signed forms in your insurance claims for doctor visits in which you give the insurance company permission to obtain the doctor's records for your treatment. This is a waiver of the privilege.

Only the patient can waive the privilege. The physician can assert the privilege on the patient's behalf but cannot waive the privilege. This is like the attorney-client privilege where, as we discussed, the attorney can assert the privilege on the client's behalf but cannot waive it.

Other Privileges

The attorney-client, husband-wife, and physician-patient privileges are the privileges you are most likely to encounter frequently. However, you should be aware that other privileges may arise. Some jurisdictions recognize a priest-penitent privilege, to protect communications with a priest or pastor. In some jurisdictions a reporter's informants, government secrets, and an accountant's records are privileged. The existence and scope of these privileges vary considerably and require accurate research. Finally, the Fifth Amendment privilege against self-incrimination may sometimes be asserted in civil proceedings.

ENDNOTES

1 *Black's Law Dictionary* 498 (5th ed. 1979).
2 *McCormick on Evidence* 171 (E. Cleary ed., 3d ed. 1984); Chapter 8 in *McCormick* contains a detailed discussion of evidentiary privileges.

5 DEVELOPMENT OF THE CASE

LITIGATION EXTRACT: You now have a background in the organization of a law firm, the structure of the court system, legal ethics, and the rules of evidence. We are ready to begin our informal investigation in the Wesser case as we move toward commencement of the lawsuit. First, in order to keep the investigation and the entire course of the litigation orderly, we will discuss how to set up, organize, and maintain files. Then we will formulate an investigation plan and consider the sources of information. Finally, we will examine the various remedies available to ensure that we request the proper relief in Mr. Wesser's complaint.

OPENING AND ORGANIZING FILES

Every law firm has its own system for opening new-client files and organizing the materials kept in those files. We will discuss the general principles that apply to file opening and organization, and you can apply them to the system in your law firm. (Note that in this chapter we discuss how to set up files, and in Chapter 10 we look at systems for retrieving filed materials.) The underlying principle in both setup and retrieval is that attorneys and paralegals must be able to find the documents in their files quickly. Fast and accurate document retrieval is especially important in litigation, where you must be able at all times to locate documents immediately, especially during depositions and trials.

Opening Files

Because every law firm has its own procedures for opening files, our discussion of the opening of files will be general. Let it serve as a useful background for learning your firm's system.

Master List of Files. When a law firm undertakes representation in a new matter, the common procedure is for the case to be assigned to a lawyer who will be responsible for all aspects of that case. Usually the case is also assigned at the outset to a paralegal who will remain responsible for paralegal duties for the duration of the case. The responsible lawyer and responsible paralegal must maintain close communication. Therefore it is imperative that each keep a master list of the files assigned to them. When a new file is assigned to you, it is imperative that you immediately add that file to your master list. Your master list should include the name of the file, the name of the responsible attorney, and the general status of the file. You and the responsible attorney should review together the status of your files at least once a month. At your meetings you can review the files and the specific tasks that need to be performed. You must update your master list regularly. As you keep track of your files, remember the docket control techniques discussed in Chapter 1.

Case Opening Sheets. Every time a file is opened, a **case opening sheet** is completed. It contains basic information that you will need throughout the course of litigation. Most of the information needed to complete the sheet will be available to you by the completion of the initial client conference, with one exception. At the time the file is opened, the name of the opposing party's attorney may not be known. When you represent the plaintiff, for example, as in the Wesser case, you may not know at the outset who will represent the defendants unless the parties' attorneys have held discussions prior to the filing of the lawsuit. Compare the Chattooga case, where the names of opposing counsel are known to Chattooga Corporation from the summons and complaint.

Figure 5-1 illustrates the case opening sheet in the Wesser case. Some law firms may include more or even less information, but our example illustrates the basic information usually necessary to open a file. First is the file number. This is the number assigned for use in the law firm's filing system. Do not confuse it with the file number assigned by the clerk of court when a lawsuit is commenced. Some law firms use file numbers that include the year in which a file was opened, and the designation may indicate the subject matter of the litigation. For example, a file opened in 1991 where the subject matter concerns immigration law may be designated as file 91-0423-I.

The next blanks to fill in are simply the name of your client and the name of the opposing party. Next are the address and phone number of your client. The next category of information is for the client contact. You may not always contact the clients themselves. For instance, when the client is a corporation, you will insert the name of the contact at the corporation, such as the president or human resources manager. Next are the name, address, and phone number of the attorney for the opposing party. As we mentioned earlier, you may not always know who the opposing attorney is when the file is opened, but you should know as soon as the defendant retains counsel.

The next designations on the case opening sheet are the names of the attorney and the paralegal responsible for the case. This is followed by the date that the file was opened. When the lawsuit is over and the file is closed, the date of closing is noted.

FIGURE 5-1 CASE OPENING SHEET

File No.: 89-1235-L

Client:

Bryson Wesser

Opposing Party:

Woodall Shoals Corporation and
Second Ledge Stores, Incorporated

Client Information

Address:

115 Pipestem Dr.
Charleston, North Carolina 28226

Phone: (704) 555-1933

Client Contact

Address:
Same

Phone:

Opposing Party

Woodall Shoals Corporation and Second Ledge Stores, Incorporated

Address:

300 West Blvd.
New York, NY 10019-0987

Phone: (212) 555-3100 (WS)
250 E. 88th St.   (212) 555-9263 (SL)
New York, NY 10019-3521

Opposing Lawyer

Address:

Phone:

Responsible Lawyer:

Leigh J. Heyward

Responsible Paralegal:

Christina Anderson

Date File Opened:

December 4, 1988

Date File Closed:

Fee Agreement:

Contingent—25%

Referred by:

Michael Buchanan

Attorney who brought case in:

Leigh J. Heyward

The next blank is for a designation of the fee agreement. The arrangement may be for a contingent fee—that is, a certain percentage of the amount the client recovers. This is the arrangement in the illustration for Mr. Wesser's personal injury lawsuit. As we discussed in Chapter 1, another common fee arrangement is the hourly rate. This is the fee arrangement that would most likely be used in the Chattooga case for the defense of Chattooga Corporation.

Finally, you enter the name of the person who referred the case to the law firm. The referral may have come from a friend of the client or from another attorney who does not handle this type of case. The attorney who brought the case in is the attorney to whom the case was referred. This is not necessarily the attorney responsible for the case. For instance, in the Chattooga case, the attorney who received the initial inquiry may have been an attorney who does only corporate law and no litigation, so the case would be assigned to an attorney who regularly litigates.

After the case opening file is completed, it is usually routed to a clerk, secretary, or bookkeeper, who enters the information into the firm's bookkeeping system so that billing information can be kept up to date. The case opening sheet may also be placed in a master litigation notebook and/or in a notebook used to track the statute of limitations for all pending cases. The procedures will vary among law firms. Usually the information is entered by computer so that in addition to having the information for billing purposes, the information is in the system for docket control and for screening potential conflicts of interest. One very common step after the case opening sheet is completed is for a clerk to prepare an index card with the basic information about the parties involved. Many firms keep this manual system in addition to their computer system. See Figure 5-2 for an example of the card made for the Wesser case.

FIGURE 5-2   SAMPLE FILE CARD

Our File No.: 89-1235-L

Client:
Bryson Wesser

Adverse Party:
Woodall Shoals Corporation and
Second Ledge Stores, Incorporated

Address:
115 Pipestem Dr.
Charleston, North Carolina 28226

Address:
Woodall:
    300 West Blvd.
    New York, NY 10019-0987

Second Ledge:
    250 E. 88th St.
    New York, NY 10019-3521

Date opened:
December 4, 1988

POINTER: Note that on the Wesser index card the corporate addresses for the defendants are used. This is because at the time the file was opened, the name of counsel for the defendants was not yet known. Once the name and address of counsel for all defendants are known, you should prepare for the file a master list for service of documents. Remember that after the complaint is filed, subsequent pleadings and motions are served on all parties by mailing them to the parties' attorneys. A master list of the proper names and addresses is particularly important when there are numerous parties to the lawsuit.

Other Documents in Newly Opened Files. Be sure that all documents are put in the newly opened file immediately. There may not be many documents initially. Usually attorneys and clients enter a written fee agreement, which should be ready when the file is opened. Notes and memoranda regarding the information obtained at the initial client conference will be ready to go in the file. You may have obtained important documents from the client that are ready to be filed, such as contracts or correspondence with adverse parties. Other documents will follow quickly, so the file must be organized at the outset, as discussed next.

Organizing Files

Files may be organized in different ways, depending largely on the complexity of the litigation. A file for a simple collections matter will not be as large as the file for a complex product liability case; therefore it may be organized more simply. The key to file organization is to ensure that any single document can be found easily. The organization of a file may have to be modified during the course of the litigation, as more documents accumulate.

Mechanics of Setting Up Files and Subfiles. The basic organizational units are similar in most files. The main file is labeled by file number and/or client name. Because a file soon grows too cumbersome if all documents are lumped together in one big folder arranged, for instance, in chronological order, the main file must be subdivided into smaller categories. Therefore within the main file are a number of smaller files called ''subfiles'' or ''working files.'' The types of subfile categories we will list here are typical in litigation.

Use a rigid jacket to enclose the subfiles, which should be self-contained in manila folders or clipped together with a cover sheet indicating the subfile category. Careful labeling and indexing are crucial.

Subfile Categories. The subfiles in a litigation file will vary somewhat, depending on the complexity of the litigation. The following categories suggest typical subfiles in a litigation file.

1. *Court papers.* Court papers are the documents filed with the court that are exchanged between and among the parties. Obviously this includes the pleadings—complaint, answer, counterclaim, and the like. Motions, together with supporting documentation, also belong in this subfile.[1] (This subfile may include discovery materials, if they are required to be filed with the court. However, in most cases it is better to maintain a separate subfile for discovery materials.) Within the subfile for court papers, documents are usually arranged in chronological

order. This is particularly true for pleadings, which need to be in chronological order to follow the progression of the litigation. This subfile will also contain the orders and judgment entered by the court, together with any judicial opinions. Consent orders and stipulations are also placed in this subfile.

 POINTER: In this section we are discussing only the subfiles typically set up at the beginning of the litigation. As the litigation progresses, you will develop further subfiles. You may develop subfiles by the name of the witness or by the issues. You may have some discovery materials that are so lengthy, such as a deposition, that they require their own subfiles. Remember that the key is easy retrieval of documents. See Chapter 10 for further discussion of document retrieval.

2. *Correspondence with court and counsel.* This subfile includes letters to the court. Usually these are general cover letters stating the documents being submitted to the court. Correspondence with counsel for all parties also belongs in this subfile. These letters generally reflect information exchanged between counsel and settlement discussions. Correspondence is arranged in chronological order.

3. *Correspondence.* In simple cases, *all* correspondence may be in this file, but when a case is complex and its file large, it may be best to separate the correspondence with the court and counsel from other correspondence. General correspondence includes correspondence with the client, with witnesses, with insurance carriers, with hospitals and doctors to obtain medical records, and with a host of other persons involved in the litigation.

General correspondence is usually arranged in chronological order. If litigation is protracted over the course of several years, the subfiles may need to be further subdivided by year and even by person. A subfile may be labeled Correspondence/Lee Smith, for instance, or Correspondence/1985-1990.

4. *File memoranda.* You will find that in the course of litigation you and the attorneys on your team will write many memoranda to the file. Paralegals write memoranda relating information to the attorney, such as synopses of initial witness interviews or the contents of telephone conversations with the client. Attorneys write many memoranda to paralegals outlining information that they want the paralegals to gather. Attorneys also write memoranda to the file, often to record facts from a conversation with a client or opposing counsel.

5. *Legal research.* This subfile may include memoranda summarizing legal research. It may also include copies of judicial opinions pertaining to the legal issues in the litigation. In a very complex case, the legal research working file may need to be further subdivided into specific legal issues.

6. *Memoranda of law.* The memoranda of law, or briefs, submitted to the court during the litigation may be lengthy and thus require a separate subfile. In simpler cases, the memoranda of law may be included with court documents.

7. *Discovery.* Discovery materials may be filed a number of ways, depending on their bulk. As we noted earlier, if you are in a jurisdiction that requires that discovery materials be filed with the court, your discovery documents may be routed to the court-documents subfile. However, when extensive discovery documents are involved, further subdivisions are usually necessary. For instance,

when the parties exchange lengthy interrogatories, you may need subfiles for each one. Thus a subfile may be labeled ''Plaintiff's Second Set of Interrogatories to Defendant Woodall Shoals—6/5/90.'' See Chapter 10 for further discussion of document retrieval from discovery documents.

8. *Lawyer's notes.* This subfile will contain the lawyer's notes, usually handwritten, concerning legal and factual research. It may also contain the lawyer's outlines of important documents or oral arguments.

9. *News clippings.* This subfile is important for cases that generate publicity. Some cases generate enough press coverage that clippings can provide information about events that gave rise to the lawsuit and about the parties in the case.

10. *Billing matters.* There may be a subfile for documents related to billing the client, especially if the law firm uses a timekeeping method that involves tearing time slips off a master sheet each day and submitting them for computer entry. Even after the computer entries are made, the slips are often retained. Copies of billing statements to the client may also be kept in this subfile.

Indexing Files

A good index is crucial to quick and accurate document retrieval. The purpose of the index is to keep a record of the subfile in which a document can be located. In simple lawsuits one index at the front of the file may be sufficient, but in more complex cases, the subfiles themselves can become so large as to require an index for each subfile.

The index may appear in different places in different files. It may be placed in the inside front cover of a folder. A common method for arranging pleadings is in groups of about 25 documents, either in a subfile or a binder, with an index placed on top. Each pleading in the group can be flagged with a separate numbered tab, which can be referenced along with the document name in the index.

The index must describe the documents very specifically. Instead of entering a document simply as ''Defendant's Answers to Interrogatories,'' for instance, call it ''Defendant Woodall Shoals' Answers to Plaintiff's Second Set of Interrogatories.''

Central Files and Working Files

Because of the large number of documents in a file and the large number of persons using the file, many law offices keep the original of each document in a central file area. The original documents generated and received in a lawsuit are stored in the central file, and cannot be removed from the central file area without formally checking them out. Employees are encouraged to make a copy of a document rather than remove it from the central file area. This reduces the dreaded risk of losing an original document.

Using this system, when an original document arrives, a copy is made immediately and placed in the working file for that case. The lawyers and paralegals use the working file for their daily activities on the case. This way they can make notations on the documents when necessary and avoid the risk of losing an original document.

ANALYSIS OF AVAILABLE REMEDIES

At the conclusion of the informal investigation and before you draft the complaint, review all the facts carefully. Determine whether the facts support the legal theories that you formulated before the investigation. Consider also whether you now have a basis for any additional theories for recovery.

 POINTER: Remember that FRCivP 11 requires attorneys to certify that the facts and law support the claim or defense asserted. A thorough investigation of the facts and review of the applicable law is essential to ensure that your attorney-paralegal team has complied with FRCivP 11.

Now that you have determined the claims that you will assert in the complaint, you should review the various remedies that may be available for your client. As we discussed in Chapter 1, the plaintiff is seeking a remedy for the wrong allegedly done by the defendant. Various remedies are available, and you must determine what remedies to request in the complaint. You should request every type of relief that is appropriate. The Federal Rules of Civil Procedure allow parties to amend their complaints to include additional requests for relief after the complaint is filed. However, it is best to try to include all appropriate forms of relief in the complaint so that the litigation will be more focused.

Money Damages

As you recall from Chapter 1, **money damages** means monetary compensation that one party pays to another party for losses and injuries suffered. We will discuss damages in the context of damages owed to the plaintiff by the defendant, but remember that other parties besides defendants may have to pay damages. For instance, a plaintiff may be ordered to pay damages to a defendant as a result of a counterclaim filed by the defendant.

Money damages constitute the most frequently requested relief and are of several types.

Compensatory Damages. As the term implies, the aim of **compensatory damages** is to compensate the injured party for the harm caused by another party. For instance, when a plaintiff is owed money by a defendant pursuant to a promissory note that the defendant failed to honor, the plaintiff requests compensation in the amount due on the promissory note. For another example, consider the Chattooga case. Here the Equal Employment Opportunity Commission asks that Sandy Ford be compensated for the damage done by Chattooga Corporation's alleged unlawful employment practices. Specifically, the complaint requests that Sandy Ford be awarded back pay, with interest, as compensation for being terminated from her job.

Compensatory damages are often termed either ''general'' or ''special'' damages. This is especially true in personal injury litigation. **Special damages** are awarded for items of loss that are specific to the particular plaintiff. Examples of special damages in a personal injury lawsuit include compensation for lost wages and medical expenses. Consider the Wesser case. Mr. Wesser's special damages include his hospital bills, doctor bills, pharmacy bills, and loss of wages while his injuries prevented him from working. Special damages can be measured accurately. Mr. Wesser can produce the bills from the hospital, doctors, and pharmacy, and can prove what he would have earned each day that he could not work. Such specific proof of the exact amount of special damages is usually required at trial.

General damages are awarded to the plaintiff as compensation for less tangible losses, such as pain and suffering, temporary or permanent disability, and temporary or permanent disfigurement. In contrast to special damages, general damages do not lend themselves to precise calculation. For instance, pain and suffering is a rather nebulous concept that encompasses factors such as the plaintiff's inability to engage in the activities and hobbies enjoyed before the injury. The emotional trauma of disfigurement is another aspect of pain and suffering. There is no fixed rule to calculate such general damages and thus there is wide latitude for the amount that may be awarded.

Punitive Damages. Punitive damages, sometimes called exemplary damages, are sometimes awarded to a plaintiff when a defendant's conduct was malicious, wanton or fraudulent. As the term implies, punitive damages are intended to punish defendants for egregious conduct and to make examples of them. These damages are based on the public policy of punishing the defendant. Punitive damages are awarded in addition to the compensatory damages and frequently equal three to five times the amount of the compensatory damages.

Equitable Remedies

Sometimes a plaintiff's loss cannot be compensated by monetary damages. **Equitable remedies** protect parties when monetary damages cannot make them whole. A common equitable remedy is an **injunction**. An injunction is a court order directing a person to refrain from doing an act.[2] As explained in Chapter 1, if your neighbor is about to cut down your trees, you do not want compensation in the form of the timber value of the trees. Rather, you want an order to prevent the neighbor from cutting down the trees.

A lawsuit may request both monetary damages and injunctive relief, as in the Chattooga case. Here the Equal Employment Opportunity Commission requests that Sandy Ford be awarded back pay as compensation for being unlawfully terminated from her job. The EEOC also requests injunctive relief in the form of an order restraining Chattooga Corporation from retaliating against employees in the future. Ford may also request reinstatement—that is, to be put back on her job. This too is a form of equitable relief.

Another common equitable remedy, **specific performance**, arises in disputes about contracts. When one party to a contract fails to comply with its provisions, and money damages cannot compensate the other party, the court can order specific performance of the contract. This means that the party in breach of the contract is ordered to comply with its terms. Specific performance is appropriate when a party contracts to sell something that is unique, such as a parcel of real estate or a painting. Even if the other party were awarded damages in the amount of the agreed purchase price, that party would not be adequately compensated because the object to be sold is unique.

Attorney's Fees

As a rule, the prevailing party is not entitled to payment of attorney's fees by the other party, in the absence of a statute providing for payment. Many plaintiffs have the mistaken notion that if they win, the other party has to pay their (the plaintiffs') attorney's fees. This question frequently arises at the initial client conference, and it is important that clients understand the general rule from the outset.

In analyzing the remedies to request in the complaint, it is important to check applicable federal and state statutes to determine whether they provide for an award of attorney's fees to the prevailing party. An example of a federal statute is the Magnuson-Moss Act, which concerns consumer products warranty protection.[3] A provision for attorney's fees appears in some statutes concerning civil rights and employment discrimination, including Title VII. Some state consumer-protection statutes also provide for attorney's fees. Other examples might include child support and alimony.

INFORMAL INVESTIGATION

Assume that your attorney/paralegal team has conducted sufficient legal research to determine the bases for Mr. Wesser's lawsuit. You have reviewed the applicable statutes and case law for a product liability case. You know that Mr. Wesser has three basic grounds for his claim: negligence, breach of express warranty, and breach of implied warranty. You will assert these grounds against the manufacturer of the blanket, Woodall Shoals, and the seller, Second Ledge. Now you must determine whether the facts support the legal theories on which you wish to base Mr. Wesser's claims.

Organizing the Informal Investigation

Before you begin interviewing witnesses and gathering extensive documentation, it is crucial to organize your investigation. You must determine the facts your client must prove and identify all the defendants against whom you will assert claims.

Determining the Facts Your Client Must Prove. Before the commencement of a lawsuit, it is imperative that you determine through informal investigation whether you can gather enough evidence to prove Mr. Wesser's claims. You have already researched the substantive law of negligence, breach of express warranty, and breach of implied warranty. From your research you determine the **essential elements** of each claim. An essential element is a fact that the law requires to exist in order to establish a particular cause of action. To establish a cause of action against Woodall Shoals based on express warranty, you must establish these essential elements: Woodall Shoals made an express warranty that the blanket would remain free of electrical and mechanical defects for a certain period of time and that the fire occurred within the warranted period; that the blanket contained electrical and mechanical defects that caused it to ignite; and that this breach of express warranty caused the injuries and property damage sustained by Mr. Wesser.

You must also establish that the facts support a claim for breach of express warranty by Second Ledge and for breach of implied warranty and negligence by both Woodall Shoals and Second Ledge. You may find it helpful to make a chart showing the bases for your claims against all defendants. See Figure 5-3 for an example. The chart for the Wesser case is fairly simple, because there are only two defendants, and the bases for the claims are the same. However, you may encounter more complex litigation with numerous defendants and several claims, with some claims asserted against some defendants but not others. In such an instance, a chart becomes indispensable.

FIGURE 5-3   BASES FOR CLAIMS

Defendant #1

Woodall Shoals Corporation

1. Breach of express warranty
2. Breach of implied warranty of merchantability
3. Negligence in design and manufacture

Defendant #2

Second Ledge Stores, Incorporated

1. Breach of express warranty
2. Breach of implied warranty of merchantability
3. Negligence in inspection and failure to warn

Determining All Defendants.   In the initial client interview, Ms. Heyward was able to ascertain the identity of both defendants in the Wesser case. Mr. Wesser knew the store at which he purchased the blanket and had his receipt. He also had the warranty that came with the blanket when he purchased it. Our investigation is greatly simplified by the fact that these important documents were not destroyed in the fire.

However, the determination of all parties to join as defendants is not always so simple. This is particularly true when the defendants are corporate entities. It is important to name the corporate defendant correctly. Many corporate entities are subdivisions of other corporations, and the names can be confusing. Some preliminary investigation may be necessary just to name the proper defendants. There are many sources for this information. The office of the secretary of state for the relevant state may be able to provide the information. Directories of corporations are available in public and university libraries.

It is important to join all parties necessary to resolve the dispute entirely. The Federal Rules of Civil Procedure seek to resolve in one lawsuit all claims arising out of the same transaction or occurrence. This is why the rules allow defendants to assert counterclaims and codefendants to assert cross-claims, as explained in Chapter 7. Rule 19 of the Federal Rules of Civil Procedure has the same goal. It provides that "those who are united in interest must be joined as plaintiffs or defendants. . . ." FRCivP 19 also allows the court to summon parties to appear in the action when a complete determination cannot be made without their presence.

However, the Federal Rules of Civil Procedure also allow the court to drop from the action a party that is not properly joined in the lawsuit. FRCivP 21 states that ". . . on such terms as are just parties may be dropped or added by order of the court on motion of any party or on its own initiative at any stage of the action." Thus it is important that you name the proper defendants. If you join the wrong party, you will incur delay and expense as a result of the motions and arguments as to whether that entity is a proper party to the action.

Consider the Rules of Evidence. As we discussed in Chapter 4, the attorney makes the final decision on objections to the admission of evidence. However, it is important for paralegals to consider the rules of evidence throughout the litigation process, even at this early stage. You may come across some evidence that is clearly protected by a privilege. You may find some evidence that does not appear to be relevant. You will not want to waste time on evidence that clearly cannot be used.

Bear in mind that when you encounter evidence that you think may not be admissible, you should discuss the matter with the attorney before abandoning that route of investigation. The attorney may know of an exception that would make the evidence admissible. Even if the evidence is not admissible, the attorney may want to pursue the avenue of investigation in hope that it will lead to other evidence that is admissible.

Sources of Information

When you investigate the facts of a case, the sources of information are limited only by your imagination. Your first and most obvious source is your client, who can tell you many facts and provide you with important documents. From there the sources of information depend to some degree on the type of case you are investigating. For instance, in an automobile accident case, you will obtain police reports and records from the Department of Motor Vehicles, interview witnesses, visit the scene of the accident, obtain emergency room and hospital records, and perhaps obtain an official weather report from the United States Weather Bureau.

In different types of litigation, your evidence will come from different sources. If a case involves the division of marital property in connection with a divorce, for instance, your goal will be to identify and determine the value of the marital assets. Thus the evidence you gather in a property division case will be quite different from the evidence in a case involving a car accident, where you will seek to determine who caused the event. In the property division case, you will gather data and analyze the parties' bank accounts, credit cards, and other financial records; you will investigate the salaries and education of the parties and analyze business records if either is self-employed. You will obtain appraisals of real estate and valuations of personal property.

Although the sources of information can vary from case to case, three sources serve as a starting point in most cases: the client, witnesses, and physical and documentary evidence.[4] And in many cases, including products liability cases, there is an important fourth source: expert witnesses. An expert witness, as we noted in Chapter 4, is one whose scientific, technical, or specialized knowledge can help persons without such knowledge to understand and form a conclusion about a technical fact in issue.

A chart of the facts you must prove and the sources for obtaining those facts can be useful. Refer to Figure 5-4, which concerns proving the claim based on breach of express warranty by Woodall Shoals in the Wesser case. The chart has three headings: elements of the claim, sources of information, and method to obtain information. When you set out your evidence in a simple form like this, any lack of evidence to support a particular element of your claim becomes very clear. Examine Figure 5-4 and you see that the Wesser case involves evidence obtained from the three major sources—the client, witnesses, and physical and documentary evidence. The Wesser case also involves expert witnesses, which is typical of a product liability case.

FIGURE 5-4   CHART OF FACTS TO PROVE

Woodall Shoals: Express Warranty

Elements of Claim	Sources of Information	Method of Obtaining Information
1. Woodall Shoals made express warranty that blanket would be free of defects for 2 years from date of purchase	Written warranty that came with blanket	Obtain from Mr. Wesser
2. Electric blanket had defects, which constitutes breach of warranty	Fire inspector Fire inspector's report Remains of blanket and control Inspection of scene Testing and testimony of expert witnesses	Interview Request by letter Obtain from Mr. Wesser Go to scene Retain expert witnesses
3. Defects caused Mr. Wesser's damages	Same as #2	

The Client.   It is important to obtain from the client as much information as possible, as soon as possible. The client is usually your first source of information. During the initial client interview the attorney/paralegal team obtains the basic facts of the case. You must then move quickly to locate and interview witnesses and preserve physical evidence. Regular contact with the client is necessary to get additional and updated information.

Clients themselves can provide many facts, so begin by letting your client tell about the incident in his or her own words. Learning exactly what happened and who was involved helps you determine the parties to the lawsuit and the liability issues. Ask clients to describe the damages they suffered—injuries to themselves and their property, lost wages, and any other damages. This requires thorough questioning about the client's injuries and the degree to which they may be permanent. The degree of pain and suffering the client has experienced is also important. Make sure your client obtains documents to prove the damages—hospital records, doctors' bills, home or car repair bills, and so on. Inquire about your client's insurance coverage, and determine whether your client has any knowledge about the other parties' insurance coverage.

In addition to gathering the pertinent facts of the case, you should obtain basic information about the client. That is, you need to know the client's age, education, occupation, salary, assets, and family history. This information helps to direct future settlement negotiations. If a client has been permanently disabled by an injury, for example, his or her age, education, salary, and work history are crucial to calculate future lost earnings.

POINTER: In all interviews with the client, but especially in the initial client interview, you should assess the client's credibility as a witness. You may observe the client's demeanor and delivery and make notes for reference in trial preparation. For instance, if a client hesitates inordinately before responding to questions, you should point this out, because a halting witness is less credible than one who answers promptly. The information on the client's background can also help you assess the client's credibility as a witness. A person who has been a police officer for seven years will be more credible to a jury than will a person who has been a drug dealer.

It is also necessary to question the client about possible defenses that may be raised. For instance, in the Wesser case, the lawyer can be sure that the defendants will assert the defense of contributory negligence. They will claim that Mr. Wesser misused the electric blanket by folding it, tucking it in, or leaving objects on top of it, contrary to the written warnings in the package when the blanket was purchased. Thus the attorney/paralegal team must find out whether Mr. Wesser did anything to affect the condition of the blanket.

Another important topic to cover with clients is whether there are witnesses to the matters in question. There may be all sorts of potential witnesses, depending on the nature of the case. Compare the Wesser case and the Chattooga case. In the Wesser case there were no eyewitnesses to the outbreak of the fire except Mr. Wesser, who was at home alone. In the Chattooga case, however, there are many witnesses who can testify about the events in question. If you interview Sandy Ford, she can tell you the name of the employee whom she helped to file a claim with the Equal Employment Opportunity Commission against Chattooga Corporation. She can tell you the name of her supervisor, the human resources personnel involved in her hiring and termination, and other employees who may have knowledge of the events surrounding her termination. If Chattooga Corporation is your client, you can find out from Sandy Ford's supervisor and human resources personnel the same basic information about persons with knowledge of the events surrounding Sandy Ford's termination.

Witnesses. Once you have determined the identity of some prospective witnesses, it is time to plan interviews with them. Careful preparation for witness interviews is crucial. Consider the type of information you need from each one. You are still in the initial investigation stage, and you are seeking information about what happened and who was involved.

Usually you will have a general idea of what a witness knows. For instance, you may know that Sandy Ford's supervisor told her in the employment interview the importance of being able to gain security clearance to enter nuclear power plants. You should consider the specific information you need from this witness. For example, you may elicit the details of Ford's statements regarding her criminal record, both before and after the discovery of her felony conviction. You may ask about the supervisor's knowledge of the claim filed with the EEOC by Ford's friend, including the names of other persons with knowledge of these events.

As you interview the initial witnesses, try to ascertain the names of others who are familiar with the events of the case. One method for eliciting witnesses' full knowledge is to let them tell everything they know, in their own words, before asking very specific questions. This may lead to new evidence and additional witnesses you would not otherwise learn about. Allowing a witness to ramble a bit may prove to be time well spent.

As you do with clients, obtain information about the witness's personal background—occupation, residence, family. This will help you assess how effective the witness is likely to be. Someone described as an excellent potential witness may turn out to be such an excessive talker that you decide against calling him or her to testify.

Physical and Documentary Evidence. In addition to testimony of witnesses, a wide array of other types of evidence may be necessary to prove your client's claim. The types of physical and documentary evidence you use depend upon the nature of the lawsuit. In litigation concerning a breach of contract, for instance, the contract itself is a crucial piece of evidence. In an action to collect on a promissory note, you need the promissory note with the debtor's original signature. You also need records of how much the debtor paid on the note and how much is still owed. The lender can provide accounting records to establish the amount paid. You may obtain the debtor's canceled checks, although you may need to do this through the formal discovery process, because the debtor is an adverse party and may not be willing to cooperate initially.

 POINTER: For most lawsuits, you cannot obtain all the documents you need in the informal investigation stage, especially documents in the possession of an adverse party. However, you usually can obtain the documents through formal discovery procedures later in the litigation process.

Documentary evidence is very important in personal injury litigation, both to establish liability and to determine the client's damages. Consider the Wesser case. One crucial document is the written warranty that came with the blanket. Reports on any tests conducted to find defects in the electric blanket are important.

Tests may also show that Mr. Wesser damaged the blanket and was himself negligent. The written report of the fire inspector is an important piece of evidence to help establish liability, because the inspector may state an opinion about the cause of the fire.

Documentary evidence is crucial to establish the amount of the damages in a personal injury lawsuit. Reports and office notes of Mr. Wesser's treating physicians help to establish the extent of his injuries, including pain and suffering. Hospital and emergency-room records are necessary evidence, and may also include results of laboratory tests performed in the hospital and physical therapy notes.

Documentary evidence in the Chattooga case would include Sandy Ford's employment application and employment contract, as well as other personnel records of Chattooga Corporation, such as notations in her file regarding the discovery of her felony conviction. It would also be necessary to obtain court records of her conviction.

Physical evidence refers to objects involved in the incident in question, such as the electric blanket in the Wesser case. Physical evidence can be crucial in many personal injury cases and includes such objects as the cars involved in an accident or a gun involved in an accidental shooting. In the case of an airplane crash, the remains of the plane and the "black box" recording what happened prior to the crash are crucial pieces of evidence. As with other types of evidence, the types of physical evidence vary according to the type of case you are litigating.

It is important to preserve physical evidence for use at trial. Some types of evidence cannot be maintained in the same condition from the time of an accident until the time of trial. For example, parties will have their cars repaired long before a trial is held or even before a settlement is reached.

Photographs are an important way of recording the condition of an object just after the incident in question. Photographs are also important to preserve the appearance of the scene of an accident. For instance, in an automobile accident case, photographs record the way an intersection looked, including such important features as skid marks left from the accident. Photographs of Mr. Wesser's burn injuries prior to plastic surgery can help to prove the extent of his injuries and his degree of pain and suffering.

Many types of physical evidence can emerge as you investigate a case. It is important to be alert for new pieces of evidence as you interview witnesses and review written reports.

Expert Witnesses. Expert witnesses are not necessary in every type of case. For instance, in a case involving an automobile accident where the issue is whether the light was red or green, you do not need an expert witness to make that determination. A person who just happened to be standing near the intersection when the accident occurred can tell a jury what color the light was. Compare this case with one involving an automobile accident in which only one car was involved where the issue is whether the car was negligently designed. This issue calls for a conclusion by a person with specialized knowledge and experience in such matters as automobile design, metallurgy, and accident reconstruction.

Expert witnesses are almost always used in lawsuits involving products liability and medical malpractice, as well as in other types of lawsuits involving negligence. Expert witnesses are important to establish that a product had defects and that the defects caused a person's damages. This is true in the Wesser case. As the outline of evidence in Figure 5-4 shows, an expert witness will be used to establish that the electric blanket had defects during the period that it was still under warranty and that these defects caused the damages suffered by Mr. Wesser in the fire in his house.

How to Locate Expert Witnesses. The attorney determines whether expert witnesses will be used in a particular lawsuit. Paralegals often help to locate appropriate experts. There are numerous ways to locate expert witnesses. First, find out whether the attorney on your team prefers any particular expert. If not, check with other litigators in the firm to see whether they know of any appropriate experts. If no one in your firm knows an appropriate expert, ask litigators in other law firms.

If no one has personal knowledge of an expert you can use, there remain many ways to locate one. Many trial lawyer associations, such as the American Trial Lawyers Association, have directories and information about experts. There are numerous publications and directories in libraries. You may consult the Technical Advisory Service for Attorneys (TASA), an organization that maintains references for experts. Local universities may have faculty with expertise in the type of issue in your case.

Professional publications such as bar association newsletters and the *ABA Journal* contain advertisements for expert witnesses. You will find it interesting to scan the ads to get an idea of the various types of expert witnesses available. Experts are available for subjects ranging from aquatic safety to vehicle crashworthiness.

Consider the types of expert witnesses that may be helpful in the Wesser case. An expert on electrical wiring and malfunctions could help establish that a defect in the electric blanket caused the fire. An expert who analyzes the readability of warning labels may be useful to examine the warnings that accompanied the blanket. A neurologist may analyze the physical aspects of Mr. Wesser's pain and suffering, and a plastic surgeon may testify about surgical procedures on scar tissue that may be necessary in the future. A rehabilitation expert may be useful to discuss the requirements and cost of therapy. Mr. Wesser's treating physicians may also be able to provide opinions about these matters.

POINTER: Our discussion focuses on finding expert witnesses to testify at trial. However, it is often advisable to have an expert review a case even before the attorney decides to undertake representation. This is particularly true with complex cases, especially ones that involve issues with which the attorney has not dealt before.

Obtaining the Evidence

The method by which you obtain a piece of evidence depends on the type of evidence involved. You interview the client and witnesses to find out facts. You obtain physical evidence at the scene or from a person who has it in his or her possession already. To gather documentary evidence, you send a letter to the person and request the information you need. These are not the only means through which to obtain evidence, but they are the most common and therefore the focus of our discussion. There are special considerations involved in each of these three methods.

As you begin to gather physical and documentary evidence, remember that you need to establish your client's damages as well as the elements of the claim. The chart in Figure 5-4 is a guide for gathering evidence to prove the elements of the claim. It is helpful to prepare another chart to plan the evidence necessary to prove the amount of your client's damages. Examine Figure 5-5, which outlines the information you need to prove Mr. Wesser's damages. You are now ready to obtain your evidence through the informal investigation process.

FIGURE 5-5 PROOF OF MR. WESSER'S DAMAGES

Type of Damage	Sources of Proof	Method of Obtaining Information
1. Property damage	List of items damaged Value of items damaged	Mr. Wesser Receipts for purchase Comparative replacement values Appraisals
2. Personal injury	Hospital records, including emergency room, lab tests, physical therapy notes	Letter to request, with authorization
	Ambulance report	Letter to request, with authorization
	Records and reports of treating physicians, including follow-up office visits	Letter to request, with authorization
	Testimony of Mr. Wesser re pain	Interview
	Testimony of friends and relatives re pain and restrictions of activities	Interviews
3. Lost wages	Records of employer re salary and days missed	Letter to request, with authorization

Interviews. Our discussion applies to interviews both of clients and of witnesses. Although certain factors are unique to each, both types of interviews require the basics of adequate preparation and interview techniques.

While the general discussion applies to both attorneys and paralegals, the role of the paralegal may be different from that of the attorney in certain respects. For example, the attorney normally conducts the initial client interview. As a paralegal, you may well be present during the interview; this is a good idea, because the client can meet you and feel comfortable sharing confidential information with you from the beginning. If anyone takes notes during the interview, it may be you. This frees the attorney to maintain eye contact and observe the person's demeanor. Initial witness interviews, however, may be conducted by paralegals by themselves, as may some follow-up interviews with both clients and witnesses.

Preparing for the Interview.   The primary differences between client interviews and witness interviews occur in preparing for the interview and in arranging to talk with the person. Preparation for the initial client interview is fairly straightforward. You know the general nature of the client's problem, and one of your primary aims in the initial client interview is to gather as much general information as possible by giving clients the opportunity to explain their problems in their own words. Before the interview you may want to make a list of the facts that you seek to elicit during the interview. Your firm may have developed checklists of the information you should obtain for a particular type of case. Review the checklist before the interview. Determine whether you need to ask the client to bring any documents to the interview. For instance, you would ask Mr. Wesser to bring the written warranty, any medical records and bills he may already have, information about his insurance coverage, and any information he has about the potential defendants, including their insurance coverage.

Preparation for witness interviews is different in the sense that the most important element of preparation is to obtain as much information as possible before the interview. You should ascertain before the interview what facts the witness might know and then direct your questions to elicit more specific information. As with clients, you may first let witnesses tell the story in their own words and then ask more specific questions. However, you may encounter witnesses who are unwilling to share much information, so be prepared to drag the information out with a series of questions. Witnesses are not generally as willing as clients to grant subsequent interviews, so you may be forced to elicit the information in one short session. Obviously, preparation is very important. Flexibility is also important in witness interviews, however, because it is more difficult to predict how a witness will respond to questioning.

Arranging the Interview.   Making arrangements to talk with your client is easy, because clients are willing, in fact eager, to talk. You can simply telephone to arrange a time for the client to come your law firm. On the other hand, witnesses may not be so eager to talk. Some witnesses may seek to avoid you simply because they do not want to get involved. Other witnesses may be openly hostile because their sympathies lie with the other side. If a witness does not want to meet with you, you may have to surprise the witness with a visit at home or after work. Remember that the witness has no obligation to talk with you, and you can arrange a deposition during the discovery phase if the witness will not talk with you. The witness may be more willing to talk if you promise to keep the interview short, which is another reason to plan your questions beforehand.[5]

 POINTER: Remember that ethical considerations pertain to talking with witnesses. As we discussed in Chapter 2, if a person is represented by counsel, you must obtain counsel's consent to talk with that person. If the person is unrepresented, the attorney/paralegal team has an ethical obligation to inform the person of the attorney's interest in the case and/or to advise the person to obtain counsel. See Chapter 2 for a review of these obligations.

Conducting the Interview. Certain interview techniques apply to interviews with both clients and witnesses. First, you should try to put people at ease so that they are more willing to share information. Assure the clients that what they say is confidential. Conduct the interview in a friendly, private setting. Do not allow interruptions, especially by telephone. Try to empathize with the person. Remember that some persons will have never talked with a lawyer or paralegal before and may feel intimidated.

One common approach is to start with a general question that allows the person to tell the story in his or her own words. Your first question may simply be "What happened?" After the person gives you a narrative of events, ask specific questions and establish the precise events in chronological order.[6]

Throughout the interview, determine how sure the persons are of the information they relate and the conclusions they reach. They may be absolutely certain the stoplight was red, or they may admit that they were actually too far away to tell. If one person gives a version of events different from the other evidence you have gathered, you may tell the person that his or her version is different and find out why.

Be sure to gather background information from witnesses as well as clients. As we discussed, occupation and other personal factors can affect a witness's credibility. During interviews you can personally observe the clients and assess their demeanor. You and the attorney can compare your impressions afterwards.

Preserving Information from the Interview. For several reasons it is important to preserve the information you gain in any interview. You cannot expect to remember indefinitely everything each person tells you, and as you prepare for discovery and trial you will need to review their prior statements. You may need exact statements to impeach the testimony of those who change their versions of the facts later.

When paralegals interview without attorneys present, they must be able to pass the information on to the attorneys. There are several methods to preserve the contents of an interview. You may actually tape-record a person's statements. However, you must obtain the person's permission beforehand, or the recording may not be admissible in evidence. You may take notes during the interview, but this is advisable only if the attorney is doing the actual questioning. If you are questioning the person and taking notes at the same time, you may lose your rapport. If you cannot take notes during the interview, you may make notes directly after the interview. You may take a dictaphone with you and dictate a memo. Whatever method you use, record your notes immediately after the interview, or you may forget crucial information.

Another method is to have the witness sign a statement. In some instances, a witness may write out and sign a short statement during the interview. Another approach is to send the witness a letter recounting the statements made, and request that the witness sign an acknowledgment at the bottom of the letter, signifying that the letter accurately reflects the statements made.

Physical and Documentary Evidence. Review Figures 5-4 and 5-5, which show the types of physical and documentary evidence we will use to establish the essential elements of our claim and the amount of damages in the Wesser case. The types of evidence needed in the Wesser case are fairly typical of evidence used in many types of cases and thus will serve as the focus of our discussion. Remember that there are many other kinds of evidence used in other types of lawsuits.

Obtaining and Preserving Physical Evidence. In the Wesser case, our primary piece of physical evidence consists of the remains of the electric blanket and its control. Assume that this evidence is still in Mr. Wesser's possession. We need only to obtain it from him. However, it is possible that by the time a client retains an attorney, the evidence may be in another person's possession. For instance, Mr. Wesser's insurance adjuster may have already picked up the blanket and control for inspection or testing, or the fire inspector may have it. Usually the person who has the evidence will allow others not only to inspect the evidence but even take it to conduct their own inspection and testing.

However, the evidence may be in the hands of an adverse party or its agent, such as its insurance adjuster. If the adverse party does not consent to your examining the evidence, you may obtain the evidence by use of a subpoena later in the litigation process. A **subpoena** is a document issued by the clerk of court directing persons to appear in a certain place at a certain time, to testify or to produce documentary or physical evidence in their possession.[7] The preferable method is to obtain the evidence by agreement as early as possible. If you have to wait for the issuance of a subpoena, the evidence may be in a different condition from its condition just after the incident in question. Further, not having immediate access hinders your informal investigation, because you do not have all the evidence needed to develop the case.

As we mentioned earlier, it is important to preserve evidence in the condition it was in at the time of the incident in question. However, it is not always possible to keep a damaged piece of property in the same condition until a trial several months later. For instance, Mr. Wesser does not want to leave his home unrepaired until after the trial, yet the jury may want to see the damage. The attorney/paralegal team must obtain photographs of the house directly after the fire. You may want to hire a professional photographer to ensure clear pictures.

When the attorney/paralegal team is able to get the actual physical evidence, it is important to preserve the evidence in its original condition. It is also important to document how, when, and where you got the evidence, plus the steps you take to preserve it. The evidence is usually labeled and kept in a protective container of some sort. Often a person other than the attorney or paralegal obtains, labels, and prepares the evidence for storage. In the Wesser case, this may be done by the fire inspector. It is imperative that the physical evidence be properly stored. You must ensure that it is not damaged or even lost. If you must let another person have temporary possession, such as an expert witness who wishes to conduct tests, document carefully when the expert took the evidence and what the expert did to it. The preservation of physical evidence and associated recordkeeping is known as establishing the **chain of custody**. In order to admit the evidence, the attorney must show the location of the evidence from the time of the accident to trial, to prove that the evidence has not been altered. This is crucial for the admission of the physical evidence at trial.

Obtaining and Preserving Documentary Evidence.   In most lawsuits there is far more documentary evidence than physical evidence. As Figures 5-4 and 5-5 show, numerous documents are necessary to establish the essential elements of a claim and the amount of a client's damages.

Most forms of documentary evidence are obtained by sending a letter requesting the documents. Consider the fire inspector's report. You need only to send the inspector a simple letter requesting a copy of the report and explaining why you need it. See Figure 5-6 for a sample letter.

Other request letters require more explanation. This is particularly true when you obtain medical records. When you request hospital records, you may need to specify the exact documents—discharge summary, patient's chart, results of all laboratory tests, physical therapy notes, x-ray reports, admission notes, and final bill for services rendered.

Even more specificity is necessary when you request information from the client's treating physicians. Be sure to specify whether you want the doctor's office records only, or a narrative of the client's treatment and prognosis as well. You may actually want different information at different stages of the litigation. At the informal investigation stage, the final outcome of the client's treatment may not be known. Thus you may simply request the doctor's office notes to date. As you approach serious settlement discussions and trial, you want more detailed information on the client's condition: in addition to the doctor's most recent office notes you want the doctor's narrative report explaining the treatment rendered, the results of the treatment, and an opinion as to any permanent disability the client may have.

Doctors may charge a minimal fee for sending copies of their office notes. However, a detailed medical narrative report may cost several hundred dollars. Thus it is imperative that you plan the information you want at each stage of the litigation and indicate the information specifically in your letter.

Medical records are confidential; therefore you need written authorization from the client before the records may be released. See Figure 5-7 for a sample authorization. You may have the client sign several authorizations at the initial interview so that you can request records as needed without having the client

FIGURE 5-6   LETTER REQUESTING DOCUMENTARY EVIDENCE

Heyward and Wilson
401 East Trade Street
Charleston, North Carolina 28226-1114
704/555-3161

Mr. John Misenheimer
Fire Inspector
Charleston Fire Department
509 Savannah Street
Charleston, North Carolina 28226-5431

Dear Mr. Misenheimer:

We represent Mr. Bryson Wesser in a lawsuit against the manufacturer and seller of an electric blanket. It appears that defects in the electric blanket caused a fire at his home on January 3, 1987.

We understand that you inspected the scene at 115 Pipestem Drive, Charleston, North Carolina, immediately after the fire. We would appreciate your forwarding a copy of your report of that investigation. We would appreciate any other information that you have concerning the cause of this fire. If you have questions or require further information, please contact me. We look forward to your prompt response.

Sincerely yours,
Heyward and Wilson

Leigh J. Heyward
Attorney at Law

FIGURE 5-7   SAMPLE AUTHORIZATION FOR RELEASE OF INFORMATION

This is to authorize you to furnish, release and give to Heyward and Wilson, Attorneys at Law, any and all information or opinions which they may request regarding my mental or physical condition and to allow them to see or copy any records which you may have regarding my treatment.

Yours very truly,

Subscribed and sworn to before me
this _____ day of _____, 19____.

_____
Notary Public

My commission expires: _____

come to the office to sign additional authorizations. However, some institutions require that the authorization be signed fairly recently, usually within 60 days of the request. Some institutions require that the client's signature be notarized, so it is a good idea to go ahead and have all the authorization forms notarized. You may encounter certain medical establishments that require you to use their own authorization form, so you will have to write or call to obtain their form. This is particularly true when you request mental health records, especially from a state institution.

POINTER: Any time you request documents from an institution, find out that institution's procedures before sending the request letter. In particular, find out the charge for sending the documents and whether the institution requires payment before releasing the records. You can easily obtain the information by telephoning the medical records department of a hospital. When you call a doctor's office, you may talk to a nurse or the office manager.

Employment records are also confidential, so again you need written authorization from the client to release the records. As with medical records, specify the precise information you need. For Mr. Wesser you would need to know his position, salary, and number of days lost from work after the fire. In the Chattooga case, the Equal Employment Opportunity Commission would request Sandy Ford's employment application, information about her position and salary, and other information about her termination. Bear in mind that some of this information may be privileged. Other information may be obtainable, but only through the formal discovery process. The EEOC will also request other information, such as further facts about the employee whom Sandy Ford assisted in filing a claim against Chattooga Corporation. The amount of information obtainable at the informal investigation stage depends on the parties involved. In some administrative procedures, such as EEOC claims, a fact-finding conference and a written statement of the employer's position are required. Thus in this type of procedure you may be able to obtain more information in the early stages of investigation than in other types of cases.

POINTER: Your law firm will most likely have on file standard authorization forms and request letters used frequently in litigation. This can save you a great deal of time and help ensure that you request all the proper information. However, you should review the forms to be sure that they include the information you need in a particular case. If you have a case unlike any the firm has handled before, you may need to modify the existing forms.

Once you receive the documents requested, review them immediately. There may be facts that you need to clarify. You may not be able to read handwritten treatment notes. You should resolve immediately any ambiguities, so that your investigation can proceed on the right course. You may require some assistance to understand some documents. For instance, medical personnel use many abbreviations. However, the abbreviations are usually standard ones, and you can use a book that explains medical abbreviations to lay persons.

Informal investigation may take many hours of the attorneys' and paralegals' time. Some lawsuits require more investigation than others do. Be tenacious and obtain all the information you can, so that your attorney/paralegal team can draft pleadings that accurately state the facts and the law. Never forget the ethical obligations to investigate fully.

ENDNOTES

1 For a discussion of the documents that are filed with the court to support motions, see Chapter 8, pp. 197–200.
2 The procedure for obtaining injunctive relief is discussed in Chapter 6, pp. 156–157.
3 15 U.S.C. §2310(d) (2).
4 For further discussion of informal investigation, especially the use of litigation charts, *see* Thomas A. Mauet, *Fundamentals of Pretrial Techniques* 17 ff. (1988).
5 *Id.* at 41.
6 *Id.* at 42.
7 See Chapter 9, p. 253, and Chapter 10, pp. 289–291 for further explanation of subpoenas in the discovery process and at trial.

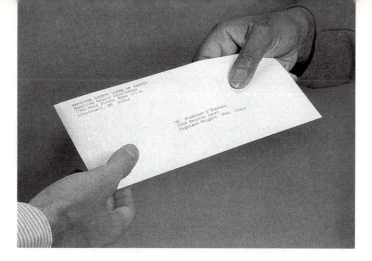

6 COMMENCEMENT OF THE PLAINTIFF'S LAWSUIT

 LITIGATION EXTRACT: We have completed our informal fact investigation and are ready to prepare the documents to commence Mr. Wesser's lawsuit against Woodall Shoals and Second Ledge. The first document we will prepare is the complaint, which states our allegations against the defendants and the relief Mr. Wesser is seeking. We also prepare a summons, which is delivered to the defendants to succinctly inform them of the lawsuit and of their need to respond within 20 days. For the use of the clerk of court, we prepare a civil cover sheet, which helps the clerk keep track of the litigation. Finally, we discuss service of process, to be sure we use the proper method for delivering the complaint and summons to the defendants.

INTRODUCTION

You have developed your case and are ready to initiate the lawsuit. Now you need to draft a complaint and prepare a summons. You will likely have to prepare other documents too, depending on the type of lawsuit you are filing.

The **complaint** is the first pleading filed in a lawsuit. **Pleadings**, as you know by now, are the formal documents in which the parties allege their claims and defenses. As we discussed in Chapter 1, the Federal Rules of Civil Procedure set forth the rules that govern pleadings in federal trial courts, including the rules for serving the pleadings on the other party. The Federal Rules of Civil Procedure ensure that each party knows the facts that the other party alleges against it by requiring that the pleadings state the claims and defenses in comprehensible language and that each party receive proper notice so that it can prepare an adequate response.

AN INTRODUCTION TO PLEADINGS

The discussion in this chapter focuses on the Federal Rules of Civil Procedure. You may wish to review the discussion in Chapter 1 of the importance of the Federal Rules of Civil Procedure and the other rules that will govern our litigation of the Wesser case in federal court. The Federal Rules of Civil Procedure most pertinent to the format and content of complaints and other pleadings will be discussed here. Recall that the federal local court rules will also affect our pleadings by regulating paper size, how many copies to file, and other small details.

Purpose and Types of Pleadings

Rule 7 of the Federal Rules of Civil Procedure states the types of pleadings that are allowed:

> . . . a complaint and an answer; a reply to a counterclaim denominated as such; an answer to a cross-claim, if the answer contains a cross-claim; a third-party complaint if a person who was not an original party is summoned under the provisions of Rule 14; and a third-party answer, if a third-party complaint is served.

Do not worry about counterclaims, cross-claims, and third-party pleadings for now. They will be explained in Chapter 7. For now just remember that a party can assert a claim in a complaint, counterclaim, cross-claim, or third-party complaint, and that Rule 8 of the Federal Rules of Civil Procedure states the general rule for the content of all four pleadings that set forth a claim.

FRCivP 8 requires a "short and plain statement of the claim showing the pleader is entitled to relief." Rule 8 reflects the concept of **notice pleading**, the concept on which the Federal Rules of Civil Procedure are based. Thus a pleading should not contain an excruciatingly detailed recitation of every fact in the case. The fine details can be ascertained in the discovery process. (See Chapter 9.) Notice pleading requires only that a party state a claim concisely and plainly enough for the other party to know the nature of the claim and prepare a defense. Rule 9 sets forth the exceptions to notice pleading and cites the matters that must be alleged specifically. For example, when alleging fraud, "the circumstances constituting fraud . . . shall be stated with particularity."

Format for Pleadings

Pleadings follow a standard format, and it is important to follow the rules governing format.

Rule 10 Requirements. Rule 10 of the Federal Rules of Civil Procedure governs the general format for pleadings. FRCivP 10 specifies the following requirements for all pleadings. They are shown in Figure 6-1.

1. *Caption.* FRCivP 10 requires a caption with the following information:
   a) The name of the court in which the action is filed.
   b) The title of the action. This is the designation of the parties in the lawsuit. It is imperative that each party be named correctly. This is

FIGURE 6-1   FRCivP PLEADING FORMAT

**IN THE DISTRICT COURT OF THE UNITED STATES
FOR THE MIDDLE DISTRICT OF NORTH CAROLINA
CHARLESTON DIVISION
CIVIL NO.: C-C-90-129-M**

MICHAEL ANDREOU AND ELIZABETH ANDREOU,
                     Plaintiffs,

                          -vs-   *COMPLAINT*

U.S. DEPARTMENT OF JUSTICE, IMMIGRATION
AND NATURALIZATION SERVICE,
                            Defendant

Jurisdiction

1. This court has jurisdiction pursuant to 8 U.S.C. Section 1329, 28 U.S.C. Section 1331, and 18 U.S.C. Section 2201.

2. Plaintiff Elizabeth Andreou is a citizen of the United States and a resident of Charleston, North Carolina.

3. Plaintiff Michael Andreou is a citizen of Greece and a resident of Charleston, North Carolina.

4. Defendant Immigration and Naturalization Service ("INS") is an agency of the United States Department of Justice empowered to implement the Immigration and Nationality Act, 8 U.S.C. Section 1101 *et seq.*

simple when only an individual is the party. However, you must take particular care when a party is a corporation or a party is acting on behalf of another party. For example, the title of a complaint when Mr. Wesser sues two corporations for injuries must be specific, as shown in Figure 6-2.

   c) The name of the pleading. Designate the type of pleading: "COMPLAINT," "ANSWER," and so on.

   d) File number. When you file a complaint with the clerk of court, the complaint is stamped with a file number, sometimes referred to as a civil action number. This file number must be on all subsequent pleadings.

   2. *Numbered Paragraphs.* Allegations and defenses must be set forth in numbered paragraphs. As far as practicable, each paragraph should contain a statement of a single set of circumstances. This requirement furthers the objective of plain and simple statements of the facts.

FIGURE 6-2   SPECIFIC TITLE IN SUIT INVOLVING CORPORATION

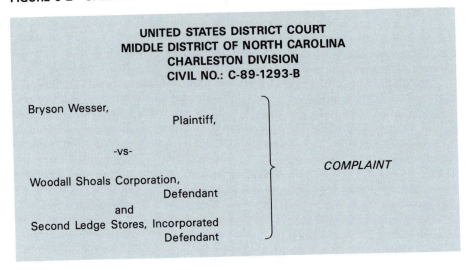

UNITED STATES DISTRICT COURT
MIDDLE DISTRICT OF NORTH CAROLINA
CHARLESTON DIVISION
CIVIL NO.: C-89-1293-B

Bryson Wesser,

                                    Plaintiff,

          -vs-

Woodall Shoals Corporation,
                              Defendant   *COMPLAINT*
                        and
Second Ledge Stores, Incorporated
                              Defendant

Other Requirements. There are other format requirements in addition to the Rule 10 requirements. The attorneys who sign the pleadings should include their addresses and telephone numbers. This appears on the last page of the pleadings beneath the signatures. See Figure 6-3. Always consult your local rules for further format requirements. A good example is Rule 106(a) of the Rules of Practice and Procedure of the United States District Court for the Middle District of North Carolina, which reads as follows:

> **Form.** Pleadings, motions, briefs, and other papers submitted for filing must be typewriten, printed, or legibly handwritten on letter size paper. The pages shall be unfolded and shall be bound at the top and numbered at the bottom, without manuscript cover. Typewritten documents should be double spaced or one and one-half spaced. Mechanically reproduced copies which bear an original signature will be accepted by the court as originals.

FIGURE 6-3   ATTORNEY'S ADDRESS AND TELEPHONE NUMBER

7. That the plaintiff be granted such other and further relief as to the Court may

    seem just and proper.

                                    Leigh J. Heyward
                                    Attorney for the Plaintiff
                                    Heyward and Wilson
                                    401 East Trade Street
                                    Charleston, NC 28226-0114
                                    Telephone: (704) 555-3161

You should be able to determine format requirements by examining recently filed pleadings in other files. However, you can never go wrong by checking the rules.

Signing and Verification of Pleadings

Signing by Attorney. Rule 11 of the Federal Rules of Civil Procedure requires that one attorney of record must sign every pleading, motion, and other paper filed with the court. Parties unrepresented by counsel sign their own pleadings.

When attorneys sign a pleading, they signify that they have read the pleading and made ''reasonable inquiry'' into the law and the facts of the case and have determined that there is a sound basis in fact and in law for the pleading and that the pleading is not interposed for delay. If a pleading is signed in violation of FRCivP 11, the court may impose sanctions on the signing attorney. Obviously, the attorney will make every effort not to violate Rule 11. The paralegal can help by assisting with a thorough investigation and detailed preparation.

Verification of Pleadings by a Party. Pleadings in federal court actions and state actions usually do not require verification by the client. However, in some cases the party is required by law to verify the pleading. For example, some states require parties to verify by affidavit every pleading filed in a divorce action or child custody action. Clients verify a pleading by signing an affidavit stating that they have read the pleading and everything in it is true. See Figure 6-4. The purpose of client verification is to prevent the filing of false claims.

FIGURE 6-4   CLIENT VERIFICATION

NORTH CAROLINA

MECKLENBURG COUNTY

Carla M. Suarez, being duly sworn, deposes and says that she is the plaintiff in this action; that she has read the foregoing Complaint and knows the contents thereof; that the same is true to her own knowledge except as to those matters and things therein stated on information and belief and as to those she believes it to be true.

_____
Carla M. Suarez

Subscribed and sworn to before me
this the _____ day of _____,

_____
            Notary Public

My commission expires: _____

(Seal)

PREPARING THE COMPLAINT

The **complaint** is the initial pleading filed by the plaintiff. The filing of a complaint commences a lawsuit under Rule 3 of the Federal Rules of Civil Procedure. In state court a lawsuit does not commence until the summons and complaint are served on the defendant.

Substance of a Complaint

FRCivP 8(a) requires three substantive elements for every complaint:

1. A statement of jurisdiction;
2. A short and plain statement of the claim showing that the plaintiff is entitled to relief; and
3. A demand for judgment for the relief sought.

Like all pleadings, the complaint must follow the format requirements discussed above. This means that the complaint will include the name of the court, the names of the parties, and the title of the pleading (''Complaint''). These appear at the top of the complaint, in the caption. See Figures 6-1 and 6-2.

After the statement of jurisdiction, statement of the claim, and demand for judgment come the name, address, and signature of the plaintiff's attorney. In addition, if the plaintiff wants a jury trial, the complaint must contain a demand for jury trial. It may be helpful at this point to turn to the Appendix and examine the complaint in the Wesser case. Now that you are familiar with the format for a complaint, we will examine the substantive elements of the complaint.

Allegation of Jurisdiction. As we discussed in Chapter 3, federal courts are courts of limited jurisdiction. Thus it is crucial to establish in the complaint that the federal court has subject matter jurisdiction to hear the plaintiff's case. The safest method to ensure that you allege jurisdiction correctly is to follow the language in the Appendix of Forms to the Federal Rules of Civil Procedure.[1] See Figure 6-5, which reprints Official Form 2. This form illustrates how to allege jurisdiction based on diversity of citizenship, a federal question, the existence of a question arising under a particular statute, and jurisdiction based on the admiralty or maritime character of the claim. The complaints in the Wesser and Chattooga cases also illustrate jurisdictional allegations in federal court actions. See also Figure 6-1, which illustrates the caption and jurisdictional allegations where individuals sue an agency of the United States government.

Statement of Claims. Now you are ready to state the facts that show that the plaintiff is entitled to judicial relief. A claim for which courts can grant relief is called a *cause of action*. Common causes of action include negligence, breach of contract, and fraud. Courts do not provide a remedy for every wrong or unkind act that a person directs against another person. For instance, Mr. Green may wish to sue Mr. Jones, because Mr. Jones called him a ''nincompoop'' when they were arguing about presidential candidates. Mr. Green may approach a lawyer and state that he wants to sue Mr. Jones for intentional infliction of emotional distress. However, most states require a showing of ''outrageous conduct'' in order to recover damages for intentional infliction of emotional distress. Because Mr.

FIGURE 6-5 FRCivP OFFICIAL FORM 2

Form 2. Allegation of Jurisdiction

(a) Jurisdiction founded on diversity of citizenship and amount.

Plaintiff is a [citizen of the State of Connecticut][1] [corporation incorporated under the laws of the State of Connecticut having its principal place of business in the State of Connecticut] and defendant is a corporation incorporated under the laws of the State of New York having its principal place of business in a State other than the State of Connecticut. The matter in controversy exceeds, exclusive of interest and costs, the sum of fifty thousand dollars.

(b) Jurisdiction founded on the existence of a Federal question and amount in controversy.

The action arises under [the Constitution of the United States, Article _____, Section _____]; [the _____ Amendment to the Constitution of the United States, Section _____]; [the Act of _____, _____ Stat. _____ U.S.C., Title _____, § _____]; [the Treaty of the United States (here describe the treaty)],[2] as hereinafter more fully appears. The matter in controversy exceeds, exclusive of interest and costs, the sum of fifty thousand dollars.

(c) Jurisdiction founded on the existence of a question arising under particular statutes.

The action arises under the Act of _____, _____ Stat. _____; U.S.C., Title _____, § _____, as hereinafter more fully appears.

(d) Jurisdiction founded on the admiralty or maritime character of the claim.

This is a case of admiralty and maritime jurisdiction, as hereinafter more fully appears. [If the pleader wishes to invoke the distinctively maritime procedures referred to in Rule 9(h), add the following or its substantial equivalent: This is an admiralty or maritime claim within the meaning of Rule 9(h).]

Green cannot establish that Mr. Jones's conduct was outrageous, he cannot establish an essential element of the tort termed intentional infliction of emotional distress.

Rule 8(e) of the Federal Rules of Civil Procedure states that a "pleading shall be simple, concise, and direct." This means you use plain English. Use short sentences and common words. This is not the place for *whereas* and *witnesseth*. Keeping the complaint simple means that you do not go into excruciating detail. You need only allege the facts necessary to establish that the plaintiff is entitled to the relief requested and to give the defendants fair notice of the claims against them.

Essential Elements of the Cause of Action. A complaint that does not properly allege a cause of action must be amended or dismissed. You must be careful to allege sufficient facts to establish all the essential elements of the plaintiff's cause of action. An **essential element** is a fact that the law requires to exist in order to establish a particular cause of action. For example, to establish a cause of action for fraud, a plaintiff must establish the essential elements of fraud, which include a false representation of a present or past fact made by the defendant, action

by the plaintiff in reliance upon the defendant's statement, and damage resulting
to the plaintiff from such misrepresentation.[2] Thus, if the plaintiff did not rely
on the defendant's false statement, the plaintiff cannot establish fraud. As a further example, if the plaintiff sues the defendant for failure to pay a $5,000 prom-
issory note, the plaintiff must allege that the defendant signed and delivered to
the plaintiff a promissory note in the amount of $5,000 payable with 8 percent
interest on August 2, 1989; that the defendant has failed to pay the note as
promised; and that the defendant owes to the plaintiff the amount of the note
and interest.

There are several ways to ensure that you allege the essential elements of
a claim. First you must know the substantive law of the jurisdiction. You can
find the essential elements by researching the case law in the jurisdiction and
by examining successful pleadings in similar cases. You can probably find similar
pleadings in files in your law firm. You can also examine files in the clerk's office
that involved the same substantive law. Second, use the Appendix of Forms to
the Federal Rules of Civil Procedure. For example, Official Form 3 (Figure 6-6)
shows a complaint on a promissory note. The Appendix of Forms to the Federal
Rules of Civil Procedure contains examples of legally sufficient pleadings.

FIGURE 6-6   FRCivP OFFICIAL FORM 3

Form 3. Complaint on a Promissory Note

1. Allegation of jurisdiction.
2. Defendant on or about June 1, 1935, executed and delivered to plaintiff a promissory note [in the following words and figures: (here set out the
note verbatim)]; [a copy of which is hereto annexed as Exhibit A]; [whereby
defendant promised to pay to plaintiff on order on June 1, 1936 the sum of
_____ dollars with interest thereon at the rate of six percent per annum].
3. Defendant owes to plaintiff the amount of said note and interest.
Wherefore plaintiff demands judgment against defendant for the sum of
_____ dollars, interest, and cost.

Signed: _____

Attorney for Plaintiff.

Address: _____

Your state rules of civil procedure may also contain an appendix of legally
sufficient pleadings. You can also find books of forms in your law library. However,
you must be cautious in using generic forms. Be sure to tailor the forms carefully
to the specific facts of your case rather than following the forms blindly.

POINTER: If you have a complex case or a case dealing with a novel question of
law, you will work closely with your supervising attorney. It may be your task to
obtain a copy of the pleadings filed in a similar case in a distant state. The office
of the clerk of court for that judicial district can copy the pleadings and mail them
to you. Call the clerk's office to find its procedure for sending copies. Find out
its mailing address, how much it charges per page for copies, and whether it will

bill you or you will need to send a check. Then follow up with a letter stating precisely the documents you need copied and enclosing a check, if necessary.

State Separate Claims in Separate Counts. Often a plaintiff relies on more than one legal theory as a basis for recovery of damages. For example, Mr. Wesser bases his claim on three theories: negligence, implied warranty, and express warranty, which are all set out in separate counts. Setting out the claims in separate counts clarifies the legal theories on which the plaintiff is proceeding.

When there are multiple defendants, as in the Wesser case, specify which count applies to which defendant. For instance, in the Wesser complaint, Count One is "BREACH OF EXPRESS WARRANTY BY THE DEFENDANT WOODALL SHOALS" and Count Four is "BREACH OF EXPRESS WARRANTY BY THE DEFENDANT SECOND LEDGE."

Note also that when you begin a second count, you incorporate by reference the allegations in the first count.

Demand for Judgment (Prayer for Relief). The third component that FRCivP 8 requires is the demand for judgment, sometimes called the prayer for relief. FRCivP 8 provides that a plaintiff may request relief of several different types or alternative forms of relief. (You learned about these in Chapter 5.) The demand for judgment should state each type of relief sought in a separate numbered paragraph. Be sure to specify every type of relief sought, including general damages, punitive damages, special damages, equitable remedies, interest, costs, and attorney fees. Figure 6-7 illustrates a demand for judgment. A demand for judgment in the Wesser complaint appears in the Appendix.

Demand for Jury Trial. A party must specifically request a jury trial. If a party fails to request a jury trial within the time limits set out in FRCivP 38, the party waives the right to a jury trial. In state court actions, you must check the state rules of procedure and other statutes concerning the right to jury trial, and comply with the state requirements for requesting a jury trial. A party is not entitled to a jury trial in every type of lawsuit. For instance, there is no right to jury trial in a lawsuit alleging a violation of Title VII, as in the Chattooga case. The right to a jury trial is a subject paralegals will frequently need to discuss with the attorneys on their team.

Rule 38 of the Federal Rules of Civil Procedure allows a party to demand a jury trial in the complaint or in writing at any time after the complaint is filed but "not later than 10 days after the service of the last pleading directed to such issue." If your supervising attorney has already determined that your client will request a jury trial, it is best to include the demand for jury trial in the complaint itself. The jury trial request is placed in a conspicuous place, often in the caption below the word "Complaint" or at the end of the complaint. The Wesser complaint (see Appendix) contains an example of the request for a jury trial.

Signing and Verification

Remember to insert after the demand for judgment the name, address, and telephone number of the attorney who signs the complaint. Double-check to be

FIGURE 6-7   A DEMAND FOR JUDGMENT

> **WHEREFORE**, the plaintiff prays the Court:
>
> 1. That the plaintiff be granted custody of Laura Hanford and Tom Hanford, the minor children of the parties.
>
> 2. That the defendant be ordered to pay into the Office of the Clerk of Superior Court for Montgomery County, North Carolina, a reasonable amount of child support to be disbursed to the plaintiff for the care and maintenance of the parties' minor children.
>
> 3. That the Court enter a preliminary injunction restraining the defendant from dissipating or disposing of any of the marital assets of the plaintiff and defendant, until such time as said property can be equitably distributed by the Court pursuant to G.S. 50-20 and 50-21.
>
> 4. That the costs of this action be taxed against the defendant, including reasonable attorney's fees for counsel for the plaintiff.
>
> 5. That the plaintiff be granted such other and further relief as to the Court may seem just and proper.
>
> (Note: This demand for judgment is offered for example only and is not intended to be an inclusive demand under the law of any state.)

sure the attorney actually signs the complaint. If client verification is required, insert the signed verification. See Figure 6-4. The simplest way to include the client verification is to put it on a separate sheet of paper and attach it after the page with the attorney's signature.

Exhibits and Appendices

Often you will attach exhibits to prove the plaintiff's claim. Some states require that a copy of the written contract on which a breach of contract action is based be attached as an exhibit. Other common exhibits include copies of promissory notes, warranty statements, invoices, and correspondence. Place the exhibits after the signature and verification pages. Retain the original of each document to be presented at trial.

Refer to the exhibit in the body of the complaint. For example:

> 11. The defendant signed and delivered to the plaintiff a promissory note in the amount of $5,000 payable with 8% interest on August 2, 1988, a copy of which is attached as Exhibit A and incorporated herein.

POINTER: If the complaint requires numerous exhibits, it is helpful to insert a List of Exhibits before the first exhibit. It is also helpful to tab each exhibit so the judge will not have to plow through 50 exhibits in her search for the crucial Exhibit 35.

PREPARING OTHER DOCUMENTS NECESSARY TO INITIATE THE LAWSUIT

The complaint is not the only document necessary to commence the lawsuit. In this section we discuss the other documents that you must prepare.

The Summons

The **summons** is the form that accompanies the complaint and explains in simple terms to the defendants that they have been sued and that they must file an answer with the clerk of court. The summons further states that if the defendants fail to file an answer in the allotted time, a **default judgment** will be entered against them. (See Chapter 7 for a discussion of default judgments.) The summons and the complaint are then served on the defendants. Service of process means that the summons and complaint are delivered to the defendants in accordance with FRCivP 4, which we will discuss throughout the remainder of this chapter. When the defendants have been properly served, the court has personal jurisdiction over them.

First the paralegal must learn how to prepare the summons. FRCivP 4(b) establishes the contents of the summons. Read Rule 4(b) of the Federal Rules of Civil Procedure, but remember that you can acquire the proper preprinted form for the summons from the clerk of court. Your law firm will probably have blank summonses on file for your use. Look at Figure 6-8, a preprinted summons form. You will see that you fill in (1) the name of the court district, (2) the name of the plaintiff(s), (3) the name of the defendant(s), (4) the address of the defendant to whom this particular summons is addressed, (5) the name and address of the plaintiff's attorney, and (6) the number of days the defendant has to file his answer. The Return of Service appears on the back of the Summons. Leave the Return of Service blank because the person who serves the complaint and summons completes this section.

When you go to the clerk's office to file the lawsuit, the clerk will "issue" the summons, as directed in FRCivP 4(a). This means that the clerk signs and dates the summons, stamps it with the court seal, and fills in the case number assigned to the lawsuit. Prepare enough summonses so that the clerk can issue one summons for each defendant, at least one summons for your file, and the proper number of summonses that the clerk's office requires for its file.

The Civil Cover Sheet

The civil cover sheet is another preprinted form that you must prepare and file with the complaint. This is a very simple form. Examine Figure 6-9, which shows a civil cover sheet filled out for the Wesser case. The civil cover sheet provides information the clerk of court needs to docket the case—that is, to record basic information about the lawsuit and keep track of its progress. You need to file one civil cover sheet. Be sure to keep at least one copy. Before filing the civil cover sheet, check to be sure that the attorney signed and dated the form.

FIGURE 6-8   A COMPLETED SUMMONS

AO 440 (Rev. 5/85)   Summons in a Civil Action ⊕

United States District Court

_____Middle_____ DISTRICT OF _____North Carolina_____

Bryson Wesser

v.

Woodall Shoals Corporation and
Second Ledge Stores, Incorporated

SUMMONS IN A CIVIL ACTION

CASE NUMBER:

TO: (Name and Address of Defendant)

Woodall Shoals Corporation
300 West Blvd.
New York, NY 10019-0987

YOU ARE HEREBY SUMMONED and required to file with the Clerk of this Court and serve upon

PLAINTIFF'S ATTORNEY (name and address)
    Leigh J. Heyward
    Heyward and Wilson
    401 East Trade Street
    Charleston, NC 28226-1114

an answer to the complaint which is herewith served upon you, within ___twenty (20)___ days after service of
this summons upon you, exclusive of the day of service. If you fail to do so, judgment by default will be taken
against you for the relief demanded in the complaint.

_____   _____
CLERK   DATE

_____
BY DEPUTY CLERK

FIGURE 6-8   A COMPLETED SUMMONS (Cont.)

AO 440 (Rev. 5/85)   Summons in a Civil Action

RETURN OF SERVICE	
Service of the Summons and Complaint was made by me[1]	DATE
NAME OF SERVER	TITLE

Check one box below to indicate appropriate method of service

☐ Served personally upon the defendant. Place where served : _____
_____   _____

☐ Left copies thereof at the defendant's dwelling house or usual place of abode with a person of suitable age and discretion then residing therein.
Name of person with whom the summons and complaint were left: _____

☐ Returned unexecuted: _____
_____
_____

☐ Other (specify): _____
_____
_____

STATEMENT OF SERVICE FEES		
TRAVEL	SERVICES	TOTAL

DECLARATION OF SERVER

I declare under penalty of perjury under the laws of the United States of America that the foregoing information contained in the Return of Service and Statement of Service Fees is true and correct.

Executed on _____   _____
              Date   *Signature of Server*

              _____
                    Address of Server

1) As to who may serve a summons see Rule 4 of the Federal Rules of Civil Procedure.

To be completed by process server

FIGURE 6-9   CIVIL COVER SHEET

JS 44
(Rev 07/86)
CIVIL COVER SHEET

The JS 44 civil cover sheet and the information contained herein neither replace nor supplement the filing and service of pleadings or other papers as required by law, except as provided by local rules of court. This form, approved by the Judicial Conference of the United States in September 1974, is required for the use of the Clerk of Court for the purpose of initiating the civil docket sheet. (SEE INSTRUCTIONS ON THE REVERSE OF THE FORM.)

I (a) PLAINTIFFS

Bryson Wesser

DEFENDANTS

Woodall Shoals Corporation
Second Ledge Stores, Incorporated

(b) COUNTY OF RESIDENCE OF FIRST LISTED PLAINTIFF __Watauga__
(EXCEPT IN U.S. PLAINTIFF CASES)

COUNTY OF RESIDENCE OF FIRST LISTED DEFENDANT _____
(IN U.S. PLAINTIFF CASES ONLY)
NOTE: IN LAND CONDEMNATION CASES, USE THE LOCATION OF THE TRACT OF LAND INVOLVED

(c) ATTORNEYS (FIRM NAME, ADDRESS, AND TELEPHONE NUMBER)

Leigh J. Heyward
Heyward and Wilson
401 East Trade Street
Charleston, NC 28226-1114

ATTORNEYS (IF KNOWN)

Not yet known

II. BASIS OF JURISDICTION (PLACE AN × IN BOX ONLY)

- ☐ 1 U.S. Government Plaintiff
- ☐ 2 U.S. Government Defendant
- ☐ 3 Federal Question (U.S. Government Not a Party)
- ☒ 4 Diversity (Indicate Citizenship of Parties in Item III)

III. CITIZENSHIP OF PRINCIPAL PARTIES (PLACE AN × IN ONE BOX FOR PLAINTIFF AND ONE BOX FOR DEFENDANT)
(For Diversity Cases Only)

	PTF	DEF		PTF	DEF
Citizen of This State	☒1	☐1	Incorporated or Principal Place of Business in This State	☐4	☐4
Citizen of Another State	☐2	☒2	Incorporated and Principal Place of Business in Another State	☐5	☐5
Citizen or Subject of a Foreign Country	☐3	☐3	Foreign Nation	☐6	☐6

IV. CAUSE OF ACTION (CITE THE U.S CIVIL STATUTE UNDER WHICH YOU ARE FILING AND WRITE A BRIEF STATEMENT OF CAUSE. DO NOT CITE JURISDICTIONAL STATUTES UNLESS DIVERSITY)   28 U.S.C. 1332

Personal injury and property damage caused by defective electric blanket

V. NATURE OF SUIT (PLACE AN × IN ONE BOX ONLY)

CONTRACT	TORTS	FORFEITURE/PENALTY	BANKRUPTCY	OTHER STATUTES
☐ 110 Insurance	**PERSONAL INJURY** / **PERSONAL INJURY**	☐ 610 Agriculture	☐ 422 Appeal 28 USC 158	☐ 400 State Reapportionment
☐ 120 Marine	☐ 310 Airplane / ☐ 362 Personal Injury—Med Malpractice	☐ 620 Food & Drug	☐ 423 Withdrawal 28 USC 157	☐ 410 Antitrust
☐ 130 Miller Act	☐ 315 Airplane Product Liability / ☒ 365 Personal Injury—Product Liability	☐ 630 Liquor Laws		☐ 430 Banks and Banking
☐ 140 Negotiable Instrument	☐ 320 Assault, Libel & Slander / ☐ 368 Asbestos Personal Injury Product Liability	☐ 640 R R & Truck	**PROPERTY RIGHTS**	☐ 450 Commerce/ICC Rates/etc.
☐ 150 Recovery of Overpayment & Enforcement of Judgment	☐ 330 Federal Employers Liability	☐ 650 Airline Regs	☐ 820 Copyrights	☐ 460 Deportation
☐ 151 Medicare Act	☐ 340 Marine	☐ 660 Occupational Safety/Health	☐ 830 Patent	☐ 470 Racketeer Influenced and Corrupt Organizations
☐ 152 Recovery of Defaulted Student Loans (Excl Veterans)	☐ 345 Marine Product Liability / **PERSONAL PROPERTY**	☐ 690 Other	☐ 840 Trademark	☐ 810 Selective Service
☐ 153 Recovery of Overpayment of Veteran's Benefits	☐ 350 Motor Vehicle / ☐ 370 Other Fraud	**LABOR**	**SOCIAL SECURITY**	☐ 850 Securities/Commodities/Exchange
☐ 160 Stockholders' Suits	☐ 355 Motor Vehicle Product Liability / ☐ 371 Truth in Lending	☐ 710 Fair Labor Standards Act	☐ 861 HIA (1395ff)	☐ 875 Customer Challenge 12 USC 3410
☐ 190 Other Contract	☐ 360 Other Personal Injury / ☐ 380 Other Personal Property Damage	☐ 720 Labor/Mgmt. Relations	☐ 862 Black Lung (923)	☐ 891 Agricultural Acts
☐ 195 Contract Product Liability	/ ☐ 385 Property Damage Product Liability	☐ 730 Labor/Mgmt. Reporting & Disclosure Act	☐ 863 DIWC (405(g)) / ☐ 863 DIWW (405(g))	☐ 892 Economic Stabilization Act
REAL PROPERTY	**CIVIL RIGHTS** / **PRISONER PETITIONS**	☐ 740 Railway Labor Act	☐ 864 SSID Title XVI / ☐ 865 RSI (405(g))	☐ 893 Environmental Matters
☐ 210 Land Condemnation	☐ 441 Voting / ☐ 510 Motions to Vacate Sentence	☐ 790 Other Labor Litigation	**FEDERAL TAX SUITS**	☐ 894 Energy Allocation Act
☐ 220 Foreclosure	☐ 442 Employment / ☐ 530 Habeas Corpus	☐ 791 Empl. Ret. Inc. Security Act	☐ 870 Taxes (U.S. Plaintiff or Defendant)	☐ 895 Freedom of Information Act
☐ 230 Rent Lease & Ejectment	☐ 443 Housing/Accommodations / ☐ 540 Mandamus & Other		☐ 871 IRS—Third Party 26 USC 7609	☐ 900 Appeal of Fee Determination Under Equal Access to Justice
☐ 240 Torts to Land	☐ 444 Welfare / ☐ 550 Civil Rights			☐ 950 Constitutionality of State Statutes
☐ 245 Tort Product Liability	☐ 440 Other Civil Rights			☐ 890 Other Statutory Actions
☐ 290 All Other Real Property				

VI. ORIGIN (PLACE AN × IN ONE BOX ONLY)

- ☒ 1 Original Proceeding
- ☐ 2 Removed from State Court
- ☐ 3 Remanded from Appellate Court
- ☐ 4 Reinstated or Reopened
- ☐ 5 Transferred from another district (specify)
- ☐ 6 Multidistrict Litigation
- ☐ 7 Appeal to District Judge from Magistrate Judgment

VII. REQUESTED IN COMPLAINT: CHECK IF THIS IS A **CLASS ACTION** ☐ UNDER F.R.C.P. 23   **DEMAND $** in excess of $50,000.00   Check YES only if demanded in complaint: **JURY DEMAND:** ☒ YES ☐ NO

VIII. RELATED CASE(S) IF ANY (See instructions):   None   JUDGE _____   DOCKET NUMBER _____

DATE _____   SIGNATURE OF ATTORNEY OF RECORD _____

UNITED STATES DISTRICT COURT

Other Forms

Check the local rules to determine whether the judicial district requires any other forms to accompany the complaint. In state court actions, determine whether the local rules require a civil cover sheet. Many state judicial districts have their own civil cover sheet, which you can obtain from the clerk's office. Your state judicial district may require special forms for certain types of lawsuits. For instance, in an action for child support, the court may require each party to file an Affidavit of Income and Expenses.

You are almost ready to go to the courthouse and file the documents to initiate the lawsuit. First, we must examine the procedure and the documents required for service of process.

SERVICE OF PROCESS

Service of process means delivery of the summons and complaint to the defendant in accordance with Rule 4 of the Federal Rules of Civil Procedure. FRCivP 4 establishes who may serve the summons and complaint and on whom these documents must be served. When the defendant is properly served, the court acquires personal jurisdiction over the defendant.

How Process Is Served

FRCivP 4 provides several methods for service of process. You need to discuss with the attorneys on your team which method is best for each defendant.

Service by Mail. FRCivP 4(c)(2)(C)(ii) provides for service on an individual or corporation by mailing a copy of the summons and complaint to the defendant, together with two copies of a notice and acknowledgment and a return envelope, postage prepaid, addressed to the sender. The **notice and acknowledgment form** must substantially conform with Form 18-A in the Appendix of Forms to the Federal Rules of Civil Procedure. Form 18-A is illustrated in Figure 6-10. If the defendant does not accept service and return the acknowledgment form within 20 days after the date of mailing, other methods of service must be used.

 POINTER: FRCivP 4(c)(2)(C)(ii) states that first-class mail (postage prepaid) is sufficient. However, it is better to send the documents by certified mail, return receipt requested. When you fill out the green card for certified mail, be sure to check the box that says "restricted delivery only." Otherwise, a person at the same address who is not qualified to accept service for the defendant under Rule 4 might sign for the documents, and service of process would not meet the Rule 4 requirements.

Personal Service by a Person Not a Party. FRCivP 4(c)(2)(A) provides that a person who is not a party to the lawsuit and is not less than 18 years of age may serve the summons and complaint on the defendant. The person who serves the defendant completes the Return of Service on the back of the summons. Your law firm may have you serve process on the defendant. Some law firms hire a process server, especially when the defendant lives far away.

FIGURE 6-10   FRCivP OFFICIAL FORM 18-A

Form 18-A. Notice and Acknowledgment for Service by Mail

United States District Court for the Southern District of New York
Civil Action, File Number _____

A.B., Plaintiff
   v.
C.D., Defendant

} *Notice and Acknowledgment
of Receipt of Summons
and Complaint*

NOTICE

To: (insert the name and address of the person to be served.)

The enclosed summons and complaint are served pursuant to Rule 4(c)(2)(C)(ii) of the Federal Rules of Civil Procedure.

You must complete the acknowledgment part of this form and return one copy of the completed form to the sender within 20 days.

You must sign and date the acknowledgment. If you are served on behalf of a corporation, unincorporated association (including a partnership), or other entity, you must indicate under your signature your relationship to that entity. If you are served on behalf of another person and you are authorized to receive process, you must indicate under your signature your authority.

If you do not complete and return the form to the sender within 20 days, you (or the party on whose behalf you are being served) may be required to pay any expenses incurred in serving a summons and complaint in any other manner permitted by law.

If you do complete and return this form, you (or the party on whose behalf you are being served) must answer the complaint within 20 days. If you fail to do so, judgment by default will be taken against you for the relief demanded in the complaint.

I declare, under penalty of perjury, that this Notice and Acknowledgment of Receipt of Summons and Complaint was mailed on (insert date).

_____
Signature

_____
Date of Signature

ACKNOWLEDGMENT OF RECEIPT OF SUMMONS AND COMPLAINT

I declare, under penalty of perjury, that I received a copy of the summons and of the complaint in the above-captioned manner[1] at (insert address).

_____
Signature

_____
Relationship to Entity/Authority
to Receive Service of Process

_____
Date of Signature

Service by United States Marshal. FRCivP 4(c)(2)(C) provides for service by a United States marshal in limited circumstances, namely, on behalf of the United States government and its agencies, on behalf of paupers, and by court order. When a United States marshal completes service of process, form USM-285 (Figure 6-11) is completed and filed with the clerk of court. (For purposes of Figure 6-11, assume that David H. Benedict is Chattooga Corporation's registered agent for service of process.) FRCivP 4(c)(2)(C) also provides that the court may specially appoint a person other than a marshal to serve the summons and complaint.

Person to Be Served

FRCivP 4(d) explains who is the proper person to serve. This differs according to the defendant's status; infants or incompetents, business organizations, and agencies of the United States or state government are served according to specific rules. FRCivP 4(d) states that service shall be made as follows:

(1) **Upon an individual other than an infant or an incompetent person**, by delivering the summons and complaint personally to the defendant or by leaving copies at the defendant's "dwelling place or usual place of abode" with a person of suitable age and discretion who resides there. The summons and complaint may also be delivered to an agent authorized by appointment or by law to receive service.

(2) **Upon an infant or an incompetent person**, in the same manner service would be made under the law of the state in which service is made. This usually means service on a parent or guardian.

(3) **Upon a domestic or foreign corporation, partnership or other unincorporated association**, by delivering a copy of the summons and complaint to an officer, a managing or general agent, or to any other agent authorized by appointment or by law to receive service of process.

POINTER: The secretary of state keeps a record of the person authorized by foreign and domestic corporations to accept service of process. As to other persons authorized by statute to accept service, see the section below on "long-arm statutes."

(4) **Upon the United States**, by delivering a copy of the summons and complaint to the United States attorney for the district in which the action is filed or a clerical employee designated by the United States attorney to accept service. A copy of the summons and complaint must also be served upon the Attorney General in Washington, D.C., by registered or certified mail. If the lawsuit attacks the validity of an action of a United States agency or officer, the agency or officer must also be served by certified or registered mail.

(5) **Upon an officer or agency of the United States**, by serving the United States as in paragraph (4) and by sending a copy of the summons and complaint by registered or certified mail to such officer or agency. If the agency is a corporation, service is made as in paragraph (3).

(6) **Upon a state or municipal corporation or other governmental organization thereof subject to suit**, by delivering a copy of the summons and complaint to the chief executive officer or by service in a manner prescribed by the law of that state.

FIGURE 6-11   FORM USM-285

U.S. Department of Justice *United States Marshals Service*	PROCESS RECEIPT AND RETURN *See Instructions for "Service of Process by the U.S. Marshal" on the reverse of this form.*

PLAINTIFF Equal Employment Opportunity Commission	COURT CASE NUMBER
DEFENDANT Chattooga Corporation	TYPE OF PROCESS Summons/Complaint

SERVE ➤ AT

NAME OF INDIVIDUAL, COMPANY, CORPORATION, ETC., TO SERVE OR DESCRIPTION OF PROPERTY TO SEIZE OR CONDEMN
David H. Benedict, Esq.

ADDRESS *(Street or RFD, Apartment No., City, State and ZIP Code)*
Benedict, Parker & Miller
100 Nolichucky Dr., Bristol, NC 28205-0890

SEND NOTICE OF SERVICE COPY TO REQUESTER AT NAME AND ADDRESS BELOW:

Edward R. Cheng, STA
Equal Employment Opportunity Commission
1301 North Union Street
Charleston, NC 28226-1114

Number of process to be served with this Form - 285	1
Number of parties to be served in this case	1
Check for service on U.S.A.	

SPECIAL INSTRUCTIONS OR OTHER INFORMATION THAT WILL ASSIST IN EXPEDITING SERVICE *(Include Business and Alternate Addresses, All Telephone Numbers, and Estimated Times Available For Service)*:
Fold   Fold

Plaintiff is an agency of the U.S. Government.

Signature of Attorney or other Originator requesting service on behalf of:	☒ PLAINTIFF ☐ DEFENDANT	TELEPHONE NUMBER (704) 555-3000	DATE

SPACE BELOW FOR USE OF U.S. MARSHAL ONLY — DO NOT WRITE BELOW THIS LINE

I acknowledge receipt for the total number of process indicated. *(Sign only first USM 285 if more than one USM 285 is submitted)*	Total Process	District of Origin No.	District to Serve No.	Signature of Authorized USMS Deputy or Clerk	Date

I hereby certify and return that I ☐ have personally served, ☐ have legal evidence of service, ☐ have executed as shown in "Remarks", the process described on the individual, company, corporation, etc., at the address shown above or on the individual, company, corporation, etc., shown at the address inserted below.

☐ I hereby certify and return that I am unable to locate the individual, company, corporation, etc., named above *(See remarks below)*

Name and title of individual served *(if not shown above)*	☐ A person of suitable age and discretion then residing in the defendant's usual place of abode.
Address *(complete only if different than shown above)*	Date of Service / Time / am pm
	Signature of U.S. Marshal or Deputy

Service Fee	Total Mileage Charges *(including endeavors)*	Forwarding Fee	Total Charges	Advance Deposits	Amount owed to U.S. Marshal or	Amount of Refund

REMARKS:

PRIOR EDITIONS MAY BE USED	**1. CLERK OF THE COURT**	FORM USM-285 (Rev. 12/15/80)

POINTER: Rule 4 is quite technical. Review it before attempting service. Especially when the lawsuit involves multiple defendants, you must keep careful records of when service is accomplished. Be sure to keep a close tab on the 20-day limit for service by notice and acknowledgment. Service on a United States government agency requires special care. After the United States attorney, Attorney General of the United States, and the agency have all been served, file an affidavit of service in the format shown in Figure 6-12.

Timeliness of Service of Process. FRCivP 4(j) requires that service of process be accomplished within 120 days of the filing of the complaint. The action against the unserved defendant will be dismissed without prejudice unless good cause is shown for failure to complete service within 120 days. The plaintiff may file a motion with the court requesting additional time to accomplish service.

Service of Process Under State Law. It is imperative that you review your state's rule for service of process. State service of process tends to be similar to Rule 4 of the Federal Rules of Civil Procedure. However, technical differences may exist. Some states may have methods of service not found in FRCivP 4, such as service by publication. In state court actions, it is common for the sheriff of the county in which the defendant lives to serve process.

Long-Arm Statutes. Long-arm statutes provide for personal jurisdiction over persons and corporations that do not reside within the state ("non-residents") by substituted service of process. For example, a nonresident corporation may be served through the secretary of state in the state where the corporation has its principal place of business. Long-arm statutes commonly provide for personal jurisdiction over nonresident persons or corporations who voluntarily transact business in the state, sign contracts in the state, and so on. If your state has a long-arm statute, read it to see the types of activities that submit a defendant to the state's long-arm jurisdiction. As we discussed in Chapter 3, if the defendant has had "minimum contacts" with a state, long-arm jurisdiction is considered to be fair. For guidance, read the case law that defines "minimum contacts."

Proof of Service

After the summons and complaint have been served on the defendants, the documents proving that service has been completed must be filed with the clerk of court. FRCivP 4(g) provides that the person who serves the summons and complaint must "make proof of service thereof to the court promptly and in any event within the time during which the person served must respond to the process." If anyone other than a U.S. marshal serves process, then that person must file an affidavit attesting that service has been effected. The summons itself has a Return of Service on the back, on which the process server indicates the date and the manner in which service was made. See Figure 6-8.

Sometimes, particularly when there are multiple defendants, a separate affidavit is necessary. Figure 6-12 illustrates an affidavit of service when the defendant is a federal agency. Note that the affidavit describes how each defendant

FIGURE 6-12   AFFIDAVIT OF SERVICE

**IN THE DISTRICT COURT OF THE UNITED STATES
FOR THE MIDDLE DISTRICT OF NORTH CAROLINA
CHARLESTON DIVISION
CIVIL NO.: C-C-90-129-M**

MICHAEL ANDREOU AND ELIZABETH ANDREOU,
                                  Plaintiffs,

                    -vs-   *AFFIDAVIT
                                                                            OF SERVICE*

U.S. DEPARTMENT OF JUSTICE, IMMIGRATION
AND NATURALIZATION SERVICE,
                                  Defendant.

The undersigned attorney for the Plaintiffs, being first duly sworn, deposes and says:

1. This is an action for declatory and injunctive relief challenging the constitutionality of 8 U.S.C. Section 1154. The Defendant has been duly served with process in this action, in accordance with Rule 4(d) (4) and (5) of the Federal Rules of Civil Procedure, as described below.

2. On July 3, 1990, the undersigned personally served a copy of the Summons and three copies of the Complaint in this action on Judith K. Wagner, in the Office of the U.S. Attorney in Charleston, North Carolina.

3. On July 3, 1990, the undersigned sent by certified mail, return receipt requested, a copy of the Summons and Complaint in this action to Gene McNary, Commissioner, Immigration and Naturalization Service, 425 "I" Street NW, Washington, DC 20536. The copy of the Summons and Complaint were in fact received on July 6, 1990, as evidenced by the Return Receipt attached as Exhibit "A."

FIGURE 6-12   AFFIDAVIT OF SERVICE (Cont.)

4. On July 3, 1990, the undersigned sent by certified mail, return receipt requested, a copy of the Summons and Complaint in this action to Richard Thornburg, Attorney General, United States Department of Justice, B-27 13th and Constitution Ave. NW, Washington, DC 20530. The copy of the Summons and Complaint were in fact received on July 6, 1990, as evidenced by the Return Receipt attached as Exhibit "B."

This the _____ day of July, 1990.

_____

Leigh J. Heyward
Attorney for the Plaintiff
Heyward and Wilson
401 East Trade Street
Charleston, NC 28226-0114
704-555-3161

Sworn to and Subscribed before me

this the _____ day of _____,

1990.

_____

Notary Public

My Commission Expires: _____

(SEAL)

was served. Here the U.S. Attorney's office was personally served, and proof of this will appear on the back of the summons, which will be filed simultaneously with the affidavit. The U.S. Attorney General and the Immigration and Naturalization Service were served by certified mail, and the return receipts from the postal service are attached as exhibits to the affidavits. Note that FRCivP 4(g) provides that when service is effected by use of notice and acknowledgment (FRCivP 4(c)(2)(C)(ii)), the acknowledgment must be filed to prove service.

THE MECHANICS OF FILING THE LAWSUIT

You have now prepared the forms necessary to file the lawsuit—the complaint and the summons. You have also determined the proper manner to serve the summons and complaint on the defendant and prepared the necessary forms. You are ready to go to the clerk of court's office to file the lawsuit. It is helpful to prepare a checklist of the items you need to take. Until you have gained experience filing lawsuits, review the documents with your supervising attorney or another paralegal in your firm. Double-check all documents for accuracy and signatures. To file the lawsuit in federal court, you need the following items:

1. The original complaint, with enough copies for each defendant, for the clerk's files (check local rules), and a copy for your file.
2. The original summons, with enough copies for each defendant to be served and a copy for your file.
3. A check for the filing fee.
4. The civil cover sheet, with a copy for your file.
5. If process will be served by a United States marshal, take Form USM-285 and a check for the service fee.

The clerk will stamp the complaint and copies "filed," stamp a date, and assign a civil case number. Some district courts assign the judge at this time. The clerk of court will issue the summons and return the summons for service on the defendants. The clerk will check over and retain the civil cover sheet.

You can also mail the complaint, summons, and other necessary documents to the clerk for filing. This is convenient if your office is in a different city from the court. If you mail the documents, send a short cover letter asking the clerk to file the complaint and return the copies with a "file-stamp." Also enclose a self-addressed, postage prepaid return envelope. The clerk will go through the same process and return the summons and copies of the summons and complaint to you.

If you serve process by mail, mail to each defendant a copy of the complaint, a summons, two copies of the Notice and Acknowledgment for Service by Mail (Form 18-A), and a self-addressed, stamped return envelope. For personal service, deliver the summons and complaint to the person who will serve process. Remember to file the documents to prove service of process.

The filing procedure in state court is generally the same, except that most often the sheriff or other appropriate law enforcement officer serves the summons and complaint. If you do serve process by mail, be sure to file an affidavit of service after service has been accomplished.

INJUNCTIONS

The litigation process takes months, sometimes years, to reach a conclusion and determine the relief that each party will get. However, in some cases your client needs immediate relief. In some situations a party will lose property forever unless a court quickly enters an order directing another party to leave the property alone. When a client needs an immediate court order directing the other party to refrain from some act, you must have ready to file with the complaint the documents seeking an injunction.

An **injunction** is a court order directing a person to refrain from doing an act. The classic example of a situation appropriate for injunctive relief is the boundary dispute involving 100-year-old trees. If Ms. Taylor's neighbor is about to cut down these trees, it is appropriate for Ms. Taylor to seek injunctive relief from the court to prevent her neighbor from cutting down the trees.

Distinguishing a Temporary Restraining Order from a Preliminary Injunction

Both a temporary restraining order (TRO) and a preliminary injunction provide injunctive relief. Injunctive relief is considered equitable relief—that is, relief appropriate when a party shows that money damages will not protect her rights. Both are governed by Rule 65 of the Federal Rules of Civil Procedure. A TRO can be issued only when a party establishes that she will suffer immediate and irreparable harm; it is issued immediately and normally is valid for only ten days. The TRO preserves the parties' rights until the court can hold a hearing to determine whether the injunctive relief should be continued. If the court elects to continue injunctive relief, the court issues a preliminary injunction, which preserves the parties' rights until the issues can be determined at trial.

Procedure for Obtaining a Temporary Restraining Order and Preliminary Injunction

FRCivP 65(b) provides that a court can issue a TRO *ex parte*—that is, without a hearing at which both parties are present. However, the attorney must try to give notice of the TRO request to the other party. The plaintiff must also post a bond to protect the defendant in case it is later determined that the defendant was wrongfully enjoined.

An application for a TRO and preliminary injunction must be submitted along with the complaint. It is customary to combine the application for TRO and preliminary injunction in the same application, because a hearing must be held on the preliminary injunction as soon as possible after a TRO is issued. Thus the title will be "Application for Temporary Restraining Order and Preliminary Injunction." The application sets forth the threatened acts and states that the plaintiff will suffer immediate and irreparable harm if the defendant is not enjoined. The application can refer to the complaint and incorporate the facts alleged in the complaint. The complaint must be verified; that is, the plaintiff must sign an affidavit stating that the facts alleged are true. The relief requested in the application reads as follows: "WHEREFORE, plaintiff requests that the court enter a temporary restraining order against defendant and set a hearing for a temporary injunction at the earliest practical time." The court issues the preliminary injunction for a specified period of time, usually until the issues can be determined at trial.

CLASS ACTIONS

A class action is a complex type of litigation. If you assist with a class action, it will no doubt be under the direction of lawyers with much experience in this complicated area. It is important for paralegals to understand the nature of class actions and when a class action is appropriate. The purpose of a class action is to allow a large group of persons with similar grievances to bring one lawsuit on behalf of themselves and other persons with the same grievance. A class of plaintiffs can include thousands of individuals, so not every plaintiff will be named.

Rather, just a few of the plaintiffs will be named, and they will serve as representatives of the thousands of other persons in the class. Note that a group of defendants can constitute a class as well.

The court must determine whether a lawsuit can be maintained as a class action. Not just any group of aggrieved persons can get together and decide that it will constitute a class. Rather, a court must decide that they meet the prerequisites to a class action set forth in Rule 23(a) of the Federal Rules of Civil Procedure. Those prerequisites include a class "so numerous that joinder of all members is impracticable" and "questions of law or fact common to the class." In addition, the claims or defenses of the representative parties must be "typical of the claims or defenses of the class" and the representative parties must "fairly and adequately protect the interests of the class."

If you are involved in class action litigation, you will refer not only to FRCivP 23, but also to reference books that address complex litigation. As we have noted, you will no doubt be working with attorneys experienced in class action litigation.

ENDNOTES

1 The Appendix of Forms is found in 28 U.S. Code, at the end of the Federal Rules of Civil Procedure.
2 *Black's Law Dictionary* 594 (5th ed. 1979).

7 SUBSEQUENT PLEADINGS

LITIGATION EXTRACT: Mr. Wesser has filed a complaint and completed service of process. It is now time to consider the responses that the defendants may assert. Defendants respond to each of the plaintiff's allegations in an answer, which may also include motions to dismiss under FRCivP 12. Chapter 7 discusses the contents and format for answers and Rule 12 motions, as well as the filing deadlines. Defendants may assert their own claims in addition to responding to the plaintiff's allegations. In a counterclaim, a defendant asserts a claim against a plaintiff and in a cross-claim a defendant asserts a claim against a codefendant. Chapter 7 also covers third-party practice, when a defendant wishes to assert a claim against a person not already a party to the lawsuit. New facts often arise as litigation progresses, and the new facts may be added by amending the pleadings. The final topic in Chapter 7 is removal, the process for transferring a lawsuit from state court to federal court.

INTRODUCTION

Review Rule 7 of the Federal Rules of Civil Procedure, which sets forth the types of pleadings allowed. So far we have discussed only one type of pleading, the complaint. Once the plaintiff asserts a claim, the defendant must either admit that the plaintiff is entitled to relief, or must assert defenses. The defenses are asserted in responsive pleadings: that is, all the other pleadings set forth in Rule 7.

This chapter also addresses defenses made pursuant to Rule 12(b), (e), and (f) of the Federal Rules of Civil Procedure. Although these Rule 12 defenses are technically denominated motions rather than pleadings, they are included in Chapter 7 because they are often filed as part of the answer.

This chapter concentrates on drafting and filing answers and Rule 12 motions, as well as counterclaims and replies to them. Counterclaims are pleadings in which defendants assert claims against plaintiffs.

Litigation paralegals are likely to be involved in more complex actions as well, involving third-party complaints and answers, and interpleader. However, because attorneys will be more involved with such complex pleadings, these are discussed only briefly.

At this time, review Rule 10 of the Federal Rules of Civil Procedure, which discusses the format requirements for pleadings. Review also Rule 8, which states the general rules of pleading. Recall especially Rule 8's requirement that pleadings be concise and direct. This rule of thumb for drafting applies to answers just as to complaints, as we discussed in Chapter 6.

TIMING

It is absolutely essential that responsive pleadings be filed on time. Failure to meet the filing deadline can result in waiver of the right to raise a defense and can actually result in entry of judgment against the party who failed to respond.

Deadlines for Filing Responses

Rule 12(a) of the Federal Rules of Civil Procedure delineates the deadlines for most responsive pleadings in federal court actions. For example, as a general rule, a defendant must file an answer within 20 days after service of the summons and complaint. For actions filed in state court, you must check your state rules of civil procedure to determine deadlines. Some state rules permit a different period for response. For instance, some states allow 30 days, rather than 20, to file an answer. The summons usually will tell the defendant how many days are allowed for filing an answer.

Computing Time for Responses

By now you are probably thinking that 20 days is not a very long time to formulate a response. Your next question may be whether you have to include weekend days and holidays in the number of days allowed for the response. Rule 6 of the Federal Rules of Civil Procedure explains precisely how to compute any period of time allowed for any response.

FRCivP 6(a) gives three general rules in computing deadlines for responses. Assume that you are figuring on what day your defendant must file an answer. First, in counting your 20 days, do not include the day on which the summons and complaint were served. This is because FRCivP 6(a) states that "the day of the act, event, or default from which the designated period of time begins to run shall not be included." Second, if the last day of your 20-day period falls on a Saturday, Sunday, or legal holiday, do not include that day. Rather, your last day to file the answer is the next day that is not a Saturday, Sunday, or legal holiday. Thus, if your 20-day period ends on the Saturday before Labor Day, your answer is due on the Tuesday after Labor Day.

The third general rule is that if the time allowed to respond is less than 11 days, intermediate Saturdays, Sundays, and legal holidays are excluded in the computation. For response periods of 11 days or more, you must include Saturdays, Sundays, and legal holidays. Thus in computing the 20-day deadline for filing the answer, you must include Saturdays, Sundays, and legal holidays.

Rule 6(a) of the Federal Rules of Civil Procedure contains the definition of ''legal holidays,'' and you should read the definition. You should keep a copy of Rule 6 handy, because its computation rules apply not just to answers, but also to all other responsive pleadings, motions, and any other filing deadlines provided by the Federal Rules of Civil Procedure, local court rules, court orders, or any applicable statute.[1] The various deadlines will make more sense after we have discussed more pleadings and motions.

Finally, Rule 6(e) of the Federal Rules of Civil Procedure states an additional rule in computing time when service is by mail. When a party receives a notice that he is required to file a response or take other action, and that notice is served by mail, three days are added to the prescribed period for the response. Thus, if you are served a complaint by mail, first calculate your response deadline according to the guidelines discussed above. Then add three days, excluding Saturdays, Sundays, or legal holidays in your computation.

Keeping a Record of Response Dates

Review the docket control discussion in Chapter 1. Remember to calculate the date a response is due as soon as you receive a document that requires a response. Enter the date in the docket control system immediately.

Extensions of Time to Respond

Sometimes an adequate response cannot be prepared within the prescribed period. For instance, a complaint may address multiple alleged grounds of liability and the attorney/paralegal team may need additional time to gather and review extensive documents before an answer can be filed.

Rule 6(b) of the Federal Rules of Civil Procedure governs the extension of time for filing responses. When the motion to extend time is filed before the prescribed period ends, the court may grant an extension of time for ''good cause.'' There is no universal definition for ''good cause.'' However, when the party expresses a legitimate reason that will not result in great prejudice to the opposing party, the court will grant an extension when the prescribed response period has not yet expired. Examples of ''good cause'' may include a trial in another case, difficulty in locating documents, or the attorney's illness.

As a practical matter, when the response period has not yet expired, before seeking the court's approval of an extension, the party seeking an extension first contacts opposing counsel to seek consent to an extension. If opposing counsel agrees, the parties submit a consent order, stating their agreement to the extension. When the parties agree to an extension, the judge usually signs the consent order. In Chapter 8 we will further discuss procedures for extension of time.

If the motion to extend time is filed after the prescribed response period has elapsed, FRCivP 6(b) requires a higher standard for granting an extension. The responding party must establish that the failure to file a timely response was the result of ''excusable neglect.'' Again, there is no universal definition, but the fact that the lawyer has a busy schedule will generally not suffice. On the other hand, if the attorney promptly asked the client to deliver extensive documentation for review, and the client failed to bring the documents until two days before the response was due, this may be an acceptable reason.

 POINTER: As with any action taken, you should check the local rules to determine whether they impose additional requirements. For instance, some federal district court local rules require a showing that the opposing attorney was contacted and her views solicited before the motion was filed.

Rules regarding extensions of time may vary in state courts. State court rules may follow exactly Rule 6(b) of the Federal Rules of Civil Procedure. However, the equivalent state rule of civil procedure may be more lenient. It may allow the clerk of court to grant the extension when the motion is filed before the prescribed period ends. The state rule may allow an extension of 20 or 30 days without court approval if all parties agree to the extension, whether the stipulation is entered before or after the prescribed period. See Figure 7-1 for an example of a motion for an extension of time to file a response to a motion to dismiss. In this instance, local rules allowed only ten days to file the response.

RULE 12 MOTIONS

Introduction

Rule 12(b) of the Federal Rules of Civil Procedure states seven defenses that can be raised by either a motion to dismiss or the answer. Rule 12(e) addresses the motion for a more definite statement, and Rule 12(f) provides for the motion to strike certain types of allegations from a pleading. It is important that you understand the Rule 12 motions so that you can review complaints and find defects which the Rule 12 motions address. The attorney/paralegal team can then discuss the Rule 12 defenses and when to raise them.

Motions to Dismiss under Rule 12(b).   The defenses that can be raised in a motion to dismiss pursuant to Rule 12(b) are as follows.

1. Lack of jurisdiction over the subject matter (Rule 12(b)(1)). This means that the type of claim that the plaintiff has brought does not address a subject matter that this particular court is authorized to hear. For instance, the bankruptcy court does not have subject matter jurisdiction to grant a divorce.

2. Lack of jurisdiction over the person (Rule 12(b)(2)). This means that the court does not have personal jurisdiction over the defendant and thus cannot enter a binding judgment over the defendant. For example, suppose that a resident of Virginia writes a check in New Jersey, and the check bounces. If the resident of Virginia does not have minimum contacts with New Jersey, the New Jersey court cannot make the Virginia resident come into court in New Jersey, because the New Jersey court lacks personal jurisdiction.

3. Improper venue (Rule 12(b)(3)). This means that the case has been filed in the wrong geographic district: in federal court, the wrong district; in state court, the wrong county. For example, a state statute may provide that when a plaintiff sues a railroad, proper venue is in the county where the cause of action

FIGURE 7-1 MOTION FOR AN EXTENSION OF TIME TO RESPOND TO DEFENDANT'S MOTION TO DISMISS

UNITED STATES DISTRICT COURT
MIDDLE DISTRICT OF NORTH CAROLINA
CHARLESTON DIVISION
CIVIL NO.: C-89-1293-B

Bryson Wesser,
                    Plaintiff,

            -vs-

Woodall Shoals Corporation,
                    Defendant,
            and
Second Ledge Stores, Incorporated,
                    Defendant

Motion

(For additional time to respond to Defendant's Motion to Dismiss)

Plaintiff, by and through his attorneys, moves that the Court grant additional time, through April 25, 1989, for filing of a response to Defendants' Motion to Dismiss and a Memorandum of Law in support of Plaintiff's response. In support of his Motion, Plaintiff shows unto the Court:

1. Plaintiff's attorneys received by mail Defendants' Motion to Dismiss and Memorandum of Law on March 30, 1989.

2. A period of ten days from date of service will not provide sufficient time for filing a response to Defendants' Motion to Dismiss and Memorandum of Law.

3. On March 31, 1989, Leigh Heyward, Esq., telephoned Ed Cheng, Esq., to inquire whether he would agree to the granting of additional time. Mr. Cheng stated that he consented to additional time, specifically, through April 25, 1989 (a period of two additional weeks), for Plaintiffs to file a response to Defendants' Motion to Dismiss and Memorandum of Law in support of Plaintiff's response.

WHEREFORE, Plaintiff, through Counsel, respectfully requests that the Court grant Plaintiff additional time, through April 25, 1989, to file a response

FIGURE 7-1   MOTION FOR AN EXTENSION OF TIME TO RESPOND TO DEFENDANT'S MOTION TO DISMISS (Cont.)

to Defendants' Motion to Dismiss and a Memorandum of Law supporting Plaintiff's response.

_____

Leigh J. Heyward
Attorney for the Plaintiff
Heyward and Wilson
401 East Trade Street
Charleston, NC 28226-1114
704-555-3161

CERTIFICATE OF SERVICE

I, Leigh Heyward, attorney for the plaintiff, do certify that service of the within and foregoing Motion for additional time to respond to Defendant's Motion to Dismiss was made upon David H. Benedict, attorney for the defendants, by enclosing a true copy in an envelope addressed to Mr. David H. Benedict, Benedict, Parker & Miller, Attorneys at Law, 100 Nolichucky Drive, Bristol, NC 28205-0890, postage prepaid, and depositing same in the United States mail at Charleston, NC, on the _____ day of April, 1989.

_____

Leigh J. Heyward
Attorney for the Plaintiff
401 East Trade Street
Charleston, NC 28226-1114

arose or where the plaintiff resided at the time of the cause of action. If the lawsuit is filed in a county other than those allowed by the statute, venue is improper.

4. Insufficiency of process (Rule 12(b)(4)). This motion challenges the form of process—that is, the content of the summons. If a defendant is misnamed on the summons, this makes the summons invalid. For instance, a corporation may be misnamed.

5. Insufficiency of service of process (Rule 12(b)(5)). This motion challenges the method of service used. FRCivP 4 specifies the correct manner of service of process. Suppose that a summons and complaint are left at a defendant's home with the defendant's brother, who is obviously schizophrenic and out of touch with reality. The brother is not a person of suitable discretion, so service of process is not sufficient.

6. Failure to state a claim upon which relief can be granted (Rule 12(b)(6)). This means that based on the facts the plaintiff has alleged and the applicable

law, no set of facts will support the plaintiff's claim under any legal theory. For example, if a lawsuit is filed after the statute of limitations has expired, this is an insuperable bar to relief, so the complaint can be dismissed.

7. Failure to join a party under Rule 19 (Rule 12(b)(7). This motion generally asserts that there is a party who has not been brought into the lawsuit without whom complete relief cannot be granted or who would be prejudiced by not being included. For instance, if two general partners own a company, and the company is sued for breach of contract, both partners are potentially liable, so they are both indispensable parties.

When you are asked to draft a motion or answer which includes Rule 12 defenses, refer to the usual sources of sample pleadings and motions: other similar files to which the attorney refers you, your firm's file of sample pleadings, form books, and the forms in the Appendix to the Federal Rules of Civil Procedure in 28 U.S. Code.

Consolidation of Rule 12(b) Motions.   Rule 12(g) and (h) provide some technical rules regarding when certain Rule 12 motions must be consolidated—that is, joined together—in order not to be waived. Some defenses cannot be asserted unless they are included in a motion to strike or an answer. Thus a party can lose the right to assert the following defenses at a later stage of the litigation if they are not asserted in one consolidated motion to dismiss: lack of personal jurisdiction, venue, insufficiency of process, and insufficiency of service of process. A detailed discussion of these waiver provisions is beyond the scope of this book, but you should read Rule 12(g) and (h) and be prepared to discuss with the attorney the combination of defenses that you recommend asserting and how to assert the defenses without waiving them.

In contrast, the defenses of failure to state a claim upon which relief can be granted (Rule 12(b)(6)) and failure to join an indispensable party (Rule 12(b)(7)) can be asserted later, in any pleading permitted by Rule 7, in a motion for judgment on the pleadings, or at the trial on the merits. Note that the defense of lack of subject matter jurisdiction (Rule 12(b)(1)) can never be waived and thus can be raised at any time.

When to File Rule 12(b) Motions to Dismiss.   Rule 12(b) defenses can be filed either in the answer or in a separate motion to dismiss. Whether the Rule 12(b) defenses are in the answer or are filed as a separate motion, the defendant must file within the time permitted for filing an answer to the complaint. Recall that this is 20 days after service of the complaint under the Federal Rules of Civil Procedure. Figure 7-2 illustrates a separate motion to dismiss. Turn to the Appendix and examine the answer in the Wesser case for an example of a motion pursuant to Rule 12(b)(6) filed as part of the answer.

As with consolidation of defenses, whether to file a separate motion to dismiss or to file the defenses in the answer is a determination you will discuss with the lawyer. However, you should be aware of the purpose of 12(b) defenses, which is to point out defects in the complaint and to terminate the litigation at an early stage if possible. You should bear in mind that many of the defects that Rule

FIGURE 7-2   A SEPARATE MOTION TO DISMISS

UNITED STATES DISTRICT COURT
MIDDLE DISTRICT OF NORTH CAROLINA
CHARLESTON DIVISION
CIVIL ACTION NO.: C-89-2388-B

Equal Employment Opportunity
Commission,
                Plaintiff,

     -vs-

Chattooga Corporation,
                Defendant

DEFENDANT'S MOTION TO DISMISS

Defendant, by its undersigned Counsel, hereby moves for dismissal of the complaint pursuant to Federal Rule of Civil Procedure 12(b) (6) on the ground that plaintiffs have failed to state a claim upon which relief can be granted.

Nancy Reade Lee
Attorney for the Defendant
Gray and Lee, P.A.
380 South Washington Street
Charleston, NC 28226-1115
704-555-2500

+ Certificate of Service

12(b) addresses can be cured. For instance, if process or service of process is defective, the plaintiff can serve process on the defendant again in the correct manner. If venue is improper, the action will usually be transferred to a proper venue rather than dismissed.

The most frequently asserted 12(b) defense is Rule 12(b)(6), failure to state a claim upon which relief can be granted. The defendant is generally given permission to amend the complaint to correct defects and state a claim upon which relief can be granted. However, if for some reason the court does not permit the plaintiff to amend the complaint or if an essential element of the claim simply does not exist, granting the 12(b)(6) motion will end the lawsuit.

Motion for a More Definite Statement

Rule 12(e) of the Federal Rules of Civil Procedure states that "(i)f a pleading to which a responsive pleading is permitted is so vague or ambiguous that a party cannot reasonably be required to frame a responsive pleading, he may move for a more definite statement before interposing his responsive pleading." This motion permits a party to request sufficient facts to determine the claim or defense asserted against him. Then the party can fashion an intelligent response and not unwittingly admit to liability for something she or he could not detect from the pleadings. Note that Rule 12(e) requires the moving party to "point out the defects complained of and the details desired." Thus the moving party cannot simply state in a motion that she or he does not know what the other party is talking about.

Paralegals should review pleadings and bring to the attorney's attention those statements that are so ambiguous that a response is difficult to formulate. Bear in mind that Rule 8 requires "short and plain statements" in pleadings. Thus not every pertinent fact will appear in the pleadings. However, not every question you have will require a motion for more definite statement. Remember that you can ascertain more details in the discovery process. If the pleading is so vague that you cannot formulate a response, discuss with the attorney whether to file a motion for more definite statement.

Finally, note that the motion for more definite statement may have a different name in some state court actions, such as a bill of particulars. Regardless of the name, the purpose remains the same.

Motion to Strike

Rule 12(f) of the Federal Rules of Civil Procedure provides that a party may file a motion asking the court to "order stricken from any pleading any insufficient defense or any redundant, immaterial, impertinent, or scandalous matter." A defendant making a motion to strike would file the motion before filing the answer. The motion would have to be filed within the period allowed to file the answer.

The purpose of the motion to strike is to keep out of the pleadings material that is unnecessary and scandalous and would therefore result in prejudice. Such language, if left in the pleading, would be harmful if the pleading were read to the jury in the course of a trial.

How to File Rule 12 Motions

The format for motions and the mechanics of filing all types of motions will be discussed in Chapter 8. The rules discussed there apply to all Rule 12 motions. Remember that every motion, together with a notice of motion, must be served on all parties.

The certificate of service must be attached to these documents. FRCivP 5 requires that every pleading filed after the complaint, and every motion, discovery request, or other document filed with the court be served on every party. The service in FRCivP 5 is different from service of process, the FRCivP 4 procedure for delivering the summons and complaint to the defendants. FRCivP 5(b) states that when a party is represented by an attorney, the motion or other document must be mailed or personally delivered to the party's attorney. The documents are usually mailed. However, documents can be hand delivered to the attorney or to the attorney's office. If a party is unrepresented, the motion or other document is mailed or personally delivered directly to the party. Figure 7-1 shows a certificate of service for a motion. The certificate of service may be attached as a separate page or it may be typed on the last page of the motion or pleading. The attorney signs both the motion or pleading itself and the certificate of service. Figure 7-3 illustrates a certificate of service for an answer. Note that the language is the same; you just change the description of the document being served and the name and addresses of the attorneys on whom the documents are served.

FIGURE 7-3   CERTIFICATE OF SERVICE

CERTIFICATE OF SERVICE

I, Leigh Heyward, attorney for the plaintiff, do certify that service of the within and foregoing Answer and Counterclaim was made upon David H. Benedict, attorney for the defendants, by enclosing a true copy in an envelope addressed to Mr. David H. Benedict, Benedict, Parker & Miller, Attorneys at Law, 100 Nolichucky Drive, Bristol, NC 28205-0890, postage prepaid, and depositing same in the United States mail at Charleston, NC, on the _____ day of April, 1989.

_____
Leigh Heyward
Attorney for the Plaintiff
401 East Trade Street
Charleston, NC 28226-1114
704-555-3161

Motions are usually accompanied by supporting **affidavits** that state the facts on which the motion is based. In fact, some states require supporting affidavits. Motions are also frequently supported by **memoranda of law**, which state the reasons why the motion should be granted. We will discuss affidavits and memoranda of law at great length in Chapter 8.

ANSWERS

An **answer** is the formal written statement in which the defendant states the grounds of his or her defense. Rule 8(b) of the Federal Rules of Civil Procedure governs the statement of defenses and provides that "(a) party shall state in short and plain terms his defenses to each claim asserted and shall admit or deny the averments upon which the adverse party relies." The precise method for stating the denial is discussed below. Note that Rule 8(b) includes the general rule for pleadings that appears throughout the Federal Rules of Civil Procedure, namely that the statements should be "short and plain."

Other general rules of pleadings that we have discussed in connection with the complaint apply equally to the answer. The Rule 10 requirements for captions and paragraphs apply, as does the the Rule 11 requirement that the attorney sign the pleading. As with complaints, you may also attach exhibits and appendices to substantiate your assertions. As always, check local rules for special requirements, especially to determine whether the client has to sign a verification for the answer.

In addition to the responses to the allegations in the complaint, an answer may contain Rule 12 motions and affirmative defenses (statute of limitations, contributory negligence, and so on). Indeed, as we discussed earlier, some defenses may have to be included in an answer if they are not to be waived. If an answer has multiple parts, each part should be set out separately and clearly. Refer to the answer in the Wesser case (see Appendix), which designates the Rule 12(b)(6) motion as the FIRST DEFENSE, the responses to plaintiff's allegations as the SECOND DEFENSE, and the affirmative defensive of contributory negligence as THIRD DEFENSE.

Timing

Rule 12(a) of the Federal Rules of Civil Procedure provides the general rule for when an answer must be filed. This discussion of time limits refers to answers. Recall, however, that if the defendant files a motion to dismiss, motion to strike, or motion for more definite statement pursuant to Rule 12, the time limit for filing the motion is the same as that for filing the answer. The general rule is that the answer must be filed within 20 days of service of the complaint and summons. As we noted, this is the general rule for federal court actions; states may have different rules.

Rule 12(a) also provides some exceptions to the general rule. For instance, when the United States or one of its agencies or officers is the defendant, the defendant is allowed 60 days to file a responsive pleading. Another exception is that a different time limit may apply if the defendant lives in another state and service is made in that other state in accordance with Rule 4(e) of the Federal Rules of Civil Procedure. Finally, a different federal or state statute may apply and alter the time limit.

Rule 12(a) also explains how filing a Rule 12 motion prior to filing an answer alters the 20-day rule. If the court denies the Rule 12 motion, then the defendant must file an answer within 10 days after notice of the court's action. If the court grants a motion for more definite statement, then the plaintiff must file an amended complaint containing the more definite information. The defendant must respond within 10 days of service of the more definite statement.

Format

Review the general format requirements in Rule 10 of the Federal Rules of Civil Procedure in Chapter 6. Refer in the Appendix to the answer in the Wesser case, which shows the caption requirements—the name of the court, the title of the action, the name of the pleading, and the file number. In this example there are two defendants, and they filed a joint answer. Often multiple defendants each file a separate answer, and the caption must specify which party is answering. Figure 7-4 illustrates how the caption would appear if defendant Woodall Shoals filed a separate answer.

FIGURE 7-4   CAPTION FOR A SEPARATE ANSWER

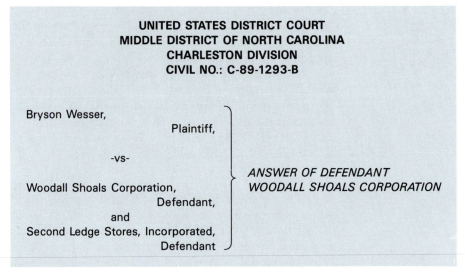

When the plaintiff has already requested a jury trial, it is not necessary for the defendant to repeat the request, although she may do so. If the defendant requests a jury trial, the request must appear in a conspicuous place. The jury demand should be placed in the caption below the word "Answer" and/or at the end of the answer. (See Chapter 6 for a review of demand for jury trial.)

As with the complaint, every paragraph is numbered. This makes the responses clearer and easier to follow.

Responses

The defendant must admit or deny every averment in the complaint. Therefore the answer must be constructed very carefully so that it is clear that every paragraph in the complaint has been addressed.

Requirement to Admit or Deny Every Allegation. Rule 8(b) of the Federal Rules of Civil Procedure provides that the defendant must admit or deny all averments in the complaint. Rule 8(d) states the consequences of failing to respond to an averment in the complaint: that the averment is deemed to be admitted when not denied.

Insufficient Knowledge. FRCivP 8(b) provides that a defendant may, as an alternative to an admission or denial, state that "he is without knowledge or information sufficient to form a belief as to the truth of an averment . . . and this has the effect of a denial.'' The statement that a defendant is without sufficient knowledge or belief must be made in good faith and not just for the purpose of avoiding a harmful response. An example of the insufficient knowledge response is paragraph 4 of the Second Defense section in the answer in the Wesser case. At this point in the pleadings the defendants do not know when or under what circumstances the plaintiff purchased the electric blanket. This information will come out during the discovery process.

Denial of Only Part of an Allegation. FRCivP 8(b) also states that ''(w)hen a pleader intends in good faith to deny only a part . . . of an averment, he shall specify so much of it as is true and material and shall deny only the remainder.'' Thus it is proper to admit part of an allegation but deny or plead insufficient knowledge as to the rest of the allegation. These partial denials must be drafted very carefully. In paragraph 9 in the Second Defense in the Wesser case, for instance, the defendant admits that the plaintiff received certain injuries. However, the defendant states insufficient knowledge to form a belief as to whether the plaintiff incurred extensive medical expenses and lost wages and whether the plaintiff suffered severe emotional distress as a result of the injuries.

Affirmative Defenses

An **affirmative defense** goes beyond a simple denial of an allegation in the complaint. It brings out a new matter, not mentioned in the complaint, that serves as a defense even if all the allegations in the complaint are admitted. A commonly raised affirmative defense is statute of limitations, which means that the plaintiff did not file the claim within the period specified by statute and therefore is barred from any recovery from the defendant. For example, in a suit on a promissory note, the defendant may admit that she signed a promissory note in May 1982 and that she did not pay the money back to the plaintiff by May 1983, as agreed in the promissory note. However, the defendant then pleads the affirmative defense of statute of limitations, because the plaintiff did not file the complaint until after the deadline for doing so. Different statutes of limitation apply to different claims. A party may have two years, for instance, to file a suit for breach of contract, and three years to file a personal injury suit.

Rule 8(c) of the Federal Rules of Civil Procedure specifies additional affirmative defenses, including such common affirmative defenses as assumption of risk, contributory negligence, discharge in bankruptcy, fraud, release, res judicata, and waiver. Rule 8(c) also refers to ''any other matter constituting an avoidance or affirmative defense.'' The substantive law of your jurisdiction may designate additional affirmative defenses. You should review with the attorney any possible affirmative defenses and determine which affirmative defenses the attorney believes will apply.

The exact format in which affirmative defenses are asserted may vary among jurisdictions. It is best to set out each affirmative defense in a separate paragraph. The language in that paragraph should specifically state the particular affirmative defense. Each paragraph should be labeled as a defense, whether the paragraph title includes the word ''affirmative'' as in Figure 7-5, or simply numbers as in the

Third Defense in the answer in the Wesser case. Note that some affirmative defenses may require more explanation than others. Compare the statement of the statute of limitations defense in Figure 7-5 with the Third Defense in the answer in the Wesser case (see Appendix).

FIGURE 7-5 ANSWER

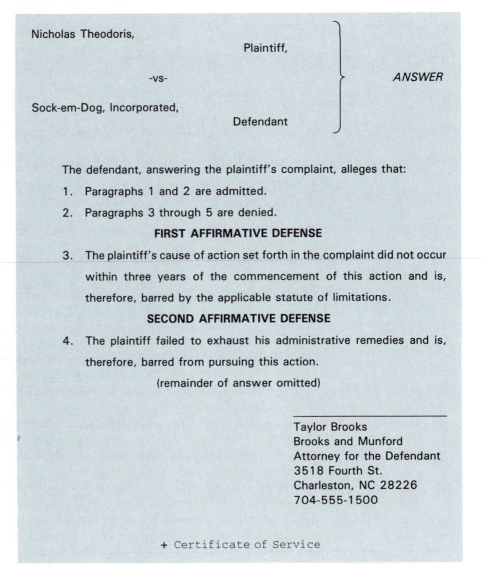

Nicholas Theodoris,

                               Plaintiff,

        -vs-   *ANSWER*

Sock-em-Dog, Incorporated,

                         Defendant

The defendant, answering the plaintiff's complaint, alleges that:

1. Paragraphs 1 and 2 are admitted.
2. Paragraphs 3 through 5 are denied.

FIRST AFFIRMATIVE DEFENSE

3. The plaintiff's cause of action set forth in the complaint did not occur within three years of the commencement of this action and is, therefore, barred by the applicable statute of limitations.

SECOND AFFIRMATIVE DEFENSE

4. The plaintiff failed to exhaust his administrative remedies and is, therefore, barred from pursuing this action.

(remainder of answer omitted)

Taylor Brooks
Brooks and Munford
Attorney for the Defendant
3518 Fourth St.
Charleston, NC 28226
704-555-1500

+ Certificate of Service

Filing the Answer

The answer, like the complaint and other pleadings, must be filed in the office of the clerk of court. Before filing, check the answer for accuracy and signatures.

Be sure the certificate of service is signed and dated and includes the attorneys for all parties. If exhibits are attached to the answer, check that they are in the correct order and properly labeled.

Generally, there is no filing fee for the answer and other pleadings subsequent to the complaint.[2] Nor is there a civil cover sheet, although local rules may require some type of cover sheet, especially if the defendant asserts a counterclaim.

The original answer stays in the clerk's office. Check your local rules to determine whether the clerk also requires an additional copy, known as a "working copy," of each pleading and motion for the file. Some judicial districts require a working copy for the judge's use. As with the complaint, the clerk will stamp the original and each copy with the date filed. After you have all copies file-stamped by the clerk, mail a copy to each party in the lawsuit. Keep a copy for your file, and send a copy to your client.

COUNTERCLAIMS AND CROSS-CLAIMS

One of the consistent guidelines in litigation is that all related claims among parties should be adjudicated in one lawsuit, if possible. This prevents multiple trials involving the same issues and facts. Suppose that Jones is injured when he falls on the stairs of the office building that he rents from Smith. Smith is the owner of the office building, and Green is the architect who designed the building.

Several issues arise from Jones's accident. Jones asserts that Smith is negligent because he did not properly maintain the stairs. Jones also asserts that Green negligently designed the stairs. Smith asserts in his answer that Jones's own behavior was negligent and caused the accident, because Jones was carrying a large box that partially blocked his vision. Smith also asserts that Green negligently designed the stairs, and therefore, if Smith is found liable to Jones, then Green must reimburse Smith for all or part of the sum paid to Jones. Green also files an answer defending against allegations of negligence. Finally, Smith asserts in a counterclaim against Jones that Jones is $55,000 in arrears in rental payment and in another counterclaim asserts property damage resulting from damage to the steps when the objects in Jones's box fell on them.

All these issues should be resolved in one trial. If a jury found that the stairs were defective either in design or in maintenance, it would be a waste of time and money to have a second trial to determine whether Smith, the owner, or Green, the architect, was responsible for the defect.

In this example, Jones files a *complaint* against both Smith and Green for their alleged negligence. Smith files an *answer* stating that he was not negligent in maintaining the office building. Smith also files a *counterclaim* against Jones for unpaid rent and for damage to the building from the materials in Jones's box hitting the steps. Smith files a *cross-claim* against Green for her alleged negligent design of the stairs. This section explains the basic rules and format for counterclaims and cross-claims. Paralegals encounter these pleadings often, especially in litigation involving multiple parties.

Counterclaims: Definitions and Timing

We have already discussed two ways a defendant can respond to a complaint—namely, by filing an answer and/or Rule 12 motions. A defendant may, in addition, file a counterclaim. In a **counterclaim** the defendant asserts a claim against the plaintiff. A counterclaim is essentially a complaint in which the original defendant takes the role of a plaintiff and the original plaintiff takes the role of a defendant. In our example, plaintiff Jones must defend against the charge that he was negligent in causing his own accident.

A counterclaim must be filed within the time prescribed for filing the answer, with certain exceptions explained in FRCivP 13(e). The counterclaim is made part of the answer, as we will explain in the discussion of format later in this section. The plaintiff must file a response to the counterclaim, and this response is called a **reply**. The plaintiff's reply is like an answer, and must be filed within the time limit allowed for an answer. The plaintiff may also file Rule 12 motions in response to a counterclaim.

Rule 13 of the Federal Rules of Civil Procedure governs counterclaims. FRCivP 13 allows two types of counterclaims.

Compulsory Counterclaims

A **compulsory counterclaim** is a claim that a defendant *must* assert against the plaintiff or else be barred from bringing the claim in a separate lawsuit. The purpose of the requirement that the counterclaim must be asserted is that the court already has jurisdiction over the plaintiff and defendant, as well as the subject matter of the lawsuit. Therefore it would be a great waste not to resolve all the issues in one lawsuit. This is the same principle we discussed earlier, sometimes referred to as judicial economy.

FRCivP 13(a) explains the factors that make a counterclaim compulsory. First, the claim must arise "out of the transaction or occurrence that is the subject matter of the opposing party's claim. . . ." Second, the claim must "not require for its adjudication the presence of third parties of whom the court cannot acquire jurisdiction." However, FRCivP 13(a) provides that a counterclaim may not be asserted if it is already the subject of another pending action.

The question whether a claim involves the same transaction or occurrence can be quite complex. In our example, it is clear that Smith's claim arises out of the same transaction as Jones's claim—that is, Jones's fall on the stairs. However, some cases may involve several complicated transactions, such as complex contracts litigation. The paralegal should be aware of the general concept of the compulsory counterclaim and know that there will arise complex situations that you will have to discuss with the attorney.

Permissive Counterclaims

A counterclaim is **permissive** when the defendant may bring a claim but does not have to bring it in the same lawsuit that the plaintiff initiates. Permissive counterclaims are governed by Rule 13(b), which explains that permissive counterclaims concern ''any claim against an opposing party not arising out of the transaction or occurrence that is the subject matter of the opposing party's claim.''

In our stairway example, at the time Jones filed the lawsuit against Smith, Jones was behind on his rental payments and owed Smith $55,000. Smith may want to assert as a permissive counterclaim the claim for the rent Jones owes. This counterclaim is permissive because it did not arise out of the stairway incident. If judgment were entered against Smith for $80,000, this amount could be offset by the $55,000 that Jones owed Smith.

There are limitations on permissive counterclaims. If the counterclaim makes the lawsuit too complex, the court can order that the counterclaim be tried separately. In addition, a permissive counterclaim must have its own separate basis of jurisdiction. This contrasts with compulsory counterclaims, which do not require an independent jurisdictional ground. This is because the court already has jurisdiction over the transaction from which both the complaint and compulsory counterclaim arose.

In our present example, suppose the complaint was filed in federal court with diversity jurisdiction as its basis—that is, the parties are residents of different states. Smith is a resident of Idaho, Jones is a resident of North Carolina, and Green is a resident of California. Smith's counterclaim requested $55,000 in damages. Next we must consider whether the permissive counterclaim meets the jurisdictional requirements. Here it does, because we have complete diversity among the parties, and the amount in the counterclaim meets the $50,000 jurisdictional amount requirement.

Cross-Claims

A **cross-claim** is a pleading that states a claim by one party against a coparty. That is, a defendant may file a cross-claim against a codefendant. If a defendant filed a counterclaim against two coplaintiffs, one plaintiff may file a cross-claim against the other plaintiff. In our stairway accident example, defendant Smith may file a cross-claim against defendant Green, the architect, claiming that if Smith is liable to Jones, then Green is liable to Smith because the accident was actually Green's fault.

Rule 13(g) of the Federal Rules of Civil Procedure governs cross-claims. FRCivP 13(g) requires that the claim by one coparty against another coparty must arise ''out of the transaction or occurrence that is the subject matter either of the original action or of a counterclaim therein or relating to any property that is the subject matter of the original action.'' This is like the test for compulsory counterclaims. The subject matter requirement gives the court the authority to order that a coparty may not file a cross-claim when the subject matter is insufficiently related to the pending lawsuit.

FRCivP 13(g) provides that a cross-claim may be contingent. That is, a party may assert that a coparty is *or may be* liable to him. The cross-claimant also has the option of asserting that the coparty is liable to him for all or part of the claim against the cross-claimant. In our example involving Jones's accident,

Smith, the owner of the building, may file a cross-claim against Green, the architect who designed the building, asserting that if Smith is liable to Jones, then Green is liable to Smith, because Green's negligent design caused the accident. There is flexibility in the assertions a coparty may make in a cross-claim.

A cross-claim is usually filed as part of the answer. The cross-claim must be filed within the time prescribed for filing the answer. A party must file a reply to a cross-claim within 20 days of service of the cross-claim.

Format and Contents of Counterclaims and Cross-Claims

The format and content of a counterclaim are like those of a complaint. This is because a counterclaim is essentially a complaint, filed by the defendant against the plaintiff. A counterclaim included with an answer will bear the title ANSWER AND COUNTERCLAIM. If multiple defendants are involved, it is important to designate which defendant is asserting the counterclaim—for example, ANSWER AND COUNTERCLAIM OF WOODALL SHOALS CORPORATION. If there are multiple plaintiffs, be sure to designate against which plaintiff the defendant is asserting the counterclaim—for example, ANSWER AND COUNTERCLAIM OF DEFENDANT TEGLASY AGAINST PLAINTIFF CARLTON. The rest of the caption has the same components as a complaint: name of the court in which the action is filed, title of the action, and file number. (See Chapter 6 for a review of these components.)

The counterclaim is inserted after the paragraphs responding to the paragraphs in the complaint. The counterclaim requires its own heading so that it will be clear that the defendant is asserting a counterclaim. This is important because the right to assert a counterclaim can be waived if not included with the answer. Because a counterclaim requests relief from the plaintiff, the defendant must include all essential elements to support her claim.

The counterclaim has the same general pleading requirements of a clear and concise statement of the claim, and an attorney signature (which appears at the end after the answer and counterclaim). Local rules may also require verification by the client, which means that the client attests to the truthfulness of the statements in the counterclaim. If the defendant demands a trial by jury for the counterclaim, this must be conspicuously noted in the counterclaim. Finally, be sure to state the relief requested in a demand section at the end of the counterclaim.

The cross-claim must also be a part of the answer. The drafting requirements are like those for a counterclaim—that is, it is much the same as a complaint. Like the complaint and counterclaim, the cross-claim will end with the demand for relief (''wherefore'' clause). The coparty will have 20 days from service to file a reply, under the Federal Rules of Civil Procedure. See Figure 7-6 for a sample cross-claim in the stairway accident case.

POINTER: An answer and counterclaim must be served on all other parties in the same manner as all pleadings and motions made after the complaint is filed. Make sure that the certificate of service states the exact document (answer and counterclaim) that is being mailed and includes the names and addresses of all attorneys to whom the document is sent.

FIGURE 7-6   A SAMPLE CROSS-CLAIM

UNITED STATES DISTRICT COURT
MIDDLE DISTRICT OF NORTH CAROLINA
CHARLESTON DIVISION
CIVIL NO.: C-89-5687-B

Joe Jones,
         Plaintiff,

         -vs-

Lee Smith,
         Defendant,
         and
Sue Green, d/b/a
Green Designs,
         Defendant

ANSWER AND CROSS-CLAIM OF
DEFENDANT LEE SMITH

*Note: only the cross-claim is shown

CROSS-CLAIM AGAINST DEFENDANT GREEN

3.   Defendant Smith incorporates by reference paragraphs 1 and 2 of his answer.

4.   Defendant Sue Green is the architect who designed the building at 110 Burnet Avenue, including the stairs upon which the plaintiff fell. Defendant Sue Green owed a foreseeable duty to users of the premises, including the plaintiff, to exercise reasonable care in the design of the premises. Defendant Sue Green failed to exercise reasonable care in the design of the premises, including the stairs, and her failure proximately caused the plaintiff's injuries.

WHEREFORE, in the event that defendant Smith is liable to the plaintiff, defendant Smith demands judgment against defendant Green for any amount that defendant Smith is required to pay to the plaintiff.

_____
Ahmad Bhat
Attorney for Defendant Lee Smith
Ahmad Bhat, P.C.
813 Cameron Ave.
Charleston, NC 28226-1714
704-555-1977

+ Certificate of Service

See also Figure 7-7, which shows Smith's simple answer and permissive counterclaim based on the stairway accident case. A complaint is not illustrated. Assume that Smith admits the paragraphs in the complaint pertaining to jurisdiction and ownership of the building and denies the paragraphs regarding liability. Note that Smith must allege jurisdiction because this is a permissive, not a compulsory, counterclaim. Remember that the plaintiff must file a reply to the answer and counterclaim within 20 days of service under the Federal Rules of Civil Procedure. See Figure 7-8 for a reply to the counterclaim.

FIGURE 7-7   ANSWER AND COUNTERCLAIM

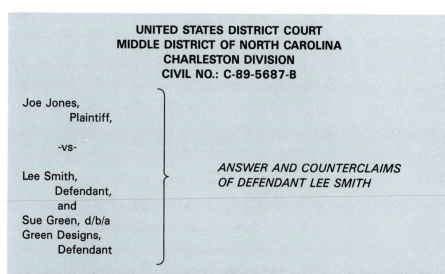

UNITED STATES DISTRICT COURT
MIDDLE DISTRICT OF NORTH CAROLINA
CHARLESTON DIVISION
CIVIL NO.: C-89-5687-B

Joe Jones,
          Plaintiff,

     -vs-

Lee Smith,
          Defendant,
          and
Sue Green, d/b/a
Green Designs,
          Defendant

ANSWER AND COUNTERCLAIMS
OF DEFENDANT LEE SMITH

The defendant Lee Smith, answering the complaint of the plaintiff, alleges and says that:

1. Paragraphs 1 through 3 are admitted.

2. Paragraphs 4 through 7 are denied.

FIRST COUNTERCLAIM

1. Plaintiff is a citizen of the state of North Carolina. Defendant Lee Smith is a citizen of the state of Idaho. Defendant Sue Green d/b/a Green Designs is a citizen of the state of California. The matter in controversy exceeds, exclusive of costs and interests, $50,000.00.

2. The plaintiff signed a lease to rent the premises at 110 Burnet Avenue, Charleston, North Carolina, for five years, at a monthly rate of $5,500.00, as shown by the signed lease, which is attached as Exhibit A.

3. The plaintiff has failed and refused to pay the agreed rent for the past ten months. The plaintiff owes defendant Lee Smith $55,000.00 for unpaid rent.

FIGURE 7-7   ANSWER AND COUNTERCLAIM (Cont.)

SECOND COUNTERCLAIM

1.   On February 23, 1990, plaintiff Joe Jones negligently carried up the stairs on the premises located at 110 Burnet Avenue a large box that obscured his vision.

2.   As a result of his negligence, plaintiff Joe Jones fell on the stairs and dropped the box, which damaged the stairs, resulting in damage to the steps in the amount of $800.00.

3.   The above described property is owned by the defendant, who has at all times properly maintained the premises.

WHEREFORE, the defendant Lee Smith prays the court that:

1.   Judgment be entered against the plaintiff for the sum of $55,000.00 for unpaid rent and $800.00 for damages to the stairs on the premises.

2.   The costs of this action be taxed against the plaintiff.

3.   The defendant Lee Smith be granted such other and proper relief as the court may deem just and proper.

Ahmad Bhat
Attorney for Defendant Lee Smith
Ahmad Bhat, P.C.
813 Cameron Ave.
Charleston, NC 28226-1714
704-555-1977

+ Certificate of Service

FIGURE 7-8   REPLY TO COUNTERCLAIM

UNITED STATES DISTRICT COURT
MIDDLE DISTRICT OF NORTH CAROLINA
CHARLESTON DIVISION
CIVIL NO.: C-89-5687-B

Joe Jones,
    Plaintiff,

-vs-

Lee Smith,
    Defendant,
    and
Sue Green, d/b/a
Green Designs,
    Defendant

*REPLY TO COUNTERCLAIM
OF DEFENDANT LEE SMITH*

The plaintiff, replying to the defendant Lee Smith's counterclaim, alleges and says that:

FIRST DEFENSE

1. The counterclaim fails to state a claim upon which relief can be granted.

SECOND DEFENSE

2. Paragraphs 1 through 4 of the reply are admitted.

3. Paragraph 5 of the reply is denied.

WHEREFORE, the plaintiff prays that the defendant Joe Green's counterclaim be dismissed.

Franklin Russell
Attorney for the Plaintiff
Russell, Moore, and Aziz
1403 Fourth Street
Charleston, NC 28226-1418
704-555-1824

+ Certificate of Service

THIRD-PARTY PRACTICE (IMPLEADER)

So far we have discussed only the original parties to a lawsuit: the plaintiff, coplaintiff, defendant, and codefendant. It is possible to bring additional parties into the lawsuit by a procedure known as **impleader** or **third-party practice**. Impleader is governed by Rule 14 of the Federal Rules of Civil Procedure. FRCivP 14(a) explains the purpose of impleader. A defendant asserts that a person who is not already a party to the action may be liable to the defendant (third-party plaintiff) for all or part of the plaintiff's claim against the defendant (third-party plaintiff).

It is important to grasp the difference between impleader and counterclaims or cross-claims. Counterclaims and cross-claims involve claims between the original parties. Recall that in a cross-claim defendant A asserts that not defendant A, but rather defendant B, should be liable for any damages and that in a counterclaim defendant A asserts that the plaintiff, not defendant A, is responsible for any damages. In contrast, impleader brings in a new party to the lawsuit.

Terminology

To understand impleader, one must understand the terms used to refer to each party in the action. Consider our stairway accident case. Defendant Smith wants to assert that Robertson, the contractor who built the building, is liable to Smith for all or part of Jones's claim against Smith. Note that Robertson is not a party to the lawsuit yet. To bring Robertson in as a party, Smith files a third-party complaint. In the complaint Jones is still called the plaintiff. Smith is now called the defendant and third-party plaintiff. Robertson is the third-party defendant. See Figure 7-9, which shows a third-party complaint in the Appendix to the Federal Rules of Civil Procedure (Form 22). This simple form helps clarify the party designations. If you become confused about the parties in a complex case, refer to a simple form like Figure 7-9, and plug each party into the appropriate slot.

Mechanics of Filing a Third-Party Complaint

A third-party plaintiff files a third-party complaint, which has the same basic components as an original complaint—allegation, a short and plain statement of the claim, and prayer for relief. See Figure 7-9, and pay special attention to the way the parties are labeled in a third-party complaint. Note that a copy of the original complaint should be attached as an exhibit to the third-party complaint.

The third-party plaintiff must serve the third-party summons and third-party complaint on the third-party defendant just as with an original complaint, following the directives of FRCivP 4. See Figure 7-9 for a sample third-party summons.[3]

Court Permission to File a Third-Party Complaint. Under FRCivP 14(a), a third-party plaintiff must file a motion to obtain court permission to file a third-party complaint unless the third-party complaint is filed within 10 days after serving the original answer. In other words, a third-party plaintiff can file the third-party complaint without court permission only if it is filed within 10 days of service of the original answer. See Figure 7-10 (Form 22-B of Appendix to FRCivP) for a simple example of a motion to obtain permission to file a third-party complaint. The proposed third-party summons and complaint should be attached as an exhibit to the motion. The motion and notice of motion must be mailed to all parties to the action.

FIGURE 7-9   THIRD-PARTY SUMMONS AND COMPLAINT (FRCivP OFFICIAL FORM 22-A)

Form 22-A. Summons and Complaint Against Third-Party Defendant

United States District Court for the Southern District of New York

Civil Action, File Number _____

A.B., Plaintiff
v.
C.D., Defendant and Third-Party Plaintiff
v.
E.F., Third-Party Defendant
} *Summons*

To the above-named Third-Party Defendant:

You are hereby summoned and required to serve upon _____, plaintiff's attorney whose address is _____, and upon _____, who is attorney for C.D., defendant and third-party plaintiff, and whose address is _____, an answer to the third-party complaint which is herewith served upon you within 20 days after the service of this summons upon you exclusive of the day of service. If you fail to do so, judgment by default will be taken against you for the relief demanded in the third-party complaint. There is also served upon you herewith a copy of the complaint of the plaintiff which you may but are not required to answer.

_____,
Clerk of Court.

[Seal of District Court]
Dated _____

United States District Court for the Southern District of New York

Civil Action, File Number _____

A.B., Plaintiff
v.
C.D., Defendant and Third-Party Plaintiff
v.
E.F., Third-Party Defendant
} *Third-Party Complaint*

1. Plaintiff A.B. has filed against defendant C.D. a complaint, a copy of which is hereto attached as "Exhibit A."

2. (Here state the grounds upon which C.D. is entitled to recover from E.F., all or part of what A.B. may recover from C.D. The statement should be framed as in an original complaint.)

Wherefore C.D. demands judgment against third-party defendant E.F. for all sums[1] that may be adjudged against defendant C.D. in favor of plaintiff A.B.

Signed: _____,

Attorney for C.D., Third-Party Plaintiff.
Address:_____

FIGURE 7-10   MOTION TO BRING IN THIRD-PARTY DEFENDANT

Form 22-B. Motion to Bring in Third-Party Defendant

Defendant moves for leave, as third-party plaintiff, to cause to be served upon E.F. a summons and third-party complaint, copies of which are hereto attached as Exhibit X.

Signed: _____,

Attorney for Defendant C.D.

Address: _____

Notice of Motion

(Contents the same as in Form 19. The notice should be addressed to all parties to the action.)

Contesting the Request for Impleader. Other parties may contest the request for impleader. FRCivP 14(a) provides that "[a]ny party at any time may move to strike the third-party claim, or for its severance or separate trial." This means that a party may object to impleader at the time the motion requesting permission to implead is made or at any time in the litigation. If the court has already granted permission to implead, any party may request that the court either strike the third-party claim completely or order that it be heard in a separate trial. The original plaintiff may object to inclusion of the third-party claim because it would make the litigation too complex or otherwise prejudice the plaintiff's claim. FRCivP 14(a) does not specify when to file a motion to strike or sever the third-party claim. However, it is best to file any motion in opposition to another motion as early as possible.

Service of Pleadings on Original Parties. Recall that FRCivP 5 requires that every pleading subsequent to the original complaint must be served on all parties to an action. Thus the third-party plaintiff effects service of process on the third-party defendant, in accordance with FRCivP 4, in the same manner as for a "regular" complaint. In addition, the third-party plaintiff serves (mails or hand delivers) a copy of the third-party complaint and summons to all the original plaintiffs and defendants, with a certificate of service, as required by FRCivP 5.

Summary of Procedure

The paralegal must be sure that all necessary documents related to the third-party complaint are filed and served properly. The procedure in summary is as follows: (1) If more than 10 days have elapsed since the defendant's answer was served, prepare a motion for court permission to bring in a third-party defendant. Attach a copy of the proposed third-party complaint and summons as Exhibit A. If less than 10 days have elapsed since the answer was filed, move directly to (3) below. (2) File the motion with the clerk of court and serve a copy on all parties. Also serve a notice of motion. (3) When the court grants the motion to file the third-party complaint, serve the filed complaint and the summons on the third-party defendant, in accordance with FRCivP 4. Be sure that the original complaint is attached as an exhibit to the third-party complaint. (4) Mark in your pleading response tracking system the date that the third-party defendant's answer is due.

 POINTER: Check your local rules and/or call the clerk of court to find out whether a filing fee is required for a third-party complaint.

Defenses to a Third-Party Complaint

FRCivP 14(a) provides that a third-party defendant may assert any of the responses that a defendant served with a "regular" complaint may assert. That is, a third-party defendant may file an answer and/or Rule 12 motions. A third-party defendant may include any defenses that the original defendant has against the original plaintiff. A third-party defendant may also assert a counterclaim against the original plaintiff or a cross-claim against another third-party defendant.

The possibilities may sound endless and confusing. For now, just be aware of the permissible pleadings and refer to FRCivP 14(a) for a listing of the third-party defendant's options. With litigation this complex, you will discuss the options with the attorneys on your team.

AMENDMENTS AND SUPPLEMENTAL PLEADINGS

Introduction

In the course of a lawsuit a party may realize that an important fact or issue has been omitted from a pleading, or some new fact may come to light that necessitates an addition to a pleading. When this occurs, parties need to change or add to the pleadings they have filed. Rule 15 of the Federal Rules of Civil Procedure allows parties to do this freely, so long as it does not cause substantial prejudice to another party. The goal of pleadings under the Federal Rules of Civil Procedure is to frame the dispute accurately and ensure that every party has fair notice and an opportunity to respond.

This same rationale applies to supplemental pleadings. Rule 15(d) provides that a party may ask the court for permission to serve a supplemental pleading. Rule 15(d) states that this is appropriate to set forth "transactions or occurrences or events which have happened since the date of the pleading sought to be supplemented."

The distinction between an amended pleading and a supplemental pleading is not always evident. Technically, a supplemental pleading adds a new fact that has come to light, and an amended pleading changes a previously pleaded fact. As a practical matter, once a complaint and responsive pleading have been filed, if the plaintiff needs to alter the complaint, the plaintiff requests permission to amend and supplement the complaint. The revised complaint will then bear the title AMENDED AND SUPPLEMENTAL COMPLAINT.

Timing and Procedure

Rule 15(a) states the rules regarding when a party needs the court's permission to amend a pleading. A party may amend a pleading once as a matter of right when no responsive pleading has yet been filed. Therefore a plaintiff may amend the complaint without court permission when the defendant has not yet filed an answer. If no responsive pleading is permitted and the action has not been placed on a trial calendar, a party may amend the pleading within 20 days after service. An example of a pleading to which no responsive pleading is permitted is a reply to a counterclaim.

In all other circumstances, a party must either request leave of the court or obtain the written consent of the adverse party in order to file an amendment. Rule 15(a) further directs that leave to amend "shall be freely given when justice so requires." While courts do generally grant leave to amend freely, the court is less likely to grant the motion to amend if the request is made far into the litigation. The rules encourage the court to be fair, and allowing a substantial amendment well into the discovery period or on the eve of trial may be too prejudicial to the adverse party.

How to File a Motion to Amend. Motions in general are discussed in Chapter 8. However, the basic procedure for filing a motion to amend a pleading is as follows. The necessary documents obviously include the actual motion asking the court's leave to amend. See Figure 7-11 for an example. State explicitly the facts that necessitate the amendment rather than a general statement that plaintiff needs to amend her complaint. Many attorneys attach the proposed amended pleading as an exhibit to the motion.

Next, prepare a notice of motion (see Figure 7-12). This informs the adverse party when the motion will be heard before the court. Often the attorneys for adverse parties will confer beforehand to determine a mutually convenient date on the court calendar. Finally, prepare a proposed order granting leave to file an amended pleading. As we note in Chapter 8, it is best to submit a proposed order. This encourages the judge to incorporate the language you prefer. See Figure 7-13 for an example. As always, file the documents with the clerk of court, and serve all filed documents on all parties to the litigation. A memorandum of law is sometimes prepared to explain the reasons why leave to amend should be granted.

If the adverse party opposes the motion to amend, that party must submit a motion requesting the court not to grant the adverse party leave to amend. The adverse party must specifically state why the motion should not be granted, including an explanation why the amendment would be unduly prejudicial.

POINTER: Note that many local court rules deem a motion unopposed if the adverse party files no response to the motion. Never assume that the court will just know that you oppose a motion if you fail to file a response. Check the local rules to determine time limits for filing responses to motions.

Filing the Amended Pleading. Suppose that the court has just granted the plaintiff's motion to amend the complaint with the clerk of court, with service on all parties. When the amendment is very slight, the body of the amended pleading may simply state, for instance, that the plaintiff amends paragraph 5 of the complaint by deleting the words "Model 6102" and inserting the words "Model 7102." If the amendment is anything more complex or extensive, a party should file

FIGURE 7-11   MOTION TO OBTAIN PERMISSION TO FILE AMENDED COMPLAINT

UNITED STATES DISTRICT COURT
MIDDLE DISTRICT OF NORTH CAROLINA
CHARLESTON DIVISION
CIVIL NO.: C-89-1293-B

Bryson Wesser,

Plaintiff,

-vs-

Woodall Shoals Corporation,

Defendant,

and

Second Ledge Stores, Incorporated,

Defendant

MOTION AND AFFIDAVIT
FOR LEAVE TO FILE
AMENDED COMPLAINT

NOW COMES the plaintiff, by and through Leigh J. Heyward, attorney of record, under the provisions of Rule 15 of the Federal Rules of Civil Procedure, and moves the Court for leave to file an Amendment to his Complaint, as set forth in ''Exhibit A'' attached hereto and incorporated herein by reference, and in support thereof, respectfully shows unto the Court that:

1.   The electric blanket which is the subject of this action was almost completely destroyed in the fire which it caused; thus, there was and is little material by which the model number identifying the blanket can be identified.

2.   In a meeting on December 30, 1988, between plaintiff attorney and Richard Olivarez, adjuster for ABC Insurance Company, carrier for the defendants, Mr. Olivarez identified the blanket as Woodall Shoals Model 6102. Since the defendant Woodall Shoals had previously had physical possession of the blanket remains and control for testing purposes, plaintiff's attorney relied upon Mr. Olivarez's identification in drafting the Complaint.

3.   In April 1989, when the defendant Woodall Shoals Corporation filed ''answers'' to plaintiff's first set of interrogatories, said defendant asserted that it had never sold Woodall Shoals Model 6102 to defendant Second Ledge Stores, Incorporated, implying and asserting that the blanket was probably not Model 6102.

FIGURE 7-11 MOTION TO OBTAIN PERMISSION TO FILE AMENDED COMPLAINT (Cont.)

4. Because Richard Olivarez may have erroneously identified said blanket, the only direct means of identification upon which plaintiff can rely is the name plate from the controller, which is attached to the proposed Amendment to Complaint ("Exhibit A-1").

5. The granting of plaintiff's motion will not surprise or prejudice the defendants, because the defendants' insurance carrier has previously had physical possession of the control and remains of the blanket, and the defendants' attorneys have had a photograph of the name plate for several months. Furthermore, only the defendants have the records, if any, to enable the parties to identify the model of the blanket, using the information on the name plate.

6. Denial of plaintiff's motion would result in substantial injustice and prejudice to plaintiff.

7. The ends of justice would best be served by granting plaintiff's motion.

WHEREFORE, plaintiff respectfully moves the Court for leave to amend the Complaint in this action in the manner and to the extent set forth in the "Amendment to Complaint" attached hereto and marked "Exhibit A."

_____

Leigh J. Heyward
Attorney for the Plaintiff
Heyward and Wilson
401 East Trade Street
Charleston, NC 28226-1114
704-555-3161

+ Certificate of Service

FIGURE 7-11   MOTION TO OBTAIN PERMISSION TO FILE AMENDED COMPLAINT (Cont.)

UNITED STATES DISTRICT COURT
MIDDLE DISTRICT OF NORTH CAROLINA
CHARLESTON DIVISION
CIVIL NO.: C-89-1293-B

Bryson Wesser,

　　　　　　　　Plaintiff,

　　-vs-

Woodall Shoals Corporation,

　　　　　　　Defendant,
　　　　　and
Second Ledge Stores, Incorporated,

　　　　　　　Defendant

AMENDMENT TO COMPLAINT

NOW COMES the plaintiff and, with leave of the Court, amends his Complaint in the above-entitled action, as follows:

1. By striking the language "Model 6102" in Paragraph 4 and adding the following sentence at the conclusion of that paragraph, "The electric blanket is further identified by data on the control unit thereof, a copy of a photograph of which is attached as 'Exhibit A-1.'

Leigh J. Heyward
Attorney for the Plaintiff
Heyward and Wilson
401 East Trade Street
Charleston, NC 28226-1114
704-555-3161

EXHIBIT "A"

FIGURE 7-12   NOTICE OF MOTION

UNITED STATES DISTRICT COURT
MIDDLE DISTRICT OF NORTH CAROLINA
CHARLESTON DIVISION
CIVIL NO.: C-89-1293-B

Bryson Wesser,

Plaintiff,

-vs-

Woodall Shoals Corporation,

Defendant,

and

Second Ledge Stores, Incorporated,

Defendant

NOTICE OF MOTION

To: David H. Benedict
Attorney for the Defendants
Benedict, Parker & Miller
100 Nolichucky Drive
Bristol, NC 28205-0890

YOU WILL TAKE NOTICE that the plaintiff in the above-entitled action will appear before His Honor, James C. Jefferson, or such other judge as may be presiding over the United States District Court for the Middle District of North Carolina, on Monday, May 15, 1989, at 10:00 a.m., or as soon thereafter as counsel may be heard, for hearing upon plaintiff's Motion for Leave to File an Amended Complaint.

YOU WILL PLEASE TAKE NOTICE thereof and be present at said time and place if you care to be heard.

This the 2d day of May, 1989.

Leigh J. Heyward
Attorney for the Plaintiff
Heyward and Wilson
401 East Trade Street
Charleston, NC 28226-1114
704-555-3161

+ Certificate of Service

FIGURE 7-13 ORDER

UNITED STATES DISTRICT COURT
MIDDLE DISTRICT OF NORTH CAROLINA
CHARLESTON DIVISION
CIVIL NO.: C-89-1293-B

Bryson Wesser,

                Plaintiff,

    -vs-

Woodall Shoals Corporation,   *ORDER*

                Defendant,

        and

Second Ledge Stores, Incorporated,

                Defendant

THIS CAUSE, coming on to be heard and being heard before His Honor, James C. Jefferson, Judge Presiding at the February 10, 1989, Civil Session of the United States District Court for the Middle District of North Carolina, upon motion of the plaintiffs under Rule 15(a) of the Federal Rules of Civil Procedure to amend their Complaint;

AND IT APPEARING TO THE COURT that the defendant Woodall Shoals Corporation's initial answers to Interrogatories raise a question as to the correct identity of the electric blanket, as given by their insurance adjuster, Richard Olivarez, and that the defendants would not be prejudiced by the proposed amendment.

IT IS, THEREFORE, ORDERED that:

1. Plaintiff's Complaint be and it is hereby amended to strike the language and term "Model 6102" from paragraph 5 thereof and to add the following sentence at the conclusion of paragraph 5:

The electric blanket is further identified by data on the control unit thereof, a copy of a photograph of which is attached as Exhibit A-1.

2. Defendants Woodall Shoals and Second Ledge be and they are hereby granted thirty (30) days within which to file answer or otherwise plead to paragraph 5 of the Complaint as so amended.

Entered in open Court and signed this 30 day of May, 1989.

                                      _____

                                        James C. Jefferson
                                        United States District Judge

the entire amended pleading—that is, the original pleading with the amendments incorporated (typed in the appropriate place). A complete amended pleading should also be filed when prior amendments have been made, when the court file is particularly thick and finding the amended complaint for reference would be difficult, or if the particular judge in your case prefers this method.

After the clerk has file-stamped each copy of the amended pleading, serve a copy on each party. Recall that service of all documents after the initial complaint is made by one of the methods prescribed in FRCivP 5. Usually you will mail a copy of the amended pleading to each party's attorney. Note that service of process (FRCivP 4) is not required for amended complaints, just for the original complaint.

Responding to the Amended Pleading. Rule 15(a) governs the time for responding to the amended pleading. It states that a "party shall plead in response to an amended pleading within the time remaining for response to the original pleading or within 10 days after service of the amended pleading, whichever period may be the longer, unless the court otherwise orders." Obviously, if the responding party needs more time to file a response, the party must seek additional time from the court.

REMOVAL

Introduction

The definition of removal is simple: Removal is the transfer of a case from a state court to a federal court. When a case is removed, the state court file is closed and the federal court takes over jurisdiction of the lawsuit. A defendant seeks removal when there is a jurisdictional basis for hearing a case in federal court and the defendant feels it is advantageous for the case to be heard in federal court rather than state court. The federal court must have concurrent jurisdiction. If the lawsuit is a type over which federal courts do not have jurisdiction, it obviously would not be proper to remove the case to federal court.

Removal is for the benefit of defendants and therefore only defendants may seek it. When a plaintiff files a lawsuit, the plaintiff chooses the court in which the litigation will take place. Removal gives defendants an opportunity to try to litigate in a court that is more advantageous for them.

You may wonder why a party would want a case transferred from state court to federal court. This is a strategy decision, and there are many reasons why a defendant might want a case heard in federal rather than state court. For example, the case may be assigned to a state court judge whom the defendant's attorney considers unfavorable to this particular type of case. The defendant's attorney may feel that a more favorable jury can be picked in federal court, which draws jurors from a larger area.

The removal procedure is fairly simple. However, determining whether removal is possible and advantageous can be complex. The decision whether to seek removal will be made by the attorney on your team, but the paralegal needs to have an understanding of when removal is proper and the procedure for requesting it.

When Removal Is Proper

The removal of actions to federal court is governed by 28 U.S.C. §§1441-1452. Recall that federal courts have limited jurisdiction; that is, they can hear only certain types of cases. For this reason, a case can be removed to federal court only if the federal court has original subject matter jurisdiction. That is, the claim must be one that the court could have heard had the suit originally been filed in federal court.

The federal jurisdiction basis must exist at the time the notice of removal is filed. Suppose that a plaintiff files a complaint for breach of warranty based on state law only, and all the parties are residents of the same state, thereby precluding diversity jurisdiction. At this point, removal is not possible, because there is no basis for federal jurisdiction. The plaintiff subsequently amends the complaint, adding a claim pursuant to the Magnuson-Moss Act, a federal statute concerning consumer protection. The defendant may now petition for removal, based on federal question jurisdiction. Note that the federal jurisdiction basis must be in the complaint. A defendant cannot base the removal petition on defenses in the answer or on counterclaims.

Another requirement is that every defendant must agree to the request for removal. Because the removal process aims to benefit defendants, every defendant must join in the notice of removal.

Timing and Procedure

The procedure for requesting removal is explained clearly in 28 U.S.C. §1446(a):

> A defendant or defendants desiring to remove any civil action or criminal prosecution from a State court shall file in the district court of the United States for the district and division within which such action is pending a notice of removal signed pursuant to Rule 11 of the Federal Rules of Civil Procedure and containing a short and plain statement of the grounds for removal, together with a copy of all process, pleadings, and orders served upon such defendant or defendants in such action.

POINTER: Note that the document requesting removal is called a "notice of removal." Formerly this document was termed a "petition for removal." You may encounter the old term is some form books or pleadings that predate the November 1988 amendments to 28 U.S.C. §1446.

Content of Notice of Removal

The notice of removal must contain a "short and plain statement of the grounds for removal." Obviously, the notice of removal must contain the statement of federal jurisdiction, since this is the crucial factor in removal. Like other pleadings, the attorney must sign the notice of removal, verifying, pursuant to FRCivP 11, that there is a sound basis in law and in fact for the removal request.

There are three general bases for removal. You are already familiar with two of them—federal question jurisdiction and diversity jurisdiction. There are also federal statutes that allow removal in certain types of actions. These include civil actions against foreign states, civil rights actions, foreclosures against the

United States, and actions involving federal officers or members of the armed forces. The statutes providing for removal in these circumstances are 28 U.S.C. §§1441, 1443, 1444, 1442, and 1442(a), respectively.

State the basis for removal clearly, citing specific statutory authority—for example, federal question jurisdiction under 28 U.S.C. §1332, based on a claim involving the Magnuson-Moss Act, 15 U.S.C. §2301, *et seq.*

Deadlines for Filing Notice of Removal

The deadlines for filing a notice of removal are set forth in 28 U.S.C §1446(b). It is crucial to understand the filing deadlines, because the effect of missing the deadline is that your client becomes barred from seeking removal and must remain in state court.

There are three rules to remember in regard to the filing deadlines. The first rule applies where the basis for removal is stated in the initial pleading stating the claim for relief. Usually the "initial pleading" means the complaint. When the complaint contains a basis for removal—for example, when the plaintiff has asserted a claim that raises a federal question—the defendant must file the notice of removal within 30 days of receiving the complaint, or within 30 days of receiving the summons when the summons is served without the complaint, whichever period is shorter.

The second rule applies when the basis for removal first appears in an amended pleading. 28 U.S.C. §1446(b) states that "[i]f the case stated by the initial pleading is not removable, a notice of removal may be filed within thirty days after receipt by the defendant . . . of an amended pleading, motion, order or other paper from which it may first be ascertained that the case is one which is or has become removable. . . ." As noted above, the first mention of a federal statute may appear in an amended complaint. In this instance, the defendant must file the notice of removal within 30 days of receipt of the amended complaint.

The third rule applies only when the basis for federal jurisdiction is diversity of citizenship of the parties. When the basis for federal jurisdiction that arises after the initial pleading is diversity of citizenship, the notice of removal must be filed within one year after the commencement of the action in state court.

Thus suppose that in a state court action in Indiana there are two defendants. One defendant is a citizen of Illinois, and one defendant is a citizen of Indiana; the plaintiff is also a citizen of Indiana. Six months after commencement of the state court action, the defendant from Indiana is dismissed from the lawsuit. There is now complete diversity of citizenship. The Illinois defendant may file a notice of removal, because less than one year has elapsed since the commencement of the state court action. If the Indiana defendant had been dismissed 14 months after commencement of the state court action, the Illinois defendant could not remove the case to federal court, because more than one year would have elapsed.

POINTER: Remember that the one-year bar applies only when jurisdiction is based on diversity. If a federal question arose for the first time 14 months after commencement of the state court action, the defendant could still file a notice of removal.

Procedure after Removal Is Complete

When the case is removed to federal court, the federal court takes full jurisdiction, and the state court has no more authority to enter orders. When a lawsuit is removed to federal court, it does not always stay in federal court for the remainder of the litigation. A party opposing removal may file a motion to remand the action to state court. A motion to remand based on a defect in the removal procedure must be filed within 30 days after the filing of the notice of removal under section 1446(a). As provided by 28 U.S.C. §1447(c), a case shall be remanded if "at any time before final judgment it appears that the district court lacks subject matter jurisdiction." This can occur when the plaintiff is permitted to add an additional defendant whose citizenship destroys diversity, and there is no federal question jurisdiction. Thus even though a defendant succeeds in having a case removed to federal court, the case may still be sent back to the state court. When a case is remanded to state court, a certified copy of the order of remand is mailed by the federal court clerk to the clerk of the state court, and the state court may then proceed with the case.

Other Rules Regarding Removal

Not every rule related to removal is discussed here. Removal can be complex. When you face a complex removal situation, review with the attorney any of the more intricate rules. Recall that the rules for removal appear in 28 U.S.C. §§1441-1450. Note that §1445 cites certain types of actions that cannot be removed from state court. So long as you understand the basic rules and procedure for removal, you can deal with the more intricate aspects in conjunction with the attorney on your team.

ENDNOTES

1 FRCivP 6(a).
2 Some judicial districts may have a filing fee for counterclaims. You must check your local rules and/or call the clerk's office.
3 Note that Form 22-A in the Appendix to the Federal Rules of Civil Procedure includes a Third-Party Summons *and* a Third-Party Complaint. They are clearly labeled as separate documents.

8 MOTION PRACTICE AND MOTIONS FOR ENTRY OF JUDGMENT WITHOUT TRIAL

LITIGATION EXTRACT: At this stage of the litigation Mr. Wesser has filed a complaint and completed service of process. Woodall Shoals and Second Ledge have filed an answer, with a motion to dismiss. In addition to the pleadings, the parties will file various motions throughout the litigation. Chapter 8 explains the process of filing motions, known as motion practice. The motions filed can range from a motion seeking additional time to file a response to a motion requesting that the court enter judgment in favor of the moving party without having a trial, known as a dispositive motion. Chapter 8 explains three motions to end the litigation without having to go through an actual trial. These include motion for default judgment, requested when the defendant does not respond to the complaint; motion for judgment on the pleadings, requested when the pleadings on their face show that the moving party is entitled to judgment; and motion for summary judgment, requested when there is no dispute as to any material fact and the moving party is entitled to judgment as a matter of law.

INTRODUCTION

Chapter 8 focuses on three types of motions: **motion for default judgment, motion for judgment on the pleadings,** and **motion for summary judgment.** The purpose of all these motions is to terminate the litigation at an early stage so that a trial will not be necessary. This can result in great savings of time and money. Before a substantive discussion of these motions, it is necessary to understand the basic rules that apply to all motions.

MOTION PRACTICE

A **motion** is an application to a court for an order directing some act in favor of the applicant.[1] Motions regulate the course of a lawsuit. Numerous motions will be filed in most lawsuits, and the process is sometimes called "motion practice." Some motions pertain primarily to procedural matters: a motion for extension of time to file a response to a pleading, for example, or a motion to amend a pleading.

Other motions ask the court to enter a judgment in favor of the moving party and thus terminate the lawsuit. These include motions for default judgment, for judgment on the pleadings, and for summary judgment. Because these motions dispose of the lawsuit, they are often referred to as **dispositive motions**. A motion to dismiss an action for failure to state a claim upon which relief can be granted (FRCivP 12(b)(6)), discussed in Chapter 7, may also terminate a lawsuit and be a dispositive motion.

Still other motions are made orally during trial (e.g., a motion for a directed verdict) or entered after trial (e.g., a motion for a new trial). Motions made at trial are discussed in Chapter 12.

Most local rules provide that if a party opposes a motion, that party must file a response to the motion. Therefore, if a wide variety of motions can be made during the course of a lawsuit, an equally wide variety of responses may be filed asking the court to deny the other party's motion.

As an example of the variety of motions and responses, consider a situation where the defendant has successfully removed the case from state court to federal court. The plaintiff then files a MOTION TO REMAND the case to state court. The defendant responds with a RESPONSE IN OPPOSITION TO MOTION TO REMAND, asking the federal court to retain the case. The court grants the plaintiff's motion to remand and orders the case sent back to state court. The defendant files a MOTION TO RECONSIDER ORDER REMANDING ACTION TO STATE COURT. The plaintiff responds with a RESPONSE TO MOTION TO RECONSIDER ORDER REMANDING ACTION TO STATE COURT, in which the plaintiff asks the court to deny the defendant's motion and affirm its earlier order to remand to state court. The court then enters an order denying the motion to reconsider, and this series of motions and responses is mercifully finished.

Form and Content of Motions

Rule 7(b) of the Federal Rules of Civil Procedure addresses the form of motions and states three requirements. First, a motion must be in writing unless the motion is made orally during a hearing or trial. Second, the motion must "state with particularity the grounds" on which the motion is based. Third, the motion must "set forth the relief or order sought."

The format for motions is the same as for the complaint and other pleadings, as you see from the motions illustrated throughout this chapter. Like a complaint, the caption includes the name of the court, title of the action (names of parties in the lawsuit), and file number. The motion also has a caption that states the specific nature of the motion. For example, a motion for summary judgment is not captioned simply "Motion." Rather, it is captioned "Motion for Summary Judgment." A caption may be lengthy, as in the preceding sample motions related to removal. Most local rules of court require such specific titles, so spell out the nature of the motion in the caption even if it looks cumbersome.

FRCivP 7(b)(2) states that the rules applicable to matters of form for pleadings apply to all motions as well. In addition to the captions, motions also contain numbered paragraphs and the attorney's signature, name, address, and telephone number. As with pleadings, a certificate of service must be attached.

The actual content of the motion itself depends on the type of motion you are filing. Be sure to state specifically the relief you seek and the specific reasons why you seek the relief. For instance, in a motion to strike, specify the exact words in the pleading that you want struck, and explain why these words are, for instance, scandalous and prejudicial. If you file a response to the plaintiff's motion to file an amended complaint, ask the court to deny the plaintiff's motion and explain why you oppose the plaintiff's motion.

Notice of Motion

Most motions require a hearing before the court to determine whether the motion should be granted. (See the subsection headed Hearings.) The moving party must inform the other parties of the time and place where the hearing will be held, so that the other parties can prepare their arguments for the hearing. FRCivP 6(d) requires that the motion and notice of motion must be served on the other parties "not later than five days before the time specified for the hearing, unless a different period is fixed by these rules or by order of the court." FRCivP 56(c) requires that motions for summary judgment be served at least 10 days before the dated fixed for the hearing. Local court rules may require more than five days notice. The motion, notice of motion, and supporting documentation should be served together.

The content of a notice of motion is short and simple. It specifies the date, time, and location of the hearing. The notice of motion also specifies the exact nature of the motion to be heard—motion for summary judgment, for example, or motion to dismiss pursuant to FRCivP 12(b)(6). (In Chapter 7, Figure 7-12 illustrated a notice of motion.) See also Figure 8-1 for an example of a preprinted form that a court may use.

Affidavits, Memoranda of Law, and Other Supporting Documents

Supporting affidavits and memoranda of law (briefs) accompany many, if not most, motions. An **affidavit** is a written statement of facts and bears the notarized signature of the person stating the facts. The person making the statement is referred to as the **affiant**. The significance of the notarized signature is twofold. First, the notary verifies the identification and signature of the affiant, so that a person reading the affidavit knows that the statement was made by the person who signed it. A notary must actually witness the affiant signing the affidavit. Second, the affiant swears that the facts in the affidavit are true. Thus affidavits are considered more reliable than simple signed statements.

Chapter 8

FIGURE 8-1   FORM THAT MAY BE USED FOR NOTICE OF MOTION

NOTICE OF MOTION

STATE OF NORTH CAROLINA   **IN THE GENERAL COURT OF JUSTICE**
COUNTY OF MECKLENBURG   _____**COURT DIVISION**
                                                               Case No. _____
Date: _____   **Jury: ( ) Yes   ( ) No**

                         Plaintiff   Defendant

                                            vs.

TO: Trial Court Administrator
          The undersigned attorney has this date filed and served a motion:
(Check type)
          (   ) To dismiss under Rule 12.
          (   ) To join additional party.
          (   ) To amend pleadings.
          (   ) For sanctions under Rule 37.
          (   ) For summary judgment under Rule 56.
          (   ) For preliminary injunction.
          (   ) Other:_____

                    _____

          It is requested that this motion be calendared for hearing.

_____   _____
Attorney for   (   ) Plaintiff   (   ) Defendant   Date

Address: _____

          _____

Telephone No. _____

_____

This motion is calendared for Hearing on _____

In Courtroom _____

                                                       _____

Affidavits are often attached to motions as exhibits. The statements in the affidavits help to explain to the court why the motion should be granted. Examine the simple motion for summary judgment and the affidavit in support of motion for summary judgment illustrated in Figures 8-17 and 8-18. This is a lawsuit by a hospital to recover an unpaid hospital bill. The information in the affidavit supports the claim stated in the complaint (which is not illustrated) that the hospital rendered services to the defendant, that the defendant agreed to pay for the services, and that the defendant has failed to pay.

With motions for summary judgment and other more complex motions, the motion itself is usually quite short, and the facts are explained in attached affidavits. Examine Figure 8-19, which is a motion for summary judgment in the Chattooga case. This motion for summary judgment refers the court to an attached affidavit, as well as to relevant parts of the pleadings and to other attached exhibits. The other exhibits include the pertinent pages of depositions and documents produced during the discovery process. Do not worry about the intricacies of discovery just now; these matters will be discussed in Chapter 9. Just note the types of documents that can be used to support motions.

To support many motions, the attorney/paralegal team will prepare memoranda of law. This is not necessary for simple motions, such as the motion for summary judgment to recover money owed on a hospital bill. Nor is a memorandum of law necessary for a motion to reschedule a hearing, particularly if all parties agree to the rescheduling. But for more complex motions, such as the motion for summary judgment in the Chattooga case, a memorandum of law is necessary. Some local court rules specify when a memorandum of law should accompany a motion. Be sure to check your local rules.

A **memorandum of law**, sometimes called a **brief**, is a written explanation of the facts, applicable statutes, and pertinent case law. Some judicial districts use the term ''statement of points and authority'' or ''memorandum of points and authority.'' This textbook uses all these terms interchangeably.

The purpose of the memorandum of law is to explain to the court why it should rule in favor of your client. Memoranda of law follow a general format that you may have already learned in your legal writing class. That format consists of cover page, table of contents, table of authorities, statement of the question(s) presented for review, procedural history, statement of the facts, argument (why the facts and law support a ruling in your favor), conclusion, signature and identification of counsel, proof of service, and any exhibits. Figure 8-20 illustrates some portions of a memorandum of law.

The length and content of the memorandum of law obviously depend on the nature of the motion. A motion based on a simple factual argument need not be lengthy. However, motions pertaining to complex fact situations and novel questions of law may be lengthy. For example, a brief in support of a motion to dismiss under Rule 12(b)(6) may be quite long when the case involves a complex question of constitutional law that has not been litigated before. The lawyers in your firm will be familiar with the fine points and strategy involved in composing a brief. However, you should remember that a good brief is thorough without being long-winded, and that your argument should be presented in a straightforward manner, explaining why the law and facts support your client.

Remember that you file memoranda of law in opposition to motions as well as in support of them. A memorandum of law in opposition to a motion follows basically the same format as one in support. You may have the option to delete the statement of facts. However, it is usually advantageous to restate the facts to help set the stage for your own argument. Be aware that the local rules may not provide a great deal of time for filing the brief, so record your deadline and begin work immediately.

POINTER: This is just a general outline of the parts of a memorandum of law. Local rules may modify or amplify these basic parts. You *must* consult your local rules regarding format for briefs, page limits (if any), how many copies to file with the court, and deadlines for filing and responding to briefs. See Figure 8-2, which reprints a portion of Rule 107 of the United States District Court for the Middle District of North Carolina.

FIGURE 8-2   PORTION OF A RULE REGARDING BRIEFS AND MEMORANDA OF LAW

RULE 107
(Middle District of North Carolina)
BRIEFS AND MEMORANDA OF LAW

   (a) **Contents.** All briefs filed with the court shall contain:
   (1) A statement of the nature of the matter before the court.
   (2) A concise statement of the facts. Each statement of fact should be supported by reference to a part of the official record in the case.
   (3) A statement of the question or questions presented.
   (4) The argument, which shall refer to all statutes, rules and authorities relied upon.
                                          . . .
   (e) **Additional Copies of Briefs for Court Use.** At the time the original of a brief is filed, a working copy of the brief for use by the judge or magistrate shall be delivered to the clerk.

Filing and Service of Motions

FRCivP 6(d) requires that the motion, notice of motion, and supporting affidavits be served on all parties not later than five days before the hearing date. It also provides that opposing affidavits be served not less than one day before the hearing. These deadlines can be altered by local rules or by other federal rules of civil procedure. Some local rules set deadlines for filing dispositive motions so that any such motions can be heard well before trial. For example, a local rule may require that a motion for summary judgment be filed within 60 days following the close of the discovery period. As we noted earlier, FRCivP 56 requires that a motion for summary judgment must be served at least 10 days before the date set for hearing.

If at all possible, the motion and accompanying papers should be filed well ahead of these deadlines. With complex motions, you must allow the court plenty of time to examine the extensive supporting documents and consider the complicated questions of law involved. You may need an extension of time for filing a motion or response to a motion. It is imperative to request court permission for an extension of time. In many jurisdictions, if a response to a motion is not filed within the stated time, the motion is deemed unopposed. Never assume that the court knows that your client opposes a motion. File an opposing motion.

POINTER: Local rules are always important. However, they are especially important in motion practice because of their specific directions regarding filing deadlines, supporting documents, etc. Read Rule 108 of the United States District Court for the District of Columbia for an example of a local rule regarding motion practice (Figure 8-3).

Every motion must have attached a certificate of service, signed by the attorney, verifying the date that the motion was served on the opposing parties. Recall that service can be accomplished by mail or by personal delivery to the office of the attorney for the other parties. FRCivP 5(c) states that service by mail is complete upon mailing.

FRCivP 5(c) provides that papers can be filed with the clerk either before service or "within a reasonable time thereafter." It is usually best to file documents with the clerk before service, for several reasons. Doing so lessens the chance of forgetting to file the papers and the chance of missing a filing deadline. Also, the document will bear the clerk's stamp showing the date filed, so the other parties will know when the documents were filed.

As always, review your checklist to be sure that all documents are prepared before you mail anything or go to the clerk's office. Be sure that for the court and for each party you have assembled the entire package necessary to decide the motion. You need to assemble the motion with supporting affidavits and other exhibits (e.g., excerpts from depositions or other discovery materials, excerpts from pleadings, applicable business records, etc.), the memorandum of law in support of the motion, and the notice of motion. Local rules may also require that you submit a proposed order for the judge. (See the upcoming subsections on orders.) When you return to the office, check by the end of the day to be sure that all motions were served at the time and in the manner stated in the certificate of service.

Responses to Motions

When a party is served with a motion, the party must respond to the motion. As we have noted, if the party does not respond at all, the motion will be deemed unopposed in most jurisdictions.

There will be times when the party in fact does not oppose the motion. This is particularly true with simple procedural motions, such as an extension of time to file a pleading or a motion to reschedule a hearing because one attorney has a schedule conflict. If you do not oppose the motion, you should inform the court in writing. You may file a simple statement that the party you represent does not oppose the motion and does not wish to appear at the hearing. Sometimes the attorneys for all the parties involved file a **consent order**. This is a proposed order signed by all the attorneys, stating that they have agreed to an extension of time or a rescheduled hearing date. See Figure 8-4 for an example

FIGURE 8-3   EXAMPLE OF A LOCAL RULE

RULE 108   MOTIONS

(a) **Statement of Points and Authorities.** Each motion shall include or be accompanied by a statement of the specific points of law and authority that support the motion, including where appropriate a concise statement of facts. If a table of cases is provided, counsel shall place asterisks in the margin to the left of those cases or authorities on which counsel chiefly relies.

(b) **Opposing Points and Authorities.** Within 11 days of the date of service or at such other time as the court may direct, an opposing party shall serve and file a memorandum of points and authorities in opposition to the motion. If such a memorandum is not filed within the prescribed time, the court may treat the motion as conceded.

(c) **Proposed Order.** Each motion shall be accompanied by a proposed order.

(d) **Reply Memorandum.** Within five days after service of the memorandum in opposition the moving party may serve and file a reply memorandum.

(e) **Page Limitations.** A memorandum of points and authorities in support of or in opposition to a motion shall not exceed 45 pages and a reply memorandum shall not exceed 25 pages, without prior approval of the court. Documents that fail to comply with this provision shall not be filed by the Clerk.

(f) **Oral Hearings.** A party may in a motion or opposition request an oral hearing, but its allowance shall be within the discretion of the court. If at the time of the hearing the moving party fails to appear, the court may treat the motion as withdrawn; if the opposing party fails to appear, the court may treat the motion as conceded.

(g) **Motions to Vacate Default; Verified Answer.** A motion to vacate an entry of default, or a judgment by default, or both, shall be accompanied by a verified answer presenting a defense sufficient to bar the claim in whole or in part.

(h) **Motions for Summary Judgment.** Each motion for summary judgment shall be accompanied by a statement of material facts as to which the moving party contends there is no genuine issue, which shall include references to the parts of the record relied on to support the statement. An opposition to such a motion shall be accompanied by a separate concise statement of genuine issues setting forth all material facts as to which it is contended there exists a genuine issue necessary to be litigated, which shall include references to the parts of the record relied on to support the statement. Each such motion and opposition must also contain or be accompanied by a memorandum of points and authorities required by sections (a) and (c) of this rule. In determining a motion for summary judgment, the court may assume that facts identified by the moving party in its statement of material facts are admitted, unless such a fact is controverted in the statement of genuine issues filed in opposition to the motion.

(i) **Motions to Amend Pleadings.** A motion for leave to file an amended pleading shall be accompanied by an original of the proposed pleading as amended. The amended pleading shall be deemed to have been filed and served by mail on the date on which the order granting the motion is entered.

(District of Columbia)

FIGURE 8-4   A CONSENT ORDER

UNITED STATES DISTRICT COURT
MIDDLE DISTRICT OF NORTH CAROLINA
CHARLESTON DIVISION
CIVIL NO.: C-89-1293-B

Bryson Wesser,

                              Plaintiff,

          -vs-

Woodall Shoals Corporation,
                    Defendant,
                and
Second Ledge Stores, Incorporated,
                    Defendant

CONSENT ORDER

The defendant having moved the Court pursuant to Rule 6(b) of the Federal Rules of Civil Procedure for an extension of time within which to file answer;

AND IT APPEARING TO THE COURT that the defendant has shown good cause for the granting of said motion for an extension of time and that the parties have agreed to said extension of time;

IT IS, THEREFORE, ORDERED that the defendant shall have twenty (20) days from the date of the filing of this Order within which to file answer in this action.

This the _____ day of June, 1989.

_____
United States District Judge

CONSENT:

_____
Leigh J. Heyward

_____
David H. Benedict

of a consent order. The judge is not obliged to sign the consent order. However, if all parties have agreed, and the consent order concerns only a simple procedural matter, the judge will likely sign it. It is best to submit the consent order as far ahead of the hearing as possible, in case the judge has questions or chooses not to sign it.

A response in opposition to a motion is prepared and filed in the same way as a motion. The format follows the general rules for motions. The response in opposition is supported by affidavits, memoranda of law, and other exhibits. Service is made pursuant to FRCivP 5, as with all documents filed after the complaint.

The content of a response to a motion will vary according to the type of motion. A motion to deny a defendant's motion to dismiss pursuant to Rule 12 (b)(6) is illustrated in Figure 8-5. The length of and detail in the memorandum of law supporting a response will depend on the nature of the motion. As we noted previously, a brief for a Rule 12(b)(6) motion involving a complex issue that has not been litigated before may be quite lengthy. The same is true for the responsive brief.

FIGURE 8-5 MOTION TO DENY A MOTION TO DISMISS

**UNITED STATES DISTRICT COURT
MIDDLE DISTRICT OF NORTH CAROLINA
CHARLESTON DIVISION
CIVIL ACTION NO.: C-89-2388-B**

Equal Employment Opportunity
Commission,

              Plaintiff,

      -vs-

Chattooga Corporation,

              Defendant

MOTION
(To deny Defendant's
Motion to Dismiss)

Plaintiff, through Counsel, moves that the Court deny the Defendant's Motion to Dismiss, for the reasons set forth in Plaintiff's Memorandum of Points and Authorities. Plaintiff, through Counsel, further requests oral argument.

This the 25th day of April, 1989.

                              Nancy Reade Lee
                              Attorney for the Defendant
                              Gray and Lee, P.A.
                              380 South Washington Street
                              Charleston, NC 28226-1115
                              704-555-2500

+ Certificate of Service

Hearings

At a hearing on a motion, the attorneys present an oral argument to the judge, stating why their motion should be granted or why the other party's motion should be denied. Usually, the attorneys present the most important points emphasized in their memorandum of law, which has already been presented to the judge. As a paralegal, you may be present at the hearing, particularly when the motion is complex and involves many documents. Your job will be to keep the documents in order and hand them to the attorney at the appropriate time.

Scheduling Hearings.   The method for scheduling varies among different courts. The first point to remember is that the court does not hold a hearing for every motion. A few types of motions are *ex parte* motions, which means that there is no hearing and only the moving party talks to the judge. An example of an *ex parte* motion is a motion for a temporary restraining order. *Ex parte* motions are not very common. With the more common motions, you must consult the clerk of court and/or the local court rules. Not all judges hold hearings on routine motions and motions to which all parties consent, such as a motion for an extension of time to file a pleading. Some local rules provide that no oral argument will be held on any motion unless the moving party specifically requests in writing that an oral argument be held.

In many judicial districts, the court schedules the hearing date and sends notice to the parties' attorneys. There are many variations on the procedure for scheduling hearings. See Figure 8-1, which is a state court form for a notice of motion. Here the attorney designates the type of motion and requests that the motion be calendared for a hearing. The trial court administrator then schedules the hearing and notifies the attorneys of the hearing date.

When the attorneys participate in scheduling, as they do in some jurisdictions (especially in state court), there are several points to keep in mind. In selecting the date, you must consult the clerk of court and/or local court rules, because scheduling procedures can vary widely. The court may hear arguments on motions only on certain days or at certain times. It is not unusual for a court to hear motions at the beginning of the day's court calendar. The hearing should be scheduled far enough in advance to give the judge time to review the motion and supporting documents.

POINTER: Although it is not usually required, it is best to consult the attorney for the opposing party before scheduling a hearing. There is no guarantee that a litigator will be available at a time that you pick, so you need to agree on a mutually convenient hearing date. Checking with the other party's attorney beforehand helps ensure that the hearing will not have to be rescheduled and the notice of motion reissued. The court and its administrators will also be pleased when the hearing does not have to be rescheduled.

Orders and Proposed Orders

When the judge decides whether to grant or deny a motion, the judge enters an **order**. An order is a written statement of the judge's decision. An important point of terminology is to distinguish an order from a **judgment**. A judgment is also a written statement of a judge's decision; however, a judgment terminates the lawsuit. That is, it resolves the entire dispute. In contrast, an order resolves only a specific issue or issues. The lawsuit continues after entry of an order.

Content of Orders. The content of an order varies, depending on the nature of the motion it addresses. In issuing an order on one of the motions that the court regularly hears, the judge may just fill in the blanks on a preprinted form kept in the courtroom. See Figure 8-6 for an example. The order does not always state in great detail why the motion is granted or denied. If a detailed explanation is necessary, the judge will likely issue a very short order accompanied by an opinion containing the rationale.

FIGURE 8-6   FORM FOR A JUDGE'S ORDER

POINTER: Opinions pertaining to some motions may be published. For example, an opinion explaining why a motion for summary judgment was denied may be lengthy and deal in depth with substantive issues of law. Such opinions may have precedential value and therefore will be published. Other opinions, which are shorter and less detailed, may be unpublished and are often called "memorandum opinions."

Proposed Orders. Along with the motion and supporting documents, it is common practice to submit to the court a proposed order. A proposed order is an order ready for the judge to sign, stating that the moving party should receive the relief requested and the reasons the moving party is entitled to that relief. Whether a proposed order is submitted may depend on local rules and the preferences of the judge. Even if a proposed order is not required, there are advantages in submitting one. If the judge is inclined to rule in your client's favor, the convenience of having an order there, requiring nothing more than a signature, may encourage the judge to enter an order in your favor. If the judge has difficulty deciding whether to grant or deny a motion, a proposed order is a vehicle for a logical presentation of the facts and law that support a ruling in your client's favor. A logical, well-organized proposed order may tip the scales in your favor.

Including a proposed order with the package of documents when you file a motion is especially important when there will be no oral argument. When there is an oral argument, the judge may direct both parties to submit proposed orders within a certain number of days. This is a good opportunity to present the argument again in written form. This practice is more common in state court where, unlike federal district court, the judge does not have law clerks to draft the orders. In state court it is common for the judge to announce the decision in open court and direct the attorney for the prevailing party to draft a proposed order. When this happens, the prevailing attorney drafts the order, sends it to opposing counsel for comments, and then submits the order to the judge for signature.

 POINTER: In the discussion of motion practice, we have referred to the actions of judges. However, in federal court it is common practice for judges to have magistrates hear and rule on routine pretrial motions. The procedure is the same as when a judge hears the motion. Federal court magistrates are court officials who have the authority to perform some, but not all, judicial duties as set forth in 28 U.S.C. §636(b)(3). Local court rules may give magistrates authority to perform additional duties. Duties frequently performed by magistrates include ruling on pretrial motions, such as motions concerning discovery.

DEFAULT JUDGMENT

We have discussed the importance of asserting a defense to a complaint within 20 days of service. FRCivP 55(a) provides that when the defendant does not "plead or otherwise defend" as provided by the Federal Rules of Civil Procedure, the defendant is in default. Thus a defendant who has not filed an answer and/or motion to dismiss within 20 days of service of the complaint is in default.

The documents filed to obtain a default judgment against the defendant are fairly straightforward, and you may be asked to prepare the appropriate forms. If you work with a law firm involved in collections, you will be very likely to prepare documents to obtain default judgments.

Procedure

FRCivP 55 explains the procedure the plaintiff must follow to obtain a default judgment against the defendant. Figure 8-7 outlines the procedure. The example is a federal court action to collect a sum certain owed to the plaintiff on a promissory note. This simple example is used rather than our sample cases, because the sample cases do not lend themselves as readily to default judgment.

The first step is to file with the clerk of court a Request to Enter Default. See Figure 8-8. Note that the request is supported by an affidavit signed by plaintiff's attorney (Figure 8-9). It explains that service of process was accomplished and that 20 days have elapsed without the defendant's pleading or otherwise defending. When the clerk determines that the defendants are in default, the clerk signs

FIGURE 8-7   OBTAINING DEFAULT JUDGMENT

PROCEDURE FOR OBTAINING DEFAULT JUDGMENT

I. Entry of Default
    Documents to file with the clerk of court:

    Request for Entry of Default
    Affidavit for Entry of Default
    Proposed Entry of Default for Clerk's signature

II. Default Judgment
    Documents to file:

    A. If the amount of judgment requested is a sum certain

                                    and

        the defendant has not entered an appearance

                                    and

        the defendant is not a minor or incompetent:

        1. Request for Default Judgment
            (to be entered by the Clerk—FRCivP 55(b) (1))

        2. Supporting affidavit (to show default judgment is proper and to prove
            amount owed)

        3. Affidavit in compliance with Soldiers' and Sailors' Civil Relief Act

    B. In all other cases
        (when further proof of the amount of damages is necessary or the defen-
        dant has entered an appearance or the defendant is a minor or
        incompetent):

        1. Request for Default Judgment
            (to be entered by the Court—FRCivP 55(b) (2))

        2. Supporting affidavit (to show that default judgment is proper and
            amount of damages plaintiff intends to prove)

        3. Affidavit in compliance with Soldiers' and Sailors' Civil Relief Act

        4. Notice of Motion for hearing on application for default judgment (must
            be served at least 3 days prior to hearing)

FIGURE 8-8   REQUEST TO ENTER DEFAULT

UNITED STATES DISTRICT COURT
MIDDLE DISTRICT OF NORTH CAROLINA
CHARLESTON DIVISION
CIVIL NO.: C-89-1250-M

Blue Mountain National Bank,
        Plaintiff,

    -vs-   *REQUEST TO ENTER DEFAULT*

Kevin Sanders,
        Defendant

To the Honorable J.P. McGraw, Clerk of the United States District Court for the Middle District of North Carolina:

    You will please enter the default of the defendant Kevin Sanders for failure to plead or otherwise defend as provided by the Federal Rules of Civil Procedure, as appears from the Affidavit of Marion Edozian hereto attached.

    This the _____ day of _____, 1989.

                           _____
                           Marion Edozian
                           Attorney for the Plaintiff
                           Edozian and Stratakos, P.C.
                           1290 Fifth St.
                           Charleston, NC
                           28226-5612
                           704-555-4777

+ Certificate of Service

FIGURE 8-9   AFFIDAVIT SUPPORTING REQUEST FOR DEFAULT

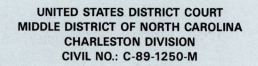

UNITED STATES DISTRICT COURT
MIDDLE DISTRICT OF NORTH CAROLINA
CHARLESTON DIVISION
CIVIL NO.: C-89-1250-M

Blue Mountain National Bank,
         Plaintiff,

     -vs-

Kevin Sanders,
         Defendant

                                          *AFFIDAVIT FOR
ENTRY OF DEFAULT*

STATE OF NORTH CAROLINA   )
)
COUNTY OF OCOEE   )

    Marion Edozian, being duly sworn, deposes and says that she is the attorney for plaintiff in the above-entitled action; that the Summons and Complaint in this action were served on defendant Kevin Sanders on February 4, 1989, as appears from the return of service of said Summons by Frank Santagata, who is not a party and is not less than eighteen (18) years of age; that the time within which the defendant may answer or otherwise move as to the Complaint has expired; that the time for defendant to answer or otherwise move was extended to August 26, 1989, but not beyond said date; and that defendant has not answered or otherwise moved.

                                       _____
                                       Marion Edozian

Subscribed and sworn to before me
this the *27th* day of *August*, 1989.

Barbara M. Pressley
          Notary Public

My Commission expires: *6-25-91*

and files an Entry of Default. See Figure 8-10. It is best to include the proposed Entry of Default with the Request for Default and affidavit, just as one encloses a proposed order with a motion.

FIGURE 8-10   ENTRY OF DEFAULT

UNITED STATES DISTRICT COURT
MIDDLE DISTRICT OF NORTH CAROLINA
CHARLESTON DIVISION
CIVIL NO.: C-89-1250-M

Blue Mountain National Bank
        Plaintiff,

        -vs-   *ENTRY OF DEFAULT*

Kevin Sanders,
                Defendant

IT APPEARING TO THE COURT that the defendants are in default for failure to plead or otherwise defend as required by law;

NOW, THEREFORE, DEFAULT is hereby entered against the defendant Kevin Sanders.

This the 11th day of September, 1989.

_____

J.P. McGraw
Clerk of the United States
District Court for the Middle
District of North Carolina

Entry of Judgment by the Clerk of Court.   After the first step, the procedure differs depending on whether the clerk or the judge must enter the default judgment. FRCivP 55(b)(1) provides that the clerk may enter the default judgment "[w]hen the plaintiff's claim against a defendant is for a sum certain or for a sum which can by computation be made certain ... if the defendant has been defaulted for failure to appear and is not an infant or incompetent person."

If all the requirements of FRCivP 55(b)(1) are met, the clerk may enter the default judgment without having a hearing. This is because the amount of damages is easily ascertainable. In the hypothetical Blue Mountain National Bank v. Kevin Sanders example with which we illustrate this chapter, the amount of damages is determined by the terms of the promissory note and is therefore easy to ascertain. In instances where the parties agreed beforehand what the amount of the damages would be or the amount can be ascertained directly from the terms of the parties' agreement, the damages are called **liquidated damages**.

The forms submitted to the clerk in the example include a Request for Entry of Default Judgment (Figure 8-11) and an affidavit to prove the amount to which

FIGURE 8-11   REQUEST FOR ENTRY OF DEFAULT JUDGMENT

UNITED STATES DISTRICT COURT
MIDDLE DISTRICT OF NORTH CAROLINA
CHARLESTON DIVISION
CIVIL NO.: C-89-1250-M

Blue Mountain National Bank,
                                  Plaintiff,

                  -vs-   *REQUEST FOR ENTRY OF*
                                                                              DEFAULT JUDGMENT

Kevin Sanders,
                                  Defendant

To: Honorable J.P. McGraw
     Clerk of the United States District Court
     Middle District of North Carolina

     Upon the Affidavit attached hereto, the plaintiff requests that you enter judgment by default against the defendant in the sum of Seventy-Six Thousand Twenty-Six Dollars Thirty-One Cents ($76,026.31), plus interest at the rate of Fifteen Dollars Eighty-Six Cents ($15.86) per day from the 5th day of July, 1989, and attorney's fees of Fourteen Thousand Four Hundred Forty-Four Dollars Ninety-Nine Cents ($14,444.99).

     This request is submitted on the ground that default has been entered against the defendant for failure to answer or otherwise defend as to the Complaint of the plaintiff, and the Affidavits of Jeffrey Hopkins and Marion Edozian, attached hereto.

                                                          _____
                                                          Marion Edozian
                                                          Attorney for the Plaintiff
                                                          Edozian and Stratakos, P.C.
                                                          1290 Fifth St.
                                                          Charleston, NC 28226-5612

                              +Certificate of Service

the plaintiff is entitled (Figure 8-12). The attorney also signs and submits an affidavit in compliance with the Soldiers' and Sailors' Civil Relief Act of 1940, as

FIGURE 8-12   AFFIDAVIT FOR DEFAULT JUDGMENT

UNITED STATES DISTRICT COURT
MIDDLE DISTRICT OF NORTH CAROLINA
CHARLESTON DIVISION
CIVIL NO.: C-89-1250-M

Blue Mountain National Bank,
                Plaintiff,

        -vs-   *AFFIDAVIT FOR*
                                                      DEFAULT JUDGMENT

Kevin Sanders,

                Defendant

JEFFREY E. HOPKINS, being duly sworn, says that:

1. He is a Vice President of the plaintiff in the above-entitled action and is familiar with and has control of the books and records of the plaintiff with regard to this claim.

2. According to the Note of the defendant and books and records of plaintiff, the defendant is indebted to the plaintiff in the sum of Seventy-Six Thousand Twenty-Six Dollars Thirty-One Cents ($76,026.31), plus interest at the rate of Fifteen Dollars Eighty-Six Cents ($15.86) per day from the 5th day of July, 1989, and attorney's fees of Fourteen Thousand Four Hundred Forty-Four Dollars Ninety-Nine Cents ($14,444.99); that the amounts stated above are justly due and owing and that no part thereof has been paid.

_____
                                                Jeffrey E. Hopkins

Subscribed and sworn to before me
this the _4th_ day of _September_, 1989.

Barbara M. Pressley
                Notary Public

My commission expires: _6-25-91_

Amended (Figure 8-13). This certifies that an investigation has been made to ensure that the defendants are not in the military service of the United States. The purpose is to prevent entry of judgment against a person in military service, because the person may well not receive notices sent to the last known address.

FIGURE 8-13   AFFIDAVIT IN COMPLIANCE WITH SOLDIERS' AND SAILORS' CIVIL RELIEF ACT

UNITED STATES DISTRICT COURT
MIDDLE DISTRICT OF NORTH CAROLINA
CHARLESTON DIVISION
CIVIL NO.: C-89-1250-M

Blue Mountain National Bank
          Plaintiff,

          -vs-   *AFFIDAVIT*

Kevin Sanders,
                    Defendant

STATE OF NORTH CAROLINA
COUNTY OF OCOEE

        Marion Edozian, being duly sworn, deposes and says that:

        1. She is the attorney for the plaintiff in the above-entitled action and makes this Affidavit pursuant to the provisions of the Soldiers' and Sailors' Civil Relief Act.

        2. She has caused careful investigation to be made to ascertain whether Kevin Sanders is in the military service of the United States, in that private investigations reveal that Kevin Sanders is not in the military service of the United States and is a civilian resident of the state in which he was served.

        3. From the facts as above set forth, she is informed and verily believes that the said defendant is not in the military service of the United States.

        4. The default of the defendant has been entered for failure to appear in this action.

                                                    _____
                                                    Marion Edozian

Subscribed and sworn to before me
this the *4th* day of *September*, 1989.
Barbara M. Pressley
          Notary Public
My commission expires: *6-25-91*

Depending on local custom, you may also submit to the clerk a proposed judgment. Because the form of the default judgment is fairly uniform in cases that the clerk handles, the clerk may use preprinted forms and fill in the blanks for the parties' names and the amount of the judgment. In other judicial districts, the attorney submits a proposed order, which when signed by the clerk of court looks like Figure 8-14.

FIGURE 8-14   DEFAULT JUDGMENT

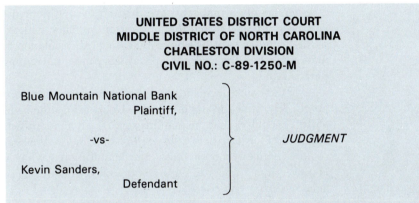

UNITED STATES DISTRICT COURT
MIDDLE DISTRICT OF NORTH CAROLINA
CHARLESTON DIVISION
CIVIL NO.: C-89-1250-M

Blue Mountain National Bank
        Plaintiff,

            -vs-   *JUDGMENT*

Kevin Sanders,
            Defendant

The defendant having failed to plead or otherwise defend in this action and his default having been entered;

Now, upon application of the plaintiff and upon Affidavit that the defendant Kevin Sanders is indebted to the plaintiff in the sum of Seventy-Six Thousand Twenty-Six Dollars Thirty-One Cents ($76,026.31), plus interest at the rate of Fifteen Dollars Eighty-Six Cents ($15.86) per day from the 5th day of July, 1989, and attorney's fees of Fourteen Thousand Four Hundred Forty-Four Dollars Ninety-Nine Cents ($14,444.99); and that the above-named defendant is not an infant or incompetent person or in the military service of the United States, it is hereby ORDERED, ADJUDGED and DECREED that Blue Mountain National Bank recover of and from the defendant the sum of Seventy-Six Thousand Twenty-Six Dollars Thirty-One Cents ($76,026.31), plus interest at the rate of Fifteen Dollars Eighty-Six Cents ($15.86) per day from the 5th day of July, 1989, and costs, including attorney's fees of Fourteen Thousand Four Hundred Forty-Four Dollars Ninety-Nine Cents ($14,444.99).

This the 24th day of September, 1989.

_____
J.P. McGraw
Clerk of the United States
District Court for the Middle
District of North Carolina

Entry of Judgment by the Court. When application must be made to the court for default judgment, file a Request for Entry of Default Judgment by the Court. This form is like the one addressed to the clerk (Figure 8-11), except that it is addressed to the court. Also submit the affidavit in compliance with the Soldiers' and Sailors' Civil Relief Act (Figure 8-13).

The important difference when the request for default judgment is before the court is that the court holds a hearing if "it is necessary to take an account or to determine the amount of damages or to establish the truth of any averment by evidence or to make an investigation of any other matter," as provided by FRCivP 55(b)(2). When the amount of damages cannot be determined by the parties' stipulation or by simple mathematical calculation from the available information, such as the terms of a promissory note, the damages are called **unliquidated damages**.

If the court deems it necessary and proper, the court can order a trial by jury to determine the amount due to the plaintiff. When a hearing is held, FRCivP 55(b)(2) requires that the plaintiff serve the defendant with written notice of the application for judgment at least three days before the hearing. FRCivP 55(b)(2) requires notice of motion only if the defaulting party has entered an appearance. However, it is prudent to serve a notice on the defaulting party even if no appearance has been entered.

Other General Rules Established by FRCivP 55

Our discussion thus far has assumed that the defaulting party is the defendant. However, FRCivP 55(d) provides that the party entitled to the judgment by default may be, in addition to the plaintiff, a third-party plaintiff or a party who has pleaded a cross-claim or counterclaim. Thus the defaulting party may be, in addition to a defendant, a third-party defendant, a codefendant in the case of a cross-claim, or a plaintiff in the case of a counterclaim.

Motion to Set Aside Default

FRCivP 55(c) provides that for "good cause" the court may set aside an entry of default or a judgment of default, if judgment has been entered.

Grounds for Setting Aside Default. FRCivP 55(c) further provides that the bases for setting aside default are those enumerated in FRCivP 60(b). Rule 60 is the general rule for relief from judgments under the Federal Rules of Civil Procedure.

"Excusable neglect" is the most common ground cited as good cause for setting aside default. The court exercises a great deal of discretion in determining what constitutes excusable neglect. Different judges have different views. You can get a general idea of how courts view excusable neglect by reviewing case law. Obviously a statement from the attorney saying "I forgot" or "I was busy" is insufficient. In contrast, good cause may be found when the attorney who was supposed to file the answer was seriously ill, or when the client failed to supply the information on which the answer was to be based. Courts do not favor default and generally prefer to allow the case to be heard on the merits.

Deadlines for Filing.   The time limit for filing a motion to set aside a default judgment is governed by FRCivP 60(b), which provides that the motion must be made within a reasonable time, but never more than one year from the date judgment is entered.[2] The one-year limitation applies to a default judgment as well as to other judgments under the Federal Rules of Civil Procedure.

Entry of default is not a judgment; it is an order, and the one-year rule does not apply absolutely to an order. The more general limitation of filing "within a reasonable time" is applied to the motion to set aside entry of default.[3] Nevertheless, it is a bad idea to wait more than a year to file the motion. In fact, you should file the motion to set aside default judgment or entry of default promptly. Not only do you avoid worry about the filing deadline, but you prevent the court from considering your firm to be dragging its feet, a habit almost universally despised by judges.

As more time elapses after entry of default, the chances of establishing good cause for setting aside the default entry grow ever slimmer. Although the court may allow the motion to be filed, the chances of the court granting the motion to set aside entry of default are not good. A court is most likely to set aside default on a set of facts as in *Johnson v. Harper*, 66 F.R.D. 103 (E.D. Tenn. 1975). Here the court found good cause where the defendant filed an answer one day after the prescribed period ended and promptly filed a motion to set aside default. In addition, the aggregate damages sought exceeded $6 million, the plaintiffs showed no prejudice from the delay, and a question as to the computation of the deadline for filing a response was resolved in favor of the defendant.

POINTER: Note that *Johnson v. Harper* is found in *Federal Rules Decisions* (*F.R.D.*). *F.R.D.* includes federal court decisions dealing with the Federal Rules of Civil Procedure and the Federal Rules of Criminal Procedure. The cases reported in *F.R.D.* address various procedural issues, ranging from complex issues concerning class actions to the simpler question of the time limit for filing motions to set aside entry of default.

Procedure.   The party seeking to set aside entry of default or default judgment files a motion that explains to the court why good cause exists. This is basically an explanation of why an answer or other defensive pleading was not filed within the prescribed time. The motion should also state that the defendant has a meritorious defense and explain the factual basis for the defense. In the Chattooga case, for instance, the defendant would state the defenses of poor work performance and false statements on the employment application and explain that these are meritorious defenses. If the motion to set aside is filed within a few days of entry of default, you should note the very brief time that has elapsed.

POINTER: You file a motion for extension of time to file an answer at the same time you file the motion to set aside default. Obviously, the prescribed time for filing the answer has elapsed, since this is the reason that default was entered in the first place.

For filing and serving the motions, follow the motion practice described previously. Be sure to serve a notice of both the motion to set aside default and the motion for extension of time to file an answer. See Figure 8-15 for an illustration of a motion to set aside default judgment.

FIGURE 8-15   MOTION TO SET ASIDE DEFAULT JUDGMENT

**UNITED STATES DISTRICT COURT
MIDDLE DISTRICT OF NORTH CAROLINA
CHARLESTON DIVISION
CIVIL NO.: C-89-1250-M**

Blue Mountain National Bank
                Plaintiff,

            -vs-   *MOTION TO SET ASIDE
                                                        DEFAULT JUDGMENT*

Kevin Sanders,

                Defendant

NOW COMES the defendant, through its undersigned attorney, pursuant to Rule 55(c) of the Federal Rules of Civil Procedure, and shows unto the Court:

1. The defendant has filed simultaneously herewith a Motion Requesting Extension of Time to File Answer wherein the posture of this civil action is set forth. The statements in the accompanying motion are incorporated herein by reference and the Court is requested to read the accompanying motion to obtain information necessary in the determination of both motions filed by the defendant.

2. The defendant contends that good cause exists to deny the plaintiff's request for entry of default, in that:

(a)
        (State the reasons that constitute good cause.)
(b)

WHEREFORE, the defendant moves the Court that entry of default and default judgment be denied, and that the defendant be allowed to present its defense to the claims of the plaintiff.

                                    _____
                                    Allison MacKethan
                                    Attorney for the Defendant
                                    Hall, MacKethan & Hoggard, P.C.
                                    300 Fourth St.
                                    Charleston, NC 28226-5612
                                    704-555-1612

                        + Certificate of Service

FIGURE 8-15   MOTION TO SET ASIDE DEFAULT JUDGMENT (Cont.)

STATE OF NORTH CAROLINA

COUNTY OF OCOEE

ALLISON MACKETHAN, being duly sworn, deposes and says that she is the attorney for the defendant in this action; that she has read the foregoing Motion and knows the contents thereof; that the same is true to her own knowledge except as to those matters and things therein stated on information and belief and as to those she believes it to be true.

————————————————————
Allison MacKethan

Subscribed and sworn to before me,

this ———— day of May, 1989.

————————————————————
Notary Public

My commission expires: ————————

JUDGMENT ON THE PLEADINGS

Rule 12(c) of the Federal Rules of Civil Procedure provides that "[a]fter the pleadings are closed but within such time as not to delay the trial, any party may move for judgment on the pleadings." As the name of the motion shows, the court may look only at the allegations in the pleadings to determine whether on the face of the pleadings one party is entitled to judgment. A motion for judgment on the pleadings can be granted only in limited circumstances. In fact, the motion for judgment on the pleadings is not a frequently asserted motion. Nevertheless, it is important to understand when the motion may be granted. Even if you do not request judgment on the pleadings, the other party may make the motion, and you will have to defend against it.

How the Court Must View the Pleadings

In determining whether to grant a motion for judgment on the pleadings, the court must consider the pleadings in the light most favorable to the nonmoving party. That is, it must, for purposes of deciding the motion, resolve any disputed fact in favor of the nonmoving party.[4] As a practical matter, this means that the court bases its decision on the undisputed facts.

The undisputed facts occasionally show that one party is entitled to judgment. Suppose that in the Chattooga case there were no charge of employment discrimination, but rather the entire controversy concerned Ford's employment contract. Assume that Ford asserted that she did not breach the employment contract by failing to disclose her felony conviction; however, the contract clearly stated that lack of felony convictions was a condition of employment. A question on the employment application asked whether Ford had any felony convictions, and in the employment interview Ford was informed that a job requirement was that she have no felony convictions. Looking at the undisputed facts and resolving all matters in favor of Ford, it is clear that she did breach the employment contract and terms of her employment. Judgment on the pleadings in favor of Chattooga Corporation would be appropriate on the question of breach of contract.

When the Court May Grant Judgment on the Pleadings

In order to prevail on a motion for judgment on the pleadings, a plaintiff must show that, if all the allegations are deemed true, the defendant's answer raises no valid defense to the plaintiff's claim. For a defendant to prevail on a motion for judgment on the pleadings, the defendant must show that the allegations in the plaintiff's complaint, if true, would not allow recovery.

A motion for judgment on the pleadings is usually granted when there is no disputed **question of fact** but only a **question of law**. A question of fact simply means that a factual dispute exists. A question of law involves applying a rule of law to the facts of the case.

In the Wesser case, for example, it is an undisputed fact that Wesser bought the defective blanket on January 3, 1986. The fire resulting from the blanket occurred in January 1987. The applicable statute of limitations is three years from the date Wesser bought the blanket. Suppose that Wesser did not file the complaint until March 15, 1989, two months after the statute of limitations expired. The application of the statute of limitations is a matter of law. There would be no dispute regarding the date that the blanket was purchased or the date that the lawsuit was commenced. If the lawsuit was commenced after the statute of limitations ran, as a matter of law Wesser would be barred by the statute of limitations from recovering any damages.

Let us consider the actual fact situation, in which the lawsuit was commenced within the three-year statute of limitations. Assume that there is no other question of law that could bar recovery. Now we must consider whether there are material facts in dispute that could bar recovery. A fact is considered "material" if it can affect the outcome of the case. For instance, the color of the electric blanket does not affect the outcome of the Wesser case and therefore is not a material fact. Review the complaint and answer in the Wesser case. Factual disputes exist as to whether the blanket was negligently designed, manufactured, packaged, or handled; whether the blanket contained defects that resulted in breach of express and implied warranties and proximately caused the plaintiffs' injuries; and the amount of damages to which the plaintiffs may be entitled. These are disputes on material factual issues, which means that judgment on the pleadings would not be appropriate for either the plaintiff or defendants.

Procedure and Timing

FRCivP 12(c) specifies that any party may move for judgment on the pleadings "[a]fter the pleadings are closed but within such time as not to delay the trial...."

Pleadings are considered closed after the complaint and answer are filed. If a counterclaim is filed, the pleadings are closed after a reply to the counterclaim is filed.

Note the difference in timing between the motion for judgment on the pleadings and motion to dismiss under Rule 12(b)(6). A 12(b)(6) motion is filed after the complaint is filed. In contrast, a motion for judgment on the pleadings cannot be filed until all the pleadings are filed—complaint, answer, and reply if a counterclaim is filed.

The procedure for filing a motion for judgment on the pleadings follows the general procedure for motions that we have discussed in preceding sections of this chapter. Remember to serve the motion and notice of motion on all parties and to calendar the time for response to the motion. Figure 8-16 illustrates how a motion for judgment on the pleadings in the Wesser case might have appeared had Wesser filed the lawsuit after the expiration of the statute of limitations.

Why Motions for Judgment on the Pleadings Are Infrequently Granted

Very few lawsuits are without a factual dispute that can affect the outcome of the case. Seldom can a defendant show that a plaintiff has alleged no set of facts that might justify recovery. Nor can a plaintiff often show that no reading of the defendant's pleadings shows a possible defense. There is a strong policy of allowing a party the opportunity to prove the facts alleged at trial. As the District of Columbia Court of Appeals has stated, judgment on the pleadings and summary judgment are properly invoked to eliminate a useless trial, but should not cut a litigant off from the right to have a jury resolve significant factual issues.[5]

Another reason why motions for judgment on the pleadings are not commonly made or granted is that the Federal Rules of Civil Procedure allow liberal amendment of pleadings. Recall our discussion of FRCivP 15. A party can easily remedy a factual omission by amending the pleading. However, a legal bar, such as a statute of limitations, cannot be cured by an amendment.

Conversion to Summary Judgment

A motion for judgment on the pleadings can be based only on the pleadings themselves. The court cannot consider any allegations outside the pleadings. FRCivP 12(c) states that if matters outside the pleadings are presented and not excluded by the court, the motion for judgment on the pleadings is then treated as a motion for summary judgment. Once a motion for judgment on the pleadings is converted into a motion for summary judgment, all parties are given the opportunity to submit documents outside the pleadings, and the court makes a ruling applying the standard of FRCivP 56, which governs summary judgment.

SUMMARY JUDGMENT

Summary judgment is a dispositive motion asking the court to rule in favor of a party on the basis that there are no genuine issues of material fact and the moving party is entitled to judgment as a matter of law (FRCivP 56). When a

FIGURE 8-16   MOTION FOR JUDGMENT ON THE PLEADINGS

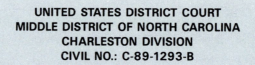

UNITED STATES DISTRICT COURT
MIDDLE DISTRICT OF NORTH CAROLINA
CHARLESTON DIVISION
CIVIL NO.: C-89-1293-B

Bryson Wesser,
                   Plaintiff

    -vs-

Woodall Shoals Corporation,
                Defendant,
        and
Second Ledge Stores, Incorporated,
                Defendant

MOTION FOR JUDGMENT
ON THE PLEADINGS

Pursuant to Rule 12(c) of the Federal Rules of Civil Procedure defendant Woodall Shoals Corporation moves the Court to enter judgment on the pleadings in favor of the defendant. On the undisputed facts in the pleadings, defendant Woodall Shoals Corporation is entitled to judgment as a matter of law.

In support of its motion, defendant states that:

1. The plaintiff filed the complaint in this action on March 15, 1989.

2. The plaintiff purchased the electric blanket which is the subject of this action on January 3, 1986.

3. The applicable statute of limitations requires that the action be commenced within three years of purchase of the allegedly defective product. The plaintiff filed the complaint one month after the statute of limitations expired and, therefore, is barred from any recovery.

WHEREFORE, defendant Woodall Shoals Corporation requests that the Court enter judgment on the pleadings in favor of the defendant.

David H. Benedict
Attorney for the Defendants
Benedict, Parker & Miller
100 Nolichucky Drive
Bristol, NC 28205-0890
704-555-8810

+ Certificate of Service

court grants a party's motion for summary judgment on all issues in the case, a judgment is entered in that party's favor without the necessity for trial. Unlike motions for judgment on the pleadings, which you will not encounter frequently, motions for summary judgment are common. Even if a motion for summary judgment is unsuccessful, preparation for the motions seeking and opposing summary judgment helps you analyze the issues and the evidence and greatly aids your preparation for trial.

How the Court Determines Whether to Grant a Motion for Summary Judgment

FRCivP 56(c) states the standard the court must use to determine if the moving party is entitled to summary judgment. Summary judgment is proper when "there is no genuine issue as to any material fact and . . . the moving party is entitled to a judgment as a matter of law." If you are thinking that the standard is similar to that for judgment on the pleadings, you are correct. However, with a motion for summary judgment, the court may look beyond the pleadings. FRCivP 56(c) provides that the court may consider the pleadings, depositions, answers to interrogatories, admissions on file, and any affidavits that the parties submit.

As FRCivP 56(c) states, the court does not determine which facts are true and which are not true. The court bases its decision only on the *undisputed, material* facts. Based on the undisputed facts, the court determines whether the law supports a conclusion that the moving party is entitled to judgment in its favor. For example, consider the case on which Figures 8-17 and 8-18 are based. Here, a person entered a hospital and signed an agreement to pay for the services rendered during the hospitalization. The amount due for the services is not in dispute. The defendants' answer is not illustrated, but assume that the defendants admitted that they owe the money, but said that they cannot pay it back yet. The issue is simply whether the defendants owe the hospital the amount stated in the complaint. Since the defendants admit that they owe the stated amount, there is no issue as to any material fact.

In simple contract cases, summary judgment is frequently granted. Consider the Blue Mountain National Bank example, which we examined in connection with default judgment. This example involves money due pursuant to a promissory note. Here the amount owed to the plaintiff is clear, because it is controlled by the terms of the promissory note. If the defendants had filed an answer admitting that they are liable on the promissory note but cannot pay the money, summary judgment would be proper.

Courts are less likely to allow summary judgment in more complex cases. Consider the Chattooga case. In Figures 8-19 and 8-20 you see a motion for summary judgment and small portions of a memorandum of law in support of the motion. Although the defendant's entire argument is not set out, you see that there are two issues. The first is whether the defendant violated Title VII. The second is whether, even if the defendant did violate Title VII, Ford is barred from recovery because she falsified her employment application. There is some factual dispute surrounding Ford's departure. Ford contends that she was ter-

FIGURE 8-17   SIMPLE MOTION FOR SUMMARY JUDGMENT

IN THE GENERAL COURT OF JUSTICE
DISTRICT COURT DIVISION

NORTH CAROLINA   **FILE NO.: 89 CVD 100**
NEW COUNTY

New Memorial Hospital,
     Plaintiff,
 	
   -vs-
 	
Richard C. Baker and
Juanita Atkins Baker,
     Defendants
	MOTION FOR SUMMARY
	JUDGMENT

    Now Comes the plaintiff, New Memorial Hospital, and moves the Court for Summary Judgment against the defendants, Richard C. Baker and wife, Juanita Atkins Baker, pursuant to Rule 56 of the North Carolina Rules of Civil Procedure on the grounds that there is no genuine issue as to any material fact and that the plaintiff is entitled to Judgment for the relief requested in the Complaint as a matter of law.

    This the 7th day of April, 1989.

                              _____
                                Marshall D. Sabat
                                Colliers & Atkinson, P.C.
                                4300 Fifth St.
                                Charleston, NC 28226-1811
                                704-555-7200

+ Certificate of Service

FIGURE 8-18   AFFIDAVIT IN SUPPORT OF MOTION FOR SUMMARY JUDGMENT

**IN THE GENERAL COURT OF JUSTICE
DISTRICT COURT DIVISION**

NORTH CAROLINA   **FILE NO.: 89 CVD 100**
NEW COUNTY

New Memorial Hospital,
       Plaintiff,

    -vs-   *AFFIDAVIT IN SUPPORT OF*
                                                  MOTION FOR SUMMARY
Richard C. Baker and   *JUDGMENT*
Juanita Atkins Baker,
       Defendants

Charles M. Garfinkel, being duly sworn, deposes and says that:

1. He is an officer of the plaintiff corporation, to-wit, its Collections Manager, and as such is familiar with the records of New Memorial Hospital.

2. That the plaintiff is a public corporation duly organized and existing under and by virtue of the laws of the State of North Carolina, with its principal place of business in Sparta, New County, North Carolina.

3. That the defendants are natural persons and are citizens and residents of the State of North Carolina and are not in the Armed Forces of the United States.

4. That on or about the 26th day of April, 1988, and on various dates thereafter, to and including the 5th day of May, 1988, the plaintiff, under an express contract with the defendants, furnished room, board and certain reasonable and necessary hospital care and professional services for and on behalf of and at the request of the defendants as prescribed by the attending physician or physicians for which services the defendants did contract and agree to pay to the plaintiff in the amount and for the agreed price set out in the itemized statement hereto attached marked "Exhibit A" and asked to be considered as a part hereof as if fully set out herein; that the balance due on the contract price amounts to the sum of $300.30, with interest at the rate of eight percent (8%) per annum from the 31st day of May, 1988 all as shown by attached Exhibit "A." The undersigned has examined the records of Cabarrus Memorial Hospital attached hereto as Exhibit "A," and attests that they are true and accurate copies thereof.

FIGURE 8-18   AFFIDAVIT IN SUPPORT OF MOTION FOR SUMMARY JUDGMENT (Cont.)

> 5. That the plaintiff has demanded payment of the defendants of the amount due aforesaid, but the defendants have refused to pay said indebtedness.
>
> This the 27th day of March, 1989.
>
>
> _____
> Charles M. Garfinkel
> Collections Manager
> New Memorial Hospital
>
>
> Subscribed and sworn to before me,
>
> this _____ day of May, 1989.
>
> _____
>   Notary Public
>
> My commission expires: _____

FIGURE 8-19   MOTION FOR SUMMARY JUDGMENT

UNITED STATES DISTRICT COURT
MIDDLE DISTRICT OF NORTH CAROLINA
CHARLESTON DIVISION
CIVIL NO.: C-89-2388-B

Equal Employment Opportunity
Commission,

               Plaintiff,

     -vs-   *MOTION FOR SUMMARY*
                                                 JUDGMENT

Chattooga Corporation,

               Defendant

     NOW COMES the defendant, Chattooga Corporation, pursuant to Rule 56 of the Federal Rules of Civil Procedure, and moves the Court for summary judgment on the grounds that there is no genuine issue as to any material fact and that the defendant is entitled to judgment as a matter of law. The defendant relies upon the pleadings in this action, and the attached exhibits, which include the pertinent pages of the deposition of Sandy Ford, marked as Exhibit "A"; Sandy Ford's application for employment with the defendant, marked as Exhibit "B"; the pertinent pages of the depositions of Lori Dehler, Forrest Pawlyk, and Ronnie Taylor, marked as Exhibits "C," "D," and "E," respectively; and the affidavit of Forrest Pawlyk, marked as Exhibit "F," in support of its motion.

     This the _____ day of February, 1989.

                                       _____

                                       Nancy Reade Lee
                                       Attorney for the Defendant
                                       Gray and Lee, P.A.
                                       380 South Washington Street
                                       Charleston, NC 28226-1115
                                       704-555-2500

+ Certificate of Service

FIGURE 8-20   SOME PORTIONS OF A MEMORANDUM OF LAW

INTRODUCTION

This is an action for an alleged violation of Sections 703 and 704(a) of Title VII of the 1964 Civil Rights Act (42 U.S.C. §2000e-2 and §2000e-3(a)). Pursuant to Rule 56 of the Federal Rules of Civil Procedure, the defendant moves for summary judgment dismissing the action on the grounds that there is no genuine issue as to any material fact and the defendant is entitled to judgment as a matter of law.

STATEMENT OF FACTS

The pleadings, depositions and affidavits show the following facts.
. . .

QUESTION PRESENTED

Is the defendant entitled to summary judgment on the grounds that there is no genuine issue as to any material fact and the defendant is entitled to judgment as a matter of law?

ARGUMENT

The granting of summary judgment in favor of the defendant is entirely proper in the case *sub judice*. Summary judgment is a procedural device designed to dispose of cases precisely like the instant case. Summary judgment is a device to dispose of actions in which there is no genuine issue as to any material fact, even though the formal pleadings may have raised such issue. *Mintz v. Mathers Fund, Inc.*, 463 F.2d 495, 498 (7th Cir. 1972). The primary purpose of a motion for summary judgment is to avoid a useless trial. *Id.* In this action, based upon the uncontroverted facts, it is clear that the defendant has not violated any section of Title VII. Further, even if the defendant had violated Title VII, Sandy Ford, on whose behalf plaintiff filed this action, would be barred from recovering any damages whatsoever.
. . .

minated because she had helped another employee file a claim with the EEOC. The defendant contends that Ford was terminated solely because she made false statements on the employment application regarding whether she had a felony conviction. In such a case, a court is likely to conclude that both parties should have the opportunity to present testimony to determine which version of events is more likely true. As a result, a summary judgment motion would be denied.

Partial Summary Judgment

FRCivP 56 allows a court to enter summary judgment "upon all or any part" of a party's claim. The most common context in which partial summary judgment is granted is when a party admits liability but the amount of damages is in dispute. Suppose that in the Wesser case, Woodall Shoals Corporation admitted that it was liable for the electric blanket fire, but did not admit that Wesser was entitled to as much as he claimed in damages. Wesser would be entitled to summary judgment on the issue of liability. However, a trial would still be necessary to determine the amount of damages to which Wesser is entitled.

FRCivP 56(d) explains the procedure after it is determined that summary judgment is proper on some but not all of the issues. It states the following:

> If on motion under this rule judgment is not rendered upon the whole case or for all the relief asked and a trial is necessary, the court at the hearing of the motion, by examining the pleadings and the evidence before it and by interrogating cousel, shall if practicable ascertain what material facts exist without substantial controversy and what material facts are actually and in good faith controverted. It shall thereupon make an order specifying the facts that appear without substantial controversy, including the extent to which the amount of damages or other relief is not in controversy, and directing such further proceedings in the action as are just. Upon the trial of the action the facts so specified shall be deemed established, and the trial shall be conducted accordingly.

Thus summary judgment narrows the issues so that a trial is necessary only on the issues that the court determines to be in dispute.

The subsequent trial will follow usual trial procedures. The right to jury trial is not abrogated by entry of an order granting partial summary judgment.

Timing

You should note at the outset that any party may move for summary judgment and that summary judgment may be entered on a counterclaim or cross-claim as well as on the initial claim. The time at which the motion for summary judgment may be filed depends on which party makes the motion. FRCivP 56(a) provides that a party seeking to recover upon a claim cannot file a motion for summary judgment until 20 days have elapsed from the commencement of the action. FRCivP 56(b) states that a party against whom a claim is asserted may move for summary judgment at any time.

Often both a plaintiff and a defendant will move for summary judgment. This is called *cross-motions* for summary judgment. If a defendant is the first to file for summary judgment, the plaintiff may file its cross-motion for summary judgment anytime thereafter.

As a practical matter, a motion for summary judgment is rarely filed by either side until well into the discovery period. Only then can one determine, in a relatively complex case, which issues are undisputed. In a simple case, a motion for summary motion could be filed fairly early in the litigation, because there are no complex issues.

Procedure and Supporting Documents

The procedure for summary judgment is straightforward. The motion itself is usually quite short, stating little more than that the moving party moves for summary judgment on the grounds that there is no dispute as to any material fact and the moving party is entitled to judgment as a matter of law. See the motions illustrated in Figure 8-17 and 8-19. Follow the usual procedure for filing the motion and supporting documents with the clerk of court and serving all the papers on all the parties in the litigation.

Affidavits in Support of Motion for Summary Judgment. As we discussed, the court may consider the pleadings, depositions, answers to interrogatories, admissions on file, and affidavits submitted by the parties. FRCivP 56 does not require the parties to submit affidavits, but parties almost always submit affidavits both in support of and in opposition to motions for summary judgment. Review the general discussion of affidavits on pages 197 and 199. Figure 8-18 shows a simple affidavit in support of summary judgment.

FRCivP 56(e)–(g) gives some specific directives concerning affidavits supporting or opposing a summary judgment motion. First, FRCivP 56(e) states that the affidavit must be based on personal knowledge. Second, the affidavit must show affirmatively that the "affiant is competent to testify to the matters stated therein." The affidavit should state at the outset who the affiant is, how the affiant has personal knowledge, and why the affiant is competent to make the statements. Note the affidavit in Figure 8-18. It states in the beginning that the affiant is the collections manager for the hospital and that he is familiar with the records of the hospital. This establishes who the affiant is, how he has knowledge of the hospital records, and why he is competent to make the statement as to how much the defendants owe.

FRCivP 56(e) further provides that the facts set forth in the affidavits must be admissible in evidence. This calls for consideration of the Federal Rules of Evidence. Take, for example, the hospital bill affidavit. Recall from Chapter 4 the "business records" exception to the hearsay rule. The hospital records were kept in the regular course of the hospital's business and the collections manager is sufficiently familiar with the hospital records to testify about them.

FRCivP 56(e) also requires that when the moving party sets forth the supporting affidavits and other supporting documents, the party opposing the motion for summary judgment cannot simply rest on its pleadings. Rather, the "adverse party's response, by affidavits or as otherwise provided in this rule, must set forth specific facts showing that there is a genuine issue for trial." As a practical matter, a party will always respond to the motion and state in a memorandum of law and affidavits the reasons for its opposition. However, sometimes a party cannot present by affidavit facts necessary to justify its opposition. In such a case, FRCivP 56(f) provides that the court may refuse the motion for summary judgment or may enter an order allowing more time to gather facts for affidavits, and may order that depositions or other forms of discovery take place.

Finally, FRCivP 56(g) addresses affidavits made in bad faith. It states that when an affidavit is presented "in bad faith or solely for the purpose of delay," the court shall order that party to pay to the other party the costs incurred in filing its affidavits (i.e., the affidavits made in good faith), and that this amount may include attorney's fees. It is clear from FRCivP 56 that the paralegal/attorney team must take great care in preparing affidavits in support of a motion for summary judgment.

Memoranda of Law. We have already discussed broadly the filing of memoranda of law in support of motions. With summary judgment, perhaps more than with any other motion, memoranda of law are very important. It is difficult, if not impossible, to convince a court that your party is entitled to summary judgment without submitting a memorandum of law. Obviously you must present the facts in a way that convinces the judge that there are no material facts in dispute. This must be followed by a discussion of the applicable law, and you must relate the facts to the applicable law in a manner to convince the court that your party is entitled to judgment as a matter of law. Figure 8-20 illustrates some of the basic components of a memorandum of law in support of a motion for summary judgment. While memoranda of law will tend to follow a common format, the content of each one must be carefully tailored to the particular facts of the case and to applicable law.

Oral Argument. Whether oral argument is held depends on the local rules and customs of your judicial district and the preferences of the presiding judge. Be aware that in some judicial districts a hearing on a motion is waived unless a party requests oral argument in writing.

If the moving party does request a hearing, FRCivP 56(c) requires that the motion for summary judgment be served at least ten days before the time fixed for the hearing. It further states that the adverse party may serve opposing affidavits prior to the day of the hearing. FRCivP 56(c) states the minimum time requirements. In practice, it is best to allow far more time than the minimum stated. Motions for summary judgment are often complex, and it is best to have time to prepare thoroughly and to allow the court ample time to consider the motion prior to oral argument.

Responses to Motions for Summary Judgment

The general rules of motion practice concerning responses apply to summary judgment. One should file a response to the motion itself, file a responsive memorandum of law, and be certain that oral argument is requested. However, the need to respond is in some respects even greater with summary judgment motions than other motions. As noted, FRCivP 56(e) specifically states that a party opposing the motion must file affidavits and cannot just rely on the pleadings. The chances of prevailing on some motions, such as a motion for judgment on the pleadings, are not as great as the chances of prevailing on a motion for summary judgment. By the stage in the litigation where an intelligent argument for summary judgment can be made, the case may well be developed enough to grant the motion. There is much to be lost—or gained—by a motion for summary judgment. As we noted earlier, even if the motion for summary judgment is not granted, a great deal of trial preparation can be accomplished in preparing an argument for or against summary judgment.

ENDNOTES

1 *Black's Law Dictionary* 913 (5th ed. 1979).

2 FRCivP 60(b) states that the one-year limitation applies only to the first three reasons listed in FRCivP 60(b) for relief from a judgment, i.e., "(1) mistake, inadvertence, surprise, or excusable neglect; (2) newly discovered evidence which by due diligence could not have been discovered in time to move for a new trial under Rule 59(b); (3) fraud (whether heretofore denominated intrinsic or extrinsic), misrepresentation, or other misconduct of an adverse party."

3 *Stuski v. U.S. Lines*, 31 F.R.D. 188 (D.C. Pa. 1962); see also *Consolidated Masonry & Fireproofing, Inc. v. Wagman Construction Corporation*, 383 F.2d 249 (4th Cir. 1967).

4 Wright & Miller, *Federal Practice and Procedure: Civil* 2d §1368 (1990).

5 *Wager v. Pro*, 575 F.2d 882, 885 (D.C. Cir. 1976).

9 DISCOVERY

LITIGATION EXTRACT: Early in the litigation process we performed informal discovery by interviewing witnesses, inspecting public records, and reviewing the documents and other information that we could obtain voluntarily through this informal process. This was only the beginning of our exploration of the facts. We obtain the bulk of our facts through the discovery process. Discovery is the principal fact-finding process in litigation. The Federal Rules of Civil Procedure provide five principal discovery methods. We will discuss how each method works and the principal tasks that paralegals perform. We will also examine the scope of the information that parties can obtain through discovery, and the limitations imposed by the Federal Rules of Civil Procedure. Finally, we will consider the methods available to compel discovery when a person or organization fails to comply with reasonable discovery requests.

INTRODUCTION TO DISCOVERY

The term discovery refers to the series of activities through which litigants obtain from one another information that enables them to prepare for trial. Although information gathering is its primary function, discovery serves several additional purposes. Discovery helps to clarify the factual and legal issues and preserve witnesses' testimony, especially when a witness might not be available for trial. Testimony obtained through discovery can be used to impeach a witness who gives contradictory testimony at trial. Another important function of discovery is that it guards against surprises at trial. Discovery has virtually eliminated the courtroom ambush, thus making the trial process more efficient.

Methods of Discovery

FRCivP 26(a) sets forth the five methods of discovery. The methods do not have to be used in the order they are listed in FRCivP 26(a). As we will discuss later in the chapter, there is great flexibility in the order in which discovery takes place, and methods may be used more than once. The first method listed in FRCivP 26(a) is the **deposition**, which consists of the oral responses of a witness to questions asked by the attorney representing another party. A deposition is taken under oath, without a judge present, and the setting is outside the courtroom. Depositions are governed by Rules 27 through 32 of the Federal Rules of Civil Procedure.

Second is the use of **interrogatories**, which are written questions submitted to another party. The party responds in writing to each question, and the answers are given under oath. FRCivP 33 governs the use of interrogatories.

The third method of discovery is through **requests for production** of documents and things and for entry upon land for inspection. This method of discovery is governed by FRCivP 34. As a paralegal, you may encounter frequent requests for the production of documents, which may be inspected and copied by the requesting party. You may also request or answer requests for the production of tangible things, such as the electric blanket in the Wesser case, for inspection and testing. Requests for entry upon land enable one party to a lawsuit to inspect, measure, survey, photograph, test, or sample the property of the opposing party.

The fourth method of discovery is through **requests for admission**, written requests asking the opposing party to admit to the truth of facts, the genuineness of documents, and the application of law to fact. Requests for admission are not appropriate for all issues related to the litigation. For instance, it would be fruitless to request that a party admit to the fact that the party is liable and should pay one million dollars to the other party. However, requests for admission are useful for parties to state in writing their agreement on certain uncontroverted facts, so that they will not have to waste time at trial. This is particularly true for admissions that documents are authentic. FRCivP 36 governs requests for admission.

The fifth method of discovery is **physical and mental examination of a person**, the request that a person undergo a physical or mental examination when her condition is at issue. FRCivP 35 governs physical and mental examination, and requires a court order for the examination if the person will not voluntarily submit to it. Obviously, this method of discovery is not applicable to every type of lawsuit. It is most common in personal injury litigation.

Rules that Govern the Discovery Process

The rules that govern the discovery process are the same that control the entire litigation process: the Federal Rules of Civil Procedure, state rules of civil procedure in state court, and local rules.

Before you examine the rules, it is important to understand that the entire discovery process is flexible. The rules are flexible and straightforward enough that the parties can usually conduct discovery without the court's intervention. However, if a serious problem arises, a party can file a motion for the court to intervene. This will be discussed at the end of the chapter.

Federal Rules of Civil Procedure. FRCivP 26 states the general provisions governing discovery. FRCivP 26(a) states the specific types of discovery methods that are available. FRCivP 26 also contains important provisions defining the scope of discovery and limitations on the information that is discoverable, as well as the sequence and timing of discovery.

The Federal Rules of Civil Procedure set forth the procedure for the various methods of discovery and the use at trial of the information gained in the discovery process. Rules 27–32 govern depositions. Rule 33 addresses interrogatories; Rule 34, production of documents and things and entry upon land for inspection; Rule 35, mental and physical examinations; Rule 36, requests for admission. Just as with pleadings, it is important that paralegals learn the exact procedures set forth in the applicable rules.

State Rules of Civil Procedure. As we discussed in Chapter 1, state rules of civil procedure are generally modeled closely after the Federal Rules of Civil Procedure. This is also true for the rules governing discovery. However, there may be important differences, so it is imperative that you consult the state rules in state court actions. For example, Rule 33 of the North Carolina Rules of Civil Procedure limits to 50 the number of interrogatories a party can ask. FRCivP 33 does not have this limitation.

Local Court Rules. Local court rules regarding discovery can vary greatly. For instance, some federal district courts have only two or three general rules that govern discovery. Others have numerous rules, ranging from restrictions on the number of interrogatories a party may ask to deadlines for the completion of discovery. Therefore it is imperative that paralegals read and follow the rules for the district in which the lawsuit is pending. This is true for both federal and state cases.

Filing Discovery Materials with the Court: an Example of Varying Rules. FRCivP 5(d) states the general rule that all papers served on the parties to the litigation must be filed with the court. However, FRCivP 5(d) gives the court the option to order that discovery materials not be filed with the clerk of court. One reason a court may not want the materials filed is that discovery documents can become massive, and the clerk's office may not have the space to hold all discovery material in all pending lawsuits.

The rules on whether to file discovery materials differ significantly in various state and federal courts. Some courts require that all discovery materials be filed with the court. In contrast, Rule 5 of the North Carolina Rules of Civil Procedure directs parties *not* to file discovery materials unless the court so orders or until the materials are actually used at trial. Local Rule 205 of the United States District Court for the Middle District of North Carolina also directs the parties not to file discovery materials, unless the court so orders or the court needs the documents in a pretrial proceeding. Local Rule 107 of the United States District Court for the District of Columbia grants the court the discretion to order that all or any portion of discovery materials not be filed. This variety in the rules makes it clear that procedural rules for discovery can differ significantly and that you must review the pertinent rules carefully.

Sequence and Timing of Discovery

The sequence and timing of the discovery process are flexible under the Federal Rules of Civil Procedure. FRCivP 26(d) provides that unless the court orders otherwise, the methods of discovery may be used in any sequence.

POINTER: It is important to understand that a discovery method may be used more than once during a lawsuit. A party may take the depositions of several witnesses. A party may submit multiple sets of interrogatories. However, parties must not abuse the discovery process by requesting unnecessary or repetitious information.

Although the rules do not specify a sequence for using the various methods of discovery, common sense does. This will become clearer as we explore the types of questions generally asked in interrogatories and depositions. The first set of interrogatories usually requests the identification of witnesses and documents. Once the documents are identified, the attorney/paralegal team can request production of the documents. After the attorney/paralegal reviews the documents, they may submit more interrogatories and/or take depositions to develop the evidence further. After a series of interrogatories and depositions has narrowed the issues and delineated the disputed and undisputed facts, a party may submit requests for admission to nail down the undisputed facts and issues. Mental and physical examinations may follow in personal injury cases.

This sequence is not set in stone. In fact, it is important to remain flexible, because the facts develop in different ways in different lawsuits. In addition, different types of lawsuits require different discovery methods. A physical examination may be necessary in the Wesser case because of Mr. Wesser's physical injuries from the fire. However, no physical examination would be needed in the Chattooga case, where the dispute centers around the reason for Sandy Ford's discharge, not her physical condition.

As for timing, FRCivP 26(d) leaves the details to the parties and to the court. Many local court rules place time limitations for the completion of discovery. For instance, a local rule may require that discovery be completed within 150 days of service of the complaint. Usually the deadlines for completion of discovery are more flexible. Often the parties meet with the judge early in the litigation process and set a deadline for the completion of discovery. This may be part of an initial pretrial conference or may be a separate conference devoted solely to discovery. Whatever deadline is imposed, its purpose is to ensure that the parties will start discovery early and complete it, so that they will not delay the trial.

As you will see in our discussion of the individual discovery methods, there are certain time limitations for making requests and for responding. For instance, FRCivP 33 provides that a party must answer interrogatories within 30 days of service, except that a defendant is allowed 45 days when the interrogatories are served with the complaint and summons. However, even with these deadlines there is some flexibility. The attorneys often agree that they will allow additional time for response. The usual practice is to state the agreement in a stipulation, which is filed with the court. See Figure 9-1 for an example. If an attorney seeks an extension and the other attorney will not agree, the attorney can file a motion asking the court for an extension.

FIGURE 9-1   STIPULATION

UNITED STATES DISTRICT COURT
MIDDLE DISTRICT OF NORTH CAROLINA
CHARLESTON DIVISION
CIVIL NO.: C-89-1293-B

Bryson Wesser,

                    Plaintiff,

      -vs-

Woodall Shoals Corporation,   *STIPULATION*
                Defendant,
         and
Second Ledge Stores, Incorporated,
                Defendant

     NOW COME THE PLAINTIFF and the defendants Woodall Shoals Corpora-
tion and Second Ledge Stores, Incorporated, and hereby stipulate and agree that
the time for responding to ''Plaintiff's First Set of Interrogatories'' shall be extended through and including the 25th day of April, 1989.

                             _____
                             Leigh J. Heyward
                             Attorney for Plaintiff

                             _____
                             David H. Benedict
                             Attorney for Defendants Woodall
                             Shoals Corporation and Second Ledge
                             Stores, Incorporated

Duty to Supplement Responses

FRCivP 26(e) requires parties to update and supplement their responses when
a prior response is no longer accurate. For instance, if Mr. Wesser answers an
interrogatory stating that the blanket model number was 6102, but later finds
out that the model number was 6100, he has a duty to supplement the answers.
FRCivP 26(e) also requires parties to supplement their responses regarding their
witnesses, including expert witnesses. Parties frequently change or add witnesses
as the case develops.

SCOPE OF DISCOVERY

The Federal Rules of Civil Procedure allow a wide range of information to be discovered. However, there are some limitations, primarily privileged information. It is crucial for paralegals to understand the scope of discovery so that the attorney/paralegal team does not accidentally turn over protected information. Before information is released to the other parties, the attorney will review it. However, paralegals are integrally involved in the screening and review of information.

The General Rule for Scope of Discovery

FRCivP 26(b)(1) states the general scope of discovery. It provides that

> [p]arties may obtain discovery regarding any matter, not privileged, which is relevant to the subject matter involved in the pending action . . . It is not ground for objection that the information sought will be inadmissible at the trial if the information sought appears reasonably calculated to lead to the discovery of admissible evidence. . . .

It is important to remember that the information requested does not itself have to be admissible evidence, but only "reasonably calculated" to lead to admissible evidence. Recall our discussion of hearsay in Chapter 4. Suppose that two weeks after the fire Mr. Wesser and his neighbor were discussing the cause of the fire. Their conversation is hearsay and most likely fits into no hearsay exception. However, the conversation is reasonably calculated to lead to discoverable evidence, such as further information about what Mr. Wesser's neighbor observed at the time of the fire. Therefore the content of their conversation could be obtained through discovery.

FRCivP 26 further states that information about the claims or defenses of any party are subject to discovery. The rule specifies that this includes "the existence, description, nature, custody, condition and location of any books, documents, or other tangible things and the identity and location of persons having knowledge of any discoverable matter."

FRCivP 26(b)(2) specifically states that insurance agreements that may be used to pay all or part of a judgment are subject to discovery. However, the rule further states that this does not mean that the existence and contents of the insurance agreements are admissible at trial.

Special Rules Concerning Expert Witnesses

To understand what information is discoverable about experts, you must split experts into two groups—experts who will testify at trial and experts who will not testify at trial.

FRCivP 26(b)(4)(A) provides the rule for experts who are expected to testify at trial. A party may use interrogatories to discover the identity of the experts, the subject matter on which they are expected to testify, and the substance of the facts and opinions about which they will testify. A summary of the grounds for each opinion may also be obtained through the use of interrogatories. However, a party must receive court permission to obtain discovery beyond the interrogatories. For instance, if a party wishes to take an expert witness's deposition, the party must file a motion and obtain court permission.

FRCivP 26(b)(4)(B) provides the rule for experts who are not expected to testify at trial. The facts known and opinions held by experts who are consulted in preparation for trial, but who are not expected to testify, are generally not discoverable. However, FRCivP 26(b)(4)(B) provides for discovery when the requesting party can show "exceptional circumstances" that make it impracticable "to obtain facts or opinions on the same subject by other means."

Limitations on Discovery

Although the scope of discovery is broad, there are limitations. That is, some information is protected from disclosure. It is crucial that paralegals be alert for privileged material so that it will not be inadvertently disclosed.

Privileged Information. Recall the discussion of privileges in Chapter 4. If information is privileged, it is protected from disclosure, even during discovery. A privilege you will frequently encounter is the attorney-client privilege. It would obviously be unreasonable to expect parties to turn over communications with their attorneys, such as letters from attorneys explaining the strategy for the lawsuit.

Another privilege that surfaces often in the discovery process is the work product privilege, set forth in FRCivP 26(b)(3). Work product is often called "trial preparation materials." Remember that this privilege precludes disclosure of the "mental impressions, conclusions, opinions, or legal theories of an attorney or other representative of a party concerning the litigation."

However, other trial preparation materials may be discoverable. A party may be able to obtain other documents and tangible things prepared in anticipation of trial, if the party can establish that "he is unable without undue hardship to obtain the substantial equivalent of the materials by other means." Suppose that the fire inspector gave Ms. Heyward a statement explaining his opinion about the cause of the fire. If Mr. Benedict wants the statement, he may not be able to obtain it through a request for the document. This is because Mr. Benedict could easily contact the fire inspector and get a statement. This would not constitute "undue hardship."

Protective Orders. Parties may file motions asking the court to enter protective orders—that is, orders to protect information that is not privileged, but the disclosure of which would cause "annoyance, embarrassment, oppression, or undue burden or expense" (FRCivP 26(c)). FRCivP 26(c) enumerates a number of ways that the court may protect the information, ranging from sealing the information and filing it with the court to allowing only certain persons to be present at a deposition.

Suppose that Woodall Shoals possesses a lengthy research paper that discusses the results of their development of advanced safety features for electric blankets. The document may mention the model of the blanket that Mr. Wesser had. Ms. Heyward requests production of the research paper. Woodall Shoals does not want to release the research paper because it discusses some advanced features that are not yet protected by patents. Mr. Benedict can file a motion for a protective order to prevent disclosure of this confidential research. The court may then order that Woodall Shoals produce those parts of the paper that do not discuss the confidential research. Of course, the court may deny the motion for a protective order and instead order Woodall Shoals to produce the entire document.

DISCOVERY PLANNING

The attorney/paralegal team must plan the discovery process carefully to make it effective. The strategy will be different in different types of lawsuits.

It is helpful to consult the chart of the essential elements to prove our claim, which we discussed in Chapter 5. Review the essential elements that our client must establish. Most discovery takes place after the complaint and answer are filed, so next we can examine the pleadings to review the contentions of the defendants and the facts that are disputed.[1]

Next we must determine the likely sources for the facts that we need to prove our claim and defeat the defendants' assertions. We listed some possible sources on our essential elements chart on page 121. We may find that we have already obtained much information through our informal investigation and will not need formal discovery for certain facts. However, formal discovery may still be necessary to develop those facts more fully or to pin down a witness's statement. Consider too whether some witnesses may be unavailable for trial. If they may disappear, it is best to pin down their statements in a deposition.

Next we must consider the most effective method for obtaining the information we need. Discovery generally moves from the general to the specific. For instance, in the first set of interrogatories, we ask the defendants to identify the witnesses. Our next step may be to take those witnesses' depositions. We may request the production of documents and after examining the documents, submit more interrogatories or take more depositions to develop some facts we find in the documents.

Time and money are considerations in discovery planning. It is best to start discovery early, so that you do not get close to the trial date and find that discovery is not complete. Also, prompt initiation of discovery sends the message to the other parties that you plan to litigate aggressively.

Remember that not every discovery method is necessary in every lawsuit. Discovery can be very expensive. If you plan depositions for 20 witnesses, this will be costly considering the amount of time the attorney and paralegal must devote. There may be additional costs such as court reporters, conference rooms at an airport, and the like. Therefore it is important to consider how much discovery your client's litigation budget can afford.

INTERROGATORIES

Now that you have an overview of discovery, we will discuss the procedures for the various discovery methods and the important duties that paralegals perform in discovery. The first step in the discovery process is usually interrogatories.

Procedure

FRCivP 33(a) explains the procedures for using interrogatories. Interrogatories may be served on any other party. It is important to remember that you can serve interrogatories only on the parties to the litigation. For instance, in the Wesser case the fire inspector is a likely witness, but he is not a party. Therefore you can take his deposition, but you cannot submit interrogatories to him.

If the party is a business organization such as a corporation, or is a governmental agency, the interrogatories are served on an officer or agent of the organization or agency. When we speak of ''serving'' interrogatories, this is not the same as service of a lawsuit. Attorneys generally mail the interrogatories to the attorney who represents the party. If the party is unrepresented, the attorney mails the interrogatories to the party.

Interrogatories may be served on the plaintiff any time after commencement of the lawsuit. They may be served on any other party to the litigation after service of the summons and complaint on that party. The party on whom the interrogatories are served must answer within 30 days. However, if the interrogatories are served on a defendant at the same time as the summons and complaint, the defendant has 45 days to answer.

POINTER: Remember that parties often need more than 30 days to prepare answers, especially answers to long, detailed interrogatories. Parties frequently seek an extension of time to answer, and the attorneys usually can agree on an extension, unless the party has been dragging its feet. A party may file a motion with the court requesting an extension if the attorneys cannot agree to an extension.

FRCivP 33 requires that each interrogatory be answered ''separately and fully in writing under oath, unless it is objected to.'' If a party objects to an interrogatory, the party must state the reason for the objection. When the answer to an interrogatory can be found in a party's business records, FRCivP 33(c) allows the party to answer the interrogatory by specifying the records in which the answer can be found. The party must then let the requesting party inspect and copy the records. For examples, see the Responses to Interrogatories in the Appendix.

Drafting Interrogatories

Paralegals sometimes prepare the first draft of the interrogatories. The attorney reviews the draft and may make revisions, just as with pleadings. When you are asked to draft a set of interrogatories, there are many sources you may consult. First you may look at other files in your office dealing with similar issues. Other attorneys and paralegals can usually point you in the right direction. Form books are available showing sample interrogatories for different types of lawsuits. As with pleadings, forms are a good starting point, but you cannot follow them slavishly. In some law libraries you can find the records on appeal for cases that were appealed in the state's appellate courts and some cases appealed to the United States Supreme Court. The record on appeal often contains some or all of the discovery materials from the trial of the case.

Topics to Include in Interrogatories. To make an initial list of the topics to include, keep in mind the facts you must establish to prove your client's claim. It may help to review once again the chart of the essential elements of the claim. Also review the pleadings and all other pertinent documents to see the facts that you already know. The documents may also give you ideas for questions you need to ask. In addition, the attorney may give you specific topics to include.

Although the topics will vary depending on the issues in question, certain categories of information will be requested in most lawsuits.

1. The identity of the person answering the interrogatories.

Note that when interrogatories are addressed to a corporation, as in the Wesser case, your question should require persons to specify their position in the company and to identify other persons in the company who provided information.

2. Ask corporate defendants whether they have been correctly designated in the pleadings.

You may not be aware that a company is a subsidiary or division of another corporation. This can be important for purposes of jurisdiction and venue.

3. The identity of witnesses.

It is important to find out the names of the party's witnesses, as well as their addresses and phone numbers. You will need this information if you take the witness's deposition. Also ask the party to describe the witness's relationship to the party.

4. Information about expert witnesses.

Remember that FRCivP 26(b)(4) allows a party to request through interrogatories the names of expert witnesses, as well as the subject matter about which they will testify and a summary of their bases for their opinions. Often interrogatories request information about the expert's qualifications. You may discover that the person does not qualify as an expert.

5. Information about pertinent documents.

Interrogatories are useful to identify the documents that are important to a party's case. There are many ways of requesting information about documents, including business records. Refer to the sample Wesser case interrogatories in the Appendix. Here many types of documents are pertinent, from the warranty that came with the blanket to quality control records to documents about the design procedures for the blanket. Usually as you cover the topics about which you need information, it will be clear what the related documents are.

6. Details of the other parties' version of the events.

Parties frequently request that other parties detail their version of the events in issue. For example, where contributory negligence is an issue, the defendant may ask the plaintiff to describe the events leading up to the accident, in the hope that the plaintiff did something negligent. In cases like the Chattooga case, the sequence of events is crucial. For instance, it is important to know when Sandy Ford helped her friend file a complaint with the Equal Employment Opportunity Commission.

7. Specific information about damages.

Recall that the Wesser complaint requests damages ''in excess of $50,000.'' Interrogatories can address the plaintiff's specific injuries and property damage, and the amount of damages attributed to each.

8. Insurance coverage.

If you do not already know the details of the defendants' insurance coverage, be sure to include a question about their insurance policies—the name of the provider, amount of coverage, and so on. You need to know right away if a defendant does not have sufficient coverage to pay a judgment.

These general topics are applicable to many types of litigation. There are many other topics that you may include, depending upon the subject matter of the lawsuit.

Guidelines for Drafting the Questions. There are several general guidelines to bear in mind when you draft interrogatories. First, make the questions clear and uncomplicated. If it is not clear what information you seek, you will not get the information that you need. If a question is too complex, it may be ambiguous or it may prompt an objection. Second, try to avoid questions that call for yes/no answers. Such questions do not draw out the details that you need from the other party. Third, ask the person answering the interrogatories to identify who is the source of the information for any answer that is not based on personal knowledge.

Format for Interrogatories. Refer to the Plaintiff's First Set of Interrogatories to Defendant Woodall Shoals in the Appendix. Interrogatories have captions like those of pleadings. It is important to indicate to which defendant interrogatories are directed. It is also important to specify which set of interrogatories you are submitting—first, second, and so forth. Most interrogatories have a simple opening paragraph stating that they are submitted in accordance with Rule 33 and that the party must submit answers in accordance with Rule 33. Especially with long, complex interrogatories, definitions follow. The illustration shows excerpts from the definitions, including ''the subject blanket'' and ''representatives.'' The interrogatories follow, with each question numbered and each subpart within the question designated. At the end is the attorney's signature, with address and phone number. Finally, there is a certificate of service.

 POINTER: State and local rules may provide strict requirements for format. For example, some rules require at least one inch of space between interrogatories to provide the respondent space to answer. If the interrogatories do not conform with the format rules, the court may strike them or require resubmission.

Answering Interrogatories

Paralegals often obtain information from clients and draft answers to interrogatories. The attorney will review the draft, but you want the draft as accurate as possible. Remember that there are two options with each interrogatory—an answer or an objection. We will discuss answers first.

The first step is to send a copy of the interrogatories to the client so that the client can gather the information you need. Obviously, this should be done immediately so that you will have time to prepare the answers and clarify any further information that you need.

Before drafting the answers, compare the information received with other information you already have from the client. If there are any inconsistencies, clarify them immediately. Remember that the opposing party will be looking for inconsistencies and anything else that can damage your case.

There are several general guidelines for drafting answers. First, do not volunteer any more information than is necessary to answer the question. You do not want to disclose any more material than you have to. Second, make the answers clear and unambiguous. Third, be consistent; do not give contradictory answers. Fourth, ask the attorney any questions that you have. Above all, discuss any material that may be privileged. Finally, remember that FRCivP 33(c) provides the option to produce business records for the opposing party to inspect and copy.

Objections to Interrogatories.   There are several grounds for objections to interrogatories. If a question seeks privileged information, this is a ground for objection. Be especially alert for information protected by the attorney-client privilege and work product privilege (trial preparation materials). An answer may call for disclosure of trade secrets, and the responding party will request a protective order. For an example, see the response to interrogatory 6, in the Appendix. A question may be irrelevant, and this is a ground for objection. See the response to interrogatory 8 in the Appendix. However, remember that the scope of discovery is broad, so it may be difficult to assert that the information sought is irrelevant.

Particularly after the first set of interrogatories, a party may seek information that is unreasonably cumulative or duplicative. This is one of the grounds for objection set forth in FRCivP 26(b)(1). Another ground for objection in FRCivP 26(b)(1) is that the discovery is unduly burdensome or expensive. The grounds in FRCivP 26(b)(1) apply to all discovery methods, but may be particularly applicable to interrogatories, especially when the parties exchange multiple sets of questions.

Procedure After Answering Interrogatories.   Be sure that the attorney signs the interrogatories. The format for signature is the same as in pleadings. See the responses in the Appendix for an example. The person who provides the answers should sign the interrogatories. This is your client or the authorized agent when your client is a business organization. The person signs a verification, the wording of which may differ depending on whether your client is an individual who has personal knowledge of the facts or an organizational agent who does not necessarily have personal knowledge. Refer to the sample verification signed by Mr. Wesser (Figure 9-2). Compare the verification signed by the designated employee of Woodall Shoals, in the Appendix. The person's notarized signature follows the verification.

FIGURE 9-2   BRYSON WESSER'S VERIFICATION

STATE OF NORTH CAROLINA
COUNTY OF MITCHELL

    BRYSON WESSER, being duly sworn, deposes and says that he is the plaintiff in this action; that he has read the foregoing Answers to Defendants' First Set of Interrogatories and knows the contents thereof; that the same is true to his own knowledge except as to those matters and things therein stated on information and belief and as to those he believes it to be true.

                                      _____
                                       Bryson Wesser

Subscribed and sworn to before me
this the _____ day of June, 1989.

_____
             Notary Public

My commission expires: _____

    Mail a copy of the interrogatories to each party, and attach a certificate of service to each set of interrogatories. Remember to check the state and local rules to determine whether the interrogatories should be filed with the clerk of court or retained by the law firm until trial.

POINTER: Always enter in the docket control system the date on which answers to interrogatories are due. Also arrange for reminders well ahead of the deadline, so you can be sure to obtain information from the client in time.

REQUESTS FOR PRODUCTION OF DOCUMENTS AND THINGS

FRCivP 34 provides that a party may request other parties to produce designated documents for inspection and copying. Documents include more than just papers such as contracts or warranties. FRCivP 34 defines documents to include "drawings, graphs, charts, photographs, phonorecords, and other data compilations...."

    FRCivP 34 also provides that a party may request tangible things for inspection and testing. This includes physical evidence such as the electric blanket in the Wesser case. The third category in FRCivP 34 is the request to enter property under another party's control, to inspect, measure, survey, photograph, test, or sample the property. If two parties have a dispute over land ownership, one party may want permission to enter the property to survey it and perhaps take photographs.

For all three categories—documents, tangible objects, and land—the item requested must be "in the possession, custody or control of the party upon whom the request is served." Assume that you request accounting records from an officer of a corporation, who replies, "Sorry, our accountant has those papers." This response is unacceptable. FRCivP 34 requires that the corporate officer get the records from the accountant and produce them, because these records are under the corporation's control. This prevents parties from giving documents to other persons to avoid having to produce them.

Our discussion focuses on document production, because this is the most frequent request. Remember that the general rules we discuss apply also to requests for tangible things and to entry and inspection of property.

Procedure

FRCivP 34(b) describes the timing and procedure for requests to produce. Requests may be served on the plaintiff any time after commencement of the lawsuit. Requests may be served on other parties with the service of the summons and complaint or any time afterward. Note that parties may make requests for documents only on other parties.

The party has 30 days to serve a written response to the requests. However, if the requests are served on a defendant along with the summons and complaint, the defendant has 45 days to serve a response. The response must state for each separate request either that the party will produce the document or that the party objects to production of the particular document or to part of it.

Format and Content of Requests to Produce

Like interrogatories, requests to produce have the case caption at the top, specifying the court, parties, and file number. See Figure 9-3. The requests must be specifically labeled; that is, they must specify to which party the requests are directed and whether this is the first, second, or some subsequent set of requests to produce. For example, the request for production in Figure 9-3 is an excerpt from the Plaintiff's First Request for Production of Documents to Defendant Woodall Shoals Corporation.

The request to produce begins with a simple statement that the defendant is requested to produce the documents in accordance with Rule 34 of the Federal Rules of Civil Procedure. This is sometimes followed by definitions. If definitions are necessary, be sure that they are consistent with the definitions in the interrogatories.

Next is the numbered list of the documents requested. There are a number of ways to describe the documents. The general guideline in FRCivP 34 is that the documents be described "with reasonable particularity." That is, the party from whom the documents are requested must be able to understand which documents the other party wants. It is not sufficient to request "all your business records." This is too vague.

FIGURE 9-3   REQUEST FOR PRODUCTION OF DOCUMENTS

UNITED STATES DISTRICT COURT
MIDDLE DISTRICT OF NORTH CAROLINA
CHARLESTON DIVISION
CIVIL NO.: C-89-1293-B

Bryson Wesser,

                  Plaintiff,

      -vs-

Woodall Shoals Corporation,

                Defendant,
       and
Second Ledge Stores, Incorporated,
               Defendant

PLAINTIFF'S FIRST REQUEST FOR PRODUCTION OF DOCUMENTS TO DEFENDANT WOODALL SHOALS CORPORATION

Pursuant to Rule 34 of the Federal Rules of Civil Procedure, the defendant Woodall Shoals is requested to produce for inspection and copying at the office of Heyward and Wilson, 401 East Trade Street, Charleston, NC, within thirty (30) days of receipt of this request, or at a time and location to be mutually agreed upon by the parties, the documents requested herein.

DEFINITIONS

(same as in interrogatories in Appendix)

REQUESTS

1. In the defendant's response to interrogatory No. 6 in the Plaintiff's First Set of Interrogatories, the defendant referred to reports on specific design/quality control tolerances for specific components of the defendant's electric blankets. Please produce reports for tolerances for the control unit for Model 6102 for the period from two years before the manufacture of the subject blanket to two years after the manufacture of the subject blanket. Note that the court entered a protective order on April 24, 1989, and that the production of documents must comply with the protective order.

This the _____ day of May, 1989.

Leigh J. Heyward
Attorney for the Plaintiff
Heyward and Wilson
401 East Trade Street
Charleston, NC 28226-1114
704-555-3161

Detailed requests for production are often the second step in the discovery process. One purpose of interrogatories is to identify the documents that you need to request. Therefore the best start for formulating the description of documents is a review of the interrogatories and answers to them. For instance, in interrogatory no. 11 (see Appendix) the plaintiff asked the defendant Woodall Shoals to describe warnings to consumers that electric blankets might overheat. Woodall Shoals replied that copies of recent examples were attached and that copies of all other instructions, warnings, and labels were available for inspection in their New York office. In a request for production you may ask for instructions, warnings, and labels used by Woodall Shoals at the time the subject blanket was manufactured and for the two years before its manufacture and the two years after its manufacture.

The description of documents differs, depending on the nature of the lawsuit. For instance, in personal injury litigation, interrogatories typically ask the plaintiffs to describe their injuries and the medical treatment they received as a result of their injuries. A request for documents related to the medical treatment may describe the documents as follows:

1. All reports, photographs, charts, diagrams and any other documents regarding the plaintiff's medical treatment as a result of the events described in the plaintiff's complaint, including but not limited to medical records and reports of the plaintiff's treating physicians; hospital and emergency room records, including the reports of x-rays and other laboratory tests; and the bills for the medical treatment obtained.

You may draft requests for production with much more detailed descriptions. For instance, in a lawsuit involving complex financial transactions, you may need quite specific descriptions, because so many documents were generated by the transactions. For instance, the defendant in a lawsuit involving allegations of fraud in the sale of securities may request from the plaintiff "documents relating to purchases by defendants in private placement transactions of unrated securities for which mortgage loans served as collateral."

FRCivP 34 requires that the request for production "specify a reasonable time, place, and manner of making the inspection and performing the related acts." This means that the parties must agree to a reasonable method for inspection and copying of the documents requested. In lawsuits that do not involve a great number of documents, a simple statement that the documents are to be produced at the office of the requesting attorney on a certain date and at a certain time will suffice (see Figure 9-3). In more complex lawsuits that involve hundreds or thousands of documents, the procedure is more involved. We will discuss these methods for production in the next section.

Both the requests for production and responses to the requests are signed by the attorneys and mailed to all parties, as with interrogatories. Remember to attach a certificate of service. Remember also to check local rules for additional requirements. In North Carolina, for instance, some courts require that a representative of the client other than the attorney attest to the accuracy of responses to interrogatories.

Production of Documents

One of the most important duties paralegals may perform is the production of documents. You may initially think that this is simple—you just put the papers in a box and take them to the other party to copy. Actually document production is much more involved than this, especially in lawsuits that involve reams of documents. Your assignment as a paralegal may be to screen the documents to help determine which ones should be produced; you may be in charge of a clerical team that helps with the copying and numbering of the documents. FRCivP 34(b) provides only a general guideline for the production of documents. It states that a party shall produce the documents "as they are kept in the usual course of business or shall organize and label them to correspond with the categories in the request." The purpose of this rule is to prevent the producing party from scrambling the documents to make discovery more difficult for the requesting party.

There are special considerations in gathering, screening and copying the documents. We will examine each step individually.

Gathering the Documents. Sometimes you already have at the law office all the documents that you need to produce. You may have a simple personal injury claim, and the client may have already brought all the documents you need.

However, with complex litigation involving many documents, your first task may be to gather the documents. This often requires a search of the client's business records, which may be in files at the corporate office or even in a warehouse. When your client is a large company, the documents may even be in several locations throughout the United States and even in offices overseas. In such a case, the attorney/paralegal team needs to meet with the client to discuss the nature of the documents requested and where the documents are located. There are many issues you may need to discuss, such as whether any of the older documents have been destroyed through the company's regular retention and disposal system.

Other questions may concern how to gain access to computer records. The attorney should explain to the client the attorney's interpretation of the description of the documents requested. For instance, the attorney may have already decided that certain documents are not covered by the request for production. He or she may have already objected to certain portions of the request for production and even obtained a protective order to prevent their disclosure. This must also be explained to the client.

The client and the attorney/paralegal team must decide who will search the client's files—the law firm personnel or the client's employees. The search may be faster if the client's employees perform it. On the other hand, the law firm personnel may be better able to determine which documents need to be produced. Whatever the decision, the person performing the search must have detailed instructions from the attorney. Paralegals may find that they are in charge of the persons performing the search. In this case, be sure you have reviewed the instructions with the attorney and clarified any questions you have about the scope of the document search.

Screening the Documents. It is imperative that you screen the documents to ensure that no protected information is released to the other party. The documents are also reviewed to be sure that no more information than necessary is released. Both the paralegal and attorney should review the documents. Sometimes the paralegal performs the initial screening, and sometimes the attorney does it. It may be more efficient for paralegals to perform the initial screening so that they can flag issues that the attorneys need to consider.

Your screening should focus on four categories of information. First, look for information that is irrelevant—that is, unrelated to the subject matter of the lawsuit. Second, screen out documents that are unresponsive. These are documents that are related to the subject matter of the lawsuit but do not fall within the description in the request for production. You may set these documents aside and may even go ahead and return them to the client.

The third category is confidential documents. These documents are generally already covered by a protective order. Remember that the court may enter orders to prevent the discovery of all or part of certain documents or to limit the discovery in other ways specified in FRCivP 26(c). Be sure to review all protective orders before producing documents. If the court has allowed the discovery of confidential documents, stamp "confidential" on them before they are copied.

The fourth category is privileged information. Recall our discussions of the attorney-client privilege and work product privilege. The attorneys make the ultimate decision whether the information is protected from disclosure by privilege. The paralegal should pull potentially privileged documents from the file and put them in a separate file for the attorney's review.

Organizing and Numbering the Documents. The first decision to make is whether to produce the original documents or to make copies. The parties generally reach an agreement on which of these to produce, and if they cannot agree, the court can decide. Parties generally produce copies but sometimes produce originals. An advantage of producing originals is saving copying costs. However, there are disadvantages to producing originals, such as the risk that they will be altered. In addition, the documents may get out of order and become confusing.

Production of large numbers of documents is unmanageable without a system to organize and identify the documents. There are a number of ways to organize documents, and the methods are often combined. For instance, all documents in a certain group may concern a common subject, and within the group they may be arranged in chronological order.

Once the attorney/paralegal team decides how to organize the documents, paralegals can put the documents in order and assign a number to each. These numbers are generally known as production numbers. There are many different systems for assigning production numbers. Some law firms begin each production number with a letter to designate which party produced the document. For instance, the plaintiff's documents may all start with "A," and the defendant's documents may start with "B."

The production number is then stamped on each document. Some law firms place a number on the front page of the document, and others number each page of the document. For instance, the third page of one of the plaintiff's documents may be "A-503-3."

Production numbers serve several purposes. First, they form the basis for an index to the documents so that you can find them easily in a sea of papers. Second, they ensure that documents are still complete when they are submitted at trial. Paralegals keep records of the number(s) assigned to a document and the number of the first and last page. Thus, if at trial the opposing party submits the document as evidence, you can make sure that the document still has all its original pages. Production numbers ensure ready access to documents, which is crucial during discovery and at trial.

The numbers may be handwritten on the documents. Some law firms use a "Bates stamp" when large numbers of documents are involved. A "Bates stamp" is a hand-held stamp that automatically advances to the next highest number each time you stamp a document. If you use a Bates stamp, watch carefully to be sure that it does not skip any numbers. If it does skip a number, insert a blank sheet of paper to mark the gap.

Copying the Documents. As paralegals organize and number the documents, they generally place them in heavy cardboard boxes to move them to the copying room. It is best to label the outside of the box with the range of numbers contained in each box.

Before copying the documents, check to be sure that confidential documents are marked "confidential." Some law firms also stamp documents with a stamp that says "Produced by _____." For instance, the documents produced by Leigh Heyward for Mr. Wesser would be stamped "Produced by Heyward and Wilson." This is helpful when there are multiple parties.

Paralegals should be sure that they have adequate clerical help for making the copies. It helps to have people to remove staples, place the documents in the copy machine, and restaple the documents. It also helps to have a person to put the documents back in the box to ensure that the documents are kept in proper order.

Some oversized documents can be reduced to standard size paper on your copy machine. However, you may have to rely on an outside copying center to handle very large documents such as blueprints.

Finally, paralegals ensure that the documents are properly indexed. There are several methods for indexing, and we will discuss them in Chapter 10.

DEPOSITIONS

Depositions are a commonly used discovery method. The Federal Rules of Civil Procedure allow two types of depositions—written and oral. Oral depositions are far more common than written depositions. In an oral deposition an attorney asks the deponent (the person whose deposition is taken) questions in much the same way that an attorney questions a witness in a trial. The deponent is under oath, and a court reporter records all the questions and answers. The court reporter then prepares a transcript of the deposition and sends a copy to the attorneys for all the parties.

Written depositions are governed by FRCivP 31, which provides that written questions may be submitted to a deponent. The deponent answers the questions under oath, and the court reporter records the answers and prepares a transcript, as with oral depositions. However, with written depositions, attorneys are not present. The deponent simply answers the written questions, and the attorney is not present to follow up with additional questions to develop the deponent's testimony. Oral depositions are more common because the attorney can develop the testimony, observe the deponent's demeanor, and get a better idea of what the deponent knows and what type of witness the deponent would be at trial. The remainder of our discussion will focus solely on oral depositions, because they are so much more commonly used.

Who May Be Deposed

Depositions are the only discovery device that can be used to get information from both parties and nonparties to a lawsuit. For instance, you cannot force a witness who is not a party to answer interrogatories. However, you can force a nonparty witness to answer questions at a deposition, by serving a subpoena in accordance with FRCivP 45.

Attorneys generally do not depose their own witnesses. That is, Ms. Heyward would not take Mr. Wesser's deposition. However, attorneys may choose to depose their own witnesses if there is a strong possibility that a witness will not be available at trial. For instance, a key witness may be terminally ill. It is wise to take that witness's deposition to preserve his or her testimony for trial. FRCivP 32(a)(3) permits this use of a deposition at trial, and Rule 804(b)(1) of the Federal Rules of Evidence allows admission of the deposition as an exception to the hearsay rule.

Procedure

FRCivP 30(a) provides that a deposition may be taken at any time after the commencement of the lawsuit without court permission, with two exceptions. Leave of court is required to take the deposition of a defendant within 30 days of the service of the summons and complaint or to take the deposition of a person confined in prison.

FRCivP 30 provides no specifications of which persons to depose or the order in which depositions should take place. Generally the attorneys for the parties can agree on matters such as when and where depositions are held. Attorneys can stipulate to other procedures in depositions, such as whether the signature of the deponent is waived.

Notice of Deposition. FRCivP 30(b) requires that attorneys give "reasonable notice" of their intent to take a deposition. The rule does not define what constitutes "reasonable notice," but local court rules may impose a specific time. In practice, most attorney/paralegal teams discuss whose depositions they wish to take and arrange a mutually convenient time.

Written notice must be given not only to the deponent, but also to all parties to the lawsuit. As a practical matter, most parties will be represented by counsel, so you send the notice to the parties' attorneys.

The notice states the name of the person to be deposed and the date, time, and location of the deposition. The attorney should include a request for production of documents if the attorney wants the deponent to bring pertinent documents.

See Figure 9-4 for an illustration of a Notice, combined with a request for production. A certificate of service is attached, and the notice and request are served on all parties.

The procedure is different when the deponent is not a party. You send a notice of the deposition to the deponent and all parties. However, you must also prepare a subpoena to compel the appearance of the nonparty deponent. See Figure 9-5 for an illustration of a subpoena. Note that you must include in the subpoena the documents that you want the nonparty deponent to produce at the deposition. Review FRCivP 45, and be sure that the subpoena complies with its requirements.

The subpoena must be personally served on the deponent. FRCivP 45(c) provides that a subpoena may be served by a marshal or by a person over 18 years who is not a party to the lawsuit. In fact, paralegals sometimes serve the subpoenas. FRCivP 45(c) also requires that a check for witness fees and mileage costs accompany the subpoena. Attach a copy of the subpoena to the notice of deposition that you send to all the parties.

When the Deponent Is a Corporation or Agency. When the deponent is a corporation or government agency, FRCivP 30(b)(6) requires that the notice or subpoena "describe with reasonable particularity the matters on which examination is requested." The corporation or agency then designates one or more persons to testify at the deposition. For instance, in the Wesser case, Ms. Heyward may want to depose an employee of Woodall Shoals about its procedures for inspecting blankets, but she may not know the name of the person qualified to give this testimony. She may address the notice to Woodall Shoals, who will designate a person such as its quality control manager to appear and testify.

Procedure During and After a Deposition. Depositions are usually held in a conference room in the office of the lawyer who instigates the deposition. The persons present may vary, but usually include the deponent, the attorneys for all parties and for the deponent, and a court reporter to record the testimony. A court reporter is also a notary public and therefore authorized to swear in the witness. After any preliminary statements, the attorney begins to question the deponent. The other attorneys may cross-examine, and the rules of evidence generally apply. The attorney representing the deponent may voice objections to questions. The attorneys often stipulate in advance which grounds may be asserted as the basis for objection at the time of the deposition, and which grounds may be reserved and asserted at trial if the other party seeks to use the deposition at that point. In accordance with FRCivP 30(c), witnesses must still answer the questions to which the attorneys object, unless the attorneys instruct otherwise. The court reporter notes the objection in the transcript. If a party seeks to use the transcript at trial, the judge can rule on the objection at that time. Refer to Figure 9-6, which illustrates excerpts of a deposition in the Chattooga case.

During the deposition, the examining attorney frequently enters documents as exhibits. The court reporter marks the documents—that is, assigns numbers or letters to them and labels them. The court reporter notes in the transcript when documents are entered as exhibits.

FIGURE 9-4   COMBINED NOTICE OF DEPOSITION AND REQUEST FOR PRODUCTION

UNITED STATES DISTRICT COURT
MIDDLE DISTRICT OF NORTH CAROLINA
CHARLESTON DIVISION
Civil Action No.: C-89-2388-B

Equal Employment Opportunity
Commission,

               Plaintiff,

     -vs-

Chattooga Corporation,
              Defendant

NOTICE TO TAKE DEPOSITION
AND
REQUEST FOR PRODUCTION
OF DOCUMENTS

To: Edward R. Cheng, attorney of record for the plaintiff:

    YOU ARE HEREBY notified, pursuant to Rule 30(b)(1) of the Federal Rules of Civil Procedure that the deposition of Sandy Ford will be taken in the offices of Gray and Lee, P.A., attorneys for the defendant, at 380 South Washington Street, Charleston, NC, before a certified reporter, at 10:00 a.m. on Tuesday, April 25, 1989, and may continue from hour to hour and day to day until completed. You are requested to produce the person above identified at said time and place. You are invited to attend and participate in the examination of said witness.

    Pursuant to Rule 30(b)(5) and Rule 34(a) of the Federal Rules of Civil Procedure the defendant requests production for copying by the defendant's attorney and for use during the deposition the documents described in the attached addendum to this notice.

    This the _____ day of _____, 1989.

_____
Nancy Reade Lee
Attorney for the Defendant
Gray and Lee, P.A.
280 South Washington Street
Charleston, NC 28226-1115
704-555-2500

(Addendum not shown)

+ Certificate of Service

FIGURE 9-5   DEPOSITION SUBPOENA

DC 9 (Rev. 10/82)   **DEPOSITION SUBPOENA**

United States District Court	**DISTRICT** MIDDLE DISTRICT OF NORTH CAROLINA

Bryson Wesser, Plaintiff

DOCKET NO.   C-89-1293-B

V.

TYPE OF CASE
☒ CIVIL   ☐ CRIMINAL

Woodall Shoals Corporation and
Second Ledge Stores, Incorporated, Defendants

SUBPOENA FOR
☒ PERSON   ☒ DOCUMENT(S) or OBJECT(S)

TO: John Misenheimer
      Charleston Fire Dept.
      200 Church St.
      Charleston, North Carolina 28226-0117

YOU ARE HEREBY COMMANDED to appear at the place, date, and time specified below to testify at the taking of a deposition in the above-entitled case.

PLACE	DATE AND TIME
The offices of Benedict, Parker & Miller 100 Nolichucky Drive Bristol, North Carolina	May 11, 1989 10:00 a.m.

YOU ARE ALSO COMMANDED to bring with you the following document(s) or object(s):[1]

Fire inspection report and all other documents concerning your investigation of the fire at the home of Bryson Wesser, 115 Pipestem Drive, Charleston, North Carolina, on January 3, 1987.

☐ *Please see additional information on reverse*

Any subpoenaed organization not a party to this suit is hereby admonished pursuant to Rule 30 (b) (6), Federal Rules of Civil Procedure, to file a designation with the court specifying one or more officers, directors, or managing agents, or other persons who consent to testify on its behalf, and shall set forth, for each person designated, the matters on which he will testify or produce documents or things. The persons so designated shall testify as to matters known or reasonably available to the organization.

U.S. MAGISTRATE (2) OR CLERK OF COURT	DATE
J.P. McGraw	April 11, 1989
(BY) DEPUTY CLERK *Glenda G. Bradford*	

This subpoena is issued upon application of the: ☐ Plaintiff ☒ Defendant ☐ U.S. Attorney	ATTORNEY'S NAME AND ADDRESS David H. Benedict 100 Nolichucky Dr. Charleston, North Carolina 28226-0117 704-555-8810

(1) If not applicable, enter "none."
(2) A subpoena shall be issued by a magistrate in a proceeding before him, but need not be under the seal of the court. (Rule 17(a), Federal Rules of Criminal Procedure.)

FIGURE 9-6   EXCERPTS FROM A DEPOSITION

1   This is the deposition of Sandy Ford

2   being taken by notice and in accordance with the Federal Rules of Civil

3   Procedure before Romelia Sanchez, Notary Public, in the offices

4   of Gray and Lee, P.A., 380 South Washington Street,

5   Charleston, NC, before a certified reporter, on the

6   3rd day of April, 1989, beginning at 10:00 a.m.

7

8   IT IS STIPULATED AND AGREED by and between counsel

9   for the parties that all objections, including those as to the form of the

10   question, and all motions to strike are reserved and may be interposed at

11   the time of trial.

12

13   IT IS FURTHER STIPULATED AND AGREED by and be-

14   tween counsel for the parties that review and signing of this transcript by

15   the witness is waived.

16

17

18

19

20

21

22

23

24

25

FIGURE 9-6   EXCERPTS FROM A DEPOSITION (Cont.)

1   EXAMINATION (by Ms. Lee)

2   Q.   State your name, please.

3   A.   Sandy Ford.

4   Q.   Do you understand what a deposition is about?

5   A.   Yes.

6   Q.   You understand that a court reporter is present taking down

7   everything that is said and that you are under oath?

8   A.   Yes.

9   Q.   Where were you employed in June 1988?

10   A.   With Chattooga Corporation.

11   Q.   Did you fill out an employment application on June 10, 1988?

12   A.   Yes.

13   MS. HEYWARD: Let's get this marked as Exhibit 1.

14   (Whereupon, the Reporter marked the document

15   referred to as Defendant's Exhibit Number 1 for

16   identification.)

17   Q.   I'll hand you a document identified as Defendant's Deposition

18   Exhibit 1 consisting of two pages and ask you to state whether

19   you can identify that document.   Can you identify it?

20   (Whereupon, Ms. Lee hands the document to the witness

21   for her review.)

22   A.   Yes.

23   Q.   What is that?

24   A.   That is the employment application I filled out for Chattooga

25   Corporation.

26   Q.   Is that your signature on page 2?

27   A.   Yes, it is.

When the deposition is over, the court reporter prepares a transcript of the deposition. The deponent reviews the deposition transcript and corrects any mistakes. The deponent then signs the deposition. FRCivP 30(f) addresses the certification of depositions and provides that the parties can waive the review and signature of the deponent. When the signature is waived, a notation is included in the statement of the parties' stipulations at the beginning of the transcript, as shown in Figure 9-6.

The court reporter attaches to the deposition a statement that the deponent was duly sworn and that the deposition is a true record of the deponent's testimony. The exhibits entered during the deposition are also attached to the deposition. FRCivP 30(f) directs the court reporter to file the transcript and attachments with the clerk of court, unless the court orders otherwise. Remember that some local rules direct that the deposition be given to the attorney who requested the deposition. State rules may also differ. For instance, Rule 30(f)(1) of the North Carolina Rules of Civil Procedure directs that the deposition be delivered to "the party taking the deposition or his attorney who shall preserve it as the court's copy."

Paralegal Tasks to Prepare for Depositions

Paralegals often prepare the notices and subpoenas for depositions. Paralegals also assist with the logistics of setting up depositions. Your first consideration is where the deposition will be held. You may need to reserve a conference room in your law office. Depositions can be lengthy, so you may need to arrange for delivery of breakfast or lunch. If the deposition is to be held at another law office, find out the contact person there and make sure that the person has arranged for a room and for the court reporter.

When you make the arrangements with the court reporter, it is simple if the deposition is held in your town. Your firm probably has one or two court reporter agencies that it uses frequently. Arrange for the court reporter to be present, and send a copy of the notice of deposition. You may also arrange the manner in which the reporter delivers the transcript. We have discussed transcripts prepared when the entire deposition is over. However, with a lengthy deposition, the lawyer may want a daily transcript. Sometimes depositions are videotaped. If the deposition is to be videotaped, check with the court reporting firm to see whether it can arrange for technicians. Otherwise, make the arrangement yourself. There are other considerations when the deposition is to be held somewhere outside your law office. Be sure that copy machines and fax machines are available. If huge numbers of documents must be copied, you may need to arrange for an outside copying service. These logistics are not so complex when the deposition is held at another law firm, but sometimes depositions are taken in conference rooms at hotels or airports.

An important task is to prepare the proper number of copies of the exhibits the attorney will use at the deposition. You will need one copy for the court reporter to stamp and show the witness, one copy for each of the attorneys on your team, one copy for yourself, one copy for each of the other attorneys present, and a few extra copies in case there are extra persons in attendance.

Although the attorney asks the questions at the deposition, you may help the attorney prepare an outline of the questions. If you help to prepare questions, review with the attorney the general areas he or she wishes to cover. Review the pleadings and discovery documents already in the file for additional issues. Keep your eyes open for statements the witness has already made. The witness may make contradictory statements at the deposition, which may help to impeach the witness's credibility at trial.

Paralegals sometimes help to prepare a client or other witness for the deposition testimony. Paralegals' duties can take many forms, depending on the law firm's procedures. Often paralegals keep the deponent informed of the schedule for the deposition, explain the general procedure for a deposition, and help coordinate meetings with the attorney. Paralegals may be present when the attorney meets with the deponent to prepare for the deposition. This generally involves reviewing questions that the deponent is likely to be asked. The attorney/paralegal team may even have the deponent go through a mock deposition. Paralegals can make suggestions to the deponent on how to be a more effective witness, such as suggesting that the deponent not pause for a long time before answering each question.

Paralegal Tasks During Depositions

Paralegals do not always attend depositions, but they can perform useful duties there. For instance, if there are many documents to be entered as exhibits, paralegals can keep the documents in order, hand them to the examining attorney, and keep track of the number or letter assigned to each document. Paralegals can also take notes that are useful for reference before the transcript is prepared. For instance, if a deposition lasts two days, you and the examining attorney may meet after the first day to discuss the testimony and refine the questions for the next day. Paralegals can also observe the demeanor of deponents and help assess their credibility as witnesses. Attorneys may be so busy thinking about the next question that they do not have the opportunity to observe a witness sufficiently.

Preparing Digests of Depositions

After the attorney/paralegal team receives the transcript of the deposition, the paralegal often prepares a digest—that is, a summary of the deposition. After you have attended depositions and read some transcripts, you will see that the meat of the deponent's testimony is not always readily apparent. Interruptions to introduce exhibits may obscure the testimony, or the attorney may have to reword a question several times, forcing you to sort through the interchange to find the real answer.

There are several reasons why it is important to summarize, or digest, depositions. The digest pulls out the deponent's actual testimony so that it is clear what the answers actually were. Inconsistent or incomplete answers then become apparent. You may find that further discovery is necessary to complete the information sought from that particular deponent. It is important to note inconsistencies, because they can be used to impeach the witness at trial.

Before you prepare a digest of a deposition, talk with the attorney to determine the format to use. The attorney may want a digest set up in paragraphs, summarizing the testimony in the order it was given. This is sometimes called a witness digest. See Figure 9-7 for an example.[2] This type of digest is most useful for short depositions. It should be a very succinct narrative of the deposition, relating the deponent's testimony in an abbreviated, clear form.

FIGURE 9-7   EXCERPT FROM A WITNESS DIGEST

Digest of Deposition of Sandy Ford (SF)
March 31, 1989
Pages 1–53

By Ms. Lee:

SF is a 29-year-old engineer. She has lived at 314 Linville Drive, Charleston, NC, since February 1986. She is married and has one daughter, age three. (pp. 1–3)

SF graduated from Greenbrier State University in December 1985, with a B.S. degree in mechanical engineering. Immediately after graduation from college, she was hired by Watauga Plastics, a company that manufactures kayaks. SF worked as a mechanical engineer for Watauga Plastics continuously until she was hired by Chattooga Corporation.

On June 15, 1988, SF filled out an employment application to work as a consulting engineer for Chattooga Corporation. Three days later she had an interview with the human resources manager for Chattooga Corporation, Leslie Gordon. She was also interviewed by Carla Fernandez, supervisor of the consulting engineers . . . .

Another format is the subject matter digest. Here, instead of paragraphs summarizing the testimony in the order it was given, the paragraphs are arranged by subject matter. Your first task is to make a list of the subjects to include. For instance, if you are preparing a digest of the deposition of Sandy Ford's supervisor, your subjects may include personal background, job experience, review of Sandy Ford's employment application, employment interview, events leading to discovery of Ford's felony conviction, events after discovery of Ford's felony conviction, and knowledge of Ford's assisting another employee with an EEOC claim. There may be other useful topics, but this gives you some indication of the types of subjects you may have.

Next, each subject is placed in a column on the left-hand side of the page, and the paragraphs digesting the testimony about that subject are in a column on the right-hand side of the page. See Figure 9-8 for an example. Be sure to include after each sentence or paragraph the page number of the transcript where this testimony is found. It is also helpful to cite exhibit numbers.

A third type of digest is the chronological digest. This type of digest is set up like a subject matter index, except that your topics on the left-hand side of the page are dates on which events occurred. The purpose is to construct a chronological history of the important events.

PHYSICAL AND MENTAL EXAMINATIONS

FRCivP 35 provides for the examination of a party's mental or physical condition when that person's condition is at issue in the litigation. FRCivP 35 requires

FIGURE 9-8   EXCERPT FROM A SUBJECT MATTER DIGEST

Digest of Deposition of Sandy Ford
March 31, 1989
Pages 1–53

SUBJECT	DIGEST
Personal background	SF is 29 years old. She has lived at 314 Linville Drive, Charleston, NC, since February 1986. SF earned a B.S. in mechanical engineering from Greenbrier State University and then worked for three years for Watauga Plastics, a company that manufactures kayaks.
Application and employment interview	On June 15, 1988, SF filled out an employment application as a consulting engineer at Chattooga Corporation. One June 18, 1988, she had an employment interview with Leslie Gordon, human resources manager, and with Carla Fernandez, supervisor of consulting engineers . . .

a court order for the examination, unless the parties stipulate to the examination. If a party files a motion for an examination, FRCivP 35 requires that the motion include the details of the examination—time, place, manner, conditions, and scope of the examination, as well as the persons who will conduct the examination. The parties may agree on all these details and include them in their stipulation. For instance, Leigh Heyward and David Benedict can file a stipulation reflecting their agreement that Mr. Wesser will undergo a physical examination by a physician they have agreed on, to evaluate the residual effects of his burns.

FRCivP 35 also provides that if the party who is examined requests the results of the examination, then the party who requested the exam must forward the results. FRCivP 35 requires "a detailed written report of the examining physician or psychologist, setting out the physician's findings, including results of all tests made, diagnoses and conclusions, together with like report of all earlier examinations of the same condition."

Physical and mental examinations are most common in personal injury lawsuits. Paralegals may assist in preparing the motion or stipulation. See Figure 9-9 for a sample motion. If you prepare a motion, remember to include a proposed order for the judge to sign.

FIGURE 9-9   MOTION FOR A PHYSICAL EXAMINATION

UNITED STATES DISTRICT COURT
MIDDLE DISTRICT OF NORTH CAROLINA
CHARLESTON DIVISION
CIVIL NO.: C-89-1293-B

Bryson Wesser,

                    Plaintiff,

       -vs-

Woodall Shoals Corporation,

                Defendant,

       and

Second Ledge Stores, Incorporated,

                Defendant

*MOTION FOR
PHYSICAL EXAMINATION*

Defendant Woodall Shoals, pursuant to Rule 35 of the Federal Rules of Civil Procedure moves the court for an order requiring the plaintiff to submit, at defendant's expense, to a physical examination, including, if necessary, X-rays, by a physician to be appointed by the court, to identify injuries allegedly sustained by the plaintiff, which are the subject of plaintiff's complaint.

The physical condition of the plaintiff is in controversy and the defendant has no means of ascertaining other than by independent medical examination, the actual nature and extent of the injuries complained of, and such examination is necessary to enable the defendant to prepare for trial.

Defendant has no reason to believe that the requested physical examination will be painful or dangerous to the plaintiff.

This the _____ day of _____ , 19____.

_____
David H. Benedict
Attorney for the Defendants
Benedict, Parker & Miller
100 Nolichucky Drive
Bristol, NC 28205-0890
704-555-8810

REQUESTS FOR ADMISSION

FRCivP 36 governs requests for admission. It provides that a party can serve on another party requests that the other party admit the truth of any matters within the general scope of discovery as defined in FRCivP 26. Thus requests for admission can cover a broad range of matters, but not if the matters are privileged or irrelevant.

FRCivP 26 sets forth three categories of requests for admission: (1) the truth of facts, (2) the application of law to facts, and (3) the genuineness of documents. These three categories are illustrated in the sample response to requests for admission in Figure 9-10. The first request is to admit that the employment application that Sandy Ford signed is authentic. This is the third category—genuineness of documents. The second request is to admit that Sandy Ford completed and signed the application on June 15, 1988. This is the first category—the truth of facts. The third request is to admit that Sandy Ford knowingly falsified her application when she stated that she had no felony convictions. This is the second category—the application of law to facts. Ford could contend that she did not "knowingly" make a misstatement.

FRCivP 36 provides that if a matter is admitted, it is admitted only for the purposes of the pending action. Thus, an admission cannot be used against the party in a different lawsuit.

The purpose of requests for admission is to eliminate the need to prove at trial those matters that are not in dispute. This discovery device is particularly helpful for the parties to acknowledge their agreement on the authenticity of documents. This can save a great deal of time at trial. Requests for admission can also give a party a preview of the issues that the other party will contest at trial.

Responses to requests for admission must be precise, and the attorney/paralegal team must be absolutely certain that the fact should be admitted. Once a matter is admitted, the admission of truth is conclusive.

Procedure

Requests for admission can be served on another party at almost any point in the litigation. Requests for admission may be served on the plaintiff any time after the commencement of the lawsuit. They may be served on any other party either with or after service of the summons and complaint. As a practical matter, requests for admission usually come later in the discovery process. They are more helpful after you have explored the other parties' positions and the facts of the case through the use of interrogatories and depositions.

A party must serve a response within 30 days of receipt of the requests for admission. A defendant is allowed 45 days to respond if the requests for admission are served together with the summons and complaint. If the party does not respond within 30 days, the matters are deemed admitted. Obviously, the consequences of letting this deadline slip by are disastrous. Paralegals must enter this deadline in the docket control system as soon as the requests for admission are received and follow up to ensure that the responses are made on time.

FIGURE 9-10   EXCERPTS FROM RESPONSE TO REQUESTS FOR ADMISSION

UNITED STATES DISTRICT COURT
MIDDLE DISTRICT OF NORTH CAROLINA
CHARLESTON DIVISION
Civil Action No.: C-89-2388-B

Equal Employment Opportunity
Commission,

Plaintiff,

-vs-

Chattooga Corporation,

Defendant

PLAINTIFF'S FIRST REQUESTS FOR ADMISSION

Pursuant to Rule 36 of the Federal Rules of Civil Procedure, the defendant Chattooga Corporation requests the plaintiff, Equal Employment Opportunity Commission, to make the following admissions, within 30 days of service of this request, for purposes of this action only:

1. That each of the following documents, exhibited with this request, is genuine:

   a. The employment contract, attached as Exhibit A, is a true and accurate copy of the employment contract signed by Sandy Ford on June 15, 1988.

   *

2. That each of the following statements is true:

   a. The employment contract, a copy of which is attached as Exhibit A, was completed by Sandy Ford on June 15, 1988, and the signature on the original is Sandy Ford's signature.

   b. Sandy Ford knew on June 15, 1988, that she had a felony conviction and knowingly falsified the employment contract when she stated that she had no felony convictions.

   *

This the _____ day of October, 1989.

*These are merely excerpts from a Request for Admission. A Request for Admission in the Chattooga case would include more references to documents and facts.

Format of Requests for Admission

Figure 9-10 illustrates the format for requests for admission. Requests for admission have the case caption at the top, specifying the court, parties and file number. As with other discovery requests, the requests for admission must be specifically labeled, specifying the party to whom the requests are directed and whether this is the first, second, or some subsequent request for admission. The requests begin with a simple statement such as "Plaintiff EEOC requests defendant Chattooga Corporation to make the following admissions within 30 days after service of this request."

Next follow the requests, individually numbered. The requests should be short and specific. A request that is too vague or complicated invites an objection from the party to whom it is directed.

Both the requests for admission and responses to the requests are signed by the attorneys and mailed to all parties. Remember to attach a certificate of service.

Drafting Requests for Admission

Requests for admission require careful planning, because the consequences of a party admitting the truth of a request are extremely significant. If a party states a fact in a deposition or interrogatory, it is still possible at trial for the party to present contradictory evidence. For instance, a party may say something damaging at a deposition, and at trial may state that she or he was confused and that something else really happened. In contrast, an admission of truth in response to a request for admission is conclusive.

When the attorney/paralegal team drafts requests for admission, they should review the pleadings and the discovery already completed. Your goal is to pick out the facts that have been admitted. Be alert for documents that will be exhibits at trial and try to establish their authenticity. By this point in the litigation process, you will be familiar with the pleadings, discovery materials including transcripts of depositions, and the documents that are potential exhibits. A paralegal's familiarity with all these materials is helpful to the attorney who is drafting and answering the requests for admission.

We emphasize again that the requests for admission must be simple and clear. A party is unlikely to admit to a vague request or a request that contains too many facts. You should try to limit each request for admission to one fact— for example, the authenticity of one document.

Responding to Requests for Admission

FRCivP 36 provides four possible responses to a request for admission. First, the party may admit the request. See Figure 9-11. Here the EEOC admitted the authenticity of Sandy Ford's employment application and admitted that she completed and signed the application on the date stated.

Second, the party may deny the request. Here the EEOC denied that Ford "knowingly" falsified the application. The party may admit part of a request and deny the other part, just as in an answer to a complaint. For instance, if

FIGURE 9-11   RESPONSE TO REQUESTS FOR ADMISSION

UNITED STATES DISTRICT COURT
MIDDLE DISTRICT OF NORTH CAROLINA
CHARLESTON DIVISION
Civil Action No.: C-89-2388-B

Equal Employment Opportunity
Commission,

                Plaintiff,

     -vs-

Chattooga Corporation,
                Defendant

DEFENDANT'S RESPONSE TO
PLAINTIFF'S FIRST REQUESTS
FOR ADMISSION

     The plaintiff EEOC, responding to the defendant Chattooga Corporation's Requests for Admission served on the 15th day of October, 1989, states as follows:

Request No. 1.a.:   The employment contract, attached as Exhibit A, is a true and accurate copy of the employment contract signed by Sandy Ford on June 15, 1988.

Response: Admitted.

Request No. 2.a.:   The employment contract, a copy of which is attached as Exhibit A, was completed by Sandy Ford on June 15, 1988, and the signature on the original is Sandy Ford's signature.

Response: Admitted.

Request No. 2.b.:   Sandy Ford knowingly falsified the above-described employment contract.

Response: Denied.

               This the _____ day of November, 1989.

_____
Kathy M. Mitchell
Regional Attorney

_____
Edward R. Cheng
Senior Trial Attorney

Equal Employment Opportunity Commission
1301 North Union Street
Charleston, NC 28226-1114
704-555-3000

Woodall Shoals asked Wesser to admit that he used the blanket regularly in a manner contrary to the instructions, Wesser may admit that he used the blanket regularly, but did not use it in a manner contrary to the instructions.

A third response is to object to a request, usually on the basis that the information is privileged or that the request is irrelevant. FRCivP 36 does not allow a party to object to a request simply by stating that it is a genuine issue for trial. Rather, the party must deny the request or explain why it cannot admit or deny the request.

A statement of the reasons why the party cannot admit or deny the request is the fourth response. A party may cite lack of information as a reason for failure to admit or deny, but not unless the party has made ''reasonable inquiry'' and still is not able to respond.

A paralegal's familiarity with the contents of a litigation file is even more helpful in responding to requests for admission than in drafting them. Paralegals are often more familiar with the detailed contents of the file than the attorney is in the pretrial stage. Therefore paralegals can easily locate the documents needed for the attorney to review to prepare responses. When you make copies of documents for the attorney to review, be sure to label them accurately—for example, ''page 3 of deposition of Sandy Ford.''

MOTIONS FOR CONTROLLING THE DISCOVERY PROCESS

From our overview of the discovery process, you can see that the parties usually can conduct discovery without the court's intervention. However, sometimes parties reach an impasse and must file motions with the court to regulate some aspects of discovery. For instance, a party may refuse to attend a deposition or to answer some interrogatories.

Parties should make every effort to resolve discovery disputes before invoking the court's authority. In fact, some local court rules require the attorney who files the motion to state the efforts that have been made to resolve the dispute. Many local court rules also require discovery conferences early in the litigation process. The parties may be able to work out the discovery scheme before disputes arise.

Procedure to Compel Discovery

The primary rule addressing discovery disputes is FRCivP 37. It is important to understand the context in which discovery disputes usually arise. Often one party objects to a discovery request, such as an interrogatory, stating that it is irrelevant or unduly burdensome. Sometimes a party gives an answer, but it is incomplete or evasive. Either way, the party has failed to respond to the discovery request. FRCivP 37(a) provides that an incomplete or evasive answer constitutes failure to respond. Thus a party cannot get off the hook by giving a vague answer that begs the question.

FRCivP 37 requires a two-step process in order for sanctions to be imposed. First, the requesting party files a motion requesting that the court order the uncooperative party to respond to the discovery request within a certain time. See Figure 9-12 for an illustration of the motion. The motion should set forth the

FIGURE 9-12   MOTION REQUESTING COURT ORDER TO COMPLY WITH DISCOVERY

UNITED STATES DISTRICT COURT
MIDDLE DISTRICT OF NORTH CAROLINA
CHARLESTON DIVISION
CIVIL NO.: C-89-1293-B

Bryson Wesser,

                          Plaintiff,

      -vs-

Woodall Shoals Corporation,   *AFFIDAVIT AND MOTION*
                     Defendant,
           and
Second Ledge Stores, Incorporated,
                    Defendant

NOW COMES the plaintiff and shows unto the Court that:

1. On February 26, 1989, Plaintiff's First Set of Interrogatories was mailed to David H. Benedict, attorney for the defendant Woodall Shoals Corporation. Interrogatories are attached as Exhibit "A". By letter dated March 19, 1989, counsel for said defendant indicated that defendant may need more than thirty (30) days to answer said Interrogatories (attached Exhibit "B"). The defendant Woodall Shoals never filed a motion for extension of time within which to answer said Interrogatories.

2. On November 30, 1989, said defendant mailed to plaintiffs' counsel defendant's so-called "Answers" to Plaintiff's First Set of Interrogatories (attached Exhibits "C" and "D").

3. The "Answers" to Plaintiff's First Set of Interrogatories Nos. 4, 12, 13, and 15–30 are so evasive and incomplete that they should be treated as a failure to answer, pursuant to Rule 37(a)(3) of the Federal Rules of Civil Procedure.

4. Defendant Woodall Shoals' objections to Plaintiff's Interrogatories are without substantial justification and without good cause, and are calculated only to evade answering the above-designated Interrogatories.

FIGURE 9-12   MOTION REQUESTING COURT ORDER TO COMPLY WITH DISCOVERY (Cont.)

WHEREFORE, the plaintiff moves the Court that:

1. This verified Motion be treated as an Affidavit.

2. The Court enter an Order compelling the defendant Woodall Shoals Corportion to answer completely Plaintiff's First Set of Interrogatories Nos. 4, 12, 13, and 15–30, within thirty (30) days of the date the Court's Order is entered.

3. The Court order the defendant Woodall Shoals Corporation to pay the reasonable expenses incurred in obtaining this Order, including attorneys' fees.

4. The plaintiff have such other and further relief as may be just and proper.

This the _____ day of December, 1989.

_____
Leigh J. Heyward
Attorney for the Plaintiff
Heyward and Wilson
401 East Trade Street
Charleston, NC 28226-1114
704-555-3161

requests that have been made and describe the other party's failure to comply with the reasonable discovery requests. For instance, in our sample motion, the uncooperative party first failed to respond at all and then filed evasive answers.

When the court grants the motion, the court then enters an order stating that the party must comply with the discovery requests by a certain date. If the uncooperative party fails to comply with the discovery requests as ordered by the court, the requesting party files a second motion. The second motion requests that the court impose sanctions on the uncooperative party. See Figure 9-13 for an illustration of the second motion.

The motions are generally filed in the judicial district where the lawsuit is pending. However, in the case of depositions, the motion is filed in the district where the deposition is held.

As with all motions, the attorney signs the motion, and a notice of motion informs all parties of the date, time and location of the hearing on the motion. The motion and notice of motion are then served on all parties in accordance with FRCivP 5.

Discovery Sanctions

FRCivP 37 gives courts the authority to impose sanctions on parties who do not comply with reasonable discovery requests. FRCivP 37(b) lists a wide array of sanctions that the court can impose on the disobedient party. See Figure 9-14.

FIGURE 9-13   MOTION FOR COURT-IMPOSED SANCTIONS ON UNCOOPERATIVE PARTY

UNITED STATES DISTRICT COURT
MIDDLE DISTRICT OF NORTH CAROLINA
CHARLESTON DIVISION
CIVIL NO.: C-89-1293-B

Bryson Wesser,

　　　　　　　　　　　Plaintiff,

　　　　-vs-

Woodall Shoals Corporation,
　　　　　　　　Defendant,
　　　　　　and
Second Ledge Stores, Incorporated,
　　　　　　　　　　　Defendant

MOTION

NOW COMES the plaintiff, Bryson Wesser, and moves the Court, under the provisions of Rule 37(b) of the Federal Rules of Civil Procedure, for the entry of sanctions against the defendant, Woodall Shoals Corporation, and in support of this Motion, respectfully shows unto the Court that:

1. On February 26, 1989, the plaintiff submitted Interrogatories to the defendant Woodall Shoals, and said defendant failed to answer Interrogatories 4, 12, 13 and 15–30.

2. On August 28, 1989, the Court, upon hearing defendant's objections to such discovery, entered an Order requiring the defendant Woodall Shoals to answer fully such Interrogatories and Request for Production by September 17, 1989, having declared that the purported Answers filed were incomplete and insufficient. Subsequently, the Court extended to November 7, 1989, the time for defendant to respond.

3. The plaintiff acknowledges receipt of informal additional responses from the defendant Woodall Shoals on November 30, 1989. However, Woodall Shoals has not submitted Answers to such Interrogatories or produced such documents as required by the Court in its Order of November 7, 1989.

FIGURE 9-13 MOTION FOR COURT-IMPOSED SANCTIONS ON UNCOOPERATIVE PARTY (Cont.)

WHEREFORE, the plaintiff moves the Court for entry of sanctions against the defendant Woodall Shoals for failure to respond to discovery in the manner and to the extent set forth in Rule 37 and to pay the reasonable expenses, including attorney fees, of plaintiff's counsel caused by the defendant's failure to respond as required by the Order of the Court.

This the _____ day of December, 1989.

_____

Leigh J. Heyward
Attorney for the Plaintiff
Heyward and Wilson
401 East Trade Street
Charleston, NC 28226-1114
704-555-3161

+ Certificate of Service

When a party refuses to answer questions about certain facts, the court can order that those facts are established for purposes of the lawsuit. For instance, if Woodall Shoals refused to answer interrogatories about its inspection procedures, the court could order that it is deemed admitted that Woodall Shoals' inspection procedures are insufficient to detect defects in the manufacture of the blanket.

The court can also order that the disobedient party is not allowed to present evidence to support or oppose claims or defenses. FRCivP 37(b) also allows the court to stay—that is, to postpone—the proceeding until the party obeys the order compelling discovery. In extreme cases, where the party has been persistently and blatantly disobedient, the court has the power to dismiss the disobedient party's claim or to enter a default judgment against the disobedient party. Thus, if Mr. Wesser refuses to attend depositions and answer interrogatories even after the court orders him to comply, the court can dismiss his claim against Woodall Shoals and Second Ledge. If Woodall Shoals and Second Ledge refuse to comply with the court's orders compelling discovery, the court can enter a default judgment against them.

FRCivP 37(b) also allows the court to find the disobedient party in contempt. An important sanction is the court's authority to order the disobedient party to pay the other party's reasonable expenses, including attorney's fees, caused by the party's failure to cooperate.

FIGURE 9-14   PROVISIONS OF FRCivP 37(b)

(b) Failure to comply with order.

(1) Sanctions by Court in District Where Deposition Is Taken.   If a deponent fails to be sworn or to answer a question after being directed to do so by the court in the district in which the deposition is being taken, the failure may be considered a contempt of that court.

(2) Sanctions by Court in Which Action Is Pending.   If a party or an officer, director, or managing agent of a party or a person designated under Rule 30(b)(6) or 31(a) to testify on behalf of a party fails to obey an order to provide or permit discovery, including an order made under subdivision (a) of this rule or Rule 35, or if a party fails to obey an order entered under Rule 26(f), the court in which the action is pending may make such orders in regard to the failure as are just, and among others the following:

(A) An order that the matters regarding which the order was made or any other designated facts shall be taken to be established for the purposes of the action in accordance with the claim of the party obtaining the order;

(B) An order refusing to allow the disobedient party to support or oppose designated claims or defenses, or prohibiting that party from introducing designated matters in evidence;

(C) An order striking out pleadings or parts thereof, or staying further proceedings until the order is obeyed, or dismissing the action or proceeding or any part thereof, or rendering a judgment by default against the disobedient party;

(D) In lieu of any of the foregoing orders or in addition thereto, an order treating as a contempt of court the failure to obey any orders except an order to submit to a physical or mental examination;

(E) Where a party has failed to comply with an order under Rule 35(a) requiring that party to produce another for examination, such orders as are listed in paragraphs (A), (B), and (C) of this subdivision, unless the party failing to comply shows that that party is unable to produce such person for examination.

In lieu of any of the foregoing orders or in addition thereto, the court shall require the party failing to obey the order or the attorney advising that party or both to pay the reasonable expenses, including attorney's fees, caused by the failure, unless the court finds that the failure was substantially justified or that other circumstances make an award of expenses unjust.

FRCivP 37(c) provides that when a party fails to admit the genuineness of a document or the truth of any other matter in a request for admissions, and the other party then proves the truth of the matter or genuineness of the document, the court can order the uncooperative party to pay the expenses of proving these matters, including attorney's fees. Of course, if the party had a good reason for failure to admit, the court will not order the refusing party to pay the other party's expenses. Note that the expenses of proof can be great. They can include attorney's fees, lodging for witnesses, and travel expenses.

FRCivP 37(d) addresses disobedient persons who are designated to appear on behalf of a party under FRCivP 30(b)(6) or 31(a). Remember that when the defendant is a corporation, the corporation must designate an officer of the company or other agent to answer questions. The court has authority to impose all the preceding sanctions except for contempt.

In conclusion, it is best for the parties to cooperate. When the parties resort to the court to referee their discovery, the consequences can be grave. Paralegals help to obtain information from clients in a timely manner and help the attorneys so that the discovery process can run smoothly.

ENDNOTES

1 For further discussion of planning discovery strategy, see Thomas A. Mauet, *Fundamentals of Pretrial Procedure* 161 ff. (1981).

2 The formats for digests illustrated here are similar to those in Brunner, Hamre, and McCaffrey, *The Legal Assistant's Handbook* (1982). There are many variations on format, so check with attorneys in your firm for the format they prefer.

10 DOCUMENT CONTROL AND TRIAL PREPARATION

LITIGATION EXTRACT: It is time for final pretrial preparation in the Wesser case. First we will examine how courts schedule trials and publish the schedules. Then we will see how to organize the case for trial, a task that involves three basic tasks: organizing the facts and outlining the case, summarizing the facts in lengthy documents, and organizing the file itself. An important facet of file organization is devising an effective document retrieval system. Other trial preparation tasks include informing witnesses of the trial date, helping to prepare them to testify, preparing demonstrative evidence, and organizing exhibits. Finally, paralegals may be involved in jury investigation.

INTRODUCTION

Discovery has been completed, most motions have been made and ruled on, and it is time for final pretrial preparation. There is still a chance that the lawsuit will be settled. For effective settlement discussions or for trial, however, the file must be well organized. Throughout the litigation process, the task of keeping an orderly file often is delegated to paralegals. Paralegals become just as familiar with the documents in the case as do the lawyers. In fact, paralegals often are the first to review the documents received from clients and other parties to the litigation.

TRIAL SCHEDULES

Before we discuss how to organize the file for trial, it is useful to understand how trials are scheduled by the court. This is crucial so that the attorney/paralegal team allows plenty of time for trial preparation, including file organization.

275

Different courts have different methods for scheduling trials. In federal court, the judge may discuss with the attorneys at the final pretrial conference when they will be ready for trial. Some courts assume that a case is ready for trial a certain number of days after the complaint is filed. Other courts require the attorneys to complete a certificate of readiness for trial, and then the case is scheduled. A sample state court certificate of readiness is shown in Figure 10-1.[1]

In some courts a specific date and time are assigned for the trial to commence. This is more common in federal court than in state court. In state court the case may be assigned to a particular session of the court, and the case will be heard during that session, if time allows. A judge may travel thoughout the state and stay in one judicial district for perhaps two weeks at a time to preside over trials, usually hearing only civil cases or only criminal cases during this two-week period. The period is called the **session** or **term** of court. The words *session* and *term* are often used interchangeably.

As we discussed in the section on docket control in Chapter 5, 50 cases may be assigned to a particular session of court. Even if your case is number 30 on the list, you must be ready for trial at the beginning of the session. Three cases ahead of you may be tried and the rest may be settled, taking number 30 to the top of the list. This uncertainty of date and time can be troublesome for witnesses, especially those who have to take time off from work or travel long distances. Most courts have a system for a **peremptory setting**—that is, a provision for setting a certain date and time due to extraordinary circumstances. For instance, some courts allow a peremptory setting if a witness has to travel more than 200 miles to attend the trial.

Once the court's schedule is established for a particular day or a particular session, the court publishes the schedule, which is called the **court calendar**. The calendar is sometimes called a **docket** or **trial list**. Different courts publish their calendars in different ways. In some cities, the calendars are published in periodicals to which attorneys subscribe. Other courts mail their calendars directly to the attorneys involved and/or post the calendars on bulletin boards in the courthouse. Other courts may require the attorneys to pick up the calendars at the office of the clerk of court. It is important that you learn the procedures used in the courts in which your attorney/paralegal team has cases pending. Often the duty of reviewing the court calendars is assigned to paralegals.

Sometimes the trial date is set by the judge to whom the case has been assigned all along. This is common in federal court, where a case is usually assigned early to a judge who hears all motions and makes all rulings throughout the litigation. This leaves the judge discretion concerning the time that the case will be scheduled and the manner in which the attorneys are informed of the date. Figure 10-2 shows Rule 111 of the United States District Court for the District of Columbia, which addresses scheduling by the judge to whom the case is assigned.

In some courts the trial dates are set by the trial court administrator or clerk of court. This is common in state court, where cases are not always assigned to one judge who rules on all motions and presides throughout the litigation. Often in state court the case is set for a certain time, and the judge is whichever one is assigned for that date or court session.

FIGURE 10-1 SAMPLE STATE COURT CERTIFICATE OF READINESS

REQUEST TO SET AND CERTIFICATE OF READINESS   CASE NO._____

☐ Jury   ☐ Non-Jury

Plaintiff/Petitioner   Defendant/Respondent

vs

_____

1. It is requested that the above cases be scheduled for:
   ☐ Motion Hearing
   ☐ Trial
   ☐ Tentative Calendar (District Court)
   ☐ Pretrial Calendar (Superior Court)

---

2. It is certified that in the above case:
   ☐ All issues have been joined.
   ☐ All discovery will be complete prior to trial.
   ☐ The case is entitled to a preferential setting in accordance with
   N.C.G.S. _____

---

3. Opposing Counsel and I have conferred and agreed, that the following dates are satisfactory:
   1._____ 2._____ 3._____ 4._____

---

4. Opposing Counsel and I have not conferred and agreed, but the following dates are satisfactory to me.
   1._____ 2._____ 3._____ 4._____

5.

_____   _____

Attorney for: ☐ Plaintiff   ☐ Defendant   Date

COPY TO:

_____   _____

Attorney for: ☐ Plaintiff   ☐ Defendant   Date

The above case is scheduled for Trial/Motion Hearing for the week/day _____
_____Time _____Courtroom No. _____

FIGURE 10-2   THE SCHEDULING RULE OF ONE DISTRICT COURT

RULE 111   SCHEDULING AND CONTINUANCES

(a) **Scheduling.** All hearings, conferences and trials shall be scheduled by the judge to whom the case is assigned, except that matters referred to a magistrate shall be scheduled by the magistrate.

(b) **Continuances.** No application for a continuance of a hearing, conference or trial shall be made unless notice of the application has been given to all other parties. An application for a continuance shall be ruled upon by the judge or magistrate before whom the hearing, conference or trial is to be held.

(c) **Notice.** The Clerk shall give notice to counsel of every matter set by the court, unless the matter is scheduled orally in open court in the presence of counsel for all parties, in which case further notice is not required. All scheduling orders pursuant to Rule 16(b), Federal Rules of Civil Procedure, must be in writing.

Continuances

The attorney/paralegal team should make every effort to be ready for trial at the scheduled time. However, sometimes circumstances beyond the team's control preclude trying a case at its appointed time. The postponement of a trial to a later date is called a **continuance**. Rules for granting continuances vary from court to court and even from judge to judge. You must know the inclinations of the various judges before whom the cases are scheduled. Some judges are lenient in granting continuances. Other judges will grant a continuance for nothing short of death of counsel.

Aside from judges' inclinations, there are some commonsense guidelines for determining whether a continuance might be granted. A case that appears on the court calendar for the first time is more likely to be continued than one that previously has been continued three times. Courts like to rid their dockets of old cases. The reason for seeking a continuance is also important. If the attorney who was going to try the case broke her leg two days before the trial date, a continuance will likely be granted. However, if the attorney seeks a continuance because she decided to go to Bermuda for three days just before trial, the chances of a continuance are slim.

Often trial attorneys have more than one case scheduled for trial at the same time. This frequently happens in state court, when the attorney has cases in both criminal and civil court on the same day. If the cases are the type that can be heard quickly, it is possible for the attorney to move between courtrooms and try the cases all in the same day. For instance, an attorney may have a child-custody hearing and two uncontested divorce actions scheduled for the same day. Divorces are frequently heard at the beginning of the court session, because they take little time if they are uncontested. The attorney can have the two divorce hearings finished by 10 a.m. and conduct the child-custody hearing afterwards.

However, sometimes the attorney would have to be cloned to dispose of all cases scheduled on a particular day. Many courts have local rules that establish which cases take precedence over which others. For instance, if an attorney has one case in state superior court and one in state district court at the same time, the case in superior court takes precedence, and the district court case has to be continued. Likewise, a case in federal court usually takes precedence over a state court case. Obviously the attorney/paralegal team must learn the local court rules thoroughly.

ORGANIZING CASES FOR TRIAL

Organizing a case for trial can be a massive undertaking, especially in a complex case that has been in litigation for several months or even years. Effective organization requires intimate familiarity with all the documents in the file. Because as a paralegal you will have read all the documents and helped to prepare many of them, you will be indispensable for trial preparation.

There is no magic formula for organizing cases for trial. The organization depends on the subject matter of the litigation and the size of the case file. Mr. Wesser's case, which involves product liability, will be organized differently from the Chattooga case, which involves employment discrimination. A case involving collection on a promissory note is smaller and less complex than an antitrust lawsuit and thus will require a different type of organization. Different lawyers prefer different methods of organization. Thus there are many variables that determine the organizational scheme for preparing a case for trial.

However, your goal is always the same—to develop a logical system for organizing documents and an effective system to retrieve the documents quickly and accurately. Regardless of the details of your system, the basic organization for trial generally involves preparing an outline of the case, organizing the documents in subfiles, and developing an effective method to retrieve the documents. You begin by outlining the case, but your three projects are so intertwined that you usually end up performing all three simultaneously. As you outline, the topics for which you need subfiles become evident. Your subfile topics become topics in your indices, and you also detect more refined subcategories that need to be indexed.

Organizing the Facts and Outlining the Case

At trial the plaintiff's objective is to present the proof to establish the essential elements of the claims asserted in the complaint. The defendant's objective is to establish that the plaintiff has not proved the essential elements of the claims. Therefore you need to pull your chart that lists the essential elements of the claims and the proof you plan to use for each element.

Beneath each element you have already listed the evidence you plan to use to establish that element. Review the chart and determine whether you have gathered additional evidence. If you have, insert it in the chart. If you find any deficiencies in the evidence, consult with the attorneys on your team immediately.

Include the names of the witnesses who will testify and the exhibits that will be introduced, including documents and photographs. In preparing the outline, it is also helpful to note exhibits and witnesses that other parties may introduce to try to refute each element of the claims.

The chart of proof of the essential elements for breach of express warranty in the Wesser case (from Chapter 5) is reprinted in Figure 10-3 so that we can work through the chart and develop part of the outline in the Wesser case. The first element to establish is that Woodall Shoals made an express warranty that the blanket would be free of defects for two years from date of purchase. Proving this element is fairly straightforward. We will present the warranty that came with the blanket, so we list that on our outline.

FIGURE 10-3 CHART OF FACTS TO PROVE

Woodall Shoals: Express Warranty

Elements of Claim	Sources of Information	Method of Obtaining Information
1. Woodall Shoals made express warranty that blanket would be free of defects for 2 years from date of purchase	Written warranty that came with blanket	Obtain from Mr. Wesser
2. Electric blanket had defects, which constitutes breach of warranty	Fire inspector Fire inspector's report Remains of blanket and control Inspection of scene Testing and testimony of expert witnesses	Interview Request by letter Obtain from Mr. Wesser Go to scene Retain expert witnesses
3. Defects caused Mr. Wesser's damages	Same as #2	

Our next consideration is how to present that exhibit. Remember that documents must be authenticated. Most likely Woodall Shoals has stipulated to the authenticity of the warranty. If not, when Mr. Wesser is testifying, we present the warranty for him to examine and ask him whether this is the warranty that came with the electric blanket that he purchased. In listing the sources of proof, review of Woodall Shoals's answer shows that Woodall Shoals admitted in the answer that it warranted the blanket to be free of defects for two years from date of purchase. Examine the partial outline in Figure 10-4 that lists this element and how we will prove it.

Ms. Heyward will use several witnesses and many exhibits to establish the other two elements. We will use the same approach. First, list the witnesses. The list will include Mr. Wesser, the fire inspector, and expert witnesses. Some of the exhibits will be the fire inspector's report and reports prepared by the expert

FIGURE 10-4   PARTIAL OUTLINE OF THE WESSER CASE

I. Breach of Express Warranty by Woodall Shoals

A. Essential Elements of the Claim

1. Woodall Shoals made express warranty that blanket would be free of defects for 2 years from date of purchase

Sources of proof:
1. Written warranty (WS stipulated to authenticity)
2. Answer WS admitted in answer that it gave express warranty for 2 years

witnesses. Physical evidence will include the remains of the blanket and its control. Ms. Heyward will also introduce photographs. The defendants will present their own expert witnesses and reports to try to refute the assertion that the blanket had defects that caused the fire. As you review the exhibits, determine which witnesses will be used to identify and discuss the documents. Also note references to discovery documents—interrogatories, transcripts of depositions, and requests for admission—that address the elements you must establish. Review the documents your opponents produced during discovery and identify pertinent information. Enter these references on your outline.

By now you will have consulted with the attorneys on your team to determine the type of outline they prefer to use and whether they have any special instructions. Some attorneys may want more detailed outlines than others want. You will have questions as you prepare the outline. Discuss your questions promptly with the attorneys on your team. The eve of trial is no time to make assumptions that may prove erroneous.

Summarizing Facts.   The outline is a very short summary of proof. As we noted earlier, to prepare it you must review many lengthy documents for pertinent facts. Reports from experts may be many pages long. You may even have to read books the experts published so that you can spot inconsistencies in their reports and testimony. You must also review lengthy discovery documents and flag the pages that pertain to the subject you are preparing for the outline.

Review the discussion of deposition digests in Chapter 9. If you have not already prepared digests of all depositions, now is the appropriate time to prepare them. You may also prepare digests or summaries of other important documents—the fire inspector's report, for example. You may assemble a large number of related documents and summarize their collective contents. For instance, you may review all Mr. Wesser's medical records and prepare a summary of his injuries, treatment received, prognosis, and total cost of treatment.

The summaries serve many purposes. You review the entire file and extract the most important facts. This helps you to prepare the outline for trial. As you prepare the summaries, the factual issues crystallize. The broad issues and the subissues emerge. You see which witnesses and documents prove which facts. Your outline falls into place, and you arrange the entire file for trial as you go. You can determine the subfiles into which the entire file needs to be divided for use at trial.

Organizing Files for Trial

For final pretrial preparation, you may need to rearrange the documents in the working files. The attorney/paralegal team must have subfiles that are arranged in a manner that will be useful at trial. At a moment's notice you must be able to locate documents pertaining to certain witnesses, issues, or specific subjects such as electrical design. You may need to create a subfile for each witness, if you have not done so already. You may take the reports written by the fire inspector, for instance, and place them with the fire inspector's deposition and even interrogatories that address his knowledge and opinions. You may create subfiles for expert witnesses containing the same information, plus information on the expert's qualifications. If the expert is a witness for the other party, include any documents that will be used to impeach the expert or question the expert's qualifications.

Assume that it has been your responsibility in the Wesser case to arrange and keep in order the file. Recall our discussion of files and subfiles in Chapter 5. As the documents have arrived, you have reviewed them and ensured that they were placed in the appropriate subfiles for ready access. You have maintained both the central file, where the originals are kept, and the working file, where the copies used daily are kept. If you have kept the documents in their proper subfiles and maintained an index, then the file should be in good working order for final pretrial preparation. However, there is a chance that someone on the attorney/paralegal team at some point in the litigation process has been in a hurry and failed to replace a few documents in their proper subfile, especially in the working file. Therefore your first step should be to go through the file, find any loose papers, and place them in the proper subfile.

It is important that paralegals arrange the case files so that the attorney/paralegal team has ready access to all documents. The specific arrangement for documents will differ depending on the subject matter and complexity of the lawsuit. One method to determine the best arrangement for document retrieval is to review the documents in the entire file and list important words, names, topics, and so on. As we have discussed, you can do this while preparing a case outline.

Next, try to fit the documents into your tentative scheme to determine whether it will work. Further refinements may be necessary. You may need to put a document in more than one group. For instance, the fire inspector's deposition may be useful in your group of documents arranged by subject matter: cause of fire. You may also place it in the group of documents concerning this particular witness: fire inspector. Your goal is to develop a system that allows quick retrieval by arranging the documents in logical groups so that you do not have to spend time trying to recall in which group a particular document may be found.

The law firm's computer programs may permit a search of the documents for certain words or names. This can help you find the most effective method to arrange the documents for quick retrieval. You can enter names of witnesses or certain subjects, such as "cause of fire," and the computer will locate all documents that contain the words you have entered. The computer search can help you in preparing the case outline and indexing documents as well.

Indices and Document Retrieval

Once you define the categories you will use to organize the file for trial, you need to prepare an index. You may already have an index of document numbers and other subfile indices. These may still be useful, particularly the document number index. However, the aim now is to prepare the documents for trial, so you need subindices that indicate how you have arranged the documents for retrieval at trial. A computer search program can create subindices by listing all documents that contain specific categories of information.

You also need to formulate the method to use for document retrieval. Document retrieval means locating documents so that you can pull them and use them. Documents may be retrieved either manually by looking at indices or by a computer search. The retrieval methods are numerous and depend on the size of the case file, the method preferred by the attorneys on your team, and the capacity of the law firm's computer system. We will not discuss specific indexing and retrieval systems in great detail, because the systems can vary so widely from law firm to law firm. However, we will cover some general guidelines that will help you adapt to whatever system your law firm uses.

Individual Document Identification. Some law firms index documents by assigning a number to each document. There are different schemes for assigning the numbers. For instance, Mr. Wesser's documents could be designated by numbers ranging from 1000 to 1999. Defendant Woodall Shoals's documents could be designated by numbers ranging from 2000 to 2999, and defendant Second Ledge's documents could be assigned numbers from 3000 to 3999. Another method is to prefix the numbers with different letters. For instance, Mr. Wesser's documents would have the prefix "A," defendant Woodall Shoals's documents "B," and defendant Second Ledge's "C."

The numbers are generally assigned to documents in chronological order—that is, by the date they are received. The assigned number gives a sure identification to a document. The documents are sometimes kept in strict numerical order in a central file. The numbers alone typically give little clue as to the content of the document.

Indices Used for Trial Organization. The documents are not useful for a working file unless they are indexed according to subject matter, issue, or the party from whom the document was received. Therefore it is important to arrange and index the documents so that they can be readily located and used for trial preparation. Actually, you have been preparing some type of useful index as you created subfiles throughout the litigation. By this stage of the litigation, you have an index in front of every subfile—court papers, correspondence, depositions, and so on. Consider an index for a subfile containing correspondence with Mr. Wesser, as illustrated in Figure 10-5. For each document in the subfile, you entered the information for each of the index headings. At a glance you know who wrote the letter, the date it was written, a summary of the content, and whether it contains confidential information.

FIGURE 10-5 SUBFILE INDEX

Doc. #	Description	Date	Author	Confidential Info.
A-1001	Letter *re* date of purchase of blanket	3-8-89	Mr. Wesser	no
A-1002	Letter transmitting medical bills	5-20-89	Mr. Wesser	no

The information in the subfile indices you have already prepared can help you to formulate the indices for final trial preparation. The short descriptions will help you flag important issues and facts. Your outline will also help. As we noted previously, a computer search for names or key words also helps to formulate index topics.

Once you have identified index headings, you need to prepare the written index. There are different methods for reducing the indices to writing, but there are two primary approaches—a manual index card system and computer programs.

The manual index card system works best when you have a relatively small number of documents. The key to a good index card system is division of documents into useful subject categories. Your outline will be helpful for picking the categories. To be sure that the categories are useful and inclusive, you should discuss the categories with the lawyers who will actually try the case. Once you have selected the categories, assign a number or key word to each.

The next step is to prepare for each document an index card that includes a document locator number, a short description of the content of the document, date of the document, and author of the document. You should be able to lift this information from the subfile indices that you prepared as the litigation progressed. The document locator number may be either the original number assigned to it, (e.g., A-101) or the exhibit number you plan to use at trial. At the top of each card write the key word or category number assigned to the document. If the document is important in more than one category, write all the numbers and make copies of the card. For instance, the fire inspector's report may fall into four categories. Make four cards, and include a card in each category.

You may also index the documents by witness, date, or author, in addition to the categories arranged by topics. Arrange the cards by categories and any other chosen designations, and you can then pick out the cards you need to pursue a particular issue or fact.

Computers are helpful, and often essential, for indexing and document retrieval in lawsuits with numerous documents. The methods for setting up the computer document retrieval system differ according to the complexity of the lawsuit and capabilities of the firm's computers. As with the manual system, first you must review the documents to determine the topics by which they need to be indexed. The topics are assigned subject codes, which are entered into the computer. Other basic information about the documents is also entered, such as date, document number, and author.

The attorney/paralegal team, together with computer personnel, must work to establish the format for entering information into the computer. Once the format is established, paralegals can enlist the aid of data-entry personnel. A well-designed computer program can create a quick and effective document retrieval system.

Trial Notebook

So far we have discussed organizing documents into subfiles for use at trial. Many attorneys like to use a trial notebook when they try a case. A **trial notebook** is a three-ring binder with tabbed dividers, and in each tabbed section are the documents needed for that portion of the trial. For instance, in a simple lawsuit concerning failure to pay a promissory note, the defense attorney's trial notebook may have the following sections: jury selection, opening statement, cross examination of plaintiff's witnesses, motion for directed verdict, direct examination of defendant's witnesses, jury instructions, and closing argument.[2] The attorney may include in the appropriate section such items as copies of case law needed to support arguments over the admission of evidence or other issues that will arise at trial. If space allows, attorneys may include in separate sections the pleadings, discovery materials, motions and orders granting or denying the motions, memoranda submitted for trial or in support of motions, and research memos.

Different attorneys arrange and use trial notebooks in different ways. Trial notebooks can be used either as a supplement to the subfiles you have created or as an alternative to them. If the documents in the lawsuit are too voluminous to place in the trial notebook, the notebook is best used as a supplement to the subfiles. Actually, the notebook is a way to organize presentation of the evidence, and the documents can be taken from the appropriate subfiles as they are needed for introduction as exhibits or for reference. This use of the trial notebook and subfiles is effective when the trial notebook outlines the use for the documents and the point at which they will be used. The subfiles are arranged so that the documents can be easily found at the time they are to be used.

When used this way, the notebook must contain an outline of the trial. It should also contain an outline of the questions to be asked of each witness on direct and cross-examination. The outline can be annotated with notes regarding arguments that will be made at trial. For instance, you may anticipate that opposing counsel will object to the admission of an important piece of evidence. The attorney/paralegal team can research case law and prepare an argument to support admission of the evidence. An annotation in the outline directs the attorney to the place in the trial notebook where the legal argument is set out or to the appropriate subfile that contains the legal argument and copies of supporting cases.

The trial notebook is a versatile tool that can make the trial go more smoothly. Paralegals who help to prepare the trial notebook need to work closely with the attorney who will try the case to determine how to make the notebook most useful for that attorney.

Review the File to Ensure that Specific Documents Are Ready

Certain documents must be ready before the attorney/paralegal team can complete preparation for trial. It is best to ensure that these documents are complete well before trial, because their completion may take a substantial amount of time.

The Trial Brief. The trial brief presents legal issues that the court will consider during the trial and an argument explaining why the judge should rule in favor of your client on these issues. The trial brief is sometimes called a **memorandum of law** or **trial memorandum**. Different attorneys prefer different formats for trial briefs, but the general format includes the following sections: cover or title sheet, statement of facts, questions presented, argument, and conclusion. The argument cites the statutes, rules, and authorities relied on. The trial brief may have a separate section that sets out the statutes and cases relied on and the page number on which there are references to each of the statutes and cases.

The format and length of the trial brief can differ depending on local court rules, judges' preferences, and the nature and complexity of the lawsuit. Be sure to check local court rules, because there may be specific requirements for the contents of briefs and the citations of cases. Rule 107 of the United States District Court for the Middle District of North Carolina sets forth such requirements, and appears as an example in Figure 10-6.

Usually the attorneys write the trial brief, at least the legal argument section. However, paralegals often contribute to the trial brief in important ways. Paralegals may prepare first drafts of the statement of facts, check case citations, and shepardize cases. Paralegals ensure that the required number of trial briefs are ready and that the brief is served on opposing counsel, complete with certificate of service.

Forms Required by Local Court Rules. Local court rules require that in certain types of lawsuits the parties must file specific forms for use at trial. For instance, in a lawsuit to divide marital property at the time of divorce, local court rules may require that each party file an affidavit stating the value they assign to each piece of property, the date the item was purchased, and so forth. An excerpt from this type of affidavit is illustrated in Figure 10-7.[3]

FIGURE 10-6   SPECIFIC REQUIREMENTS FOR THE CONTENTS OF BRIEFS:
NORTH CAROLINA

> ### RULE 107.   BRIEFS
>
> **(a) Contents.** All briefs filed with the court shall contain:
>
> (1) A statement of the nature of the matter before the court.
>
> (2) A concise statement of the facts. Each statement of fact should be supported by reference to a part of the official record in the case.
>
> (3) A statement of the question or questions presented.
>
> (4) The argument, which shall refer to all statutes, rules and authorities relied upon.
>
> **(b) Citation of Cases.** Cases cited should include parallel citations, the year of the decision, and the court deciding the case. If a petition for certiorari was filed in the United States Supreme Court, disposition of the case should be shown with three parallel citations (e.g., *Carson v. Warlick*, 238 F.2d 724 (4th Cir. 1956), cert. denied, 353 U.S. 910, 77 S.Ct. 665, 1 L.Ed.2d 664 (1957)).
>
> **(c) Citations of Unpublished Decisions.** Unpublished decisions may be cited only if the unpublished decision is furnished to the court and to opposing parties or their counsel when the brief is filed. Unpublished decisions should be cited as follows: *Wise v. Richardson*, No. C-70-191-S (M.D.N.C., Aug. 11, 1971).
>
> **(d) Citation of Decisions Not Appearing in Certain Published Reports.** Decisions published in reports other than the West Federal Reporter System, the official North Carolina reports and the official United States Supreme Court reports (e.g., C.C.H. Reports, Labor Reports, U.S.P.Q., reported decisions of other states or other specialized reporting services) may be cited only if the decision is furnished to the court and to opposing parties or their counsel when the brief is filed.
>
> **(e) Additional Copies of Briefs for Court Use.** At the time the original of a brief is filed, a working copy of the brief for use by the judge or magistrate shall be delivered to the clerk.

Another example is a state court action for child support. The party seeking child support files an affidavit of income and expenses, which itemizes monthly income and lists expenses for shelter, food, clothing, and so on. Most of these forms are filed long before the trial date approaches. However, it is best to check the file to ensure that no required forms were overlooked.

Pretrial Order. Pretrial orders set forth guidelines for the trial and list the witnesses and exhibits the parties will present. Pretrial orders are discussed in detail in Chapter 11. The procedure for preparation of the pretrial order can differ. Particularly in state court the attorneys often prepare the pretrial order before their final pretrial conference with the judge. In federal court the pretrial order is formulated largely at the final pretrial conference. Paralegals should check

FIGURE 10-7   EXCERPT FROM MARITAL PROPERTY AFFIDAVIT

AFFIDAVIT OF (Husband) (Wife) / (Pl.) (Def.) PART I, Page _____

SUMMARY

(Note: This page is a summary of the values given in the rest of the Affidavit. Complete this page after the rest of the Affidavit is completed. Do **not** omit or leave this page blank.)

PART I — MARITAL PROPERTY

CATEGORY		NET FMV OF PROPERTY AT DATE OF SEPARATION	NET FMV OF PROPERTY AT PRESENT
I.	Realty	$_____	$_____
II.	Transportation	_____	_____
III.	Stocks and Bonds	_____	_____
IV.	Bank Accounts	_____	_____
V.	Artwork, Metals and Other Collectibles	_____	_____
VI.	Miscellaneous Notes and Income-Producing Assets	_____	_____
VII.	Silverware, China and Crystal	_____	_____
VIII.	Jewelry	_____	_____
IX.	Animals	_____	_____
X.	Patents, Copyrights	_____	_____
XI.	Business Interests	_____	_____
XII.	Household Goods	_____	_____
XIII.	Any Other Item Not Listed	$_____	$_____
	TOTAL NET FMV — MARITAL PROPERTY	$_____	$_____

PART II — SEPARATE PROPERTY

	TOTAL NET FMV — SEPARATE PROPERTY	$_____	$_____

PART III — PROPERTY ACQUIRED AFTER SEPARATION

	TOTAL NET FMV — PROPERTY ACQUIRED AFTER DATE OF SEPARATION		$_____

court rules for deadlines pertaining to pretrial orders and ensure that the orders are prepared on time. Some rules require that the attorneys meet and exchange information before they meet with the judge and make the final determinations that are written in the pretrial order. This is another deadline of which the paralegals must remain aware.

PREPARATION OF WITNESSES

Witnesses need as much advance notice of the trial date as possible. They often have to arrange to be absent from work. They may have to make transportation arrangements.

Paralegals generally perform several tasks to ensure that witnesses have proper notice and are present for trial at the proper time. For instance, you may be responsible for making reservations for lodging if the witnesses have to stay for several days. Whatever your tasks, your goal is to ensure that all witnesses are present at the proper time and place to testify. Therefore there are several tasks you must perform in advance of trial.

Inform Witnesses of the Trial Date

As soon as possible, contact all witnesses, inform them of the trial date, and make sure that they will be available. It is best to subpoena all witnesses, so explain to them that they will be served with subpoenas closer to trial. Confirm the witnesses' addresses and phone numbers. Especially be sure to confirm the phone number at which the witnesses can be reached during the trial. Explain that it is not always possible to know the exact hour and minute that they will testify, but that you will call them and give them as accurate a time estimate as possible.

Subpoena Witnesses

All witnesses should be served with a subpoena before trial. The subpoena commands the witness to be present. The subpoena gives the judge the authority to order the witness's attendance. If the witness fails to attend after being properly subpoenaed, the witness can be held in contempt.

It is important to serve a subpoena on every witness, whether the witness is friendly or hostile. Even if the witness is your client's mother, subpoena her. Many persons have been known to promise to appear and testify, but when the trial date comes, they never appear. You cannot take this risk. Judges are reluctant to grant a continuance simply because a witness does not appear, and the attorney/paralegal team can be forced to proceed without important witnesses. Paralegals should contact all witnesses and explain that they will receive a subpoena.

In federal court actions, refer to FRCivP 45 for issuance and service of subpoenas. The clerk of court issues the subpoena. The subpoena must be personally served on the witness. Review FRCivP 45 to ensure that your subpoena is correctly issued and served. If you require the witness to bring any documents, list them on the subpoena. See Figure 10-8 for a sample subpoena.

FIGURE 10-8   A SAMPLE SUBPOENA

AO 89 (Rev. 5/85) Subpoena

United States District Court

Middle ——————— **DISTRICT OF** ——————— North Carolina

Bryson Wesser, Plaintiff

V.

Woodall Shoals Corporation and
Second Ledge Stores, Incorporated, Defendants

SUBPOENA

CASE NUMBER: C-89-1293-B

TYPE OF CASE	SUBPOENA FOR
[X] CIVIL [ ] CRIMINAL	[X] PERSON [X] DOCUMENT(S) or OBJECT(S)

TO:

John Misenheimer
Charleston Fire Dept.
200 Church St.
Charleston, North Carolina 28226-0117

YOU ARE HEREBY COMMANDED to appear in the United States District Court at the place, date, and time specified below to testify in the above case.

PLACE	COURTROOM
Federal Courthouse
1018 East Trade Street
Charleston, North Carolina 28226-1201	Courtroom No. 4
	DATE AND TIME
June 10, 1990
10:00 A.M.

YOU ARE ALSO COMMANDED to bring with you the following document(s) or object(s): *

Fire inspection report and all other documents concerning your investigation of the fire at the home of Bryson Wesser, 115 Pipestem Drive, Charleston, North Carolina, on January 3, 1987.

[ ] *See additional information on reverse*

This subpoena shall remain in effect until you are granted leave to depart by the court or by an officer acting on behalf of the court.

| U.S. MAGISTRATE OR CLERK OF COURT
J. P. McGraw | DATE |
| (BY) DEPUTY CLERK
Barbara J. Montgomery | May 20, 1990 |

This subpoena is issued upon application of the:

[X] Plaintiff   [ ] Defendant   [ ] U.S. Attorney

QUESTIONS MAY BE ADDRESSED TO:
Leigh J. Heyward
Heyward and Wilson
401 East Trade St.
Charleston, North Carolina 28226-1114
ATTORNEY'S NAME, ADDRESS AND PHONE NUMBER

*If not applicable, enter "none".

Procedures may differ in state court actions. For instance, in some states the attorney can issue the subpoena. The form of the subpoena is likely to be the same as the federal court subpoena. Be sure to check state rules of civil procedure and local court rules for issuance and service of subpoenas.

After the subpoenas are served, file copies with the clerk of court. The subpoenas will become part of the court file, and the judge can then readily see when witnesses have been subpoenaed.

Preparing Witnesses to Testify at Trial

Generally the attorneys meet with the witnesses to prepare them to testify at trial. However, paralegals may help in several ways. Paralegals may help to prepare the questions to be asked at trial. Paralegals may also set up the appointments for the witnesses to come to the office to meet with the attorneys. It is a good idea to take a witness to the courtroom to see what it looks like, especially if the witness has never been to court before. You can take the witnesses to the courthouse and show them around. This will help them to be more relaxed at trial.

Paralegals may be present when the attorneys meet with the witnesses. If you are present, you can help by sharing your observations about the witness with the attorneys. For instance, you may notice that the witness pauses too long before answering a question. This makes witnesses less credible, because they appear either to have insufficient knowledge or to be planning their answer too thoroughly, as persons may do when they are not telling the truth.

There are some practical guidelines that the attorney/paralegal team should share with witnesses before they testify. Witnesses should always tell the truth. If they do not know the answer to a question, they should say that they do not know rather than hazard a guess. Witnesses should answer the question and then be quiet; they should not ramble and volunteer extra information. This is not an effort to hide information. Rather, a clear, concise answer is more effective than chatter, and provides less ammunition for cross-examination. Instruct witnesses to stop talking as soon as the attorney objects to a question. They can resume their testimony after the judge has ruled on the objection. Advise witnesses to review their depositions carefully before trial. This will minimize contradictions, which are damaging. These are just a few guidelines. The attorneys on your team can provide even more guidelines for effective testimony in a particular case.

It is important to talk to witnesses about appropriate dress for the courtroom. Witnesses' attire should be neat and formal, but not too formal. Tuxedos and cocktail dresses are not appropriate. Nor are shorts appropriate. Judges have been known to eject people because their attire does not reflect proper respect for the courtroom. A witness's clothes affect the way she or he is perceived by the jury, another important consideration.

PREPARATION OF EXHIBITS

As you organized the documents for trial preparation using the chart of essential elements, you listed the exhibits that the attorney/paralegal team will use at trial. Go back through the documents and complete the organization of the exhibits.

Be sure that you have not overlooked any exhibits. You may need to expand the chart to show which exhibits will be used to establish which points at trial. Your goal is to compose a complete list of exhibits. After you have a tentative list, review it with the attorneys on your team to ensure that the list is complete.

By now the attorney/paralegal team has probably decided on the numbering scheme to use to keep track of the documents. As we discussed on page 283, the exhibits are assigned a number in the document retrieval system that the team develops.

Assemble all the exhibits in the order that they will be introduced at trial. The next step is to make sure that sufficient numbers of copies of each exhibit are made. Generally, you need one copy for the attorneys on your team, one copy for each attorney representing the other parties, one copy for the judge, and often one copy for the judge's law clerk. Check local court rules for any special rules regarding the number of copies needed. The court may require one copy for the judge and one working copy that may be used by the judge's law clerk.

 POINTER: Preparing the copies for trial can be a massive undertaking. Paralegals should arrange for sufficient clerical support to get all the copies made. After the copies are made, double-check to ensure that all exhibits are put back in their proper order.

PREPARATION OF DEMONSTRATIVE EVIDENCE

As we discussed in Chapter 4, demonstrative evidence consists of charts and other visual aids to explain the facts and assist in the presentation of evidence. For instance, a chart of Mr. Wesser's house may show the location of his bedroom and the areas affected by the fire. Suppose that one of the expert witnesses has prepared drawings of electrical design that would be useful for the jury to understand the alleged defects in the wiring of the electric blanket. You may enlarge the drawings so that the jury can look at them while the expert witness points to areas in the design that were defective. This will make the expert's testimony much more comprehensible to the jury.

Paralegals may be responsible for preparation of demonstrative evidence. This can involve preparing simple charts yourself, or employing graphic artists for more complex drawings. You may also need to make arrangements with a graphics company to enlarge certain drawings, if the copy machines at your office do not have the capacity. Start well ahead of time so that you do not have to spend the day before the trial on the telephone trying to locate a graphic artist who does not mind staying up all night to complete the charts you need.

 POINTER: Before trial it may be helpful for the attorneys to present the demonstrative evidence to persons not involved in the lawsuit, in order to test its effectiveness.

JURY INVESTIGATION

As we will discuss more fully in Chapter 12, on the first day of trial the attorneys pick a jury from the pool of jurors selected at random for that session of court. From the jury pool, the attorneys want to select the persons whom they think will view their clients' version of the facts most favorably.

The more you know about the persons in the jury pool, the more accurately you can gauge how they will react to your client's version of the facts. This is the purpose of jury investigation—to gather information about the potential jurors in order to analyze them and try to determine which persons you want to sit on the jury in your client's case. Useful information may include where the persons live, where they work, clubs to which they belong, religious beliefs, and so forth.

Many factors determine how much jury investigation the attorney/paralegal team is able to conduct. One factor is whether the clerk of court releases a list of the jury pool before the court session begins. If the list is released several weeks in advance, the attorney/paralegal team has the opportunity to conduct a thorough investigation. There is, however, another important factor that can limit the scope of the jury investigation: your client's budget. Detailed jury investigation can be expensive. Firms are available that will gather facts on the members of the jury pool, and some consultants can even arrange a mock jury—that is, a jury composed of persons similar to those in the jury pool. The attorneys then can conduct a mock trial to see how the jury decides the case and why, which may suggest what arguments are likely to be most effective at trial.

Some law firms hire psychologists to help them determine the best characteristics for a potential juror for a particular trial. This is known as developing a jury profile. This too can be expensive.

Unfortunately, many clients cannot afford such an elaborate approach. There are many other, less expensive ways to gather information about jurors that paralegals may perform. You may check public records such as tax listings to find out general information about the potential jurors' property holdings. Some courts use juror questionnaires, which are available to the attorneys before trial. These generally contain basic information about the potential juror, such as occupation, marital status, and so on. See Figure 10-9 on page 294, which illustrates a juror questionnaire used in Hamilton County, Ohio.

Although jury investigation can prove helpful, it must be done discreetly. If a potential juror finds out that your law firm is compiling information, and the juror feels that this is intrusive, this can hurt your client at trial.

ENDNOTES

1 This form is used in Mecklenburg County, North Carolina.
2 If you do not fully understand these terms, refer to Chapter 12, where they are explained.
3 In this affidavit, FMV means fair market value.

FIGURE 10-9   A SAMPLE JUROR QUESTIONNAIRE

COURT OF COMMON PLEAS
Hamilton County, Ohio
JUROR QUESTIONNAIRE

PRINT CLEARLY   DO NOT FOLD

1) NAME & AGE: _Michael_____ _T._____ _Jumpstart_____ _29_____
        (First)   (Middle Initial)   (Last)   (Age)

2) HOME ADDRESS _6310 Roundup Ct._____ HOW LONG? _all my life_
   CITY _Cincinnati_____ ZIP CODE _45224_____

3) YEARS OF RESIDENCE IN HAMILTON COUNTY: _all my life_ PLACE OF BIRTH: _Cincinnati Ohio_

4) EDUCATION: Completed to: Grade School _____ High School _____ College _1 yr._ Grad. Stud. _____
       (Indicate completion by "X", or uncompleted by years attended)

5) YOUR OCCUPATION & EMPLOYER _truck driver; self-employed_____
       (If retired, write "RETIRED" and give last occupation and employer)

6) IF YOU ARE A WIDOW OR A WIDOWER GIVE LATE SPOUSE'S OCCUPATION AND EMPLOYER _____
   _____

7) MARITAL STATUS: Married _✓_____ Separated _____ Widow _____ Number of
   (Please Check) Single _____ Divorced _____ Widower _____ Children _____

8) LIST LIVING MEMBERS OF YOUR FAMILY: (Spouse and Children only)

RELATIONSHIP	AGE	LIVING WITH YOU YES	NO	OCCUPATION	EMPLOYER
wife	26	✓		homemaker	——
son	4	✓		——	——
son	7	✓		——	——

9) Have you served as a juror before?   Yes _____ No _✓_
   If yes, when and where _____

10) Have you ever been convicted of a State or Federal crime punishable by
    imprisonment for more than one year?   Yes _____ No _✓_

11) Have you, or any member of your family listed above, been sued, or sued
    another person?   Yes _✓_ No _____
    If "Yes" complete the following: Type of Lawsuit _small claim for rent_
    When? _1984_____ What Court? _small claims_

12) Have you, or any member of your family listed above, been the victim
    of a crime?   Yes _____ No _✓_

13) Has a claim for personal injury ever been made by you or against you
    or your family, NOT involving a lawsuit?   Yes _____ No _✓_

14) Are you related to or a close friend of any law enforcement officer or
    prosecutor?   Yes _____ No _✓_

15) Do you drive an automobile?   Yes _✓_ No _____

               Michael T. Jumpstart
                (Juror Signature)

11 PRETRIAL CONFERENCES, ARBITRATION, AND SETTLEMENT

LITIGATION EXTRACT: Our pretrial preparation is nearly complete. As the scheduled day approaches, the attorney/paralegal team must prepare for the final pretrial conference, in which the judge and attorneys meet and set guidelines for the trial. However, even at a late stage in the litigation process, a lawsuit can be settled. We will discuss how to determine a settlement value for a lawsuit and the documents used to reduce the parties' agreement to writing. We will also discuss arbitration, an alternative to trial in which the litigants submit their dispute to a neutral third party who examines the evidence and reaches a resolution. We will discuss the various types of arbitration and the procedures they involve.

PRETRIAL CONFERENCES

We have saved our discussion of pretrial conferences until now, just before our discussion of trial, because just before trial is when the final pretrial conference takes place. Usually, however, at least one pretrial conference precedes the final conference, and there may be several pretrial conferences before the final pretrial conference.

Rule 16 of the Federal Rules of Civil Procedure addresses pretrial conferences. Refer to Figure 11-1, which shows FRCivP 16. Note that FRCivP 16 grants the judge a great deal of discretion in conducting pretrial conferences.

In part because FRCivP 16 provides so much flexibility, many judicial districts have local rules that delineate more specifically their procedure for pretrial conferences. Most local rules operate within the broad guidelines of FRCivP 16 but state with greater particularity the exact procedure and deadlines. In addition, judges have personal preferences concerning the conduct of pretrial conferences,

FIGURE 11-1   FRCivP 16

RULE 16.   Pretrial Conferences; Scheduling; Management

(a) Pretrial Conferences; Objectives. In any action, the court may in its discretion direct the attorneys for the parties and any unrepresented parties to appear before it for a conference or conferences before trial for such purposes as

(1) expediting the disposition of the action;

(2) establishing early and continuing control so that the case will not be protracted because of lack of management;

(3) discouraging wasteful pretrial activities;

(4) improving the quality of the trial through more thorough preparation, and;

(5) facilitating the settlement of the case.

(b) Scheduling and Planning. Except in categories of actions exempted by district court rule as inappropriate, the judge, or a magistrate when authorized by district court rule, shall, after consulting with the attorneys for the parties and any unrepresented parties, by a scheduling conference, telephone, mail, or other suitable means, enter a scheduling order that limits the time

(1) to join other parties and to amend the pleadings;

(2) to file and hear motions; and

(3) to complete discovery.

The scheduling order also may include

(4) the date or dates for conferences before trial, a final pretrial conference, and trial; and

(5) any other matters appropriate in the circumstances of the case.

The order shall issue as soon as practicable but in no event more than 120 days after filing of the complaint. A schedule shall not be modified except by leave of the judge or a magistrate when authorized by district court rule upon a showing of good cause.

(c) Subjects to be Discussed at Pretrial Conferences. The participants at any conference under this rule may consider and take action with respect to

(1) the formulation and simplification of the issues, including the elimination of frivolous claims or defenses;

(2) the necessity or desirability of amendments to the pleadings;

(3) the possibility of obtaining admissions of fact and of documents which will avoid unnecessary proof, stipulations regarding the authenticity of documents, and advance rulings from the court on the admissibility of evidence;

(4) the avoidance of unnecessary proof and of cumulative evidence;

(5) the identification of witnesses and documents, the need and schedule for filing and exchanging pretrial briefs, and the date or dates for further conferences and for trial;

(6) the advisability of referring matters to a magistrate or master;

(7) the possibility of settlement or the use of extrajudicial procedures to resolve the dispute;

(8) the form and substance of the pretrial order;

(9) the disposition of pending motions;

(10) the need for adopting special procedures for managing potentially difficult or protracted actions that may involve complex issues, multiple parties, difficult legal questions, or unusual proof problems; and

FIGURE 11-1   FRCivP 16 (Cont.)

> (11) such other matters as may aid in the disposition of the action. At least one of the attorneys for each party participating in any conference before trial shall have authority to enter into stipulations and to make admissions regarding all matters that the participants may reasonably anticipate may be discussed.
>
> **(d) Final Pretrial Conference.** Any final pretrial conference shall be held as close to the time of trial as reasonable under the circumstances. The participants at any such conference shall formulate a plan for trial, including a program for facilitating the admission of evidence. The conference shall be attended by at least one of the attorneys who will conduct the trial for each of the parties and by any unrepresented parties.
>
> **(e) Pretrial Orders.** After any conference held pursuant to this rule, an order shall be entered reciting the action taken. This order shall control the subsequent course of the action unless modified by a subsequent order. The order following a final pretrial conference shall be modified only to prevent manifest injustice.
>
> **(f) Sanctions.** If a party or party's attorney fails to obey a scheduling or pretrial order, or if no appearance is made on behalf of a party at a scheduling or pretrial conference, or if a party or party's attorney is substantially unprepared to participate in the conference, or if a party or party's attorney fails to participate in good faith, the judge, upon motion or the judge's own initiative, may make such orders with regard thereto as are just, and among others any of the orders provided in Rule 87(b)(2)(B), (C), (D). In lieu of or in addition to any other sanction, the judge shall require the party or the attorney representing the party or both to pay the reasonable expenses incurred because of any noncompliance with this rule, including attorney's fees, unless the judge finds that the noncompliance was substantially justified or that other circumstances make an award of expenses unjust.

whether published or not, and the attorney/paralegal team must be familiar with any special procedures that a particular judge requires. One pretrial task for paralegals is to ensure that the attorneys have all local rules and special judicial requirements before them and prepare for the pretrial conferences in accordance with those rules and requirements.

POINTER: In federal court actions, paralegals may need to check with the judge's law clerks for special procedures. In state courts, after you check local rules of practice, you may need to check with the clerk of court and/or with attorneys in your firm who have appeared before the judge to whom the case is assigned.

Types of Pretrial Conferences

Two types of pretrial conferences are commonly required by the federal court. The first type is often called the **initial pretrial conference**. An initial pretrial conference is held early in the litigation, and its purpose is to set guidelines to control the remainder of the litigation process. The guidelines include deadlines for completion of discovery and stipulations of matters not in dispute.

The second type is the **final pretrial conference**, which is usually held a few weeks before trial. At the final pretrial conference the judge rules on all pending motions and discusses trial procedures such as the filing of requests for jury instructions. The attorneys and judge discuss settlement possibilities and other matters.

An important part of pretrial procedure is the **pretrial order**, an order setting out matters decided at the pretrial conference. FRCivP 16(e) requires that after any pretrial conference an order be entered reciting the action taken. FRCivP 16(e) states that the pretrial order controls the "subsequent course of the action unless modified by a subsequent order." We will discuss the content of pretrial orders as we examine the conferences themselves.

The Initial Pretrial Conference

Under this heading we will discuss all pretrial conferences except the final one. A judge may hold multiple conferences if they become necessary. Suppose, for instance, that two months after an initial pretrial conference opposing attorneys have clashed repeatedly because one party refuses to cooperate with discovery requests. One option is to file motions to compel discovery and schedule formal hearings in open court, but a better alternative may be for the attorneys to set up a conference with the judge and work out their difficulties. Suppose that in the conference, the judge alters the deadline for completion of discovery and instructs a party to appear at a deposition before a certain date. These decisions are then entered in an order that modifies the original pretrial order.

Frequently only one pretrial conference is necessary before the final pretrial conference. The precise procedure for the initial pretrial conference may differ according to local court rules and the judge's special instructions. However, the aim of the initial pretrial conference is the same regardless of the procedure. FRCivP 16(a) sets forth the general purposes: to expedite the disposition of the action, to establish early control so that the case will not be protracted because of lack of management, to discourage wasteful pretrial activities, to improve the quality of trial preparation, and to facilitate settlement.

The goal of the initial pretrial conference is the preparation of a pretrial order that sets forth the schedule for the litigation and states certain matters on which the parties agree, such as that there is no question that the court has jurisdiction. If the initial pretrial conference is held early enough in the litigation process, all these matters can be discussed and resolved then. Some local court rules allow the parties to prepare a pretrial order and stipulate to the required matters without actually meeting with the judge. For instance, Rule 204 of the Rules of Practice and Procedure of the United States District Court for the Middle District of North Carolina provides that the clerk of court schedule an initial pretrial conference and send a notice to the parties' attorneys at least 20 days before the date of the conference. If the attorneys submit to the court satisfactory stipulations at least 10 days before the scheduled conference, the judge may allow entry of the initial pretrial order and not require the attorneys to appear for a conference.

The Middle District of North Carolina's rules contain a suggested form for the attorneys to follow. This form appears as Figure 11-2. It is instructive to

FIGURE 11-2   SUGGESTED FORM FOR INITIAL PRETRIAL ORDER

FORM 1

(See Local Rule 204)

IN THE UNITED STATES DISTRICT COURT
FOR THE MIDDLE DISTRICT OF NORTH CAROLINA
_____ DIVISION

Plaintiff
vs.   Civil Action
Defendant   No._____

INITIAL PRETRIAL STIPULATIONS AND ORDER

In accordance with Local Rule 204, counsel for each of the parties in the above-entitled action hereby stipulates that:[1]

(1) All parties defendant have been properly served with process.

(2) The court has jurisdiction over the parties and over the subject matter.

(3) All parties plaintiff and defendant have been correctly designated.

(4) No third-party complaint or impleading petition is contemplated.

(5) There is no question concerning misjoinder or nonjoinder of parties.

(6) There is no present need to join other parties or to amend the pleadings.

(7) There is no need for, or question concerning the validity of, the appointment of a representative for any party.

(8) There are no pending motions which the parties wish the court to consider.

(9) A trial by jury has (not) been demanded within the time provided by the Federal Rules of Civil Procedure.

(10) There is no need at this time to separate issues for purposes of discovery or trial, and discovery shall proceed on all issues.

(11) There are no related actions pending or contemplated in this or any other court.

(12) To the extent presently known, the parties estimate that a trial of this action will last approximately ____ days.

(13) The parties need _____ months to complete discovery.[2]

Stipulated and consented to:

_____   _____
Counsel for Plaintiff   Counsel for Defendant
Address   Address
Telephone Number   Telephone Number
N.C. State Bar No.   N.C. State Bar No.

FIGURE 11-2   SUGGESTED FORM FOR INITIAL PRETRIAL ORDER (Cont.)

IT IS ORDERED that all discovery be completed by the ____ day of _____19____. IT IS FURTHER ORDERED that any motion for leave to amend pleadings must be filed on or before the ____ day of _____19____. IT IS FURTHER ORDERED that the scheduled initial pretrial conference is hereby canceled.

Notice of any intention to file a dispositive motion, including a motion for summary judgment, shall be filed within ten (10) days from the close of discovery. See Local Rule 206(a). The motion must be filed within thirty (30) days from the close of discovery. See Local Rule 206(b).

_____
United States District Judge or
Magistrate

1. When no stipulation is reached on a particular matter, the parties shall state with specificity their respective positions. For example: (1) All parties defendant have been properly served with process, except defendant X does not so stipulate and claims . . .

2. The standard discovery period is 120 days. If the parties propose a longer period, they must set forth their reasons for believing an extended period is required. The discovery period must include time for identification of experts and discovery with respect thereto. In appropriate cases, the parties may wish to provide that experts be identified at the close of a "general" discovery period, with a subsequent 60 day discovery period with respect to experts only.

examine the form, because the form is representative of the matters contained in an initial pretrial order regardless of the procedure by which the order is crafted. Note the procedural matters to which the attorneys stipulate: that all defendants have been properly served, that the court has subject matter and personal jurisdiction, that all parties are properly designated, and that there is not any question that a party needs to be joined or has been improperly joined.

In addition to important procedural stipulations, the initial pretrial order contains important deadlines, including the deadline for completing discovery. Note that the model form in Figure 11-2 provides that dispositive motions, such as motions for summary judgment, must be filed within 30 days from the close of discovery. Note also that the parties estimate how long they think the trial will take. This helps the court plan its calendar.

Procedures differ among judicial districts. In some districts the judge or a magistrate enters a **scheduling order** before holding an initial pretrial conference. A scheduling order sets deadlines for joining other parties, amending pleadings, filing and hearing motions, and completing discovery. The scheduling order may also set a time for the initial pretrial conference, the final pretrial conference, and the trial.

FRCivP 16(b) requires that the scheduling order be issued as soon as practicable, but within 120 days after the complaint is filed. This leaves the judge the option of entering a separate scheduling order or including the scheduling in the comprehensive initial pretrial order.

POINTER: The initial pretrial conference procedures may take place with a United States magistrate, rather than with the judge assigned to the case. The Federal Rules of Civil Procedure allow magistrates to preside over a wide range of pretrial activities, and this includes pretrial conferences.

When the attorneys meet with the judge or magistrate, the manner in which the meeting is held can vary considerably. Some judges have informal meetings in chambers with no court reporter in attendance. Other judges hold more formal conferences in the courtroom, with a court reporter present. The attorney/paralegal team should know the method the judge or magistrate uses, so that it can prepare properly.

The Final Pretrial Conference

FRCivP 16(d) states the primary purpose for the final pretrial conference: to "formulate a plan for trial, including a program for facilitating the admission of evidence." Another general purpose of the final pretrial conference is to discuss any possibilities for settlement before trial.

The final pretrial conference is usually held several weeks before the scheduled trial date. By this time the attorneys have completed sufficient trial preparation to know each party's position and whether settlement may still be possible. Chances are that the attorneys will have discussed settlement already, but the final pretrial conference is a time when many cases are settled. Sometimes the attorneys have frank discussions with the judge about the merits of each party's contentions, and this can facilitate settlement.

The procedure for the final pretrial conference may differ among judicial districts. Just as they do with initial pretrial conferences, judges may conduct formal hearings in open court or hold informal discussions in chambers.

Local court rules often require opposing attorneys to meet prior to the final pretrial conference in order to prepare for it. One purpose of the final pretrial conference is for the attorneys to state the matters on which the parties stipulate agreement. When the attorneys meet before the conference, they can determine the matters to which they can stipulate. In particular, they can determine the documents for which they are willing to stipulate authenticity. Bear in mind that the purpose of the final pretrial conference and preparations for it is to make the trial itself go smoothly by narrowing the issues and exchanging information. The resolution of evidentiary questions before trial can eliminate the need for lengthy arguments regarding evidence during trial, resulting in a happier jury and judge.

An example of a rule that sets out points that attorneys are required to cover in their meeting before the final pretrial conference is Rule 207 of the Rules of Practice and Procedure of the United States District Court for the Middle District of North Carolina. The rule provides that the attorneys are required to bring to the meeting and exchange a short statement of their client's contentions and suggested stipulations, a list of exhibits, a list of witnesses, and a list of issues for trial. The attorneys are instructed to exchange exhibits. They are also required to include with their list of witnesses a brief statement of what the attorneys propose to establish by the testimony of each witness. In addition, Rule 207 requires the attorneys to have a frank discussion of settlement possibilities. Finally, the plaintiff's attorney is required to prepare a final pretrial order for use at the final pretrial conference.

The Middle District of North Carolina rules contain a suggested form for the final pretrial order, and the order must substantially conform to the suggested form. The form appears in Figure 11-3. It illustrates the topics generally included in final pretrial orders. Review the order, and note that it includes a number of lists: stipulations, plaintiff's exhibits, defendant's exhibits, plaintiff's witnesses, and defendant's witnesses. The order also contains the plaintiff's and the defendant's lists of contested issues.

At the final pretrial conference, the judge and attorneys may have to modify the proposed order. Once the final pretrial order is approved by the judge, it governs the procedure for the trial. The judge may also inform the attorneys of certain procedures for the trial, such as the number of copies of exhibits the attorneys must have available, the manner of marking exhibits, and the procedure for giving the judge proposed jury instructions. The judge sets a tentative or actual trial date. Finally, the judge rules on pending motions, such as motions on the admission of evidence.

Throughout our discussion we have referred to the presence of attorneys. In cases where parties are not represented by counsel, the parties themselves must perform the attorney tasks described. Even when parties are represented by counsel, they should be available either in person or by telephone to discuss settlement possibilities.

Pretrial Conferences in State Court Actions

Pretrial conferences in state court actions vary according to the state rules of civil procedure and local court rules. The goals are the same as those at the federal level: to facilitate a smooth trial and a possible settlement of the case. The content of the final pretrial order is likely to be substantially similar to the order shown in Figure 11-3.

However, the procedures for the attorneys and the judge may be different from those of federal court. In state court there may be only one pretrial conference—the final conference. Attorneys in a state court action may meet and prepare a final pretrial order without ever actually meeting with the judge. State rules usually provide that the final pretrial order must be filed a certain number of days before the first day of the session in which the case is scheduled to be tried. Final pretrial conferences may be brief and may be held the morning that trial begins. Local rules often require the attorneys to inform the trial court administrator well ahead of trial if they anticipate a lengthy final pretrial conference so that the conference can be scheduled before the court session begins. This minimizes disruption and prevents the judge from being tied up with pretrial conferences when she or he could be in the court hearing the cases.

Some state courts implement status reports in addition to pretrial conferences. The purpose of status reports is to inform the court of the status of

FIGURE 11-3   SUGGESTED FORM FOR FINAL PRETRIAL ORDER

FORM 2. ORDER ON FINAL PRETRIAL CONFERENCE

(See Local Rule 207)

IN THE UNITED STATES DISTRICT COURT
FOR THE MIDDLE DISTRICT OF NORTH CAROLINA
_____ DIVISION

Plaintiff
vs.
Defendant

Civil Action
No._____

ORDER ON FINAL PRETRIAL CONFERENCE

Pursuant to the provisions of Rule 16 of the Federal Rules of Civil Procedure and Local Rule 207, a final pretrial conference was held in the above-entitled cause on the _____ day of _____ , 19____ . _____ appeared as counsel for the plaintiff, and _____ appeared as counsel for the defendant.

(1) It is stipulated that all parties are properly before the court and that the court has jurisdiction of the parties and the subject matter, except:

(2) It is stipulated that all parties have been correctly designated, and there is no question as to misjoinder or nonjoinder of parties, except:

(3) It is stipulated that there is no question concerning the validity of the appointment of the representative of any party, except: [Letters or orders of appointment should be included as exhibits.]

(4) In general, the contentions of the plaintiff as to the basis of recovery are as follows:*

(5) In general, the contentions of the defendant as to the basis of its defenses and counterclaims are as follows:*

(6) Any third party defendant or cross-claimant should follow the same procedure as set out in paragraphs (4) and (5) for plaintiff and defendant.*

(7) In addition to the other stipulations contained herein, the parties hereto stipulate to the following undisputed material facts:

(a)
(b)

(8) The following is a list of the exhibits, with pretrial identification markings and a brief description of each exhibit, which plaintiff may offer at the trial:

(a)
(b)

(9) It is stipulated that opposing counsel has been furnished a copy of, inspected, or waives inspection of, each exhibit identified by the plaintiff, except:

(10) It is stipulated that each of the exhibits identified by the plaintiff is authentic and admissible and, if relevant and material, may be received in evidence without further identification or proof, except: [Set out with particularity the basis of objection to specific exhibits.]

(11) The following is a list of the exhibits, with pretrial identification markings and a brief description of each exhibit, which the defendant may offer at the trial:

(12) It is stipulated that opposing counsel has been furnished a copy of, inspected, or waives inspection of each exhibit identified by the defendant, except:

(13) It is stipulated that each of the exhibits identified by the defendant is authentic and admissible and, if relevant and material, may be received in evidence without further identification or proof, except: [Set out with particularity the basis of objection to specific exhibits.]

FIGURE 11-3   SUGGESTED FORM FOR FINAL PRETRIAL ORDER (Cont.)

(14) Any third-party defendant and cross-claimant should follow the same procedure with respect to exhibits as above outlined for plaintiff and defendant.

(15) The following is a list of the names and addresses of the witnesses plaintiff may offer at the trial, together with a brief statement of the material points that counsel proposes to establish by the testimony of each witness:
(a)
(b)

(16) The following is a list of the names and addresses of the witnesses defendant may offer at the trial, together with a brief statement of the material points that counsel proposes to establish by the testimony of each witness:
(a)
(b)

(17) Any third-party defendant and cross-claimant should follow the same procedure with respect to witnesses as above outlined for plaintiff and defendant.

(18) There are no pending or impending motions, and neither party desires further amendments to the pleadings, except:

(19) Additional consideration has been given to a separation of the triable issues, and counsel for all parties are of the opinion that a separation of issues in this particular case would (would not) be appropriate.

(20) The plaintiff contends that the contested issues are as follows:

(21) The defendant contends that the contested issues are as follows:

(22) Any third-party defendant and cross-claimant contends that the contested issues are as follows:

(23) Counsel for the parties announce that all witnesses are available, and the case is in all respects ready for trial. The probable length of the trial is estimated to be _____ days.

(24) Counsel for the parties represent to the court that, in advance of the preparation of this order, there was a full and frank discussion of settlement possibilities and that prospects for settlement appear to be (excellent) (good) (fair) (poor) (remote). Counsel for the plaintiff will immediately notify the clerk in the event of material change in settlement prospects.

_____
Counsel for Plaintiff
Address
Telephone

_____
Counsel for Defendant
Address
Telephone

APPROVED AND ORDERED
FILED:

Date _____

_____
United States District Judge or
Magistrate

(The notations beneath Form 2 are not reproduced.)

the lawsuit and ensure that the litigation is proceeding in a timely manner. Instead of appearing before the judge to report their progress, the attorneys may submit a written status report to the judge's clerk.

The Paralegal's Pretrial Conference Duties

Tasks performed by paralegals for initial and final pretrial conferences depend mainly on the procedures used by the court. Paralegals may prepare drafts of the lists of witnesses and exhibits, together with summaries of the witnesses' testimony. Paralegals may gather exhibits and organize and number them for use at the pretrial conference. Paralegals may gather and present to the attorney all motions on which the judge needs to rule. As part of their docket control systems, paralegals also keep track of the dates that pretrial conferences will be held and deadlines for exchanging information or submitting proposed orders. Paralegals can ensure that the attorneys know the exact procedures used in a particular court and by a particular judge. They should ensure that files are in order and that all needed documents can be located easily. As they do throughout litigation, paralegals keep clients informed of developments in their cases and make sure clients are present when needed.

ARBITRATION

Arbitration is a method of dispute resolution that serves as an alternative to a full-blown trial. Instead of bringing a matter to trial, the parties agree on a neutral third party who examines the evidence and decides how to resolve the dispute. The neutral third party is called the **arbitrator**. The arbitrator is most often an attorney who has several years of experience in the particular area of law that applies to the dispute.

Arbitration is becoming increasingly popular, because it is faster and more economical than ordinary litigation. Some courts actively encourage arbitration, and the court rules in some judicial districts require the parties to submit certain types of cases to arbitration. Many types of lawsuits may be resolved by arbitration—from child custody to automobile accident injuries to contract disputes.

The Purpose of Arbitration

The purpose of arbitration is to avoid the expense, delay, and formalities of ordinary litigation. Arbitration differs from trial in several ways. Although trials follow a set process dictated by the rules of civil procedure, there are numerous ways to conduct arbitration. Arbitration is more relaxed than a conventional trial. Even the setting is less formal; arbitration may take place in a conference room in an attorney's office or a meeting room in a county government building. Arbitration is a more expedited process than trial. Parties may agree to enter arbitration early in the litigation process, and they may have a hearing with the arbitrator long before the case could be placed on a trial calendar.

Types of Arbitration

Before we explore the various procedures that can be used for arbitration, it is important to understand some basic definitions. Arbitration may be either *binding* or *nonbinding.*

Binding arbitration means that the parties agree to abide by the decision of the arbitrator. The parties agree before arbitration begins that they will be bound by the arbitrator's decision and that they will not bring the dispute to trial even if they are unhappy with the outcome.

Nonbinding arbitration means that the parties will not be bound by the arbitrator's decision. If they do not accept the arbitrator's decision, they may proceed with a regular trial before a judge or jury. You may wonder why parties participate in arbitration if they may not accept the arbitrator's resolution of their dispute. The reason is that at the very least it is worth a try to resolve the dispute through arbitration and thus avoid the time and expense that a trial requires. Through arbitration the parties can test their respective strengths and weaknesses, but they should enter arbitration with the sincere intent of resolving the dispute rather than using the arbitration process as a means of discovery.

Arbitration may be either *mandatory* or *voluntary.* **Mandatory arbitration** means that the parties must try to resolve their dispute through arbitration before they are granted a full-blown trial. **Voluntary arbitration** is when the parties agree to try arbitration even though it is not required.

Arbitration may be *court-annexed* or *private.* In **court-annexed arbitration**, the arbitration procedure is governed by local court rules that set forth that court's arbitration process. Parties generally file with the clerk of court a statement that they wish to enter arbitration, and the court maintains a list of approved arbitrators from whom the parties may choose. **Private arbitration** is often administered through centers such as the Private Adjudication Center at Duke University. Private arbitration centers maintain a list of approved arbitrators from whom the parties may choose. The centers establish some procedural guidelines, such as rules governing the advancement of the costs for arbitration and the filing of prehearing briefs.

Parties may also set up their own private arbitration procedure—for example, by signing a settlement contract that provides that they will dismiss their lawsuits and settle their dispute by binding arbitration. The parties' attorneys then choose an arbitrator or panel of arbitrators and present their evidence in a manner agreed on by the parties, their attorneys, and the arbitrator. If the parties agree on binding arbitration and one party fails to comply with the arbitrator's decision, the other party can file a lawsuit for specific performance of the settlement contract.

With both private and court-annexed arbitration, the rules often are flexible, giving the parties some choices about the manner in which their arbitration will proceed. For instance, the parties may have some flexibility in the manner in which they present their evidence to the arbitrator. They may have a formal hearing like a trial, or they may submit their written evidence and then meet to allow the arbitrator to ask questions in a fairly informal setting. Other arbitration programs allow only the submission of written evidence and briefs, and no hearing.

Procedure for Arbitration

The procedure for arbitration can vary considerably, depending on the arbitration program in which you are involved. It is important to get a copy of the rules for your particular program and to follow the rules carefully. Some rules may allow certain choices, but other rules are mandatory. Failure to follow the rules can result in the loss of important rights, such as the right to a conventional trial after the completion of nonbinding arbitration.

An Example of Procedure in Court-Annexed Arbitration. Perhaps the best way to understand the nature of arbitration is to examine the procedural rules in an actual arbitration program. The United States District Court for the Middle District of North Carolina requires that certain types of civil actions be submitted to nonbinding arbitration. The rules that govern the arbitration procedure are part of the Middle District's local rules of practice and procedure, and an overview of these rules gives you an overview of the arbitration process.[1]

Rule 601 explains well the purpose of the court-annexed arbitration: to provide for "the speedy, fair, and economical resolution of controversies by informal procedures while preserving the right of all parties to a conventional trial."

Rule 602 sets forth the types of actions subject to mandatory arbitration. Included are civil actions in which "the relief sought consists only of money damages not in excess of $150,000 exclusive of punitive damages, statutory multiple damages, costs, and interest." The rule then sets out the exceptions—that is, civil actions that fit the preceding description but do not have to be submitted to arbitration. Examples of the exceptions include class actions, actions based on alleged violations of rights secured under the U.S. Constitution, and certain actions in which the United States is a party, such as claims arising under the Federal Tort Claims Act.

Attorneys are allowed to file motions to exempt from the arbitration requirement certain types of actions, such as cases involving complex or novel legal issues. Attorneys may certify that the relief in issue exceeds $150,000 and request an exemption on this basis. To request an exemption, a party must file a motion for exemption within 20 days of the entry of the initial pretrial order or any other order that selects the case for arbitration.

Rule 603 of the Middle District's rules sets out the preliminary procedure. First, the clerk enters an initial pretrial order that selects the case for arbitration, sets a 20-day deadline for filing motions for leave to amend pleadings or to join parties, and establishes a 90-day deadline for the conduct of discovery. The clerk also notifies the parties that they may either choose an arbitrator from the clerk's list of attorneys or choose their own arbitrator. Within 15 days of entry of the initial pretrial order, the parties must file a written statement with the clerk, identifying the arbitrator they have selected. The parties then conduct discovery.

Subsequent rules address arbitrators' eligibility requirements and the schedules for their payment, as well as procedures for selecting an arbitrator when parties fail to file their statement of selection.

Next, the clerk sends the arbitrator a complete copy of the court file. Local Rule 606, reprinted in Figure 11-4, provides the guidelines for conduct of the arbitration hearing. Note that at least 10 days before the hearing, each party must submit a statement identifying the issues to be determined, its witnesses, and its exhibits. Subpoenas may be used to compel the attendance of witnesses and production of documentary evidence. Witnesses testify under oath. The court reporter usually present in federal court proceedings is not present, but a party may hire its own court reporter, if it wishes.

At the actual hearing, the arbitrator presides; the plaintiff presents exhibits and witnesses, who are subject to cross-examination. Then the defendant makes its presentation. The parties may present oral arguments and may present briefs, if the arbitrator decides to accept them.

The arbitrator assesses the relevance and trustworthiness of the evidence. Local Rule 606(g) provides that the Federal Rules of Evidence shall not apply. Thus the formal rules of evidence are relaxed, and some of the lengthy arguments that occur over the admission of evidence in the courtroom do not occur here. In the more relaxed environment of arbitration, some evidence may be admitted that might not be admitted in a jury trial. One example is hearsay. However, if the arbitrator is a seasoned trial lawyer, expect the general principles of the rules of evidence to guide him or her, even though their application may be less rigid.

Within 15 days of the closing of the hearing or the submission of posthearing briefs, the arbitrator mails to the parties the written decision, known as the *award*. The prevailing party then files with the clerk of court the original copy of the award, which is sealed. The award is sealed so that the judge will not be influenced by the arbitrator's decision if the parties elect to reject the arbitration decision and proceed with a trial de novo.

The parties then have 30 days to file with the court a written demand for a trial de novo. If neither party files stipulation of dismissal or a written demand for a trial de novo within the 30-day period, the award is unsealed. The award is then entered as the judgment in the case, and it cannot be appealed to a higher court.

This has been an overview of some of the rules governing an actual arbitration procedure. Although not all the rules were discussed, you now have a picture of the arbitration process. From the deadlines noted here, you can see that arbitration is a much faster process than an ordinary trial. For many disputes, arbitration provides a speedy and economical resolution.

Variations in Arbitration Procedures. The actual procedures for arbitration vary. As an example, the rules governing court-annexed arbitration in the United States District Court for the Eastern District of New York provide some interesting contrasts to the rules we have just examined in the United States District Court for the Middle District of North Carolina.[2]

FIGURE 11-4   NORTH CAROLINA MIDDLE DISTRICT LOCAL RULE 606

RULE 606.   ARBITRATION PROCEDURE

(a) No Ex Parte Communication. There shall be no ex parte communication between the arbitrator and any counsel or party on any matter touching the proceeding, except with regard to scheduling matters. Nothing in this rule prevents the arbitrator from engaging in ex parte communications, with consent of the parties, for the purpose of assisting settlement negotiations.

(b) Prehearing Exchange of Information. No later than 10 days prior to the hearing date, each party shall file with the clerk and serve on the arbitrator and other parties a statement which sets forth for such party the following information:

(1) identification of the issues to be determined;

(2) identification of all witnesses to be called at [the] arbitration hearing; and

(3) identification of all exhibits to be presented at the hearing.

Each party may, at the same time, file and serve a prehearing brief.

(c) Record. No official record of the arbitration hearing will be made. Any party desiring the attendance of a reporter shall make the necessary arrangements with a reporting agency. The costs of the reporter's attendance fee, record, and all transcripts thereof, shall be prorated equally among all parties ordering copies, unless they shall otherwise agree, and shall be paid for by the responsible parties directly to the reporting agency.

(d) Subpoenas. Fed.R.Civ.P. 45 shall apply to subpoenas for attendance of witnesses and the production of documentary evidence at an arbitration hearing under these rules.

(e) Testimony Under Oath or Affirmation. All witnesses shall testify under oath or affirmation administered by the arbitrator or any other duly qualified person.

(f) Conduct of Hearing. Parties are required to be present at the arbitration hearing unless excused, in exceptional circumstances, by the arbitrator. At the opening of the hearing, the arbitrator shall make a written record of the place, time, and date of the hearing, and the presence of the parties and counsel. The arbitrator and the parties shall review the written statements concerning issues, witnesses, and exhibits filed with the clerk pursuant to section (b) of this rule. Plaintiff may then present its exhibits (copies only) and witnesses, who may be cross-examined. Defendant may then present its exhibits (copies only) and witnesses, who may be cross-examined. The arbitrator may, in the arbitrator's discretion, vary the order of presentation of evidence.

(g) Evidence. The arbitrator shall weigh all evidence presented upon assessment of its relevance and trustworthiness. The Federal Rules of Evidence shall not apply, except for rules concerning privilege or protection.

(h) Conclusion of Hearing. When the parties state that they have no further exhibits or witnesses to offer, the arbitrator shall declare the hearing closed. Counsel may make oral argument, but the filing of posthearing briefs will ordinarily not be permitted. If the arbitrator decides to accept briefs, such briefs must be filed with the clerk and served upon the arbitrator and other parties within 14 days or less, as determined by the arbitrator.

(i) Sanctions for Failure to Proceed. For any failure of a party or its counsel to proceed in good faith in accordance with these rules, the court may impose sanctions pursuant to Local Rule 122.

North Carolina rules provide for compulsory arbitration in civil cases where damages do not exceed $150,000. New York rules provide for compulsory arbitration in civil cases with damages not exceeding $50,000. The New York rules provide that the case will be decided by a panel of three arbitrators, unless the parties agree to a single arbitrator. Arbitrators are chosen at random by the clerk of court from a list of certified arbitrators. This contrasts with the North Carolina system, which uses only one arbitrator and allows the parties to choose their arbitrator.

These are just a few examples of how arbitration procedures may differ. In some programs the parties submit only written evidence and summaries, and no hearing is held. Other programs schedule hearings that amount to informal discussions among the parties and the arbitrator; such encounters are designed to help the arbitrator develop the facts. Still other arbitration programs feature hearings similar to trial before a judge.

The procedure for submission of briefs may vary. The parties may be subject to page limits for their briefs. The arbitrator may choose whether or not to allow the submission of post-hearing briefs.

Time limits for filing motions, completing discovery, and submitting written evidence may also vary. It is imperative that the attorney/paralegal team determine the applicable rules and follow them carefully.

Our discussion has emphasized cases submitted to arbitration early in the litigation process. In some arbitration systems parties may submit their dispute to arbitration later in the litigation process, such as after the completion of discovery.

Types of Disputes Submitted to Arbitration

The types of disputes that may be submitted to arbitration are controlled by the rules of the particular arbitration process. Commonly referred to arbitration are the more routine disputes such as automobile accidents and breaches of contract. A novel question of constitutional law is not an appropriate candidate for arbitration.

However, lawsuits may concern common sources of disputes and still be complex. Lawsuits that involve hundreds of exhibits can be difficult to try, especially in a jury trial. The actual process of submitting document after document into evidence can prove cumbersome and can confuse or bore a jury. Such lawsuits are sometimes good ones to submit to arbitration. For instance, the construction of a building can lead to disputes between the contractor and the owner, as well as between the contractor and numerous subcontractors. These cases can be difficult to try because so many parties are involved and so many documents must be introduced. Such a case would be a good one to submit to arbitration, with a lawyer who has experience in construction lawsuits serving as the arbitrator. This would save a lot of background explanation and ensure a knowledgeable finder of fact.

Submission of All or Some Issues. Parties may submit to arbitration all or only some of the issues in their lawsuit. For instance, the parties in an automobile accident case may submit only the issue of liability. After the question of liability is established by the arbitrator, the parties may have a trial to determine the amount of damages, or the parties may settle the amount of damages themselves.

Another issue that may be submitted to arbitration is the question of insurance coverage. For instance, an insurance company may assert a defense that damage from a fire is not covered under the policy because the fire was the result of arson. The arbitrator could decide the issue of whether the fire was the result of arson. If the arbitrator decided that the fire was caused by arson, there would be no need for a trial to determine damages.

Paralegal Tasks in Arbitration

Paralegal duties in lawsuits submitted to arbitration are basically the same as pretrial duties in ordinary litigation. Paralegals may assist with discovery and draft pleadings. However, as the attorney/paralegal team prepares for the actual arbitration procedure, the paralegal duties may differ. This will depend primarily on the rules governing your arbitration. If the rules call for submission of written evidence, paralegals will not spend time preparing witnesses for testimony. If prehearing briefs are limited to five pages, paralegals may assist the attorneys in reviewing the evidence so as to identify the most essential information to argue in the brief.

During a hearing, paralegal duties will vary, depending upon the nature of the hearing. Paralegals may simply be present and take notes. If the hearing allows the parties to present numerous witnesses, paralegals may be responsible for scheduling the witnesses. If the hearing allows the submission of numerous exhibits, paralegals may help to keep track of the exhibits during the hearing. However, if all the exhibits must be prepared and submitted before the hearing, then paralegals will help arrange the exhibits in a logical order and label the exhibits so that the arbitrator can follow them easily.

SETTLEMENT

A **settlement** is the resolution of a dispute by negotiation between the parties rather than by a judge or jury. The attorneys representing the parties negotiate the settlement, with the permission of their clients. If a party is unrepresented by counsel, then that party negotiates directly with the other party's attorney or the other unrepresented party. Once a settlement is reached and the settlement documents are signed, the parties dismiss their lawsuit.

Your clients must expressly approve the terms of the settlement. Often the attorneys exchange several settlement proposals, and it is crucial that the attorney/paralegal team inform the client promptly of each offer of settlement. Remember the ethical duty to keep the client informed of all developments.

Paralegals perform many tasks in the settlement process, such as compiling information so that the attorney/paralegal team can determine a suitable figure to request in settlement negotiations. Paralegals also help to prepare the settlement documents. Often paralegals inform the client of settlement offers. Remember the ethical obligation to refrain from giving legal advice. Any opinions about whether the client should accept a settlement offer should clearly be those of the lawyer, not the paralegal.

More than three-fourths of all civil lawsuits are settled. A lawsuit may be settled at any time, even during the trial. However, many lawsuits are settled around the time of the pretrial conference, when discovery is complete and the attorney/paralegal team has compiled all the information needed to formulate a figure for settlement. At the pretrial conference, many judges actively encourage settlement. If a large number of cases were not settled, the court system would be overwhelmed.

Determination of a Settlement Value

Before the commencement of serious settlement discussions, the attorney/paralegal team must determine the settlement value, that is, the dollar amount for which your client will agree to settle the case. This is the amount the plaintiff is willing to accept or the amount the defendant is willing to pay, depending on which party you represent. There is no precise formula for determining the settlement value of a lawsuit. We will discuss general guidelines, with emphasis on evaluation of a personal injury claim, such as Mr. Wesser has.

Damages Evaluation

To the extent possible, the attorney/paralegal team needs to calculate the dollar value of a party's claim. Both tangible factors and intangible factors must be considered in performing the calculation. We will use a personal injury lawsuit as an example in analyzing the types of damages that may be claimed. It is helpful to start with the more concrete type of damages—special damages.

Special Damages. Recall from our discussion of special damages on page 116 that special damages are awarded for items of loss that are specific to the particular plaintiff. Special damages may include items such as lost wages. If the party is a salaried employee, for instance, you may take the party's average monthly salary and multiply it by the number of months you expect the party to be unable to work on account of the injuries that gave rise to the litigation. If a party does not receive a steady salary, such as a self-employed professional, the calculation of lost wages is more difficult. Generally you calculate an average of the party's past earnings and try to project the future profits the party would have made during the time that injuries prevented work. Bear in mind that some persons are so badly injured that they may not be able to return to their past work. If a party will have to take a lower-paying job because of the injuries in dispute, compensation should be paid for the reduction in earnings. This involves trying to calculate the loss of earnings over the remainder of the party's working life.

Another type of special damages is medical expenses. This includes doctor and hospital bills, as well as medications and assistive devices such as wheelchairs and braces. This category may also include travel expenses to distant treatment facilities. If future medical expenses are anticipated, the attorney/paralegal team obtains a written description of the anticipated services and an estimate of the cost from the party's doctors. Assigning a dollar value to medical expenses is fairly straightforward because the actual bills are available.

General Damages. It is more difficult to assign a dollar value to general damages, because they include less tangible concepts, such as disability (impairment of normal physical and/or mental function), disfigurement, and pain and suffering. Obviously there is no formula for calculating the amount of compensation due to a person for pain and suffering. No two persons suffer exactly the same injury and feel exactly the same amount of pain.

Often doctors give patients a disability rating. For instance, the doctor may write that a person's limitation of function resulting from a back injury constitutes a 10% permanent impairment of the function of the person's entire body. As for disfigurement, the scars from a burn or limp from a severe fracture are obvious. However, it is still difficult to assign a dollar value to the compensation due to a person for the disfigurement. The surest approach for paralegals is to discuss the amount with the experienced trial attorneys on your team.

Other Types of Lawsuits. We have discussed only personal injury actions, but you as a paralegal will assist with lawsuits covering a wide range of subjects—from breach of contract to consumer fraud. If you review our discussion of remedies in Chapters 1 and 5, you will see that some types of damages are easily calculated, as in actions for failure to pay a promissory note, or suits for damage to an automobile. Consider Mr. Wesser's claim for fire damage to his home. He can produce the repair bills and prove the amount of damages that he suffered. Other types of damages, such as loss of future profits, are not so easy to evaluate. As with personal injury cases, discuss the potential value with the attorneys on your team.

Punitive Damages. Recall that punitive damages are sometimes awarded for particularly egregious behavior. In determining whether to include punitive damages in your calculations, review the file to see whether a statute may provide for punitive damages. If there is an applicable statute, it should be mentioned in your pleadings. For instance, some consumer protection statutes provide for punitive damages in cases of consumer fraud.

Punitive damages usually amount to three to five times the award of compensatory damages. Be sure to add punitive damages into your final calculations when you have a lawsuit in which punitive damages could be awarded.

Trial Expenses

For purposes of determining a settlement value, you should subtract from the amount of damages sought the amount of your anticipated trial expenses. The biggest trial expense will probably be expert witness fees. When doctors take a day off to testify, their fee is likely to equal the amount of money they would have earned at their office that day. Other experts, such as real estate appraisers, are likely to charge a substantial hourly fee.

Other trial expenses include travel and lodging expenses for the experts and other witnesses. If the attorney is being paid an hourly rate, the estimated time for the trial should be multiplied by the hourly rate and included in trial expenses. Many plaintiffs' attorneys are paid a contingent fee, but attorneys for the defendants are often compensated on an hourly rate. Other expenses include copies of exhibits, and this can add up when there are numerous parties and numerous exhibits. Finally, include the court costs.

Evaluate the Likelihood of Prevailing at Trial

After the attorney/paralegal team has calculated the amount necessary to compensate the plaintiff and has subtracted the trial expenses, the team must now consider the likelihood of prevailing at trial. If your client has a claim where the defendant's liability is practically unquestionable, the settlement value is greater than a claim where liability is unclear. Therefore, the first question to consider is the likelihood that your client can establish that the defendant is liable for damages. For instance, if the attorney/paralegal team determines that there is a 75 percent chance that they can establish liability, they subtract 25 percent from their settlement calculation, to account for their 25 percent chance of losing.

Many factors go into determining the likelihood of establishing liability at trial. This is a good time to review your chart of the essential elements of the claims. Review the evidence you have accumulated for establishing the essential elements of each claim. Consider how *credible* your witnesses are. Remember that honesty and sincerity do not necessarily ensure credibility. The most truthful, sincere person may be terrified of the courtroom and pause for a long time before answering each question. If that witness does not seem credible, your chance of prevailing at trial is diminished.

Consider whether any of the parties engaged in any outrageous behavior. For instance, if the defendant was drunk at the time of an automobile accident, this will make the plaintiff more sympathetic to a jury. Consider other factors that may make the plaintiff sympathetic. Very young and very old persons usually evoke sympathy. Consider the defendant also. If the defendant is a large corporation, a jury may award higher damages than it will if the defendant is an individual.

Another consideration for the plaintiff's counsel is whether the plaintiff was partially at fault. In a jurisdiction that retains contributory negligence as a defense, the plaintiff's negligence can bar recovery entirely. In a jurisdiction with comparative negligence, if 30 percent of the fault is attributed to the plaintiff, the plaintiff's recovery is reduced by 30 percent. This is an important factor that may necessitate lowering the amount you request in a settlement.

Evaluate the Likelihood of Collecting the Judgment

Remember that entry of a judgment against a defendant does not guarantee payment. If the defendant has no assets and no insurance, you are unlikely to be able to collect the judgment. One important factor is the defendant's insurance coverage. This fact is usually disclosed early in the discovery process. Review the file and determine the amount of the defendant's insurance coverage. You may need to research the defendant's assets, particularly if the defendant has little or no insurance. See the discussion of asset investigation in Chapter 13.

Miscellaneous Factors

Many other factors may differ from case to case. One important factor may be the amount of the judgments that have been awarded in cases similar to yours. Damages awards can differ significantly in different regions. For instance, a jury in a large metropolitan area may award much larger verdicts than a jury in a rural area where the cost of living and wages are lower. In some areas you may find reporter services that publish verdicts entered in that area. However, no two lawsuits are alike; you cannot assume that the verdict in your case will be the same. If no publications are available, you can get an idea of the range of verdicts from lawyers who have tried many lawsuits in a certain geographical area.

Presentation of Settlement Offers

There are many approaches to settlement negotiations. Each party may make multiple settlement offers throughout the litigation process. Negotiations may range from amicable discussions to terse "take it or leave it" letters. The tone of the negotiations depends on the personalities and negotiation styles of the lawyers.

There are several methods for the parties to communicate their settlement offers through their lawyers. At any stage, the lawyers can discuss the offers on the telephone. Sometimes the lawyers and parties meet at one lawyer's office and discuss the case. Discussions frequently take place just before trial, even the day the trial is scheduled to start. While the parties' highly charged emotions may make them unwilling to discuss settlement at the beginning of the litigation, their attitudes may change as the trial approaches. That is when parties realize the costs of litigation. The very fact that they are in the courthouse can have an effect on their willingness to discuss settlement. Many parties who display amazing bravado in the early stages of litigation lose some wind from their sails when they enter the courthouse and view the imposing setting of the courtroom. At this point some parties begin to understand that they may not prevail at trial. Thus many cases are settled "on the courthouse steps."

Particularly in state court cases that have not been pending long, the parties may suddenly want to discuss settlement as they sit in the courtroom, waiting for their case to be called. In state court the pretrial conference may not take place until the day of trial. Recall that during pretrial conferences, some judges actively encourage settlement. This too can affect the willingness to negotiate. As for the procedure for negotiating at the courthouse, often the lawyers put their clients in separate conference rooms, and the lawyers shuttle between the rooms, informing their clients whether the other party accepted the offer or informing them of a counteroffer. If the parties reach an agreement, the lawyers immediately get the terms in writing and have the parties sign an agreement.

The parties' attorneys also exchange formal written presentations of their settlement offers prior to trial. The attorneys may exchange letters outlining their proposals for settlement. Sometimes a party presents a more formal and elaborate presentation of an offer in the form of a settlement brochure.

Settlement Brochures. In large personal injury cases, the plaintiff's attorney may present a settlement brochure. Because the preparation of the brochure itself may be fairly expensive, the settlement brochure is not so often used in lawsuits requesting smaller damages.

There is no set format for settlement brochures. The brochure typically contains an opening statement outlining the accident and the plaintiff's injuries, information on the plaintiff's background (marital status, education, employment history, etc.), a summary of the evidence on liability, and a summary of the evidence on damages. The summaries are amply supplemented with photographs, such as pictures of the plaintiff's injuries and scars and pictures of damaged property. Other supplemental documents include copies of the plaintiff's medical expenses, doctors' reports on the plaintiff's injuries and prognosis for recovery, and employers' statements on lost wages. Other documents and reports may be included, with the goal of presenting a comprehensive presentation of the plaintiff's damages and convincing proof of the defendant's liability.

Settlement brochures should be a convincing presentation of the defendant's liability and the plaintiff's damages. An effective brochure illustrates the case's jury appeal and can encourage settlement.

Offer of Judgment. FRCivP 68 provides that a defending party may serve upon the adverse party an offer for judgment to be entered against the defending party. The defending party specifies the amount of the judgment that he is willing to have entered against him. See Figure 11-5 for an illustration of an offer of judgment.

The offer of judgment must be served on the plaintiff at least 10 days before trial. The plaintiff may accept or reject the offer of judgment. If the plaintiff accepts the offer of judgment, the plaintiff notifies the defendant in writing, and the parties file with the clerk of court the offer and the notice of acceptance, together with proof of service. The clerk of court enters judgment in the amount the defendant offered, plus costs accrued.

If the plaintiff fails to accept the offer of judgment, the offer is withdrawn. However, if the plaintiff prevails at trial but the judgment obtained is less than the offer of judgment, then the plaintiff must pay to the defendant the costs incurred after the offer of judgment. In the Offer of Judgment in Figure 11-5, defendants Woodall Shoals and Second Ledge offered Mr. Wesser $50,000. Suppose that Mr. Wesser rejected the offer and the case went to trial, resulting in entry of judgment in favor of Mr. Wesser, but only in the amount of $30,000. According to FRCivP 68, Mr. Wesser must now pay the costs incurred after the offer of judgment was made.

The costs may be fairly minimal if they include only the usual court costs— filing fees, marshal fees, court reporter fees, and witness fees. However, sometimes ''costs'' may be defined as including attorney's fees. When costs include attorney's fees, the amount can be formidable. Attorney's fees for a long trial can amount to many thousands of dollars.

FIGURE 11-5   AN OFFER OF JUDGMENT

UNITED STATES DISTRICT COURT
MIDDLE DISTRICT OF NORTH CAROLINA
CHARLESTON DIVISION
CIVIL NO.: C-89-1293-B

Bryson Wesser,

                    Plaintiff,

          -vs-   *OFFER OF JUDGMENT*

Woodall Shoals Corporation,
                    Defendant,
              and
Second Ledge Stores, Incorporated,
                    Defendant

Now come the defendants, Woodall Shoals Corporation and Second Ledge Stores, Incorporated, through counsel, and pursuant to Rule 68 of the Federal Rules of Civil Procedure, do offer to allow the plaintiff to take judgment against them, jointly and severally, in the sum of $50,000, together with costs accrued at the time this offer is filed.

Pursuant to Rule 68, the plaintiff shall have ten days after service hereof to accept this offer by serving written notice that the offer is accepted. If the plaintiff does not accept this offer within ten days after the service hereof, the offer shall be deemed withdrawn and evidence of the offer shall not be admissible except in a proceeding to determine costs.

This the _____ day of _____ , 1989.

_____
David H. Benedict
Attorney for the Defendants
Benedict, Parker & Miller
100 Nolichucky Drive
Bristol, NC 28205-0890

+ Certificate of Service

FRCivP 68 has an important application in lawsuits based on statutes that allow a victorious plaintiff to recover attorney's fees from the defendant as part of "costs." Certain civil rights statutes define "costs" to include attorney's fees. If the plaintiff in such a civil rights case rejects an offer of judgment and as a result of the trial receives a judgment smaller than the defendant's offer, then the plaintiff cannot recover attorney's fees incurred after the offer of judgment was rejected.

The United States Supreme Court addressed this issue in *Marek v. Chesny,* a civil rights case in which the plaintiff rejected the defendant's offer of judgment, and the plaintiff received a judgment smaller than the defendant's offer. The civil rights statute provided that a plaintiff could recover "costs," which included attorney's fees. The Court held that the plaintiff, who had rejected the offer of judgment, could not recover from the defendant the plaintiff's attorney's fees incurred subsequent to the offer of judgment. This included the attorney's fees for the entire trial, a significant amount.[3]

However, courts have generally held that in cases where statutes provide that costs include recovery of attorney's fees, the plaintiff does not have to pay the defendant's attorney's fees incurred after the offer of judgment.[4] Although offers of judgment are intended to encourage settlement, to require a plaintiff who prevails in a civil rights lawsuit to pay the attorney's fees for the defendant who violated her civil rights would seriously undermine the purpose of the civil rights statutes.

Defendants usually present offers of judgment when settlement negotiations have broken down and trial is approaching. Where the potential costs are great, an offer of judgment can be an effective tool to get the plaintiff to reconsider settlement negotiations.

Settlement Documents

Once the parties reach an agreement to settle a lawsuit, it is important that their agreement be put in writing. If the parties change their minds after reaching an oral agreement but before signing the settlement documents, the entire settlement may fall apart and everyone returns to square one. There are several ways to memorialize the parties' settlement agreement. Regardless of what type documents are used, their purpose is to state the terms of the settlement and terminate the lawsuit. The wording of the documents must be precise so that the settlement is given the effect that the parties desire. Applicable statutes may impose certain requirements for the settlement documents, such as those that address contribution among joint tortfeasors—that is, determination of how much money each of multiple defendants must pay to the plaintiff. Be sure to consult with the attorneys on your team to determine whether statutes impose any special requirements.

POINTER: Most local rules require that the parties notify the clerk of court of any settlement immediately, and there may be additional rules. Local rules of court may also impose specific requirements for the content or format of settlement documents.

Consent Judgments

When all claims against all parties have been settled, the parties may file a **consent judgment** with the court. This is a document that sets out briefly the terms of the agreement and states the amount of the judgment to be entered. A consent judgment has the same effect as a judgment entered by a judge after a trial—namely, it is the final decision resolving the dispute and determining the rights and obligations of the parties.

Examine Figure 11-6, which illustrates a consent judgment that might be entered in the Wesser case. The consent judgment is a concise document that states three main points. First it states that the parties have resolved the dispute and agreed that one party shall pay the other party a certain amount of money. Here the defendants have agreed to pay Mr. Wesser $70,000. Second, the consent judgment states that a judgment in the amount of $70,000 shall be entered against the defendants. Third, the consent judgment states which party pays the costs of the action. Here the defendants have agreed to pay the costs. Note that the parties can split the costs, if they so agree.

The consent judgment is filed with the court, so the parties' settlement is a matter of public record. If the defendants fail to carry out the terms of the agreement stated in the consent judgment, Mr. Wesser can file a motion to enforce the judgment. This and other post-trial motions will be discussed in Chapter 13.

Note that the plaintiff and all the attorneys sign the consent judgment. Finally, the judge signs the consent judgment to make it effective. Judges do not have to approve consent judgments if, for instance, they find the terms unreasonable. However, most judges sign their approval unless a particular consent judgment is really outrageous.

A variation of the consent judgment is the **consent decree**. The force of the consent decree is the same as the consent judgment. It is a statement of the parties' agreement and terminates the lawsuit. The distinction is that a consent decree states that the defendant will refrain from certain activities that the government has deemed illegal.[5] Examine the sample consent decree in the Chattooga case, illustrated in the Appendix.

Stipulation of Dismissal and Release or Settlement Agreement

A second method for memorializing the parties' agreement involves two documents. First is the stipulation of dismissal, illustrated in Figure 11-7. This is a simple statement that the parties have settled all matters in controversy and that the plaintiff dismisses the action. Because the parties have settled all the issues in dispute, the dismissal is usually **with prejudice**, which means that the plaintiff is barred from filing a subsequent action based on these same claims.

As you see, the stipulation of dismissal does not reveal the terms of settlement. The terms of the settlement are usually written in either a release or a settlement agreement. Releases and settlement agreements serve the same purpose. They state that the parties have settled all their claims in the lawsuit, state the amount that the defendant agrees to pay the plaintiff, and state that the defendant is released from all future liability for the claims that are the subject of the lawsuit. Both releases and settlement agreements are basically contracts between

FIGURE 11-6   A CONSENT JUDGMENT

UNITED STATES DISTRICT COURT
MIDDLE DISTRICT OF NORTH CAROLINA
CHARLESTON DIVISION
CIVIL NO.: C-89-1293-B

Bryson Wesser,

                Plaintiff,

    -vs-

Woodall Shoals Corporation,

                Defendant,
        and
Second Ledge Stores, Incorporated,

                Defendant

CONSENT JUDGMENT

    THIS CAUSE coming on to be heard and being heard before the undersigned Judge presiding, and it appearing to the Court that all matters in controversy between the parties have been compromised and settled, and that the plaintiff has agreed to accept and the defendants have agreed to pay the sum of $70,000 in settlement of the plaintiff's claims;

    NOW, THEREFORE, IT IS ORDERED, ADJUDGED AND DECREED that the plaintiff shall have and recover judgment against the defendants in the amount of $70,000 and that the payment of said amount by the defendants shall constitute a full and final settlement and discharge of any and all claims which the plaintiff may have against the defendants arising out of the facts alleged in the Complaint or which might have been alleged therein to the same extent as if the issues in this action had been tried before a jury and the judgment had been entered upon the verdict of the jury in the amount provided herein.

    It is further ordered that the defendants shall pay the costs of this action.

    This the _____ day of _____ , 1990.

_____
United States District Judge

FIGURE 11-7 A STIPULATION OF DISMISSAL

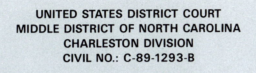

UNITED STATES DISTRICT COURT
MIDDLE DISTRICT OF NORTH CAROLINA
CHARLESTON DIVISION
CIVIL NO.: C-89-1293-B

Bryson Wesser,

Plaintiff,

-vs-

Woodall Shoals Corporation,

Defendant,

and

Second Ledge Stores, Incorporated,

Defendant

STIPULATION OF DISMISSAL

Pursuant to Rule 41(a) of the Federal Rules of Civil Procedure, Bryson Wesser, plaintiff, and Woodall Shoals Corporation and Second Ledge Stores, Incorporated, defendants, hereby stipulate and agree that this civil action is hereby dismissed, *with prejudice.*

This the _____ day of _____ , 1990.

Leigh J. Heyward
Attorney for Plaintiff
Heyward and Wilson
401 East Trade Street
Charleston, NC 28226-1114

David H. Benedict
Attorneys for Defendants
Benedict, Parker & Miller
100 Nolichucky Drive
Bristol, NC 28205-0890

CONSENTED TO:

Bryson Wesser, Plaintiff

the parties, providing that if the defendant pays a certain amount of money to the plaintiff, the plaintiff will dismiss the lawsuit and release the defendant from any future liability for the claims asserted.

Examine the sample release in Figure 11-8 and the sample settlement agreement in Figure 11-9. The release is a shorter document and basically recites the

FIGURE 11-8   A RELEASE

RELEASE OF ALL CLAIMS

For and in consideration of the sum of Seventy Thousand and no/100 Dollars ($70,000), to the undersigned paid, and other good and valuable consideration, receipt whereof is hereby acknowledged, Plaintiff agrees to release Defendants Woodall Shoals Corporation and Second Ledge Stores, Incorporated, from all claims, actions, or suits that have been brought or in the future might be known, arising from the fire at 115 Pipestem Drive, Charleston, North Carolina, on January 3, 1987.

It is understood and agreed that this settlement is the compromise of a disputed claim and that the Defendants have denied liability and the extent of damages claimed by the Plaintiff.

This agreement is a release and shall operate as a discharge of any claims Plaintiff has or may have in the future arising out of the fire on January 3, 1987.

Plaintiff and Defendants agree to file, within ten (10) days of the signing of this Release, a Stipulation of Dismissal, with prejudice, in Civil Action 89-1293-B, now pending in the United States District Court for the Middle District of North Carolina.

This Release contains the entire agreement between the parties hereto, and the terms of this Release are contractual and not a mere recital.

Witness our hands and seals this _____ day of _____ , 1990.

_____LS
Bryson Wesser, Plaintiff

Woodall Shoals Corporation

_____LS
by: William H. Cameron, President

Second Ledge Stores, Incorporated

_____LS
by: Marcia Stuart, President

STATE OF NORTH CAROLINA
COUNTY OF WATAUGA

I, _____ , a Notary Public, do hereby certify that BRYSON WESSER, WILLIAM H. CAMERON, and MARCIA STUART, appeared before me this day and executed the foregoing Release.

This the _____ day of _____ , 1990.

_____
Diane M. Miller

My commission expires: _____

FIGURE 11-9   A SETTLEMENT AGREEMENT

SETTLEMENT AGREEMENT

This action is presently calendared for trial in the United States District Court for the Middle District of North Carolina on April 2, 1990. The plaintiff, Bryson Wesser, is represented by Leigh J. Heyward. The defendants, Woodall Shoals Corporation and Second Ledge Stores, Incorporated, are represented by David H. Benedict.

The parties agree that this is an action instituted by the plaintiff when the plaintiff was burned in a fire in his home, allegedly caused by an electric blanket malfunction, said blanket having been allegedly manufactured by the defendant Woodall Shoals Corporation, and that the defendants deny all liability for said injuries.

The parties further agree that the plaintiff and defendants have agreed to compromise and settle all matters in controversy between them for and in consideration of the following payments, terms and conditions:

1. That the plaintiff agrees to accept the sum of $70,000 in full satisfaction of all claims in Civil Action 89-1293-B, now pending in the United States District Court for the Middle District of North Carolina.

2. That the defendants shall pay the sum of $70,000 to the plaintiff at the rate of $5,000 a month, beginning March 10, 1990, and on the 10th day of every month thereafter until the sum of $70,000 is paid in full.

3. That the plaintiff shall execute any and all releases prepared by the defendants' attorney which are not inconsistent with the provisions of this agreement, including the execution and filing of an appropriate dismissal with prejudice of any and all claims as the plaintiff has against the defendants in Civil Action 89-1293-B filed in the United States District Court for the Middle District of North Carolina.

4. That the defendants shall pay the sum of $17,000 to Leigh J. Heyward of Heyward and Wilson, as compensation for her fees and expenses in representing the plaintiff.

5. That the defendants shall pay the costs of this action.

This the _____ day of _____ , 1990.

_____
Witness

_____
Bryson Wesser, Plaintiff

_____
Witness

_____
Leigh J. Heyward, Attorney for the Plaintiff

WOODALL SHOALS CORPORATION and SECOND LEDGE STORES, INCORPORATED

by: _____

_____
Witness

David H. Benedict, Attorney for the Defendants

parties' agreement releasing the defendant from future liability on the claims in the lawsuit and setting forth the damages to be paid.

The settlement agreement is a longer document, different from the release in that it recites in detail the exact arrangement for payment of money to the plaintiff. Here the defendant will pay the plaintiff specified amounts of money at specified times, instead of one lump sum. Settlement agreements are often used in **structured settlements**, where the plaintiff receives periodic payments instead of a lump sum. Frequently, the first payment is large, so that the plaintiff can pay expenses that accrued prior to the settlement, such as large medical payments. The plaintiff then receives periodic payments until the entire amount of the settlement is received.

Final Remarks on Settlement Documents

As noted above, statutes in different jurisdictions, as well as local court rules, may impose specific requirements for the content of documents that state the terms of the parties' settlement. The illustrations in the text are only examples; as with any examples, you must take care to adapt them to the facts of your case and the requirements of your jurisdiction. This is especially important when there are multiple defendants who might seek contribution from one another—that is, reimbursement from other defendants who are also liable to the plaintiff. Be sure to discuss with the attorneys on your team the content of the documents you use.

ENDNOTES

1 These arbitration rules are published in Rules 601–608 of the Rules of Practice and Procedure of the United States District Court for the Middle District of North Carolina.
2 The rules are published in the Rules of the United States District Courts for the Southern and Eastern Districts of New York, Civil Rules, Appendix C.
3 *Marek v. Chesny*, 473 U.S. 1 (1985).
4 See, e.g., *Crossman v. Marciocco*, 806 F.2d 329 (1st Cir. 1986).
5 The term "consent decree" may also refer to agreements between the parties resolving lawsuits involving equitable remedies.

12 TRIAL

LITIGATION EXTRACT: The big day is finally here. After months or perhaps years of pretrial preparation, it is time for the trial. The parties are ready to present their evidence. Both jury and nonjury trials follow the same general order, and we will discuss each step in the general procedure that trials follow. Jury trials have more steps than nonjury trials, and we will include all the steps in our discussion. We will also consider the various tasks that paralegals perform during the trial.

INTRODUCTION

Trial is the culmination of all the attorney/paralegal team's preparation of the case. You have prepared your witnesses and exhibits, and now it is time to present your evidence to the finder of fact. Remember that the purpose of the trial is to determine which version of the facts is true. In a jury trial, the jury is the finder of fact; in a nonjury trial, the judge performs this function.

The atmosphere of a trial can be fast-paced, and paralegals may find themselves performing many tasks simultaneously. However, trials sometimes bog down. For instance, one party may have thousands of documents to introduce into evidence. This can be slow and laborious. While paralegals will remain busy keeping track of the thousands of exhibits, do not be surprised to look into the jury box around 2:30 in the afternoon and see some jurors fading into an afternoon nap.

Although the purpose of the trial is for the judge or jury to determine the outcome of the case, the parties may still settle the case during the trial itself. Suppose that a trial is in its third day, and the plaintiff's attorney is fairly certain that the jury is dead set against the plaintiff. The plaintiff's attorney may approach the defendant's attorney during a recess to discuss settlement. Lawsuits may even be settled while the jury is out deliberating, after all the evidence has been presented.

Paralegals perform many duties during trial. Some duties are performed only at certain stages, and others are performed throughout the trial. After we discuss the stages of the trial, we will discuss more specifically the duties that paralegals typically perform during trial.

THE COURTROOM

Before we examine procedure, let's take a minute to picture the courtroom scene. The trial is ready to begin. All the parties, attorneys, and paralegals are in their seats in the courtroom. The judge is seated at the front of the courtroom and probably looks quite imposing in a black judicial robe. The large, raised desk-like structure behind which the judge sits is called the **bench**. Throughout the trial you will hear lawyers ask if they may "approach the bench." What they are asking is permission to approach the judge to present something, often a copy of an exhibit. Sometimes both lawyers will request or be asked to approach the bench for a **bench conference**. Both attorneys will go up to the judge, and in lowered voices discuss some matter with the judge. For instance, the judge may tell the attorneys that their courtroom demeanor is unacceptable and that they should quit shouting at one another. If the discussion is going to be lengthy, the judge will usually excuse the jury until after the discussion is over.

Most courtrooms are set up with a table for each party, and the attorneys and paralegals sit behind the tables with their clients. Some state and federal local rules require that the attorneys stay behind the tables at all times unless they approach the bench or they are making opening statements or closing arguments. Other court rules allow the attorneys to stand almost anywhere in the courtroom, and you may see the attorneys get close to persons on the witness stand during questioning. The amount of dramatic embellishment is influenced by the tolerance or intolerance of the local court rules and the attitude of the judge. You may also observe some dramatic poses near the jury box at critical times. During a jury trial the jurors sit in the jury box, which is usually located on one side of the courtroom. The jury box consists of two rows of seats, surrounded by waist-high wooden panels.

TRIAL PROCEDURE

As we noted, trials typically follow a set procedure—that is, the stages usually occur in the same order. Local rules of practice may alter some parts of the standard procedure, but the order of presentation of evidence is generally uniform. We will discuss the stages from beginning to end.

Conference with the Trial Judge

This first step in the trial may vary, depending on whether the case is tried in federal court or in state court, and depending on local rules of practice. In many federal district courts, the trial judge and attorneys have already held their final pretrial conference and entered a pretrial order, as we discussed in Chapter 11. If a final pretrial conference has been held, the attorneys may meet only briefly with the judge to discuss whether further settlement possibilities have arisen since that time. Parties may have added or lost witnesses, and this may be a subject of discussion. The content of the conference just before the trial begins depends in large part on the trial judge's personal preferences, as does the manner in which the conference is conducted. The attorneys may simply have a casual conversation with the judge in chambers. In other cases, a judge may have the court reporter record the conference and make it a part of the trial transcript.

There may be even more variation in the content and procedure for the conference just before trial when the lawsuit is tried in state court, depending on state and local rules of practice and on the personal preferences of state court judges. In fairly routine lawsuits tried in state courts, there may be no formal pretrial conference of the sort discussed in Chapter 11. State and local rules sometimes give the judge the authority to dispense with the pretrial conference. Some state and local rules provide that the attorneys meet and prepare a pretrial order and submit it, without necessarily meeting with the judge before trial.

If no formal pretrial conference has been held, the attorneys may discuss for the first time with the judge the possibility of settlement. The parties may discuss with the judge the evidence they will present. The attorneys may also ask the judge to rule before the trial on the admission of evidence, when the attorneys contend that certain evidence would be prejudicial or otherwise inadmissible. These motions before trial on the admission of evidence are called **motions in limine**. As in formal pretrial conferences, the objective is to establish any issues or facts that are not in dispute and to rule on appropriate motions to make the trial smoother.

Jury Selection (Voir Dire)

Seated in the courtroom is a group of perhaps 40 persons, who constitute the **jury panel**: the pool of prospective jurors. These are adults residing in the jurisdiction, and their names have been chosen at random for jury duty. From them the attorneys pick the persons to serve as the jury. This process of selecting jurors is called **voir dire**.

The number of jurors may vary, depending on whether the trial is in state court or federal court and on the local rules of practice. For instance, each district of a federal court in a state is usually given the choice of how many jurors to require in a civil trial. In some states the districts have different requirements. Twelve jurors is the number traditionally required, but many districts require only six jurors now. One or two alternate jurors are usually picked, in case jury members become ill or have to leave the trial for some other important reason.

The procedure for voir dire also differs according to whether the trial is in state court or federal court, and according to the local rules of practice. Some judges even have their own particular method for conducting voir dire. Regardless of the exact procedure used, the purpose of voir dire is the same—to select a jury that the attorneys (often with the aid of paralegals) think will be most receptive to their client's version of the facts.

To begin voir dire, the clerk assisting the judge calls out twelve names, and these persons take a seat in the jury box. Then each prospective juror in the jury box is asked a series of questions designed to elicit basic information about the juror and often his or her views on certain pertinent subjects. Recall from our discussion of jury investigation in Chapter 10 that at this point you may know a great deal about the jurors, or you may know nothing at all, depending largely upon what local court rules allow. Recall that some local rules do not allow the clerk of court even to release the names of the persons on jury duty until the beginning of that session of court.

In voir dire the questions may be asked by either the judge or the attorneys, again depending on local rules. Some federal court local rules specifically state that the judge asks the questions. When the judge asks the questions, the attorneys submit to the judge before trial the questions they would like asked. Another method for voir dire is that the judge asks some preliminary questions and then the attorneys are allowed to ask follow-up questions. In some courts the attorneys ask all the questions, and the judge takes very little part in voir dire. It is important to know the local rules so that the attorney/paralegal team can prepare its questions well in advance.

Questions include general background questions such as how long persons have lived at their present address; whether they have children and if so, some general questions about the children; what a person's occupation is and how long the person has worked at a particular place; whether the persons know any of the parties or attorneys; and perhaps whether a person has hobbies or belongs to any organizations. The questions may be much more specific, depending on the nature of the case and the questions the judge allows. For instance, in the Wesser case it would be important to know whether any prospective juror has ever been injured in a fire. A person injured in a fire may be very sympathetic to Mr. Wesser and prejudiced against the defendants.

After the questions are asked to the twelve persons in the jury box, each party's attorney has the opportunity to request that particular persons not serve on the jury. This is known as exercising a **challenge**. There are two types of challenges. First is the **peremptory challenge**, which gives the attorney the right to excuse a juror without stating the reason. The second type of challenge is the **challenge for cause**, where the attorney must state the reason for not wanting the person on the jury. Common bases for challenges for cause are that a person is related to one of the parties, is a friend of one of the attorneys, or has stated a prejudice against one of the parties. The judge must approve the dismissal of a prospective juror for cause. If one attorney challenges a person for cause, and the other attorney opposes the challenge, the judge decides whether the person should be excused for cause. If the judge rules against the challenge for cause, the moving attorney may still exercise a peremptory challenge.

Each party may exercise only a certain number of peremptory challenges. The number of peremptory challenges allowed differs among courts, but usually in federal court each party is allowed three peremptory challenges in civil cases.[1] The number of challenges for cause is generally unlimited. However, most attorneys do not challenge for cause unless absolutely necessary, because of the risk of antagonizing other members of the jury.

Assume that the attorneys are selecting twelve jurors, and five persons are excused from the first twelve seated in the jury box. Five more names are called, and the process is repeated for these five persons. If two of these five are excused, then two more names are called, and the process is repeated for these two. Eventually twelve persons and one or two alternates are selected. The jury is then sworn in, and the trial proceeds.

During voir dire the attorney and paralegal keep a chart of the persons in the jury box. See Figure 12-1 for a sample chart. When a person is excused, they strike that person's name and insert the name of the next person called who sits in that chair. Paralegals help attorneys keep track of the prospective jurors and offer suggestions when they think a juror should be excused. For instance, an attorney may be busy asking questions and fail to notice antagonistic conduct by a prospective juror, such as icy stares at the attorney or other body language that shows that the prospective juror does not like the attorney.

When a trial receives a great deal of media coverage, the judge will take steps to shield the jury from media exposure. If a trial is particularly sensational or for some reason the judge feels that someone might try to tamper with (unduly influence) the jury, the judge will likewise take steps to shield the jury. The judge may **sequester** the jury—that is, require that they stay at a hotel during the trial rather than returning home at night. This protects members of the jury from hearing views about the ongoing trial on the news or having persons talk to them about the case. Even if a jury is not sequestered, the judge will admonish members not to discuss the case outside the courtroom. The jury should consider only what it hears at trial and should ignore what persons outside the courtroom think about the case.

Opening Statements

Throughout the remainder of our discussion of the trial, we will assume that there are only two parties—plaintiff and defendant. Although many lawsuits do involve more than two parties, our focus here is on understanding the usual trial procedure.

After the jury is sworn in, the attorney for the plaintiff makes an opening statement. The defendant's attorney then makes an opening statement, although the defendant is usually given the option of reserving the opening statement until just before the defendant presents evidence. In **opening statements** the attorneys talk to the jury, explaining what the case is about. The general purpose of the opening statement for both the plaintiff and defendant is the same, but we will speak in terms of the plaintiff for simplicity's sake. The purpose of the opening statement is to give a comprehensive but succinct account of the evidence that the plaintiff will present. The attorney interweaves a preview of the evidence with an explanation of the points the plaintiff will prove. The attorney seeks to implant in the jurors' minds the plaintiff's version of the facts.

The first impression made by opening statements is crucial. If jurors believe the plaintiff's version of the facts and find the defendant's attorney's opening statement unconvincing, the jurors are likely to filter their view of the evidence

FIGURE 12-1 SAMPLE CHART OF JURORS

Bryan Wasser

vs.

Woodale Shade Corporation and
Second Ridge Stores, Incorporated

JURY

File No. *C-89-1293-B*

BACK ROW

1 Carla Handshaw	2 James Bierksha	3 Harry Poplin Jim Chen	4 Greg Hardie	5 Rachel Fowler Steve Haar	6 Anita Overy
7 Teresa Garcia Elsa Mitlman	8 Esther Flanagan Carol Barbee	9	10 Florence Angelo	11 Kevin O'Neill	12 Angela Klaze

FRONT ROW

CHALLENGES

For Cause	0
Plaintiff	2
Defendant	1

during the trial in favor of the plaintiff. Note that opening statements are not arguments. Arguments are reserved for closing. Most attorneys use a straight-forward, sincere presentation, without the bombastic flourishes of raising their voices and waving their fists. In general, attorneys strive to state the facts clearly and forcefully, explain who the parties are and try to make their client sympathetic, and develop the theory of the case. Most attorneys avoid overstating their case. If they promise evidence but then fail to deliver, the jury remembers the failure and probably will conclude that the attorney failed to prove the client's case.

Presentation of the Plaintiff's Case

Now it is time to present the evidence that you and the attorneys on your team worked so hard to gather. We will include our overview of the procedure for present-ing evidence in the discussion of the plaintiff's case, but the procedure is the same for defendants. A rundown on the duties of paralegals throughout the trial will conclude the chapter.

The Plaintiff's Burden of Proof. Throughout our trial preparation we have discussed the necessity of proving the essential elements of each claim for relief. This is precisely what the plaintiff must now do at trial. The plaintiff has the **burden of proof**. In a civil lawsuit the plaintiff's burden of proof is to present evidence sufficient to prove by the "preponderance of the evidence" the facts necessary to support the essential elements of the plaintiff's claims for relief.[2] For instance, in the Wesser case, one claim for relief is breach of express warranty by the defendant Woodall Shoals. Leigh Heyward must present evidence to con-vince the jury by the "preponderance of the evidence" that Woodall Shoals made an express warranty that the electric blanket would remain free of electrical and mechanical defects for a certain period of time and that the fire occurred within the warranted period; that the blanket contained electrical and mechanical defects that caused it to ignite; and that this breach of express warranty caused the injuries and property damage sustained by Mr. Wesser.

Note that proving the facts by the preponderance of the evidence does not require that there be no doubt whatsoever in the jurors' minds that Mr. Wesser has established the essential elements of his claims. It means that Mr. Wesser must establish that it is more probable than not that Woodall Shoals breached the ex-press warranty, and this caused Mr. Wesser's injuries and property damage. Mr. Wesser's evidence must outweigh Woodall Shoals' evidence that there was no breach of express warranty that caused Mr. Wesser's injuries and property damage.

Presentation of Evidence. The two primary means of presenting evidence are the testimony of witnesses and the submission of exhibits—that is, documentary evidence. Remember from our discussion of discovery that the parties may admit to certain facts that are not in dispute. If the parties have stipulated to uncon-tested facts, these facts must be recited to the jury. The attorney usually does this. The facts may be read into the record at the beginning of the presentation of evidence or later, if the facts fit in better later in the trial. The bulk of the evidence, however, is presented by witness testimony or the presentation of documentary evidence.

Presentation of Witnesses. Leigh Heyward has called Mr. Wesser to the stand as her first witness. Mr. Wesser is sworn in. Ms. Heyward asks Mr. Wesser questions. This is known as **direct examination**—that is, examination of the witness by the attorney who called the witness. Ms. Heyward asks Mr. Wesser a series of questions designed to show what happened. These address basic facts such as where and when he bought the electric blanket, who manufactured the blanket, and how Mr. Wesser took care of the blanket.

Ms. Heyward will use a series of open-ended questions, such as "What happened after you went to bed on January 3, 1987?" On direct examination attorneys are not supposed to use **leading questions**—that is, questions that suggest that there is only one true answer to the question. For instance, the question "You never read the instructions for operating the blanket, did you?" is leading, because it seems to ask the witness simply to confirm what the attorney has said. Rule 611 of the Federal Rules of Evidence provides that attorneys should ask leading questions only when the witness is hostile. This occurs when attorneys call the other party's witnesses to the stand.

POINTER: The Federal Rules of Evidence do not set out an exact pattern to follow for presentation of evidence. Rather, FRE 611(a) states that the court "shall exercise reasonable control over the mode and order of interrogating witnesses and presenting evidence so as to (1) make the interrogation and presentation effective for the ascertainment of the truth, (2) avoid needless consumpton of time, and (3) protect witnesses from harassment or undue embarrassment." Thus presentation of evidence commonly follows an accepted pattern, but the court can intervene if an attorney presents an endless string of witnesses who all say the same thing, or if the attorney harasses a witness. Think of the judge's role as that of the director of a Shakespearean play, giving instructions not about the *order* in which lines are delivered, but about the *manner* in which they are delivered.

During Mr. Wesser's testimony, Ms. Heyward will also introduce exhibits such as the written warranty, medical bills, and home repair bills. The method for entering these documents as exhibits is discussed below.

After Mr. Wesser has answered all Ms. Heyward's questions, Mr. Benedict is given the opportunity to ask questions. This is **cross-examination**, when the defendant's attorney asks questions of the witnesses called by the plaintiff. Of course, the plaintiff's attorney also gets to cross-examine the defendant's witnesses.

The purpose of cross-examination is to undermine the witness's testimony. The defense attorney will try to show that Mr. Wesser really is not so sure of the facts he stated on direct examination. Cross-examination is the time for impeachment. If Mr. Wesser has made prior statements inconsistent with his testimony, Mr. Benedict will bring out these inconsistencies. This is also the time for impeachment by showing bias, if appropriate.

On cross-examination, the attorney does ask leading questions. In fact, the attorney tries to fashion the questions in such a way that the witness has to give a yes or no answer without the opportunity to explain or qualify the answer. Generally attorneys do not ask on cross-examination any questions to which they do not already know the answer. Taking the chance with the unknown may result in damaging testimony that hurts their case.

After Mr. Benedict has completed cross-examination, Ms. Heyward may ask additional questions, if she wishes. This is known as **redirect examination**. Redirect examination is generally limited to matters raised during cross-examination. The purpose of redirect is to allow Mr. Wesser to explain certain points so as to "rehabilitate" his testimony—that is, counteract any negative impressions that may have been created during cross-examination.

The same procedure of direct examination, cross-examination, and redirect examination is used for all the remainder of Ms. Heyward's witnesses, including expert witnesses. Recall from our discussion of discovery that when a witness is unavailable, the witness's deposition may be presented at trial. The general procedure is for a person to take the witness stand and read the answers given in the deposition, in response to the attorney's questions. Paralegals sometimes perform this task.

Presentation of Documentary Evidence. Most trials involve the presentation of numerous documents, and some trials involve as many as hundreds or thousands. One important task of paralegals at trial is to keep the documents in order so that the proper document will be ready when the attorney is ready to introduce it into evidence. The last thing the attorney/paralegal team wants to do at trial is sift through a pile of papers to find the next exhibit, while the jury stares in amazement at their disheveled table.

There is a generally accepted procedure for introducing documents into evidence. Before going through the procedure, you should understand that every document presented by every party has to be identified. For example, the plaintiff's first exhibit may be labeled P-1 and the defendant's third exhibit is labeled D-3. Sometimes a party's exhibits may be identified by letters; for instance, the plaintiff's first exhibit may be labeled Exhibit A. However, when more than 26 exhibits are involved, the use of letters may get confusing.

Sometimes all the exhibits are labeled before the trial begins. For example, the attorneys may have the exhibits labeled during the pretrial conference. This can make presentation of numerous documents proceed more smoothly.

Turning now to the procedure for introducing exhibits, the attorneys first lay the foundation for relevance. For instance, Ms. Heyward asks Mr. Wesser when and where he purchased the electric blanket. If the parties have already stipulated that the receipt is authentic, Ms. Heyward is ready to introduce the receipt into evidence. Assume that this is the first exhibit she introduces and that the exhibits were not labeled before trial. Ms. Heyward says that she would like to have the receipt marked as Exhibit P-1. She then walks to the clerk who marks the exhibit as P-1. Ms. Heyward gives a copy of the exhibit to Mr. Benedict and, after asking for permission to approach the bench, gives a copy to the judge.

At this point, if authenticity has not been stipulated, Ms. Heyward shows Mr. Wesser the receipt and asks him to identify it. Assume that at the end of the presentation of all the plaintiff's evidence, Ms. Heyward has presented 45 exhibits. She requests that the judge enter Exhibits P-1 through P-45 into evidence.

If there are no objections to entry of the exhibits, the judge states that Exhibits P-1 through P-45 are entered into evidence, and the jury takes the exhibits with it for its deliberations at the conclusion of the presentation of all the evidence.

Objections to Evidence. Before discussing the next step in the trial, it will be useful to examine how the court handles objections to the introduction of evidence. An attorney may object to testimony that a witness is going to give or to the entry of certain exhibits into evidence.

In regard to testimony, assume that Ms. Heyward has asked Mr. Wesser what, in his opinion, was the cause of the fire. Before Mr. Wesser answers the question, Mr. Benedict says, ''I object.'' The judge then allows Mr. Benedict to state why he objects. Assume that he says that Ms. Heyward has not laid a sufficient foundation to show that Mr. Wesser had personal knowledge of the cause of the fire. After Mr. Benedict explains the basis for his objection, Ms. Heyward is given the opportunity to explain how she has laid a proper foundation. The judge then decides whether Mr. Wesser may answer the question.

In regard to exhibits, assume that Mr. Benedict objects to the entry of Exhibits 10 and 26 into evidence. Mr. Benedict explains the grounds for his objections, and Ms. Heyward explains why the exhibits should be entered into evidence. For instance, Ms. Heyward may argue that the evidence fits an exception to the hearsay rule. The judge then rules on whether the exhibits may be entered into evidence. Assume that the judge allows both exhibits to be entered. Mr. Benedict has to accept the judge's ruling for now and proceed with the trial. If he thinks the judge erred in allowing the exhibits into evidence, he may identify this as a ground for appeal.

Sometimes the debate over the admissibility of evidence can be lengthy. If the debate promises to be lengthy or will contain statements that should not be heard by the jury, the judge will send the jury out of the courtroom while the attorneys present their arguments.

Motion for Directed Verdict. Ms. Heyward has presented all the plaintiff's evidence. She states that the plaintiff rests. This means that the plaintiff rests his case, having presented all his evidence.

At this point Mr. Benedict makes a motion for a **directed verdict**. A directed verdict is granted when a party has not presented sufficient evidence to establish a **prima facie** case. Mr. Wesser has established a prima facie case if he has presented sufficient evidence to allow the jury to rule in his favor. Assume that because he had lost the receipt and had no other evidence to establish the place of purchase, Mr. Wesser did not establish that he bought the blanket at Second Ledge Stores. A directed verdict in favor of Second Ledge might be appropriate, since there may be insufficient evidence for the jury to find that the blanket was purchased at Second Ledge.

The effect of a directed verdict is to take the decision away from the jury. If the judge decides that there is not sufficient evidence for the jury to find that Mr. Wesser bought the blanket at Second Ledge, then the judge enters a verdict in favor of Second Ledge. If the judge denies the motion for a directed verdict, the trial proceeds.

FRCivP 50(a) allows either the plaintiff or defendant to move for a directed verdict at the close of the other party's evidence. FRCivP 50(a) requires that the moving party specifically state the grounds for the motion. Attorneys usually make a motion for a directed verdict even when they are relatively sure that the judge will deny the motion. This is because they want to preserve the denial as a possible ground for appeal.[3]

Presentation of Defendant's Case

The procedure for presenting the defendant's evidence is the same as the procedure for the plaintiff. The defendant presents witnesses, who undergo direct examination, cross-examination, and redirect examination. The defendant's attorney presents documents and introduces them as exhibits, following the same procedure described for the plaintiff.

Although the defendant uses the same procedure as the plaintiff, the defendant has some different considerations in presenting evidence. In the Wesser case, Mr. Benedict's goal is to show that the defendants' version of the facts is true. Although he seeks to point out the weaknesses in the plaintiff's case, Mr. Benedict must primarily emphasize the strengths of the defendants' case. If Mr. Benedict appears too defensive, the jury may assume that he has a weak case.

A defendant who has asserted a counterclaim has different concerns. Remember that a counterclaim is like a complaint, only it is directed against the plaintiff. Because the defendant seeks to establish a claim against the plaintiff, the defendant has the burden to present a prima facie case against the plaintiff. Thus the defendant's requirements in a counterclaim are like those discussed earlier for plaintiffs.

After Mr. Benedict has presented all his witnesses and introduced all his exhibits, he makes a motion that his exhibits be entered into evidence, just as Ms. Heyward did. Mr. Benedict then rests the defendants' case.

Rebuttal Evidence

After the defense has rested, the plaintiff is allowed to present rebuttal evidence. Rebuttal evidence should be carefully planned so that it specifically rebuts points raised by the defendant. This is not an opportunity for the plaintiff to present additional general evidence. The testimony should be tailored to rebut specific points and is generally not lengthy. Unduly lengthy rebuttal evidence may aggravate the jury or the judge, because they are likely to be restless by now.

Motions at the Close of the Evidence

After all the evidence is presented, either or both parties may move for a directed verdict. Mr. Benedict renews the defendants' previous motion for a directed verdict. Ms. Heyward moves for a directed verdict in favor of the plaintiff. As noted earlier, the judge decides whether there is sufficient evidence for the case to go to the jury.

Closing Arguments

Closing argument is a summary of the evidence presented in a manner that persuades the jury that your client's version of the facts is true. In closing arguments, the attorneys try to persuade the jury to rule in their client's favor. Different attorneys have different styles of delivery for their closing arguments. Some attorneys give a casual, forthright presentation, as if they were conversing with friends. Other attorneys try to wax eloquent, giving vent to their best dramatic qualities. Often the style of the presentation depends on the nature of the case. An attorney may be dramatic and display more emotion in talking about the severe injuries a small child suffered than in recounting three witnesses' statements about whether a stoplight was red or green.

Attorneys are not allowed to go beyond the evidence presented at trial in making their closing arguments. Rather, they recap the evidence, summarizing what the witnesses said and what the exhibits show. The attorneys weave their summary in with their theory of the case. Even as the trial winds down, the attorneys are still trying to show that their clients have established the essential elements of their claims.

The plaintiff's attorney generally gives the first closing argument. The defendant's attorney then presents a closing argument, followed by a brief opportunity for rebuttal. The length of the closing argument varies from case to case, but the judge usually tells the attorneys beforehand if there is a limit on the amount of time allowed for closing arguments.

Jury Instructions

The jury is ready to perform its duty to determine the facts. First it must resolve the disputes concerning the facts and then it must apply the applicable law.

The purpose of jury instructions is for the judge to explain what law the jury must apply. The judge gives the instructions after the completion of closing arguments. However, the judge and attorneys discuss the jury instructions before closing arguments. In fact, some judges require that attorneys submit in writing before trial any special instructions they wish the judge to give. FRCivP 51 provides that the attorneys may submit their written requests for instructions at the close of evidence or at an earlier time during the trial, as the judge directs.

An attorney may object to some instructions that the other attorney submits. The judge listens to the arguments of the attorneys, and then decides whether to include the requested information. This process is completed before closing arguments and generally takes place in the judge's chambers, outside the hearing of the jury.

Generally judges have written instructions, which they read to the jury. Judges often base their instructions largely on pattern jury instructions. Because the failure to instruct the jury properly is ground for appeal, states have developed standard pattern jury instructions for judges to use. These instructions explain the applicable law and reduce the chance that the judge will omit anything essential. Attorneys may submit refinements of the pattern instructions, tailoring the instructions to their client's favor, without altering the substance of the law.

The judge's instructions cover procedural and substantive matters. The procedural matters include an explanation of burden of proof, including the meaning of preponderance of the evidence. The judge also explains the effect of impeachment evidence and addresses other procedural issues. The explanation of substantive matters is an explanation of the law that applies. Here the judge explains the essential elements that the plaintiff must establish. The judge also instructs the jury on the effect of affirmative defenses, such as contributory negligence, and the effect of comparative negligence.

Jury Deliberation and Verdict

The jury retires to the jury room to begin its deliberations. During deliberations, the jury may have additional questions to submit to the court, usually to clarify the explanation of a point of law. The jury sends out the written questions to the judge, who considers the questions with the attorneys and returns answers to the jury.

When the jury has reached its conclusions, the verdict is delivered in writing to the judge, who reads it aloud in open court. There are two types of verdicts—general verdicts and special verdicts. In a **general verdict** the jury reports only which party wins and the amount of damages to which the prevailing party is entitled. In a **special verdict** the jury must answer specific written questions for each issue of fact. The judge submits the written questions in whatever form the judge deems appropriate, in accordance with FRCivP 49.

FRCivP 49 also permits general verdicts accompanied by answers to interrogatories. The jury returns a general verdict and answers the interrogatories, which require it to state its conclusions about certain issues of fact. If the answers to the interrogatories are not consistent with the verdict, the judge may order the jury to return to the jury room and deliberate further, or the judge may order a new trial.

Entry of Judgment

Assume that the jury in the Wesser case returned a verdict in favor of Mr. Wesser, directing that Woodall Shoals and Second Ledge pay damages in the amount of $175,000. The judge states in open court that judgment is entered in favor of the plaintiff in the amount of $175,000. The next step is the preparation and filing of a written judgment. We will discuss this subject in detail in Chapter 13. For now, note that the attorney for the prevailing party usually prepares a judgment and then submits it to opposing counsel to review. The judgment is then given to the judge to sign, and it becomes part of the written record, along with the pleadings and the other documents in the court file.

The judgment must be legally sufficient, as discussed in Chapter 13. Otherwise, parts of the judgment may be grounds for appeal. Therefore judgments may be many pages long.

Although the trial is over, the litigation process may go on for some time. The prevailing party is ready to go home and relax. However, the losing party may file several types of post-trial motions and may take the case up on appeal. The post-trial motions and appeal procedure are discussed in Chapter 13.

Differences Between Jury and Nonjury Trials

In nonjury trials, the judge is the finder of facts. Most of the differences between jury and nonjury trials are obvious. For instance, in a nonjury trial, certain steps in the trial process such as voir dire and jury instructions are not necessary.

The logistics of nonjury trials are less complicated in some respects. For instance, the jury does not have to be removed from the courtroom while the attorneys make lengthy arguments about the admission of evidence. However, the procedure for presenting evidence is the same as in jury trials, and the attorneys give opening and closing statements in order to persuade the judge of their client's version of the facts.

There are some procedural differences. For instance, at the close of the plaintiff's evidence, the defendant's attorney does not move for a directed verdict. In nonjury trials, the defendant's attorney moves for an involuntary dismissal, pursuant to FRCivP 41(b). To prevail on a motion for involuntary dismissal, the defendant must show that the plaintiff "has shown no right to relief" (FRCivP 41(b)). If the judge grants the motion for involuntary dismissal, judgment is entered against the plaintiff. If the motion is denied, the trial continues with the presentation of the defendant's evidence.

PARALEGAL DUTIES AT TRIAL

We have discussed some of the tasks that paralegals perform at specific stages of the trial, such as voir dire. However, there are certain duties that paralegals perform throughout trial.

Paralegals are invaluable at trial. Often paralegals are at least as familiar with the case as the attorneys are. In fact, you may be more familiar with the content of documents, such as depositions, because you recently reviewed the documents and summarized them. We will discuss some of the tasks that paralegals perform throughout the trial. The aim of paralegals is to assist the attorneys to give a smooth presentation of evidence and keep track of the evidence presented at trial.

Witnesses

Paralegals should keep a running log of the witnesses who testify for each party. You must pay particular attention to the order of witnesses that your side is going to present. As a paralegal, you may even be responsible for ensuring that the witnesses are present in the courtroom when they are needed.

In pretrial preparation paralegals give the witnesses a general indication of what time they will need to be present at trial. During the trial paralegals monitor the progress of the trial and inform witnesses of the exact time they must be present at the courtroom. Of course, you cannot calculate this to the minute, but you need to give the witness a definite time to arrive. Allow some lead time for the witness to find a parking place and get to the courtroom. It never hurts to give witnesses an arrival time 30 minutes before you expect to need them.

Paralegals take notes of the questions that the attorneys ask and the answers that witnesses give. You may keep an outline of the questions that the attorney plans to ask each witness, and let the attorney know if any questions are skipped. Paralegals can help pinpoint the inconsistencies on which witnesses may be impeached. For instance, a witness may testify about an incident, and you recall that the account of the incident was different in the witness's deposition. You can locate the page in the deposition and bring it to the attorney's attention so that the witness can be impeached.

In some trials the court reporter prepares a daily transcript of the trial testimony. This is expensive, however, so it is not always done. When there is no daily transcript, paralegals may prepare digests of the day's testimony for the attorney/paralegal team to review before the next day's testimony. Follow the same guidelines you used for digesting depositions, especially keeping the digest limited to the most important points. You may find inconsistencies in a witness's testimony as you prepare the digest, and you can bring these to the attorney's attention.

Exhibits

Paralegals can render invaluable help with document control during the trial. As we noted, it looks bad for an attorney to refer authoritatively to a document and then take five minutes plowing through a pile of papers to find it. Paralegals can keep the exhibits in order for the attorneys and be prepared to hand the exhibits to the attorneys when they need them. For instance, when Ms. Heyward is ready to present the written warranty that came with the blanket, a paralegal will have the copies ready for her, so she can present a copy to Mr. Benedict and to the judge.

 POINTER: As we noted in our discussion of pretrial preparation, be sure that you bring enough copies of each exhibit and perhaps one or two extra copies. Check well before trial to ensure that you have sufficient copies.

Paralegals should keep a list of the exhibits that the parties have introduced. List the number assigned to the exhibit and a short description of the document. It is important too to check off each document as it is received into evidence. When the judge says that Exhibits 1–20 are admitted into evidence, mark it on your list of exhibits. At the end of your party's presentation of evidence, double-check your list to be sure that all your exhibits have been admitted into evidence. If some exhibits were not admitted, bring this to the attorney's attention, so that the attorney can move that the exhibits be admitted.

At the end of each day, paralegals should be sure that they have a complete set of exhibits—both their own and their opponent's. Be sure that all the exhibits are identified by the number assigned.

Trial Notes

Paralegals keep notes of the questions asked and answers given by witnesses. Some persons take notes by drawing a vertical line down the middle of a legal pad and writing the questions on the left half and the answers on the right half. There are other ways to take notes; just be sure that your notes are legible. Check with the attorneys on your team to see if there is a certain method they prefer.

Observations

Often at the end of each trial day, the attorney/paralegal team meets to discuss the events of the day. Paralegals share their observations about the trial. This may include observations about testimony or about jurors' reactions to certain evidence. Did a juror sleep for an hour? Did any jurors exhibit facial expressions that let you know what they were thinking? Did jurors roll their eyes and sigh when the other side's witnesses gave boring, repetitive testimony? Did the judge turn beet red when one of the attorneys repeatedly objected to certain evidence? The attorneys may not observe these things, because they are busy thinking of the next question to ask. Paralegals' observations can be extremely helpful.

Trials can be tense, but they can also be fun. After months of preparation, it is rewarding to pull together your hard work. Remember that trials are usually fast-paced and are often full of surprises. Be ready to respond quickly to the surprise turns that the trial takes.

Finally, here are a few practical tips. Take extra supplies to the courtroom: paper clips, staples, pens, and legal pads. Observe how the attorneys on your team react to trials. Some are very tense, but others are very relaxed and would rather try a case than take a vacation. Be ready to deal with these different types of personalities. Trials can make for very long days. At lunch time you may have to run to the office or meet with witnesses. You may find that you have no time to eat, so you may want to put some fruit or other snacks in your briefcase. Some attorneys never leave home without granola bars in their briefcases. Just remember to take out the bananas you have not eaten by the end of trial!

ENDNOTES

1 28 U.S.C. §1870.

2 Preponderance of the evidence is not the only standard of proof that is used in civil litigation. However, it is the most common. Another standard of proof sometimes used is ''clear and convincing evidence.'' This is a higher standard to prove, but not as demanding as the standard used in criminal trials—proof beyond a reasonable doubt.

3 In addition, making a motion for a directed verdict is a prerequisite for making a motion for a judgment notwithstanding the verdict, which is discussed in Chapter 13.

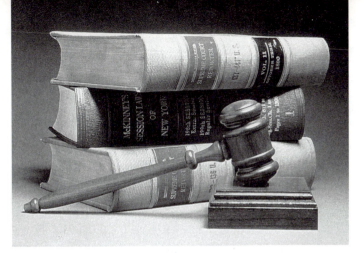

13 POST-TRIAL PROCEDURES AND APPEALS

 LITIGATION EXTRACT: Assume that in the Wesser case the jury returned a verdict in favor of Mr. Wesser in the amount of $100,000. If you are the paralegal working with Ms. Heyward, you are delighted because your client has won. However, your work is not over. After the judgment is entered against the defendants, the plaintiff must collect on the judgment. We will discuss the procedure for collecting judgments. If you are the paralegal working with Mr. Benedict, you are obviously not so delighted, because the verdict is unfavorable to your clients. Your work is definitely not over. Your attorney/paralegal team has to decide whether to file further motions. We will discuss two post-verdict motions—motion for judgment notwithstanding the verdict (JNOV) and motion for a new trial. Your team also has to decide whether to appeal the case to the appellate court. We will discuss considerations in determining whether an appeal is worthwhile and the procedure for taking an appeal.

POST-VERDICT MOTIONS

The two post-verdict motions most commonly filed are the motion for judgment notwithstanding the verdict (JNOV) and motion for a new trial. You may file either or both motions. Many attorneys file both motions, so that if the motion for JNOV is denied, all is not lost. The moving party may still prevail on the motion for a new trial.

 POINTER: Most post-verdict motions are filed by the party against whom judgment is entered at trial. If your client prevails at trial, you will likely file post-verdict motions only if your client is extremely unhappy with the amount of the verdict.

Motion for Judgment Notwithstanding the Verdict

You may wonder what the letters JNOV stand for. The term ''notwithstanding the verdict'' translates to *non obstante veredicto* in Latin. Thus judgment *non obstante veredicto* is shortened to JNOV.

FRCivP 50(b) addresses motions for judgment notwithstanding the verdict. As a prerequisite to making a motion for JNOV, a party must move for a directed verdict at the close of all evidence, as we discussed in Chapter 12. FRCivP 50(b) requires that a motion for JNOV be filed within 10 days after entry of judgment. The motion for JNOV asks the judge to set aside the jury's verdict on the ground that there was insufficient evidence for the jury to reach its verdict.

A judge does not grant a motion for JNOV simply because she or he disagrees with the jury's interpretation of the facts presented at trial or its evaluation of a witness's credibility. Rather, the judge determines whether there is sufficient evidence to support the jury's verdict. The judge considers the evidence in the light most favorable to the party against whom the motion is made. It is difficult to state an exact formula that judges use to determine when there is sufficient evidence to support the jury's verdict. The attorney/paralegal team needs to research case law in the appropriate state or circuit for an explanation of the exact standard that judges have used.

Motion for a New Trial

Motions for new trials are made and granted more frequently than are motions for JNOV. This is because the grounds to support a motion for a new trial are much broader. FRCivP 59 does not enumerate specific grounds for granting a motion for a new trial. Rather, it provides that new trials may be granted for the reasons that courts have used before to grant new trials. This broad statement gives judges much latitude.

The concept behind FRCivP 59 is that a judge should grant a new trial when necessary to prevent injustice. A few examples of grounds for granting new trials will help you understand this concept. One ground for granting a new trial is that damages awarded are too large or too small. Suppose that Mr. Wesser had not been home at the time of the fire and therefore had not been injured. Suppose too that at trial he established that the repairs to his home cost $40,000. If the jury found the defendants liable but returned a verdict for only $5,000, the judge might find the verdict excessively low and grant a new trial on the issue of damages. Judges are allowed to grant new trials on certain limited issues, such as damages, if they deem it appropriate.

Other grounds for granting new trials include misconduct by the attorneys during trial, obvious failure of the jury to follow the judge's instructions, and newly discovered evidence—that is, important evidence that was not known at the time of trial. With such a wide range of grounds available, it is important to research the case law in the appropriate jurisdiction to identify the instances in which new trials have been held to be justified.

Harmless Error. One important concept is that even if an error was made at trial, it may not be ground for a new trial. Many errors may occur at trial, such as the admission of hearsay that does not fit into an exception to the hearsay rule. However, if the error is not serious, it is not ground for a new trial. This is the important concept known as **harmless error**. FRCivP 61 addresses harmless error and provides that an error is not a ground for a new trial or for otherwise disturbing the verdict ''unless refusal to take such action appears to the court inconsistent with substantial justice.'' FRCivP 61 further states that at every stage of the proceeding the court ''must disregard any error or defect in the proceeding which does not affect the substantial rights of the parties.''

The terms used in FRCivP 61 are subject to interpretation, so again it is important to research the case law in the appropriate jurisdiction. Even if a similar error in a similar case was found to be prejudicial error, it may be harmless error in your case, when it is considered in the context of everything that transpired at trial. Although case law is helpful, experience in trying cases before a particular judge is probably a better indicator of what the judge might consider harmless error. Thus the attorney/paralegal team must rely on experience in addition to research.

Procedure for Motion for a New Trial. A motion for a new trial must be filed no later than 10 days after entry of judgment. FRCivP 59(c) sets strict time limits for the submission of affidavits in support of the motion; you should review that section.

FRCivP 59(d) allows the court on its own initiative to order a new trial. Thus the judge may decide to order a new trial even if none of the parties requested it. The grounds for the court granting a new trial on its own initiative include any grounds for which the court could grant a new trial when a party files a motion for a new trial.

Finally, it is important to understand that a motion for a new trial is not the same as appealing the case. If a party wins an appeal, the party gets a new trial and thus the outcome is the same as a FRCivP 59 motion for a new trial. However, as discussed below, an appeal is taken to a higher court—that is, an appellate court—to decide whether prejudicial errors occurred at trial. In contrast, the motion for a new trial under FRCivP 59 requests that the trial judge make such a determination. This is significant because an appellate court is often required to grant considerable deference to a decision at trial.

JUDGMENTS

A judgment is the court's final decision that resolves all matters in dispute among the parties to the litigation. The judgment states the parties' rights and liabilities—for example, that the defendants in the Wesser case are liable to Mr. Wesser in the amount of $100,000. We will address three broad topics about judgments: how a judgment is drafted, how a judgment becomes effective, and how a judgment is enforced. The general guidelines are set forth in FRCivP 58, which is shown in Figure 13-1.

FIGURE 13-1   GUIDELINES FOR ENTRY OF JUDGMENT

Rule 58.   ENTRY OF JUDGMENT

Subject to the provisions of Rule 54(b): (1) upon a general verdict of a jury, or upon a decision by the court that a party shall recover only a sum certain or costs or that all relief shall be denied, the clerk, unless the court otherwise orders, shall forthwith prepare, sign, and enter the judgment without awaiting any direction by the court; (2) upon a decision by the court granting other relief, or upon a special verdict or a general verdict accompanied by answers to interrogatories, the court shall promptly approve the form of the judgment, and the clerk shall thereupon enter it. Every judgment shall be set forth on a separate document. A judgment is effective only when so set forth and when entered as provided in Rule 79(a). Entry of the judgment shall not be delayed for the taxing of costs. Attorneys shall not submit forms of judgment except upon direction of the court, and these directions shall not be given as a matter of course.

Drafting the Judgment

At the conclusion of a trial, the judge announces the judgment to be entered in the lawsuit. In a nonjury trial the judge announces his or her decision. In a jury trial the judge repeats the jury's verdict. The judgment is then reduced to writing and signed by the judge.

The method for drafting the judgment differs from court to court and judge to judge. In federal court, for instance, it is usually the judge's law clerk who drafts the judgment, and the judge reviews and signs it. However, the judge may request that the attorney for the prevailing party draft the judgment. FRCivP 58 states that the judge may direct the attorneys to submit forms of judgment but that the judge should not direct this as a matter of course, presumably reflecting a fear that the attorneys may not submit their proposed judgments in a timely manner. In practice, when the judge requests that an attorney submit a proposed judgment, the judge often imposes a deadline for submission.

The practice of having the attorneys draft the judgments is more prevalent in state court, where judges rarely have law clerks to do the job. When state court judges hear several cases in one day, they have insufficient time to prepare the judgments, which can be quite long. Regardless of who drafts the judgment, the judge has to review it, approve it, and sign it.

Content of Judgments.   Judgments range in length from one or two paragraphs to numerous pages, depending on the number of issues and general complexity of the lawsuit. Some lawsuits require that only a few facts be determined and perhaps one rule of law applied. Refer to Figure 13-2, which illustrates a judgment in a divorce action. Here the only issues were whether the plaintiff and defendant had been married and whether they had lived completely separate and apart for one year from the date of their separation. This is a short, straightforward judgment because of the simple nature of the lawsuit. A judgment entered

FIGURE 13-2   JUDGMENT IN A DIVORCE ACTION

IN THE GENERAL COURT OF JUSTICE
DISTRICT COURT DIVISION

NORTH CAROLINA
MITCHELL COUNTY

FILE NO.: 90 CVD 3504

Vivian Jones Atlas,
    Plaintiff,

    -vs-

Charles T. Atlas

JUDGMENT

THIS CAUSE OF ACTION for absolute divorce on the grounds of one (1) year's separation under G.S. 50-6, coming on to be heard, and being heard before the undersigned Judge Presiding at the May 21, 1990, Session of District Court for Mitchell County, NC;

AND IT APPEARING TO THE COURT that service of Summons and verified Complaint was accepted by the defendant, Charles T. Atlas, on the 28th day of February, 1990;

AND IT FURTHER APPEARING TO THE COURT and the court finding as a fact that Answer was filed by the defendant on March 26, 1990; that no request for a jury trial has been filed with the Clerk of this court or with this court prior to the call of this action for trial, so that under the provisions of G.S. 50-10, and G.S. 1A-1, Rules 38 and 39, the parties have waived the right to have the facts determined by a jury, and the court is authorized to determine the issues of fact;

And the court, after hearing testimony of the witnesses for the plaintiff, the defendant having offered no evidence, finds from the evidence and by the greater weight thereof, that the plaintiff Vivian Jones Atlas has been a bona fide resident of the State of North Carolina for at least six (6) months next preceding the commencement of this action; that the plaintiff, Vivian Jones Atlas, and the defendant, Charles T. Atlas, were lawfully married in Mitchell County, North Carolina, on the 2nd day of April, 1977; that the plaintiff and the defendant separated on the 25th day of January, 1989, and have lived continuously separate and apart from each other at all times since said date;

FIGURE 13-2   JUDGMENT IN A DIVORCE ACTION (Cont.)

BASED ON THE FOREGOING FINDINGS OF FACT, the Court concludes as a matter of law that the plaintiff, Vivian Jones Atlas, is entitled to an absolute divorce from the defendant, Charles T. Atlas.

IT IS NOW, upon motion of Connie McFayden, Esq., attorney for the plaintiff, CONSIDERED, ORDERED, ADJUDGED and DECREED by the Court that the plaintiff, Vivian Jones Atlas, be and she is hereby granted an absolute divorce from the defendant, Charles T. Atlas, and the marriage heretofore existing between the plaintiff and the defendant be and the same is hereby dissolved.

IT IS FURTHER ORDERED that the costs of this action be and the same are hereby taxed against the plaintiff, Vivian Jones Atlas.

This the *21st* day of *May*, 1990.

_____
William C. Horton
Judge Presiding

in a lawsuit involving many complex legal issues would be many pages long. Because a mistake in a judgment can be a valid ground for appeal, it is essential that judgments be complete and accurate.

Judgments commonly open with a short paragraph stating the name of the judge and the designation of the session in which the trial was held. This is followed by the *Findings of Fact*, in which the court states the pertinent facts that were found to be true. In the Wesser case, for instance, the Findings of Fact would state that Mr. Wesser bought a Woodall Shoals blanket on January 3, 1987, and continue with a statement of the facts as to how long he used it, when the fire occurred, and so forth. The Findings of Fact would also state that defendant Woodall Shoals manufactured the blanket, would specify how Woodall Shoals failed to design and/or manufacture the blanket properly, would indicate what Second Ledge did improperly, and would set forth the facts that showed that Mr. Wesser was not contributorily negligent.

The Findings of Fact must state all the facts necessary to support the Conclusions of Law. The *Conclusions of Law* constitute the second major part of the judgment. They state the judge's conclusions on the legal issues that form the basis of the plaintiff's complaint. For instance, the conclusions of law in the Wesser case would state that the defendants breached their express and implied warranties and were negligent, and that their actions caused the fire. If liability were found solely on the basis of breach of express warranty, the Conclusions of Law would state this as the only basis of liability.

Finally, the judgment states the exact relief to which the plaintiff is entitled. For instance, the divorce judgment states that the plaintiff is granted an absolute divorce from the defendant and that their marriage is dissolved. The final section also states which party bears the costs of the action.

Paralegals may sometimes prepare drafts of judgments. The best guideline is usually a judgment prepared by your law firm for a similar case. Remember to take great care to include all necessary Findings of Fact and Conclusions of Law. Rarely is the trial transcript available at this time, so the attorney/paralegal team will have to rely heavily on notes taken at trial.

How the Judgment Becomes Effective

After the judge signs the judgment, it is filed with the clerk of court, just as pleadings are filed. The judgment becomes effective only when it is entered as provided in FRCivP 79. FRCivP 79 directs the clerk of court to keep a book called the civil docket and to record in the book the substance of the judgments rendered in that county or judicial district. The docket book is actually a series of books, dating back many years. The judgments are entered in the civil docket in chronological order. The entry consists of the court file number, names of the parties, the date the entry is made, and the substance of the judgment. See Figure 13-3 for an illustration of how the Wesser judgment would be entered in the civil docket. The judgment is now effective because it has been entered in the civil docket in accordance with FRCivP 79.

FIGURE 13-3   ENTRY OF THE WESSER JUDGMENT IN THE CIVIL DOCKET

Date	File No.	Parties	Judgment
June 30, 1990	C-89-1293-B	Bryson Wesser -vs- Woodall Shoals Corporation and Second Ledge Stores, Incorporated	$100,000 Jury

Note that the clerk of court keeps an index to the civil docket. This is obviously necessary, because thousands of judgments are entered. The judgments are usually indexed both by the plaintiffs' and the defendants' names. The index itself usually consists of multiple volumes, with different sets covering certain spans of years. Thus if in the year 2000 someone wanted to find the entry of judgment in the Wesser case, they would locate the civil index for 1990 and look for Wesser, Woodall Shoals, or Second Ledge.

Bill of Costs

The judgment states which party pays the costs of the lawsuit. FRCivP 54(d) provides that the nonprevailing party pays the costs unless a statute or another rule of civil procedure provides otherwise.

The prevailing party tallies up the costs, using the Bill of Costs. A preprinted court form for calculating the costs is illustrated in Figure 13-4. The task of preparing the Bill of Costs sometimes falls to paralegals. The costs generally include filing fees, witness fees, fees for service of pleadings, fees for court reporters, and the other fees shown on the Bill of Costs. Check to see whether the clerk of court has a standard fee for each applicable cost. If there is not a standard fee, then the general guideline is that the amount must be reasonable.

Enforcement of Judgments

Judgments become effective when they are entered by the clerk of court in the civil docket. However, entry of the judgment does not automatically mean that the nonprevailing party is willing or able to pay the judgment. The attorney/paralegal team may need to take the necessary steps to enforce the judgment.

Before you examine the procedure for enforcing judgments, it is necessary to understand the meaning of some terms used in the enforcement process. The first term is **judgment creditor**, which refers to the prevailing party—that is, the party to whom the judgment is to be paid. The **judgment debtor** is the nonprevailing party, the party who is supposed to pay the judgment. The process for enforcing a judgment is generally called **execution** on the judgment.

Taking the steps to execute on the judgment is not always necessary. Some judgments are **self-executing**. This means that the action the court directs in the judgment is accomplished when the judgment is entered. An example is the divorce judgment. The divorce is official when the judgment is entered, and the plaintiff needs to take no further action. Often execution is not necessary because the nonprevailing party makes immediate arrangements to pay the judgment. For instance, in the Wesser case the insurance company of the defendants is expected to pay the judgment promptly and without further action by the plaintiff.

Ways to Prevent Defendants from Disposing of Assets before Execution

The purpose of execution is to seize the judgment debtor's property and use its value to satisfy the judgment. However, the judgment debtor may try to dispose of property prior to entry of judgment, to prevent the property from being seized and sold later. FRCivP 64 provides that at the commencement of the lawsuit or at any time during the lawsuit, a party may pursue remedies to keep the defendants from disposing of property. FRCivP 64 allows the plaintiffs to use the remedies available under state law or any applicable federal statute. Thus the attorney/paralegal team generally uses the remedies available under the law of the state in which the federal court sits. In a state court action, you use the laws of the state in which your lawsuit is filed. FRCivP 64 mentions some of the remedies for preserving defendants' assets.

The purpose of all these remedies is to prevent the defendants from disposing of their property. For instance, attachment is a remedy that allows the sheriff to seize personal property physically and keep it, pending the outcome of the litigation. Measures this drastic are not always used. When the defendant owns

Post-Trial Procedures and Appeals

349

FIGURE 13-4   A BILL OF COSTS

AO 133
(Rev 7/82)

BILL OF COSTS

United States District Court

	DISTRICT
	DOCKET NO.
v.	
	MAGISTRATE CASE NO.

Judgment having been entered in the above entitled action on _____ against
date

_____ the clerk is requested to tax the following as costs:

BILL OF COSTS

Fees of the clerk ....$_____

Fees for service of summons and complaint .... _____

Fees of the court reporter for all or any part of the transcript necessarily
    obtained for use in the case .... _____

Fees and disbursements for printing .... _____

Fees for witnesses (itemized on reverse side) .... _____

Fees for exemplification and copies of papers necessarily obtained
    for use in case .... _____

Docket fees under 28 U.S.C. § 1923 .... _____

Costs incident to taking of depositions .... _____

Costs as shown on Mandate of Court of Appeals .... _____

Other costs (Please itemize) .... _____

_____

_____

_____

                                     TOTAL $_____

SPECIAL NOTE: Attach to your bill an itemization and documentation for requested costs in all categories. Briefs should also be submitted supporting the necessity of the requested costs and citing cases supporting taxation of those costs.

DECLARATION

    I declare under penalty of perjury that the foregoing costs are correct and were necessarily incurred in this action and that the services for which fees have been charged were actually and necessarily performed. A copy hereof was this day mailed with postage fully prepaid thereon to:

SIGNATURE OF ATTORNEY _____

FOR: _____   DATE _____
        Name of claiming party

Please take notice that I will appear before the clerk who will tax said costs on the following day and time:	DATE AND TIME
Costs are hereby taxed in the following amount and included in the judgment:	AMOUNT TAXED $

CLERK OF COURT	(BY) DEPUTY CLERK	DATE

FIGURE 13-4   A BILL OF COSTS (Cont.)

WITNESS FEES (computation, cf. 28 U. S. C. 1821 for statutory fees)							
NAME AND RESIDENCE	ATTENDANCE		SUBSISTENCE		MILEAGE		Total Cost Each Witness
	Days	Total Cost	Days	Total Cost	Miles	Total Cost	
						TOTAL	

NOTICE

Section 1924, Title 28, U.S. Code (effective September 1, 1948) provides:
"Sec. 1924. Verification of bill of costs."
   "Before any bill of costs is taxed, the party claiming any item of cost or disbursement shall attach thereto an affidavit, made by himself or by his duly authorized attorney or agent having knowledge of the facts, that such item is correct and has been necessarily incurred in the case and that the services for which fees have been charged were actually and necessarily performed."

See also Section 1920 of Title 28 which reads in part as follows:
   "A bill of costs shall be filed in the case and, upon allowance, included in the judgment or decree.'

The Federal Rules of Civil Procedure contain the following provisions:
Rule 54 (d)
   "Except when express provision therefor is made either in a statute of the United States or in these rules, costs shall be allowed as of course to the prevailing party unless the court otherwise directs, but costs against the United States, its officers, and agencies shall be imposed only to the extent permitted by law. Costs may be taxed by the clerk on one day's notice. On motion served within 5 days thereafter, the action of the clerk may be reviewed by the court."

Rule 6 (e)
   "Whenever a party has the right or is required to do some act or take some proceedings within a prescribed period after the service of a notice or other paper upon him and the notice or paper is served upon him by mail, 3 days shall be added to the prescribed period."

Rule 58 (In Part)
   "Entry of the judgment shall not be delayed for the taxing of costs."

real property that is the subject of the litigation, the plaintiff can file a **notice of lis pendens**. This is a simple form filed with the clerk of court, stating that the property is currently the subject of litigation. The clerk enters the notice of lis pendens in the public records so that potential buyers will have warning that the property is the subject of litigation. If a person purchased the real property and the lawsuit resulted in a judgment against the defendant who owned the property, the buyer would be bound by the adverse judgment. No buyer wants to take this risk, so the notice of lis pendens serves to prevent the defendant from selling the real property. Of course, if the defendant prevails at trial, the notice of lis pendens is cancelled.

Procedure for Execution on a Judgment

FRCivP 64 (Figure 13-5) states that the procedure for execution on a judgment is the procedure of the state in which the district court is held. If a federal statute is applicable, then the federal statute governs to the extent that it is applicable. Generally, the attorney/paralegal team follows the state procedure. Therefore you must be familiar with the state's procedures. It is necessary to read the state statutes and consult with the clerk of court for any special procedures or forms that must be used.

FIGURE 13-5 GENERAL RULE FOR PROCEDURE FOR EXECUTION

> **Rule 64. SEIZURE OF PERSON OR PROPERTY**
>
> At the commencement of and during the course of an action, all remedies providing for seizure of person or property for the purpose of securing satisfaction of the judgment ultimately to be entered in the action are available under the circumstances and in the manner provided by the law of the state in which the district court is held, existing at the time the remedy is sought, subject to the following qualifications: (1) any existing statute of the United States governs to the extent to which it is applicable; (2) the action in which any of the foregoing remedies is used shall be commenced and prosecuted or, if removed from a state court, shall be prosecuted after removal, pursuant to these rules. The remedies thus available include arrest, attachment, garnishment, replevin, sequestration, and other corresponding or equivalent remedies, however designated and regardless of whether by state procedure the remedy is ancillary to an action or must be obtained by an independent action.

An Example of Procedure

Although procedures differ from state to state, it is instructive to go through an example to get an idea of how the execution process works. We will discuss the procedure used to execute on judgments entered in the United States District Court for the Western District of North Carolina, including forms commonly used by the clerk of court for the Western District. It is important to note at the outset that the procedure for execution against an individual is different from the procedure for execution against a corporation. This is because the North Carolina Constitution and statutes allow certain property of individuals to be exempt from execution. Corporations are not afforded this protection.

Execution on a Judgment Against an Individual. After ten days from entry of judgment, the judgment creditor may file a preexecution demand. The preexecution demand consists of three documents that are served on the judgment debtor. First is the notice of petition (or motion) to set off debtor's exempt property, which is illustrated in Figure 13-6.[1] This notice tells the judgment debtor in straightforward language that the judgment creditor is taking action to collect the judgment and that the North Carolina Constitution and statutes allow the judgment debtor to designate certain property to be exempt from execution.

The notice of petition to set off property alerts the judgment debtor to the forms that are attached. One of the forms is the motion to give notice of right to have exemptions designated. This is a form signed by the judgment creditor's attorney, illustrated in Figure 13-7. Read the form, and note that it states certain information about the judgment entered and requests that the form for the judgment debtor to use to claim exempt property be served on the judgment debtor. This form is the schedule of debtor's property and request to set aside exempt property, excerpts of which are shown in Figure 13-8.

These three forms are served on the judgment debtor, together with a copy of the judgment itself. The judgment debtor has 20 days to file the schedule of debtor's property. If the judgment debtor fails to file the schedule within 20 days, the attorney for the judgment creditor files a motion for final execution and order to preclude exempt property rights, illustrated in Figure 13-9. The attorney also submits a proposed order for final execution and preclusion of exempt property, shown in Figure 13-10.

The judgment creditor may now proceed with the writ of execution. This includes two certified copies of the judgment, two certified copies of the order for final execution and preclusion of exempt property, the original and one copy of the writ of execution issued by the clerk, and the U.S. marshal's form 285. The writ of execution form is shown in Figure 13-11.

If the judgment debtor does file the schedule of debtor's property and request to set aside exempt property, then a U.S. magistrate must determine what property is actually exempt. The judgment creditor may contest the question whether certain property is exempt, and the magistrate can hold a hearing. After the magistrate designates the exempt property, the U.S. marshal serves on the judgment debtor two certified copies of the judgment, two certified copies of the order designating exemptions, the original and one copy of writ of execution issued by the clerk, and the U.S. marshal's form 285.

The actual execution involves seizing and selling the judgment debtor's nonexempt property to satisy the judgment. For instance, the marshal can seize the judgment debtor's car or freeze the assets in her bank account.

FIGURE 13-6 NOTICE OF PETITION TO SET OFF EXEMPT PROPERTY

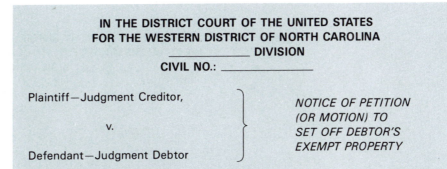

**IN THE DISTRICT COURT OF THE UNITED STATES
FOR THE WESTERN DISTRICT OF NORTH CAROLINA
_____ DIVISION
CIVIL NO.: _____**

Plaintiff—Judgment Creditor,

v.

Defendant—Judgment Debtor

*NOTICE OF PETITION
(OR MOTION) TO
SET OFF DEBTOR'S
EXEMPT PROPERTY*

GREETINGS:

The Judgment Creditor is now seeking to collect the Judgment against you in the above entitled action and has asked that this Notice from the Court be served upon you advising you of your rights under the Constitution and laws of North Carolina to have property designated which is exempt from execution. A "judgment debtor" is a person who, a court has declared, owes money to another, a "judgment creditor."

It is important that you respond to this Notice no later than twenty (20) days after you receive it because you may lose valuable rights if you do nothing. You may wish to consider hiring an attorney, at your own expense, to help you with this proceeding to make certain that you receive all the protections to which you are entitled under the Constitution and laws of North Carolina.

The procedure in this Court concerning execution of a Judgment for the payment of money and in proceedings on and in aid of execution is in accordance with the practices and procedure of the State of North Carolina. Therefore, the Court will honor your right to have certain property set off as exempt from execution pursuant to Article X of the Constitution of North Carolina and Article 16 of Chapter 1C of the General Statutes of North Carolina, if you proceed to have your exempt property designated.

Accordingly, under North Carolina law, you are required to complete and file a Schedule of Debtor's Property and Request to Set Aside Exempt Property within twenty (20) days after service of this Notice and appear at any requested hearing, or make a written request within twenty (20) days after service of this Notice for a hearing before the Court to complete the form; otherwise, the Court may determine that you have waived your exemptions provided under the Constitution and the laws of the State of North Carolina. There are attached to this Notice a copy of the Judgment in this action, and a copy of the Motion to Give Notice of Right to have Exemptions Designated, as well as the form for you to complete and file of your Schedule of Debtor's Property and Request to Set Aside Exempt Property.

This _____ day of _____,19____.

_____
Clerk, United States District Court

FIGURE 13-7   MOTION TO GIVE NOTICE OF RIGHT TO HAVE EXEMPTIONS DESIGNATED

**IN THE DISTRICT COURT OF THE UNITED STATES
FOR THE WESTERN DISTRICT OF NORTH CAROLINA
_____ DIVISION
CIVIL NO.: _____**

Plaintiff,

v.

Defendant

*MOTION TO GIVE
NOTICE OF RIGHT TO
HAVE EXEMPTIONS
DESIGNATED*

COMES NOW the Judgment Creditor and Plaintiff herein, by and through its Attorney, and moves the Court for an order to issue giving the Defendant Debtor herein Notice of Right to Have Exemptions Designated, together with Schedule of Debtor's Property and Request to Set Aside Exempt Property, on the following grounds:

1. Judgment was entered on _____ in favor of the Judgment Creditor against the Defendant Debtor for recovery of the sum of $_____, plus interest and costs.
2. The Judgment Debtor resides within the jurisdiction of this Court.
3. The Judgment in favor of the Judgment Creditor has not been satisfied, vacated, or reversed and is one on which execution may properly be issued.
4. The Judgment Creditor is the only judgment creditor of the Judgment Debtor known to the Judgment Creditor.
5. The Judgment Creditor is entitled to have its Motion granted pursuant to Rule 69, Federal Rules of Civil Procedure, and Articles 28 and 31, Subchapter X, Chapter 1, as modified by Article 16 of Chapter 1C, General Statutes of North Carolina.

WHEREFORE, Judgment Creditor prays that the Notice of Right to Have Exemptions Designated, together with Schedule of Debtor's Property and Request to Set Aside Exempt Property, be issued by this Court and served upon the Judgment Debtor as provided by law.

This _____ day of _____, 19____.

_____
Attorney for Judgment Creditor

FIGURE 13-8 EXCERPTS FROM SCHEDULE OF DEBTOR'S PROPERTY AND REQUEST TO SET ASIDE EXEMPT PROPERTY

**IN THE DISTRICT COURT OF THE UNITED STATES
FOR THE WESTERN DISTRICT OF NORTH CAROLINA
_____ DIVISION
CIVIL NO.: _____**

Plaintiff,

v.

Defendant

*SCHEDULE OF DEBTOR'S
PROPERTY AND REQUEST
TO SET ASIDE EXEMPT
PROPERTY*

I, _____, being the Judgment Debtor in the above captioned matter, submit the following information and Schedule of Debtor's Property and Request to Set Aside Exempt Property pursuant to G.S. 1C-1603 and do hereby declare under the penalties of perjury that the following is true and correct.

1. I am a citizen and resident of _____ County, North Carolina.

2. I was born on _____ (date of birth).

3. I am married to _____ (spouse's name) or (not married).

4. The following persons live in my household and are in substantial need of my support:

Name	Relationship to Debtor	Age
_____	_____	_____
_____	_____	_____
_____	_____	_____

(Attach an additional sheet, if necessary.)

5. I (own) (am purchasing) (rent) (choose one; mark out the other choices) a (house) (trailer) (apartment) (choose one; mark out the other choices) located at _____

(address, city, state, zip code), which is my residence.

6. I (do) (do not) own any other real property. If other real property is owned, list that property on the following lines; if no other real property is owned, mark "not applicable" on the first line.

(Attach an additional sheet, if necessary.)

FIGURE 13-8 EXCERPTS FROM SCHEDULE OF DEBTOR'S PROPERTY AND REQUEST TO SET ASIDE EXEMPT PROPERTY (Cont.)

7. The following persons are, so far as I am able to tell, all of the persons or companies to whom I owe money:

_____

_____

_____

_____

_____

(Attach an additional sheet, if necessary.)

8. I wish to claim my interest in the following real or personal property that I use as a residence or my dependent uses as a residence. I also wish to claim my interest in the following burial plots for myself or my dependents. I understand that my total interest claimed in the residence and burial plots may not exceed $7,500. I understand that I am not entitled to this exemption if I take the homestead exemption provided by the Constitution of North Carolina in other property.

Address _____

Names of Owners of Record _____

Estimated Value _____

Amount of Liens _____

Amount of Debtor's Interest _____

9. I wish to claim the following life insurance policies whose sole beneficiaries are (my wife) (my dependents) to work or sustain health:

Name of Insurer	Policy No.	Face Value	Beneficiary(ies)

10. I wish to claim the following items of health care aid necessary for (myself) (my dependents) to work or sustain health:

Item	Purpose	Person Using Item

FIGURE 13-9   MOTION FOR FINAL EXECUTION AND ORDER TO PRECLUDE EXEMPT PROPERTY RIGHTS

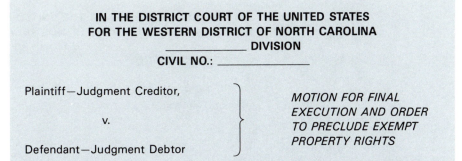

**IN THE DISTRICT COURT OF THE UNITED STATES
FOR THE WESTERN DISTRICT OF NORTH CAROLINA
_____ DIVISION**
CIVIL NO.: _____

Plaintiff—Judgment Creditor,

v.

Defendant—Judgment Debtor

MOTION FOR FINAL EXECUTION AND ORDER TO PRECLUDE EXEMPT PROPERTY RIGHTS

NOW COMES the Plaintiff who is the Judgment Creditor herein, by and through the undersigned attorney, and moves the Court for an Order of Final Execution to be issued against the Judgment Debtor and that none of the Judgment Debtor's property be set aside as exempt from execution and, in support of this Motion, shows unto the Court upon oath the following:

1. That Judgment was entered on _____ in favor of the Judgment Creditor against the Judgment Debtor for recovery of the sum of $_____ plus interest and costs.

2. That Judgment in favor of the Judgment Creditor has not been satisfied, vacated, or reversed.

3. That Judgment Creditor is the only judgment creditor of the Judgment Debtor known to the Judgment Creditor.

4. That Notice of Right to Have Exemptions Designated was duly issued by this Court on _____ and that a copy of said Notice together with Schedule of Debtor's Property and Request to Set Aside Exempt Property were served upon the Judgment Debtor according to law.

5. That Judgment Debtor has failed to respond within the time allowed and that his failure to respond should be considered a waiver of his right to have property set aside as exempt from execution of Judgment.

WHEREFORE, the Judgment Creditor respectfully requests that an Order of Final Execution be issued for the collection of the Judgment entered herein and that none of the Judgment Debtor's property be set aside as exempt from the execution of said Judgment.

This _____ day of _____, 19____.

_____
Attorney for Judgment Creditor

SWORN TO AND SUBSCRIBED before me, this _____ day of _____, 19____.

_____
Notary Public

My commission expires: _____.

FIGURE 13-10 ORDER FOR FINAL EXEMPTION AND PRECLUSION OF EXEMPT PROPERTY

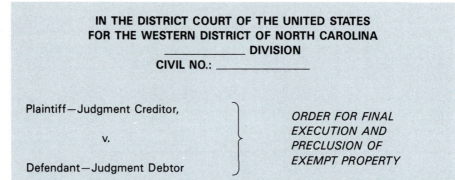

IN THE DISTRICT COURT OF THE UNITED STATES
FOR THE WESTERN DISTRICT OF NORTH CAROLINA
_____ DIVISION
CIVIL NO.: _____

Plaintiff—Judgment Creditor,

v.

Defendant—Judgment Debtor

ORDER FOR FINAL
EXECUTION AND
PRECLUSION OF
EXEMPT PROPERTY

THIS MATTER coming on to be heard and being heard before the undersigned Judge or Magistrate of the United States District Court for the Western District of North Carolina upon Judgment Creditor's Motion for an Order of Final Execution in this matter; and

IT APPEARING to the Court that Judgment Debtor has been duly served with copy of the Judgment together with copy of Notice of Right to Have Exemptions Designated and Schedule of Debtor's Property and Request to Set Aside Exempt Property and that the Judgment Debtor has failed to file a Schedule of Debtor's Property and Request to Set Aside Exempt Property and has failed to request a hearing to set aside exempt property or otherwise respond within the time allowed. The Court, therefore, finds that the Judgment Debtor has had a reasonable opportunity to assert the exemptions provided by law and that the Judgment Debtor's failure to respond should be considered a waiver of his right to have property set aside as exempt from the execution of the Judgment in this case.

IT IS, THEREFORE, ORDERED that Judgment Debtor is precluded from having any of his property set aside as exempt from Judgment in this case.

IT IS FURTHER ORDERED that a final execution be issued by the Clerk of this Court for the collection of the Judgment in this case.

This _____ day of _____, 19____.

_____

_____, United States District Court

FIGURE 13-11 THE WRIT OF EXECUTION FORM

DC 11 ⊕
Rev. 7/82

WRIT OF EXECUTION

United States District Court	DISTRICT

TO THE MARSHAL OF:

YOU ARE HEREBY COMMANDED, that of the goods and chattels, lands and tenements in your district belonging to:

NAME

you cause to be made and levied as well a certain debt of:

DOLLAR AMOUNT	DOLLAR AMOUNT
	and

in the United States District Court for the _____ District of _____ ,
before the Judge of the said Court by the consideration of the same Judge lately recovered against the said,

and also the costs that may accrue under this writ.
   And that you have above listed moneys at the place and date listed below; and that you bring this writ with you.

PLACE	DISTRICT
CITY	DATE

Witness the Honorable _____
                        (United States Judge)

DATE	CLERK OF COURT
	(BY) DEPUTY CLERK

RETURN

DATE RECEIVED	DATE OF EXECUTION OF WRIT

This writ was received and executed.

U.S. MARSHAL	(BY) DEPUTY MARSHAL

Execution on a Judgment Against a Corporation. The procedure for execution against a corporation is less complicated. Ten days after judgment is entered, the judgment creditor's attorney arranges for execution. The necessary forms are two certified copies of the judgment, an original and one copy of the writ of execution issued by the clerk, and the U.S. marshal's form 285.

Identifying Assets. Even if the judgment debtor files a schedule of property, disputes may arise about the property that the judgment debtor actually owns. The judgment creditor may believe that the judgment debtor has failed to disclose assets or is actually hiding assets. FRCivP 69 allows the judgment creditor to conduct post-trial discovery to gain information about the judgment debtor's assets. This generally involves submitting interrogatories to the judgment debtor, just as is done in pretrial discovery.

Paralegals may conduct some research to try to locate assets of the judgment debtor. This may involve a search of public records, such as tax listings. If the judgment debtor files a schedule of property, this may indicate some additional avenues of investigation.

One final concept is the **judgment-proof** judgment debtor. Persons are judgment proof when they own no property that is subject to execution. Usually this means that all their property is exempt. For this reason, it is best to investigate defendants' assets at the beginning of the litigation, if possible. Think of all the work that has gone into obtaining the judgment. It would be a waste of time and money if the judgment debtor is judgment proof.

POINTER: One clue that persons may be judgment proof is to review the clerk's civil docket. If you find many judgments entered against a person, that person may well be judgment proof. Note that if a judgment was entered and subsequently paid, the clerk of court cancels the judgment. This means that the clerk writes in the entry that the judgment has been paid and the date that it was paid.

APPEALS

If your client is unhappy with the judgment of the trial court, he or she may wish to appeal. In an **appeal**, the party who is unhappy with the judgment tries to convince the appellate court that the trial court committed **reversible error**, which entitles the party to a new trial. Reversible error is the opposite of harmless error, which we discussed earlier. Harmless error is a mistake, but not a mistake that deprived any of the parties of substantial rights or a fair trial. In contrast, reversible error is a mistake of law that has deprived a party of a fair trial. For instance, the judge may make a mistake in giving the jury instructions, and the mistake causes the jury to misapply the law. This is reversible error.

An appeal is not appropriate in every lawsuit where a party is unhappy with the outcome of the trial. There may not have been sufficient error made at trial to warrant an appeal. Prevailing on appeal is not easy, because trial judges are generally vested with great discretion. Appellate courts are frequently hesitant to overturn the decision of a trial judge who was there, who heard the testimony and legal arguments, and who had the opportunity to assess the credibility of the witnesses.

Clients should think hard about filing an appeal for another important reason: Appeals are time-consuming and expensive. If a judgment is rendered against a defendant in the amount of $1,000, an appeal can scarcely be justified; the attorney's fees alone will exceed the judgment many times over.

Applicable Court Rules

Once a case goes up on appeal, the trial court no longer has jurisdiction. The appellate court has jurisdiction. Therefore it is imperative that the attorney/paralegal team follow the rules of procedure for the court in which the appeal is taken. In federal court, the Federal Rules of Appellate Procedure control. They are supplemented by internal operating procedures of the various circuit courts of appeals. The internal operating procedures are analogous to local court rules in the trial courts. All these rules are published in 28 U.S. Code and in commercial publications.

In state court, the state rules of appellate procedure apply. These are published in the state statutes and in commercial publications. The rules are generally the same for the lower appellate court and the higher appellate court, but there may be differences, so check the rules carefully.

POINTER: Some state rules provide for an accelerated docket to speed up the appellate process. Such procedures may allow the filing of shorter briefs in a shorter period of time, as well as less time for oral argument.

Definitions

In connection with appeals there are many terms paralegals must understand. The **appellant** is the party that files the appeal and seeks to overturn the judgment of the trial court. The party who asserts that the judgment should be affirmed is the **appellee**.

The **final decision rule** is an important concept. The appellate courts generally do not have jurisdiction over a case until the final decision or judgment is entered. After entry of the final judgment, the appellant may appeal the judgment on the basis of all the errors committed at trial. It would be a colossal waste of time and energy to allow an appeal at each point in the trial where a party objects to an action of the court and asserts that the court has committed an error. Thus the final decision rule, stated in 28 U.S.C. §1291, provides that no appeal can be taken until the court's final decision. Courts enter many orders during the course of litigation, from ruling on the right to a jury trial to ruling on the admissibility of evidence.

Orders that are not final orders are called **interlocutory orders**; these orders do not dispose of the entire controversy. The appeal of an interlocutory order under certain narrow circumstances is permitted under 28 U.S.C. §1292(b). The district judge (trial judge) must "be of the opinion that such order involves a controlling question of law as to which there is substantial ground for difference of opinion and that an immediate appeal from the order may materially advance the ultimate termination of the litigation." If the district judge feels that an interlocutory order meets this criterion, the judge states this in an order and asks the court of appeals to permit an appeal to be taken. Note that the application for an appeal under 28 U.S.C. §1291(b) does not stay proceedings in the trial court unless either the district judge or the court of appeals orders a stay.

The Function of Appellate Courts

As we discussed in Chapters 1 and 3, appellate courts do not rehear testimony and retry the lawsuit. Rather, they examine the record of the trial to determine whether the trial court committed reversible error. Appellate courts review the record of appeal, which is defined in Rule 10 of the Federal Rules of Appellate Procedure as ''the original papers and exhibits filed in the district court, the transcript of proceedings, if any, and a certified copy of the docket entries prepared by the clerk of the district court.''

POINTER: Under the Federal Rules of Appellate Procedure, the clerk of court prepares the record on appeal. In state court, the attorneys are often required to prepare the record on appeal, and paralegals may assist. Consult carefully the state rules of appellate procedure that govern the record on appeal. The content of the record and the deadline for filing the record are usually quite specific.

Thus appellate courts review the record of the proceedings in the trial court to determine whether reversible errors were made. The appellate court either affirms (upholds) the lower court's decision or reverses (overturns) the decision and remands the case for correction of the errors. This can require a new trial.

Appellate Procedure

There are two constant guidelines for paralegals assisting with appeals, no matter which appellate court is hearing the appeal. First, you must maintain a precise docket control system. As we have discussed, the time allowed for filing documents in an appeal can be short, and extensions are not readily granted. Second, you must follow the applicable rules of appellate procedure to the letter. Ensure that forms and briefs follow the format prescribed by the appellate rules and that they are timely filed.

We will discuss the general procedure followed for appeals. There may be differences in procedure, depending on the rules of the state appellate court or circuit court of appeals. We will not discuss every step, but rather the major steps, in which paralegals are most likely to participate. Our discussion will focus on appeals in federal court—that is, to the circuit courts of appeal. The Federal Rules of Appellate Procedure (FRAP) and rules for internal operating procedures for the individual circuits guide the procedure. These rules are published in 28 U.S. Code.

Notice of Appeal. In an appeal as of right—that is, where no permission to appeal is required—the first step is to file a notice of appeal. This is a short document that is filed with the clerk of court for the trial court in which the final judgment was entered. The notice of appeal basically states that the appellant is filing an appeal with the appropriate appellate court.

Paralegals may draft the notice of appeal, which follows a standard format. Requirements for the notice of appeal are set forth in FRAP 3, and a sample Notice of Appeal is set forth in the appendix of the Federal Rules of Appellate Procedure. The sample notice of appeal is reprinted here in Figure 13-12.

FIGURE 13-12   A SAMPLE NOTICE OF APPEAL

Form 1.

**Notice of Appeal to a Court of Appeals
From a Judgment or Order of a District Court**

United States District Court for the _____
District of _____

File Number _____

A.B., Plaintiff

v.   *Notice of Appeal*

C.D., Defendant

        Notice is hereby given that C.D., defendant above named, hereby appeals to the United States Court of Appeals for the _____ Circuit (from the final judgment) (from the order (describing it)) entered in this action on the _____ day of _____, 19____.

                                                        (S) _____

                                                        _____
                                                        (Address)
                                                        Attorney for C.D.

It is imperative that the notice of appeal be timely filed. FRAP 4 requires that the notice of appeal be filed with the clerk of court for the trial court within 30 days of the entry of the judgment or order appealed from. If the United States or one of its officers or agencies is the appellant, 60 days are allowed for filing the notice of appeal. FRAP 4 states some variations on the deadline—for example, when a motion for a new trial pursuant to FRCivP 59 is pending. Read FRAP 4 carefully, and always discuss with the attorneys on your team any questions you have about deadlines.

Variation in Procedure for Appeals for Which Permission Is Required Under 28 U.S.C. §1292(b). FRAP 5 varies the procedure for appeals of interlocutory orders, for which permission is required under 28 U.S.C. §1292(b). The appellant files a petition for permission to appeal with the clerk of the court of appeals within 10 days after the entry of the order from which the appeal is taken. FRAP 5 states requirements about the form of the petition and number of copies to file, as well as some other rules. FRAP 5 specifically provides that a notice of appeal need not be filed. This is because the petition for permission to appeal gives notice to the trial court and all parties.

Docketing Requirements. When the notice of appeal is filed with the clerk of court for the trial court, the clerk sends a copy of the notice to the clerk of court for the circuit court of appeals (FRAP 3(d)). The clerk of the court of appeals enters the appeal upon the docket (FRAP 12). The appellant pays a docket fee, as required by FRAP 3(e).

Some circuit courts of appeals have internal operating procedures that require further action by the appellant at the time the appeal is docketed. For instance, the Fourth Circuit Court of Appeals requires the appellant to file a docketing statement within ten days of filing the notice of appeal. The Fourth Circuit's docketing statement is shown in Figure 13-13. It provides basic information about the appeal and helps the court ascertain the nature of the appeal at the outset.

Costs and Cost Bonds. Appellate costs are different from the costs at the trial level. Appellate costs include the cost of the court reporter's transcript, the fee for filing the notice of appeal, the fee for preparing and transmitting the record, the docketing fee, the cost of duplicating briefs and appendices, and fees paid for appeal bonds. FRAP 7 allows the trial court to require an appellant to file a bond or provide other security to ensure payment of costs on appeal in civil cases. The appellant usually bears the costs if the trial court's judgment is affirmed. The appellee usually pays the costs if the trial court's judgment is reversed (FRAP 39).

Transcripts. We have noted that an important part of the record on appeal is the transcript of the trial. FRAP 10 requires the appellant to order all or the pertinent parts of the transcript from the court reporter within 10 days of filing the notice of appeal. Consult FRAP 10 for more detailed procedures when the appellant deems only part of the transcript to be necessary to understand the issues on appeal. FRAP 11 requires the court reporter to submit the transcipt within 30 days of receipt of the order, unless the reporter seeks an extension. Internal operating procedures of the individual circuits may alter this deadline. For instance, IOP 11.1 of the Fourth Circuit Court of Appeals allows 60 days, with some exceptions.

Preparation and Filing of Briefs. Paralegals frequently help with the preparation of briefs. The brief is of critical importance because it is the primary tool for persuading the appellate court that the trial court committed reversible error. The Federal Rules of Appellate Procedure, internal operating procedures of the circuit courts, and state appellate rules give definite guidelines for the contents and format of briefs. It is imperative that paralegals know these rules and ensure that they are followed.

FIGURE 13-13   A DOCKETING STATEMENT

United States Court of Appeals
for the Fourth Circuit

Tenth & Main Streets
Richmond, Virginia 23219

DOCKETING STATEMENT

4CCA Docket No. _____

Caption of Case   **Type of Action**

_____ Civil
v.   _____ Criminal/Prisoner
_____ Cross Appeal

District _____ Judge _____
District Court Docket Number _____
Statute or other authority establishing jurisdiction in the:
    District Court _____
    Court of Appeals _____

A. Timeliness of Appeal
    1. Date of entry of judgment or order appealed from _____
    2. Date this notice of appeal filed _____
            If cross appeal, date first notice of appeal filed _____
    3. Filing date of any post-judgment motion filed by any party which tolls
        time under FRAP 4(a)(4) or 4(b) _____
    4. Date of entry of order deciding above post-judgment motion _____
    5. Filing date of any motion to extend time under FRAP 4(a)(5) or 4(b)
        _____
            Time extended to _____
B. Finality of Order or Judgment
    1. Is the order or judgment appealed from a final decision on the merits?
        yes (   ) no (   )
    2. If no, a) Did the district court order entry of judgment as to less than
                  all claims or all parties pursuant to FRCP 54(b)? yes (   ) no (   )
               b) Is the order appealed from a collateral or interlocutory order
                  reviewable under any exception to the finality rule? yes (   )
                  no (   )
                  If yes, explain _____
    (Criminal only)
    3. Has the defendant been convicted? yes (   ) no (   )
    4. Has a sentence been imposed? yes (   ) no (   )
        Term _____
    5. Is the defendant incarcerated? yes (   ) no (   )
C. Has this case previously been appealed? yes (   ) no (   ) If yes, give the case
    name, docket number, and disposition of each prior appeal on a separate sheet.

FIGURE 13-13   A DOCKETING STATEMENT (Cont.)

D. Are any related cases or cases raising related issues pending in this court, any district court of this circuit, or the Supreme Court? yes ( ) no ( ) If yes, cite the case and the manner in which it is related on a separate sheet.

E. State the nature of the suit, the relief sought, and the outcome below.

F. Issues to be raised on appeal. Attach one additional page if necessary.

G. Is settlement being discussed? yes ( ) no ( )

H. Is disposition on motions, memoranda, or an abbreviated briefing schedule appropriate? yes ( ) no ( ) If yes, explain on a separate sheet. Is oral argument necessary? yes ( ) no ( )

I. Were there any in-court proceedings below? yes ( ) no ( ) Is a transcript necessary for this appeal? yes ( ) no ( ) If yes, is transcript already on file with district court? yes ( ) no ( ) If transcript is not already on file, attach copy 1 of transcript order.

J. List each adverse party to the appeal. Attach additional sheets if necessary. If no attorney, give address and telephone number of the adverse party.
   1. Adverse party _____
      Attorney _____
      Address _____
      Telephone _____
   2. Adverse party _____
      Attorney _____
      Address _____
      Telephone _____

K. Appellant(s) Name _____
   If incarcerated, give identification number _____
   Address (If incarcerated, give institution address)

   _____
   _____ Telephone _____

L. Attorney or pro se litigant filing Docketing Statement. Will you be handling the appeal? (In criminal cases counsel below will handle the appeal unless relieved by this court.) yes ( ) no ( )
   Name _____ Attorney ( ) Pro se ( )
   Firm _____
   Address _____
   _____ Telephone _____

Examine FRAP 28(a)–(f), shown in Figure 13-14. This very important rule sets forth the requirements for the content of briefs and limitations. Appellate courts do not merely encourage short briefs; they require them. Note that FRAP 28(a) and (b) explain the format that the appellant's and appellee's briefs must follow. FRAP 28(e) deserves special attention because it instructs you how to refer to the record in the brief.

The format and content of the appellate brief is not altogether alien; it bears some similarity to the trial briefs that you have already helped to prepare. Paralegals

FIGURE 13-14   REQUIREMENTS FOR THE CONTENT OF APPELLATE BRIEFS

FRAP 28.   BRIEFS

(a) **Brief of the Appellant.** The brief of the appellant shall contain under appropriate headings and in the order here indicated:

(1) A table of contents, with page references, and a table of cases (alphabetically arranged), statutes and other authorities cited, with references to the pages of the brief where they are cited.

(2) A statement of the issues presented for review.

(3) A statement of the case. The statement shall first indicate briefly the nature of the case, the course of proceedings, and its disposition in the court below. There shall follow a statement of the facts relevant to the issues presented for review, with appropriate references to the record (see subdivision (e)).

(4) An argument. The argument may be preceded by a summary. The argument shall contain the contentions of the appellant with respect to the issues presented, and the reasons therefor, with citations to the authorities, statutes and parts of the record relied on.

(5) A short conclusion stating the precise relief sought.

(b) **Brief of the Appellee.** The brief of the appellee shall conform to the requirements of subdivision (a)(1)–(4), except that a statement of the issues or of the case need not be made unless the appellee is dissatisfied with the statement of the appellant.

(c) **Reply Brief.** The appellant may file a brief in reply to the brief of the appellee, and if the appellee has cross-appealed, the appellee may file a brief in reply to the response of the appellant to the issues presented by the cross appeal. No further briefs may be filed except with leave of court. All reply briefs shall contain a table of contents, with page references, and a table of cases (alphabetically arranged), statutes and other authorities cited with references to the pages of the reply brief where they are cited.

(d) **References in Briefs to Parties.** Counsel will be expected in their briefs and oral arguments to keep to a minimum references to parties by such designations as ''appellant'' and ''appellee.'' It promotes clarity to use the designations used in the lower court or in the agency proceedings, or the actual names of parties, or descriptive terms such as ''the employee,'' ''the injured person,'' ''the taxpayer,'' ''the ship,'' ''the stevedore,'' etc.

(e) **References in Briefs to the Record.** References in the briefs to parts of the record reproduced in the appendix filed with the brief of the appellant [see Rule 30(a)] shall be to the pages of the appendix at which those parts appear. If the appendix is prepared after the briefs are filed, references in the briefs to the record shall be made by one of the methods allowed by Rule 30(c). If the record is reproduced in accordance with the provisions of Rule 30(f), or if references are made in the briefs to parts of the record not reproduced, the references shall be to the pages of the parts of the record involved; e.g., Answer p. 7, Motion for Judgment p. 2, Transcript p. 231. Intelligible abbreviations may be used. If reference is made to evidence the admissibility of which is in controversy, reference shall be made to the pages of the appendix or of the transcript, at which the evidence was identified, offered, and received or rejected.

(f) **Reproduction of Statutes, Rules, Regulations, Etc.** If determination of the issues presented requires the study of statutes, rules, regulations, etc. or relevant parts thereof, they shall be reproduced in the brief or in an addendum at the end, or they may be supplied to the court in pamphlet form.

perform many of the same tasks as with trial briefs—drafting a statement of facts, conducting legal research, shepardizing cases, checking citations, and proof-reading.

FRAP 30 requires the appellant to prepare an appendix to the brief. The appendix contains the relevant docket entries from the proceeding from which you are appealing; relevant portions of the pleadings, charge, findings, or opinion; the judgment or order in question; and any other parts of the record to which the parties wish to direct the court's attention.

Note that there are three briefs filed in an appeal. First is the appellant's brief, which explains why the trial court committed reversible error. The appellee's brief is a response that tries to convince the appellate court that the trial court did not commit reversible error. The appellant is then allowed to file a reply brief, which responds to the appellee's brief.

POINTER: You may have heard of another type of brief, the brief of an *amicus curiae* (''friend of the court''). These are briefs filed by persons or organizations who are not appellants or appellees but who have a strong interest in the outcome of the litigation. Amicus curiae briefs are often filed in cases of far-reaching consequences, such as civil rights actions. FRAP 29 controls the filing of amicus curiae briefs and provides that amicus briefs may be filed only with the consent of all parties or at the request of the court.

FRAP 31 is a very important rule. It states the deadlines for serving and filing briefs. The appellant's brief must be served and filed within 40 days after the date on which the record is filed. The appellee then has 30 days from service to file and serve a brief. If the appellant files a reply brief, it must be served and filed within 14 days after service of the appellee's brief. Paralegals must also be familiar with FRAP 34, which states the form that must be used for the briefs and appendix.

Oral Argument. Oral argument is the attorneys' opportunity to appear before the appellate court and argue why the judgment should either be reversed or affirmed. Oral argument generally is not lengthy, perhaps 30 minutes at most. Thus the attorneys should not repeat their entire argument on appeal. Rather, they should emphasize their strongest points.

As FRAP 34 provides, oral argument may be waived by the appellate court. State rules of appellate procedure usually contain provisions for waiver of oral argument.

Oral argument in the circuit courts of appeal is before three judges. The number of judges or justices before whom oral arguments are presented in state appellate courts may differ, depending on the rules of appellate procedure and the level of the appellate court. For instance, oral argument in the lower appellate court may be before three judges, while oral argument in the state's highest appellate court may be before all the justices.

Entry of Judgment. After oral arguments, the judges who heard the arguments hold conferences to determine how they will rule. One judge is designated to write the opinion. The written opinion may not issue for several months, depending upon the complexity of the issues and case load of the court.

FRAP 36 provides that the clerk of court for the appellate court shall prepare and enter a judgment after the clerk receives the court's decision. The court does not always issue a lengthy written explanation of its rationale. However, if the court does issue a written decision, the clerk mails a copy to each party. If there is no written decision, the clerk mails only a copy of the judgment and notice of the date it was entered.

Petition for Rehearing.   The party that fails to prevail on appeal may file a petition for rehearing. FRAP 40 provides that the petition "shall state with particularity the points of law or fact which in the opinion of the petitioner the court has overlooked or misapprehended and shall contain such argument in support of the petition as the petitioner desires to present." FRAP 40 does not permit oral argument. The petitioner may also request that the rehearing be **en banc—** that is, that the entire panel of judges on the appellate court participate in the decision, not just the three judges who originally heard the appeal. Petitions for rehearing are not frequently granted. The petitions should be filed if there is a compelling argument to show that the appellate court erred, but should never be filed for the purpose of delay.

ENDNOTES

1 The author acknowledges the kindness of the Clerk of Court for the United States District Court for the Western District of North Carolina, Thomas J. McGraw, and Cindy Gipson, Deputy Clerk, for their help and for sharing the forms commonly used in the Western District.

APPENDIX

WESSER CASE

Complaint

Defendants' Answer

Plaintiff's First Set of Interrogatories

Responses to Plaintiff's First Set of Interrogatories

CHATTOOGA CORPORATION CASE

Complaint

Consent Decree

UNITED STATES DISTRICT COURT
MIDDLE DISTRICT OF NORTH CAROLINA
CHARLESTON DIVISION
CIVIL NO.: C-89-1293-B

Bryson Wesser,

                                  Plaintiff,

          -vs-

Woodall Shoals Corporation,
                                  Defendant,
                    and
Second Ledge Stores, Incorporated,
                                  Defendant

COMPLAINT
(Jury Trial Requested)

The plaintiff, complaining of the defendant, alleges and says that:

1. The plaintiff is a citizen and resident of Watauga County, North Carolina.

2. The defendant Woodall Shoals Corporation (hereinafter ''Woodall Shoals'') is a corporation incorporated under the laws of the State of Delaware, having its principal place of business in a state other than the State of North Carolina, and is licensed to do business and is doing business in the State of North Carolina.

3. The defendant Second Ledge Stores, Incorporated (hereinafter ''Second Ledge'') is a corporation incorporated under the laws of the State of Delaware, having its principal place of business in a state other than the State of North Carolina, and is licensed to do business and is doing business in the State of North Carolina.

4. The matter in controversy exceeds, exclusive of interest and costs, the sum of $50,000 (Fifty Thousand Dollars).

5. On or about January 16, 1986, the plaintiff purchased from the defendant Second Ledge, Store No. 289 in Charleston, North Carolina, an electric blanket, Model 6102 (hereinafter ''the electric blanket'') manufactured by defendant Woodall Shoals.

6. On or about January 3, 1987, at approximately 11:30 p.m., the plaintiff used the electric blanket to cover himself when he went to bed in his residence at 115 Pipestem Drive, Charleston, NC. In so doing and prior thereto, the plaintiff carefully followed all instructions as to the proper use of the electric blanket. The plaintiff turned the blanket on and went to sleep.

7. Shortly thereafter a defect in the blanket or its control caused the blanket to overheat and ignite. The plaintiff kicked the blanket off his body but nonetheless was severely burned.

8. The flaming blanket caused the area around the plaintiff's bed to catch fire. The plaintiff ran from his bedroom, receiving burns on his body in the process. By the time the fire was extinguished, the walls and ceiling of the plaintiff's bedroom were burned beyond reuse and the entire living area of the plaintiff's house was damaged by smoke.

9. As a consequence of the fire, the plaintiff suffered severe third-degree burns over twenty percent (20%) of his body, requiring his hospitalization for one month for treatment of his wound, resulting in extensive medical expenses for his care, and lost wages. The plaintiff has suffered severe emotional distress as a result of the fire and his injuries.

I.

COUNT ONE—BREACH OF EXPRESS WARRANTY BY THE DEFENDANT WOODALL SHOALS

10. The plaintiff incorporates by reference and realleges paragraphs 1–9 of the Complaint and, in addition, alleges as follows:

11. At the time of the sale of the electric blanket, Woodall Shoals made certain express warranties to the plaintiff including an express warranty that, for two years from the date of purchase, the blanket would be free of electrical and mechanical defects in material and workmanship.

12. The electric blanket in fact contained numerous electrical and mechanical defects which caused the blanket to overheat and ignite, causing the plaintiff's injuries and damages.

13. Because of the defects, Woodall Shoals breached the express warranties made to the plaintiff.

14. Woodall Shoals' breach of the aforementioned express warranties directly and proximately caused the injuries and damages sustained by the plaintiff.

15. The plaintiff gave Woodall Shoals timely notice of the aforementioned breach of warranties.

16. By reason of the injuries directly and proximately caused by the breach of express warranties by Woodall Shoals, as their interests appear, the plaintiff is entitled to recover from this defendant for medical and hospital expenses, past and future; pain, suffering, humiliation, embarrassment, and mental anguish, past and future; loss of life's pleasures and loss of well-being, past and future, through physical handicap; extensive property damage to his home, loss of income and other damages, all in an amount greatly in excess of Fifty Thousand Dollars ($50,000).

II.

COUNT TWO—BREACH OF THE IMPLIED WARRANTY OF MERCHANTABILITY BY THE DEFENDANT WOODALL SHOALS

17. The plaintiff incorporates by reference and realleges paragraphs 1–9 of the Complaint and, in addition, alleges as follows:

18. Woodall Shoals regularly engages in the sale of electric blankets of the type that injured and damaged the plaintiff.

19. At the time of sale Woodall Shoals impliedly warranted to the plaintiff that the electric blanket was "merchantable" within the meaning of North Carolina General Statute §25-2-314.

20. Woodall Shoals breached this warranty by selling an electric blanket that was not merchantable.

21. The electric blanket at the time of sale was not merchantable in that the numerous defects in material and workmanship, which existed in the blanket and caused it to ignite, made the blanket unfit for the ordinary purpose for which electric blankets are used.

22. As a direct and proximate result of Woodall Shoals' breach of its implied warranty of merchantability to the plaintiff, the blanket ignited and caused serious injuries to the plaintiff.

23. The plaintiff gave timely notice of the breach of the implied warranty of merchantability to the defendant Woodall Shoals.

24. By reason of the injuries directly and proximately caused by Woodall Shoals' breach of the implied warranty of merchantability, the plaintiff is entitled to recover from this defendant for medical and hospital expenses, past and future; pain, suffering, humiliation, embarrassment, and mental anguish, past and future; loss of life's pleasures and loss of well-being, past and future, through physical handicap; extensive property damage to his home, loss of income and other damages all in an amount greatly in excess of Fifty Thousand Dollars ($50,000).

III.
COUNT THREE—NEGLIGENCE IN DESIGN AND MANUFACTURE BY THE DEFENDANT WOODALL SHOALS

25. The plaintiff incorporates by reference and realleges paragraphs 1–9 of the Complaint and, in addition, alleges as follows:

26. Woodall Shoals designed, manufactured, and assembled the Model 6102 electric blanket that injured the plaintiff.

27. Woodall Shoals owed a duty to foreseeable users of the electric blanket, including the plaintiff, to exercise reasonable care in the design, manufacture and assembly of the blanket.

28. Due to Woodall Shoals' failure to exercise reasonable care in the design of the electric blanket, when it left Woodall Shoals' possession and control the electric blanket posed an unreasonable risk of harm to users because of its propensity to overheat and ignite.

29. Woodall Shoals knew or should have known that the electric blanket as designed posed an unreasonable risk of harm to foreseeable users like the plaintiff.

30. Owing to Woodall Shoals' failure to exercise reasonable care in the manufacture and assembly of the electric blanket, at the time it left Woodall Shoals' possession and control, the electric blanket posed an unreasonable risk of harm to users because of its propensity to overheat and ignite.

31. Woodall Shoals knew or should have known that the electric blanket as manufactured and assembled posed an unreasonable risk of harm to foreseeable users like the plaintiff.

32. Woodall Shoals' failure to exercise reasonable care in the design, manufacture and assembly of the electric blanket proximately caused the plaintiff's injuries and damages.

33. By reason of the injuries proximately caused by Woodall Shoals' failure to exercise reasonable care in the design, manufacture and assembly of the electric blanket, the plaintiff is entitled to recover from Woodall Shoals for medical and hospital expenses, past and future; pain, suffering, humiliation, embarrassment, and mental anguish, past and future; loss of life's pleasures and loss of well-being, past and future, through physical handicap; extensive property damage to his home, loss of income, and other damages, all in an amount greatly in excess of Fifty Thousand Dollars ($50,000).

IV.
COUNT FOUR—BREACH OF EXPRESS WARRANTY BY THE DEFENDANT SECOND LEDGE

34. The plaintiff incorporates by reference and realleges paragraphs 1–9 of the Complaint and, in addition, alleges as follows:

35. At the time of the blanket's sale to the plaintiff, Second Ledge made certain express warranties to the plaintiff, including an express warranty that, for two years from the data of purchase, the blanket would be free of electrical and mechanical defects in material and workmanship.

36. At the time of sale, the electric blanket in fact contained numerous electrical and mechanical defects which caused the blanket to overheat and ignite, causing the plaintiff's injuries and damages.

37. By reason of these defects, Second Ledge breached the express warranties made to the plaintiff.

38. Second Ledge's breach of the aforementioned express warranties directly and proximately caused the injuries and damages sustained by the plaintiff.

39. The plaintiff gave Second Ledge timely notice of the aforementioned breach of warranties.

40. By reason of the injuries directly and proximately caused by the breach of express warranties by Second Ledge, the plaintiff is entitled to recover from this defendent for medical and hospital expenses, past and future; pain, suffering, humiliation, embarrassment and mental anguish, past and future; loss of life's pleasures and loss of well-being, past and future, through physical handicap; extensive property damage to his home, loss of income, and other damages, all in amount greatly in excess of Fifty Thousand Dollars ($50,000).

V.

COUNT FIVE—BREACH OF THE IMPLIED WARRANTY OF MERCHANTABILITY BY THE DEFENDANT SECOND LEDGE

41. The plaintiff incorporates by reference and realleges paragraphs 1–9 of the Complaint, and, in addition alleges as follows:

42. Second Ledge regularly engages in the retail sale of electric blankets of the type that injured and damaged the plaintiff.

43. At the time of the electric blanket's sale, Second Ledge impliedly warranted to the plaintiff that the electric blanket was "merchantable" within the meaning of North Carolina General Statutes §25-2-314.

44. Second Ledge breached this warranty by selling an electric blanket that was not merchantable.

45. At the time of sale the electric blanket was not merchantable in that the numerous defects in material and workmanship that existed in the blanket and caused it to ignite made the blanket unfit for the ordinary purpose for which electric blankets are used.

46. Second Ledge had a reasonable opportunity to inspect the blanket prior to sale.

47. A reasonable inspection of the blanket would have revealed its defective condition.

48. As a direct and proximate result of Second Ledge's breach of its implied warranty of merchantability to the plaintiff, the blanket ignited and caused serious injuries to the plaintiff.

49. The plaintiff gave timely notice of the breach of the implied warranty of merchantability to Second Ledge.

50. By reason of the injuries directly and proximately caused by Second Ledge's breach of the implied warranty of merchantability, the plaintiff is entitled to recover from this defendant for medical and hospital expenses, past and future; pain, suffering, humiliation, embarrassment and mental anguish, past and future; loss of life's pleasures and loss of well-being, past and future, through physical handicap; extensive property damage to his home, loss of income, and other damages, all in an amount greatly in excess of Fifty Thousand Dollars ($50,000).

VI.

COUNT SIX—NEGLIGENCE OF THE DEFENDANT SECOND LEDGE

51. The plaintiff incorporates by reference and realleges the allegations contained in paragraphs 1–9 of the Complaint and, in addition, alleges as follows:

52. At the time the electric blanket left Second Ledge's possession and control, the blanket was in a defective condition and posed an unreasonable risk of harm to users in that:

(a) the blanket had a propensity to overheat and ignite; and

(b) the blanket lacked adequate warnings and instructions.

53. Second Ledge owed a duty to foreseeable users of the electric blanket, including the plaintiff, to exercise reasonable care in inspecting the blanket for defects.

54. Second Ledge had a reasonable opportunity to inspect the electric blanket for defects.

55. A reasonable inspection of the electric blanket would have revealed its defective condition and that it posed an unreasonable risk of harm to users.

56. Because Second Ledge failed to exercise reasonable care in inspecting the electric blanket, the plaintiff is entitled to recover from this defendant for medical and hospital expenses, past and future; pain, suffering humiliation, embarrassment and mental anguish, past and future; loss of life's pleasures and loss of well-being, past and future, through physical handicap; extensive property damage to his home, loss of income, and other damages, all in amount greatly in excess of Fifty Thousand Dollars ($50,000).

WHEREFORE, the plaintiff prays the Court as follows:

1. The plaintiff have and recover of the defendants, jointly and severally, damages substantially in excess of Fifty Thousand Dollars ($50,000) for personal injury, medical expenses, lost wages, pain and suffering, and emotional distress and property damage.

2. The costs of this action be taxed to the defendants.

3. The plaintiff be granted a trial by jury on all issues of fact.

4. The plaintiff be granted such other and further relief as the court may deem just and proper.

This the 2d day of January, 1989.

Leigh J. Heyward
Attorney for the Plaintiff
Heyward and Wilson
401 East Trade Street
Charleston, NC 28226-1114
704-555-3161

UNITED STATES DISTRICT COURT
MIDDLE DISTRICT OF NORTH CAROLINA
CHARLESTON DIVISION
CIVIL NO.: C-89-1293-B

Bryson Wesser,

                        Plaintiff,

     -vs-

Woodall Shoals Corporation,
                    Defendant,
          and
Second Ledge Stores, Incorporated,
                    Defendant

DEFENDANTS'
ANSWER

FIRST DEFENSE

The defendants respectfully move that the plaintiffs' Complaint be dismissed pursuant to Rule 12(b)(6) for failure to state a cause of action upon which relief can be granted.

SECOND DEFENSE

The defendants, for answer to plaintiff's Complaint, state as follows:

1. Paragraph 1 is admitted.

2. Paragraph 2 is admitted.

3. Paragraph 3 is admitted.

4, 5, and 6. The defendants deny the allegations contained in Paragraphs 4, 5, and 6 for lack of sufficient information or knowledge to form a belief as to the truth thereof.

7. Paragraph 7 is denied.

8. Paragraph 8 is denied.

9. The defendants, upon present information and belief, admit that the plaintiff suffered first, second, and third-degree burns over approximately 20% of his body, requiring hospitalization and medical treatment. The defendants deny the remaining allegations contained in Paragraph 9 for lack of sufficient information or knowledge to form a belief as to the truth thereof.

I. COUNT ONE—BREACH OF EXPRESS WARRANTY BY DEFENDANT WOODALL SHOALS CORPORATION

10. The defendants repeat, reallege and incorporate by reference their answers to Paragraph 1 through 9 of the Complaint, as if repeated herein, word for word, paragraph by paragraph.

11. Defendants admit that Woodall Shoals expressly warranted to the purchaser of the electric blanket that, for two years from the date of purchase, the blanket would be free of electrical and mechanical defects in material and workmanship.

Except as specifically admitted, the allegations contained in Paragraph 11 are denied.

12, 13, 14, 15, and 16. Paragraphs 12, 13, 14, 15, and 16 are denied.

II. COUNT TWO—BREACH OF IMPLIED WARRANTY OF MERCHANTABILITY BY DEFENDANT WOODALL SHOALS

17. The defendants repeat, reallege and incorporate by reference their answers to Paragraphs 1 through 9 and Paragraphs 10 through 16 of Count One of the Complaint, as if repeated herein, word for word, paragraph by paragraph.

18. The defendants admit that Woodall Shoals regularly engages in the manufacture and wholesale sales and distribution of electric blankets. Except as specifically admitted, the allegations contained in Paragraph 18 are denied.

19. The defendants admit that certain warranties may be implied to exist regarding the electric blanket as a matter of law, by operation of statute or otherwise. Except as specifically admitted, the allegations contained in Paragraph 19 are denied.

20, 21, 22, 23, and 24. Paragraphs 20, 21, 22, 23, and 24 are denied.

III. COUNT THREE—NEGLIGENCE IN DESIGN AND MANUFACTURE BY THE DEFENDANT WOODALL SHOALS

25. The defendants repeat, reallege and incorporate by reference their answers to Paragraphs 1 through 9, Paragraphs 10 through 17 of Count I and Paragraphs 18 through 24 of Count II of the Complaint, as if repeated herein, word for word, paragraph by paragraph.

26. Defendants admit, upon present information and belief, that Woodall Shoals designed, manufactured and assembled an electric blanket designated as Model 6102. Except as specifically admitted, the allegations contained in Paragraph 26 are denied.

27. The defendants deny the allegations contained in Paragraph 27 for the reason that the same set forth nothing more than conclusions of law and are therefore improper. The defendants further state that they met and exceeded any and all duties or obligations imposed upon them by operation of law or otherwise in the manufacture and sale of electric blankets.

28, 29, 30, 31, 32, and 33. Paragraphs 28, 29, 30, 31, 32, and 33 are denied.

IV. COUNT FOUR—BREACH OF EXPRESS WARRANTY BY THE DEFENDANT SECOND LEDGE

34. The defendants repeat, reallege and incorporate by reference their answers to Paragraphs 1 through 9, Paragraphs 10 through 16 of Count I, Paragraphs 17 through 24 of Count II, and Paragraphs 25 through 33 of Count III, as if repeated herein, word for word, paragraph by paragraph.

35. The defendants deny that Second Ledge sold any electric blanket, in particular an electric blanket manufactured by Woodall Shoals designated as Model No. 6102, to the plaintiff for lack of sufficient information or knowledge to form a belief as to the truth thereof. The defendants deny the remaining allegations contained in Paragraph 35.

36, 37, 38, 39, and 40. Paragraphs 36, 37, 38, 39, and 40 are denied.

V. COUNT FIVE—BREACH OF IMPLIED WARRANTY OF MERCHANTABILITY BY THE DEFENDANT SECOND LEDGE

41. The defendants repeat, reallege and incorporate by reference their answer to Paragraphs 1 through 9, Paragraphs 10 through 16 of Count I, Paragraphs 17 through 24 of Count II, Paragraphs 25 through 33 of Count III, and Paragraphs 34 through 40 of Count IV of the Complaint as if repeated herein, word for word, paragraph by paragraph.

42. The defendants admit that Second Ledge regularly engages in the retail sale of electric blankets. Except as specifically admitted, the defendants deny the remaining allegations of Paragraph 42.

43. The defendants admit that certain warranties may be implied to exist relative to the sale of electric blankets as a matter of law, by operation of statute or otherwise. Except as specifically admitted, the defendants deny the allegations contained in Paragraph 43 for the reason that the same set forth nothing more than conclusions of law and are therefore improper.

44 and 45. Paragraphs 44 and 45 are denied.

46. The defendants deny the allegations contained in Paragraph 46 for the reason that those allegations are so vague and unclear in the manner and form alleged that the defendants are precluded from properly formulating an answer thereto. Defendants further allege that defendant Second Ledge met and exceeded any and all duties or allegations imposed by operation of law or otherwise relative to the sale of electric blankets.

47, 48, 49, and 50. Paragraphs 47, 48, 49, and 50 are denied.

VI. COUNT SIX—NEGLIGENCE OF THE DEFENDANT SECOND LEDGE

51. The defendants repeat, reallege and incorporate by reference their answers to Paragraphs 1 through 9, Paragraphs 10 through 16 of Count I, Paragraphs 17 through 24 of Count II, Paragraphs 25 through 33 of Count III, Paragraphs 34 through 40 of Count IV, and Paragraphs 41 through 50 of Count V, as if repeated herein, word for word, paragraph by paragraph.

52. The defendants deny the allegations contained in Paragraph 52 and subparagraphs (a) and (b) contained therein.

53. The defendants deny the allegations contained in Paragraph 53 for the reason that the same set forth nothing more than conclusions of law and are therefore improper. The defendants further allege that defendant Second Ledge met and exceeded any and all duties or obligations imposed by operation of law or otherwise relative to the sale of electric blankets.

54. The defendants deny the allegations contained in Paragraph 54 for the reason that those allegations are so vague and unclear in the manner and form alleged that the defendants are precluded from properly formulating an answer thereto. The defendants further allege that defendant Second Ledge met and exceeded any and all duties and obligations imposed by operation of law or otherwise relative to the retail sale of electric blankets.

55 and 56. Paragraphs 55 and 56 are denied.

THIRD DEFENSE

57. The defendants affirmatively plead that the plaintiff was careless and negligent in the matters set forth in the Complaint. To the extent that any product manufactured, distributed and/or sold by the defendants, or either of them, in particular an electric blanket, was involved in any accident relating to the plaintiff, knowledge of which is presently lacking and which has been and is again specifically denied, then said electric blanket was abused and/or misused in that, on present information and belief, the electric blanket was or may have been folded, tucked under mattresses, used underneath other bed coverings or otherwise misused, and that such abuse and/or misuse was the sole proximate cause of any and all injuries sustained by the plaintiff, and the defendants affirmatively plead such abuse and/or misuse as a complete bar to recovery by the plaintiff.

58. The defendants affirmatively plead the contributory negligence of plaintiff as a complete bar to recovery by plaintiff.

59. The defendants affirmatively plead that the contributory negligence of plaintiff superseded any and all alleged negligence or breach of warranties by the defendants, which negligence and breach of warranties has been and is

again specifically denied, and that the negligence of the plaintiff was the sole, superseding and/or intervening proximate cause of any and all damages sustained by the plaintiff and acts as a complete bar to recovery by the plaintiff.

WHEREFORE, the defendants, having moved to dismiss plaintiff's Complaint, having fully and completely answered the allegations contained in plaintiff's Complaint, and having asserted their further affirmative defense, respectfully pray unto this honorable Court that:

1. Plaintiff's Complaint be dismissed with prejudice;

2. The plaintiff has and recovers nothing of the defendants;

3. All costs and the defendants' attorneys' fees in this action be taxed against the plaintiff;

4. The defendants be afforded such other relief as may appear to the Court to be just and proper.

Submitted this 20th day of January, 1989.

David H. Benedict
Attorney for the Defendants
Benedict, Parker & Miller
100 Nolichucky Drive
Bristol, NC 28205-0890
704-555-8810

+ Certificate of Service

UNITED STATES DISTRICT COURT
MIDDLE DISTRICT OF NORTH CAROLINA
CHARLESTON DIVISION
CIVIL NO.: C-89-1293-B

Bryson Wesser,

                    Plaintiff,

        -vs-

Woodall Shoals Corporation,

                 Defendant,
           and
Second Ledge Stores, Incorporated,
                 Defendant

PLAINTIFF'S FIRST SET OF INTERROGATORIES TO DEFENDANT WOODALL SHOALS CORPORATION

The plaintiff requests that the defendant Woodall Shoals Corporation answer under oath, in accordance with Rules 33 and 34 of the Federal Rules of Civil Procedure, the following Interrogatories. Since said defendant is a corporation, the defendant is required to select such officer or agent of said corporation as can best furnish information and answers to each interrogatory. The defendant is required to have these interrogatories answered separately and fully in writing under oath and to serve a copy of its answers on counsel for the plaintiffs within the time provided in said Rules.

DEFINITIONS

(a) "The subject blanket" means the electric blanket, Model 6102, manufactured by the defendant Woodall Shoals Corporation and purchased by Bryson Wesser on or about January 16, 1986, from the defendant Second Ledge Stores, Incorporated, Store No. 289, in Charleston, North Carolina.

(b) As used herein, "representatives" means counsel, agents, investigators, legal assistants and all persons acting on behalf of the defendant.

INTERROGATORIES

1. Please give the names, titles and addresses of the persons answering these interrogatories.

2. Does the defendant manufacture, distribute, provide component parts for, or sell Woodall Shoals Model 6102 electric blankets? Please designate specifically each of these activities in which the defendant participates.

3. Please state the year and place of manufacture of the subject blanket.

4. Please state the date and place at which the subject blanket was assembled as a finished product by the defendant, immediately before the subject blanket was placed in the path of distribution.

5. Please identify the person(s) who actually designed the subject blanket or had the overall responsibility for the design of said product.

6. Please state the design objectives for the subject blanket and describe in detail how the design criteria were established.

7. Please state the name, address and relationship to the defendant of the person(s) who defined or described the design criteria for the subject blanket.

8. Does the defendant subscribe to or purport to follow standards established by the American National Standards Institute or any other governmental or non-governmental group or association? If so, please identify and describe each such set of standards, with specific reference to the title of the standards, the date, author, and present location of the standards.

9. Did the defendant consult any outside individual, partnership, corporation, or other entity in the design or manufacture of the subject blanket? If so, please state the name and address of the entity and the phase of design or manufacture in which the entity was involved.

10. Please list every purchase made by the defendant from a named supplier, for use in manufacturing the subject blanket, and for each item purchased, please state the address of the named supplier, and describe the material purchased.

11. Was any warning given to any purchaser, including private individuals, distributors or retailers selling such model of electric blanket to inform them that the electric blanket might overheat or malfunction in any other manner so as to cause a fire? If so, state the contents of the warnings and instructions and how they were communicated to the individual purchasers, distributors, or retail stores.

These Interrogatories shall be deemed continuing in nature so as to require seasonal, supplemental answers as information becomes available to defendant.

This 26th day of February, 1989.

_____

Leigh J. Heyward
Attorney for the Plaintiff
Heyward and Wilson
401 East Trade Street
Charleston, NC 28226-1114
704-555-3161

+ Certificate of Service

Note: These interrogatories are designed to give an overview of a set of interrogatories. A full set of interrogatories would have additional definitions and questions. This overview does not contain all the basic questions that a first set of interrogatories should include.

UNITED STATES DISTRICT COURT
MIDDLE DISTRICT OF NORTH CAROLINA
CHARLESTON DIVISION
CIVIL NO.: C-89-1293-B

Bryson Wesser,

Plaintiff,

-vs-

Woodall Shoals Corporation,

Defendant,

and

Second Ledge Stores, Incorporated,

Defendant

RESPONSES TO PLAINTIFF'S FIRST SET OF INTERROGATORIES TO DEFENDANT WOODALL SHOALS CORPORATION

Defendant Woodall Shoals Corporation, for its responses to Plaintiff's interrogatories, states as follows:

1. Robert W. Carlton

    Manager of Consumer Relations

    Woodall Shoals Corporation

    300 West Blvd.

    New York, NY 10019-0987

    Victoria McGee, Counsel

    Woodall Shoals Corporation

    Leslie Miller

    Woodall Shoals Corporation

    Youghigheny, North Carolina

2. Yes. Woodall Shoals Corporation manufactures all components of Model 6102 blankets and sells such blankets.

3. Model 6102 blanket was manufactured in Youghigheny, North Carolina.

4. Model 6102 blanket was assembled and manufactured in Youghigheny, North Carolina.

5. Electric blankets manufactured by Woodall Shoals Corporation consist of a number of components which have been designed and developed separately, and the designs have changed and improved over the years. For each model, a

single individual has final "sign-off" responsibility for the overall design; the identity of this individual changes over time. The individual who currently has sign-off responsibility for Woodall Shoals Corporation's thermostat blankets is Joel Marcus, Designer Engineer–Comfort Products Manager.

6. Essentially the "design criteria" for Woodall Shoals Corporation's electric blankets are those described in response to interrogatory 15. There are a number of design/quality-control tolerances which are applicable to each of the various components and assemblies. To list each of these tolerances would require numerous pages and would require information that is proprietary in nature and which Woodall Shoals Corporation considers to constitute trade secrets. Woodall Shoals Corporation will provide information on specific design/quality-control tolerances for specific components upon a specific request, and subject to the provisions of an appropriate protective order. A reasonable number of requested documents can be photocopied and provided through the mail. Otherwise, Woodall Shoals Corporation will produce such documents for examination and photocopying at plaintiff's expense at its offices in New York, New York or at its facilities in Youghigheny, North Carolina, depending upon the documents requested.

7. The design objectives and design/quality-control tolerances for all electric blankets manufactured by Woodall Shoals Corporation have been established by employees of Woodall Shoals Corporation. It is impossible to identify individual employees without reference to specific component(s), model(s) and period(s) of manufacture.

8. Objection. The information sought is irrelevant and immaterial and not likely to lead to admissible information.

9. Electric blankets that are manufactured for and sold to specific customers are manufactured in compliance with that specific customer/retailer's specifications as to size, color, labeling, packaging and number of controls.

10. Woodall Shoals Corporation manufactures every component of every electric blanket it manufactures. A list of every supplier of every raw material (i.e., yarn, thread, wire, plastic (raw), plastic tubing, bi-metal, fasteners, etc.) would require numerous pages. Upon receipt of a specific request identifying the component(s), model(s), and period(s) of manufacture, Woodall Shoals Corporation will make such specific information available.

11. Instructions are designed to prevent and/or minimize, and warnings specifically address the risk of overheating and/or ''hot spots'' and/or burn injuries which can occur due to improper use or maintenance of electric blankets. Instructions and warnings are not provided in contemplation of ''malfunction'' of the electric blanket. Copies of recent examples of instructions and warnings are attached. All instructions, warnings and labels provided with or attached to Woodall Shoals Corporation electric blankets are available for inspection by plaintiff's counsel at Woodall Shoals Corporation offices.

Verification

Robert W. Carlton, having been first duly sworn, states that he is Manager-Consumer Relations for Woodall Shoals Corporation and verifies these supplemental responses to interrogatories and request for production in that capacity and is authorized to do so. The information contained in these responses is not within the personal knowledge of the verifying officer.

_____
Robert W. Carlton

Sworn to and subscribed before me this _____ day of April, 1989.

_____
Notary Public

My commission expires: _____

(SEAL)

+ Certificate of Service

UNITED STATES DISTRICT COURT
MIDDLE DISTRICT OF NORTH CAROLINA
CHARLESTON DIVISION
CIVIL NO.: C-89-2388-B

Equal Employment Opportunity
Commission,

          Plaintiff,

       -vs-   *COMPLAINT*

Chattooga Corporation,

          Defendant

JURISDICTION AND VENUE

1. Jurisdiction of this Court is invoked pursuant to 28 U.S.C. Sections 451, 1343 and 1345. This is an action authorized and instituted pursuant to Section 706(f)(1) and (3) and (g) of Title VII of the Civil Rights Act of 1964, as amended, 42 U.S.C. §2000e, *et seq.* (hereinafter, ''Title VII'').

2. The unlawful employment practices alleged below were and are now being committed within the State of North Carolina and the Middle Judicial District.

PARTIES

3. Plaintiff, Equal Employment Opportunity Commission (hereinafter, the ''Commission'') is an agency of the United States of America charged with the administration, interpretation and enforcement of Title VII and is expressly authorized to bring this action by Section 706(f)(1), 42 U.S.C. §2000e-5(f)(1).

4. Since at least June 23, 1988, Chattooga Corporation (hereinafter the ''Corporation'') has continuously been a private corporation licensed to do business and doing business in the State of North Carolina and city of Charleston. The Defendant Corporation is an engineering consulting firm and has continuously employed more than fifteen (15) employees.

5. Since at least June 23, 1988, the Corporation has continuously been and is now an employer engaged in an industry affecting commerce within the meaning of Section 701(b), (g), and (h) of Title VII, 42 U.S.C. §2000e-(b), (g) and (h).

STATEMENT OF CLAIM

6. More than thirty (30) days prior to the institution of this lawsuit, Sandy Ford filed a charge with the Equal Employment Opportunity Commission alleging violations of Title VII by the Defendant Corporation. All conditions precedent to the institution of this lawsuit have been fulfilled.

7. Since June 23, 1988, and continuously up until the present time, the Defendant has intentionally engaged in unlawful employment practices at its Charleston, North Carolina, facility, in violation of Sections 703 and 704(a) of Title VII. These policies and practices include but are not limited to retaliating against Sandy Ford by discharging her because she had accompanied another employee of the Defendant Corporation to the Commission's local office to assist the employee in filing a charge with the Equal Employment Opportunity Commission, alleging employment discrimination in violation of Title VII.

8. The effect of the policies and practices complained of in Paragraph 7 above has been to deprive Ms. Ford of equal employment opportunities and otherwise adversely affect her status as an employee because she opposed a practice made unlawful under Title VII or because she participated in a proceeding under Title VII.

PRAYER FOR RELIEF

WHEREFORE, the Commission respectfully prays that this Court:

1. Grant a permanent injunction enjoining Defendant, its officers, agents, employees, successors, assigns and all persons in active concert or participation with them, from retaliation against employees who complain of acts believed to be unlawful under Title VII.

2. Order Defendant to make whole Sandy Ford, by providing appropriate back pay, with interest, in an amount to be proved at trial and other affirmative relief necessary to eradicate the effects of its unlawful employment practices.

3. Grant such further relief as the Court deems necessary and proper.

4. Award the Commission its costs in this action.

_____
Kathy M. Mitchell
Regional Attorney

_____
Edward R. Cheng
Senior Trial Attorney

Equal Employment Opportunity Commission
1301 North Union Street
Charleston, NC 28226-1114
704-555-3000

UNITED STATES DISTRICT COURT
MIDDLE DISTRICT OF NORTH CAROLINA
CHARLESTON DIVISION
CIVIL NO.: C-89-2388-B

Equal Employment Opportunity
Commission,

                Plaintiff,

     -vs-

Chattooga Corporation,

                Defendant

CONSENT DECREE

    The Equal Employment Opportunity Commission (hereinafter "Commission") instituted this action against the Defendant, Chattooga Corporation (hereinafter "Chattooga"), pursuant to Sections 706(f)(1) and (3) of Title VII of the Civil Rights Act of 1964, as amended, 42 U.S.C. Section 2000e, *et seq.* (hereinafter "Title VII") to remedy alleged unlawful employment practices as set forth in the Complaint filed in this action.

    The Court has jurisdiction of the subject matter of this action and of the parties to this action.

    It is understood that this Consent Decree does not constitute an admission by Chattooga of the allegations in the Complaint.

    The Commission and Chattooga desire to resolve this action and all issues raised by the Complaint without the time and expense of contested litigation, and have formulated a plan to be embodied in a Consent Decree which promotes and effectuates the purposes of Title VII.

    The Court approves the Consent Decree as one which will promote and effectuate the purposes of Title VII.

    NOW, THEREFORE, this Court being fully advised in the premises, it is hereby ORDERED, ADJUDGED, AND DECREED:

I. DISCLAIMER OF VIOLATION

It is understood and agreed that the negotiation, execution and entry of this Consent Decree, and the undertakings made by Chattooga hereunder, are in settlement and compromise of disputed claims of alleged retaliation in employment, the validity of which is expressly denied by Chattooga. Neither the negotiation, execution, nor entry of this Consent Decree shall constitute an acknowledgment or admission of any kind by Chattooga that their officers, agents or employees have violated or have not been in compliance with Title VII or any rules and regulations issued under or pursuant to Title VII or any other applicable law, regulations, or order.

II. TERM OF DECREE

This Consent Decree shall continue to be effective and binding upon the parties to this action for the period of 18 months immediately following the entry of the Decree. Each party to this Consent Decree shall have a right within the period of 19 calendar months from the date of the entry of this Decree, to move the Court to reopen this case for the purpose of clarifying and enforcing this Decree.

III. OTHER GENERAL PROVISIONS

A. By and with the consent of the Defendant, Chattooga and its officers, agents, employees, successors and assigns are enjoined and restrained for the term of this Decree from harassing, intimidating, or otherwise retaliating against any person who has participated in any fashion in the investigation or litigation of this action, or who has or may file a charge of discrimination or participate in any fashion in the investigation of any charge filed with the Equal Employment Opportunity Commission.

B. Chattooga shall maintain at its facility in Charleston, North Carolina, the notice attached to this Decree as Exhibit 1.

C. The Commission shall have a right to visit Chattooga's facility for the purpose of ensuring that Chattooga is in compliance with Section 5 of this Decree.

IV. NOTICE REQUIREMENT

The Defendant shall post notices directed to its employees in conspicuous places throughout its facility advising its employees that the Defendant supports and will comply with Title VII and that it will not take any action against any employee because they have exercised their rights under the law.

V. COMPENSATION PROCEDURE

Chattooga has agreed to pay Sandy Ford $3,000 minus legal deductions, with such payment to be considered as full, complete and final satisfaction of the disputed claim which the EEOC now has against Chattooga on account of any alleged failure of Chattooga to comply with Title VII, which arose or may have arisen from the subject matter of Civil Action No. C-89-2388-B. Chattooga shall make said check payable to Sandy Ford and shall mail said check to the address contained in Section VII of this Decree.

VI. MAILING AND NOTICE REQUIREMENTS

Chattooga shall furnish the Commission with a report within 30 days following the date of entry of this Decree, stating the dates on which the notices are placed and their location. The report shall be sent via certified mail to the following address:

Equal Employment Opportunity Commission
1301 North Union Street
Charleston, NC 28226-1114

VII. FULL SETTLEMENT

This Decree shall be a full settlement of all issues raised between the parties to Civil Action No. C-89-2388-B. Entry of this Decree shall consitute dismissal with prejudice of Civil Action C-89-2388B, subject to the provisions of Section III of the Decree.

This the _____ day of _____ , 1990.

Counsel for Defendant: Counsel for Plaintiff:

_____   _____
Nancy Reade Lee   Kathy M. Mitchell
Gray and Lee, P.A.   Regional Attorney
380 South Washington St.
Charleston, NC 28226-1115   _____

                                              Edward R. Cheng
                                              Senior Trial Attorney

                                              Equal Employment Opportunity
                                              Commission
                                              1301 North Union Street
                                              Charleston, NC 28226-1114

GLOSSARY

ABA Model Code of Professional Responsibility Guidelines for the ethical conduct of attorneys, promulgated by the American Bar Association in 1969.

ABA Model Rules of Professional Conduct Revised rules to guide the ethical conduct of attorneys, adopted by the American Bar Association in 1983.

Admissible Admissible evidence is evidence that may be introduced at trial and considered by the finder of fact.

Affidavit A written statement of facts, with the notarized signature of the person stating the facts.

Affiant The person who makes the statements and signs the affidavit.

Affirmative defense A defense raised in an answer that goes beyond a denial of allegations in a complaint, bringing out a new matter that serves as a defense even if the matters alleged in the complaint are true.

Answer The formal written allegations of the defendant, stating defenses to the matters raised in the complaint.

Appeal The process of requesting a higher court to review the unfavorable decision of the trial court or inferior appellate court.

Appellant The party that files the appeal and seeks to overturn the judgment of the trial court or inferior appellate court.

Appellee The party that opposes the appeal, asserting that the judgment of the inferior court should be affirmed.

Arbitration A method of dispute resolution that serves as an alternative to a full-blown trial.

Arbitrator A neutral third party who resolves the parties' dispute in the arbitration process.

Attorney-client privilege The evidentiary privilege that protects from disclosure confidential communications between clients and attorneys.

Authentication The methods in the rules of evidence for establishing that a document is what it purports to be.

Breach of contract Where one party fails to honor an obligation under a contract, often giving rise to litigation.

Brief A written explanation of the facts, applicable statutes, and pertinent case law, with an argument to convince the judge to rule in favor of the party submitting the brief; sometimes called a *memorandum of law* or *statement of points and authorities*.

Burden of proof The requirement that a party present evidence sufficient to prove the facts in dispute.

Calendar   The court's schedule of cases to be heard during a certain session of court; also called *docket* or *trial list*.

Canons   In the ABA Code of Professional Responsibility, the broad statements of the standard of conduct expected of lawyers.

Cause of action   The event or state of facts which gives rise to a claim for which a party seeks relief from a court.

Certiorari   The process in which an appellant petitions the appellate court to exercise its discretion to hear an appeal of the lower court's decision.

Chain of custody   The preservation of physical evidence and associated record-keeping to establish that evidence has not been altered.

Challenge   In picking a jury, a request that a particular person not serve on the jury.

Circuit courts of appeal   In the federal court system, the courts that hear appeals from the federal district courts, divided into geographical regions termed circuits.

Class action   A lawsuit in which a large group of persons with similar grievances brings one lawsuit on behalf of themselves and others with similar grievances.

Closing argument   After all the evidence has been presented at trial, an attorney's oral summary of the evidence and argument why his or her client should prevail at trial.

Compensatory damages   Money paid as compensation to the injured party for the harm caused by another party.

Complaint   The initial pleading filed by the plaintiff, setting forth the reasons that the plaintiff is entitled to relief and the damages requested.

Concurrent jurisdiction   When jurisdiction is not limited to one court; i.e., when both state and federal courts have jurisdiction.

Consent order   An order in which the attorneys for the parties state the terms to which they agree, and the judge approves and signs the order. When the parties state their agreement on all matters in issue, the document is a *consent judgment*.

Contingent fee   A fee arrangement in which the attorney receives an agreed percentage of the recovery if and when the plaintiff prevails.

Continuance   The postponement of a hearing or trial to a later date.

Contract   An agreement between parties that one party is obliged to perform an act in exchange for something from the other party.

Counterclaim   A pleading in which a defendant asserts a claim against a plaintiff.

Court of record   A court in which all transactions and arguments that take place in the courtroom are recorded by a court reporter.

Cross-claim   A pleading in which one party states a claim against another party—e.g., codefendant against codefendant.

Damages   Monetary compensation to a party for a loss or injuries.

Default judgment   A judgment entered against a defendant who fails to respond to a complaint within the allotted time.

Deposition   A form of discovery that consists of the oral testimony of a witness, taken under oath, in response to questions asked by the attorney representing another party, and transcribed by a court reporter.

Disciplinary rules   In the ABA Code of Professional Responsibility, the statements of mandatory conduct.

Discovery   The stage of litigation in which the parties gather facts from each other to prepare for trial, using the discovery methods of interrogatories, depositions, requests for admission, mental and physical examinations, and requests for production of documents and things and for entry upon land for inspection.

Dispositive motions   Motions that, when granted, terminate the lawsuit before trial, including motions for summary judgment, judgment on the pleadings, and default judgment.

Diversity of citizenship   One of the two major categories of federal subject-matter jurisdiction, allowing jurisdiction where the plaintiffs and defendants are citizens of different states and the claim involves more than $50,000.

Docket   A court's schedule for hearing motions and trials; also called the *court calendar* or *trial list*.

Docket control   The procedure in law offices for maintaining a system for keeping track of deadlines and the status of cases.

Domicile   The place where a person has his or her permanent home and intends for the permanent home to remain, used to determine the state of which a person is a citizen.

Due process of law   The constitutional protection providing that persons may not be deprived of life, liberty, or property without proper notice and the opportunity to defend themselves.

Equitable remedies   Remedies available to parties whom monetary damages cannot make whole—e.g., specific performance.

Essential elements   The facts that the law requires to exist in order to establish a particular cause of action.

Ethical considerations   In the ABA Code of Professional Responsibility, the sections that explain in more detail the statements in the canons, giving guidance for specific situations.

Evidence   The testimony of witnesses, documents, and physical objects that a party presents at trial to prove facts.

Ex parte   An *ex parte* hearing is one at which only one party is present, and that party seeks relief from the court without notice to the other party—e.g., when a party seeks a temporary restraining order.

Exclusive jurisdiction   When only one court has jurisdiction—e.g., the federal court has jurisdiction to hear a matter and the state court does not.

Execution   The process for enforcing a judgment.

Exemplary damages   Another term for punitive damages.

Expert witness   A witness who has scientific, technical, or other specialized knowledge and who explains technical matters and gives opinions to help the jury understand matters outside the general knowledge of lay persons.

Federal question   A category of federal court jurisdiction that includes cases that involve federal laws, treaties, or the U.S. Constitution.

Final decision rule   The rule that a party may not take an appeal until the court has entered a final decision.

Finders of fact   The persons who consider the evidence and determine which party is entitled to a favorable judgment; juries in jury trials and judges in non-jury trials.

Forum state   The state in which the lawsuit is commenced.

Foundation   The evidentiary requrement that before presenting witnesses' testimony, an attorney must ask preliminary questions to establish the witnesses' personal knowledge of the facts.

General damages   In contrast to special damages, general damages compensate a party for less tangible losses that are presumed to result from the injury, such as pain and suffering.

General jurisdiction   Refers to courts with jurisdiction not limited to certain matters provided by statute; the opposite of limited jurisdiction.

General verdict   A verdict in which the jury reports only the party that wins and the amount of damages awarded to that party.

Harmless error   A trial court error not serious enough to constitute reversible error.

Impeachment evidence   Evidence introduced to impeach the credibility of a witness.

Impleader   See *Third-party practice*.

Inferior courts   Courts below the higher appellate level; e.g., trial courts are inferior courts.

Injunction   A court order directing a person to refrain from doing an act.

Interlocutory orders   Orders that are issued before final judgment and do not dispose of the entire controversy.

Interrogatories   A discovery method in which one party submits written questions to another party, who answers the questions under oath.

Judgment   The court's final decision that resolves all matters in dispute among the parties to the litigation.

Judgment creditor   The party to whom the judgment is to be paid.

Judgment debtor   The party who is supposed to pay the judgment.

Judgment notwithstanding the verdict (JNOV)   A post-verdict motion in which the nonprevailing party asks the judge to set aside the jury's verdict on the ground that there was insufficient evidence for the jury to reach its verdict.

Judgment on the pleadings   A pretrial motion in which a party asks the court to determine that on the face of the pleadings the moving party is entitled to judgment.

Jurisdiction   The authority of a court to preside over claims and enter judgment in a judicial proceeding.

Jurisdictional amount   The requirement that the amount in controversy be in excess of a certain figure before a court has jurisdiction to hear a case, as in federal diversity jurisdiction.

Limited jurisdiction   A court of limited jurisdiction can hear only the specific types of cases allowed by statute.

Liquidated damages   A type of damages in which the parties agree beforehand what the amount of damages will be in the case of a breach of their agreement, or where the amount can be ascertained directly from the terms of the parties' agreement.

Lis pendens   A notice filed with the clerk of court and entered in the public records stating that real property is the subject of pending litigation.

Long-arm statute   A law authorizing jurisdiction over an out-of-state defendant because the defendant has been involved in certain transactions in the forum state.

Memorandum of law   See *Brief.*

Motion   An application to a court for an order directing some act in favor of the applicant.

Motions in limine   Motions usually made at the beginning of a jury trial for ruling on the admission of evidence that could be prejudicial or otherwise inadmissible.

Money damages   Monetary compensation paid by one party to another party for the losses and injuries the party has suffered.

Negligence   One party's failure to exercise due care in conduct toward others, resulting in injury to others.

Notice pleading   The concept on which the Federal Rules of Civil Procedure are based, requiring a short and plain statement of the claim instead of a detailed account of every act giving rise to the claim.

Offer of judgment   A judgment in which the defending party has agreed to allow entry of judgment against him or her in a certain amount.

Opening statement   Presentation to the jury at the beginning of the trial, designed to give an overview of the evidence to be presented and explanation of the points a party will prove during the trial.

Order   The written statement of the judge's decision to grant or deny a motion.

Original jurisdiction   The court that has jurisdiciton to hear the lawsuit initially; the trial court as opposed to the appellate court.

Peremptory setting   Scheduling a trial for a specific date and time due to extraordinary circumstances, rather than scheduling for a certain week or session only.

Personal jurisdiction   The power of a court to bring a party before it and enter a judgment against that party.

Plaintiff   The party who files a complaint seeking relief from the court.

Pleadings   The formal documents in which parties allege their claims and defenses (complaint, answer, etc.).

Pleadings record   A written record of every pleading filed and received and the response dates, usually kept in the front of the office file.

Preliminary injunction   A court order directing a party to refrain from certain action and maintaining the status quo until the issues can be resolved at trial.

Pretrial conference   Conference between the judge and the parties' attorneys to resolve certain pretrial procedures. *Initial pretrial conferences* usually cover procedural matters such as stipulations of matters not in dispute and agreements on discovery issues. *Final pretrial conferences* usually cover matters such as requests for jury instructions and other matters concerning the actual trial.

Pretrial order   An order setting out matters decided at pretrial conferences.

Prima facie case   A prima facie case has been established when a party has presented enough evidence to allow the jury to rule in the party's favor.

Protective order   An order to protect information that is not privileged but the disclosure of which would cause ''annoyance, embarrassment, oppression, or undue burden or expense'' (FRCivP 26(c)).

Punitive damages   Damages in addition to compensatory damages; punitive damages are designed to punish a party for malicious or fraudulent behavior.

Question of fact   An issue that requires resolving the facts in dispute; determined by the jury in a jury trial.

Question of law   An issue that requires applying the law to a set of facts; determined by the judge in a jury trial.

Record on appeal   The testimony at trial, pleadings, and other documents from the litigation at the trial level, all of which the appellate court reviews to determine whether to uphold or overturn the judgment of the trial court.

Rehearing en banc   In appellate procedure, a request for a hearing or rehearing before the entire panel of judges of the appellate court rather than the more usual practice of hearings before a panel of only some of the judges.

Requests for admission   A method of discovery in which one party submits written requests that another party admit to the truth of facts, the genuineness of documents, and/or the application of law to fact.

Reversible error   An error by the trial court of sufficient significance to entitle a party to a new trial.

Service of process   The delivery of the summons and complaint in accordance with FRCivP 4 so that defendants have proper notice of the lawsuit filed against them.

Session   A period of time during which a certain court transacts business—i.e., hears motions and holds trials; court calendars are generally issued for a particular session, during which the cases on that calendar will be heard, time permitting. Sometimes referred to as the *term of court*.

Settlement   Agreement between the parties to resolve a lawsuit without having a trial.

Special damages   Damages awarded for items of loss that are specific to the particular plaintiff, such as lost wages.

Special verdict   A jury verdict in which the jurors are required to answer specific written questions for each issue of fact.

Specific performance   A form of equitable relief in which the court orders a party to comply with the terms of a contract.

Statute of limitations   The time within which a lawsuit must be commenced, or else the plaintiff may never bring suit.

Stipulation   A statement that the parties agree on a certain issue and will not contest it.

Subject matter jurisdiction   A court's authority to hear a particular type of case, such as a case arising from a federal statute.

Subpoena   A document issued by the clerk of court directing persons to appear in a certain place at a certain time, to testify or to produce documentary or physical evidence in their possession.

Substantive evidence   Evidence introduced to prove a fact in issue.

Summary judgment   A dispositive motion asking the court to rule in favor of a party on the basis that there are no genuine issues as to any material fact and the moving party is entitled to judgment as a matter of law.

Summons   A form that accompanies the complaint and explains in simple terms to the defendants that they have been sued and must file an answer with the clerk of court.

Temporary restraining order (TRO)   A court order directing a party to refrain from certain action temporarily, usually for ten days, after which the moving party seeks an extension of the TRO in the form of a preliminary injunction.

Term of court   See *Session*.

Testimonial evidence   Testimony by witnesses concerning the facts in issue, as opposed to written, or documentary, evidence.

Third-party practice (impleader)   The procedure by which a defendant brings in a new party to the lawsuit, asserting that the new party is liable for all or part of the plaintiff's claim against the defendant.

Torts   Injuries to a person or property, usually the result of a person's negligent conduct.

Trial courts   The courts in which lawsuits are commenced and the actual trials held.

Trial de novo   A new trial granted as the result of appeal.

Trial memorandum (trial brief)   A written presentation of the legal issues that the court will consider during the trial and an argument explaining why the judge should rule in favor of the party presenting the memorandum.

Trial notebook   A method of organizing materials for trial, in which pertinent documents and notes are put in a binder under the appropriate tabbed section.

Unliquidated damages   Damages that cannot be determined by the parties' stipulation or by simple mathematical calculation from the available information.

Venue   The particular county or court district in which a court with jurisdiction may hear a lawsuit.

Voir dire   The process of selecting a jury from the jury pool.

INDEX